The Korean War

The Korean War:
No Victors, No Vanquished

Stanley Sandler
US Army Special Operations Command

THE UNIVERSITY PRESS OF KENTUCKY

Publication of this volume was made possible in part
by a grant from the National Endowment for the Humanities.

Published by The University Press of Kentucky

Scholarly publisher for the Commonwealth,
serving Bellarmine College, Berea College, Centre
College of Kentucky, Eastern Kentucky University,
The Filson Club Historical Society, Georgetown College,
Kentucky Historical Society, Kentucky State University,
Morehead State University, Murray State University,
Northern Kentucky University, Transylvania University,
University of Kentucky, University of Louisville,
and Western Kentucky University.

Editorial and Sales Offices: The University Press of Kentucky
663 South Limestone Street, Lexington, Kentucky 40508-4008

03 02 01 00 99   5 4 3 2 1

Library of Congress Cataloging-in-Publication Data

Sandler, Stanley, 1937-
      The Korean War : no victors, no vanquished / Stanley Sandler.
         p.   cm.
      Includes bibliographical references and index.
      ISBN 0-8131-2119-1 (cloth : alk. paper).—ISBN 0-8131-0967-1
      (paper : alk. paper)
      1. Korean War, 1950-1953—Campaigns. I. Title.
   DS918.S24   1999   99-12412
   951.904'24—dc21

This book is printed on acid-free recycled paper
meeting the requirements of the American National Standard
for Permanence of Paper for Printed Library Materials.

Contents

v

List of illustrations

Maps

1. *East Central Asia.* (B. C. Mossman, *Ebb and flow* [1990])

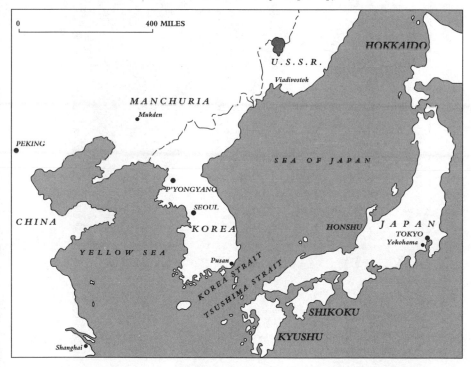

2. *How the UN Command saw Korea.* (US Army)

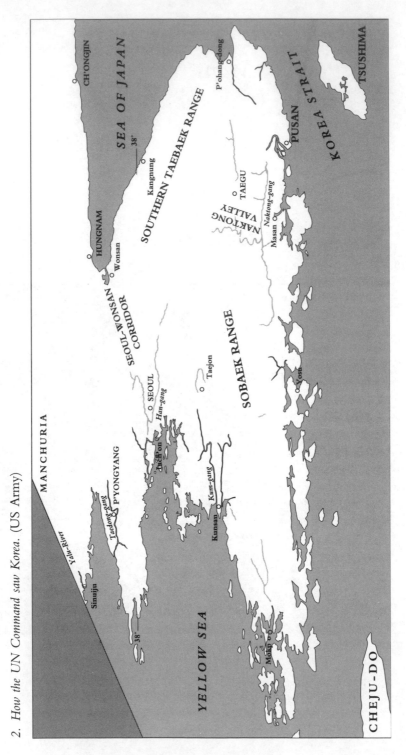

3. *How the Communist Command saw Korea.* (US Army)

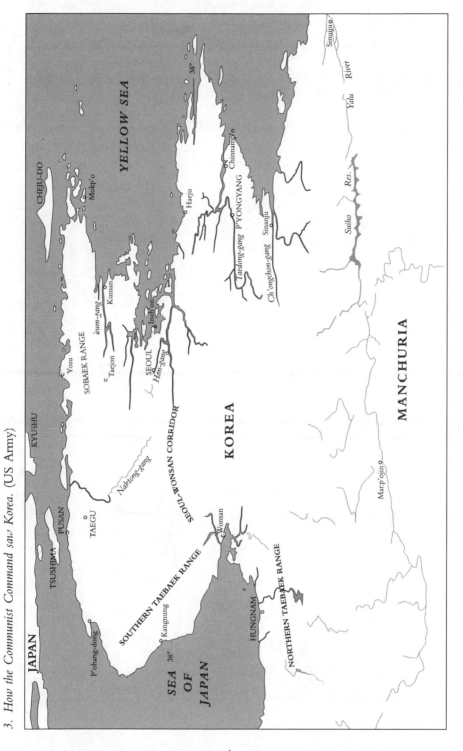

4. *The Pusan Perimeter, August–September 1950.* (US Army)

5. *Maximum advance by UNC forces, 24 November 1950.* (US Army)

6. *Demilitarized Zone as determined in the Armistice Agreement of 27 July 1953.* (US Army)

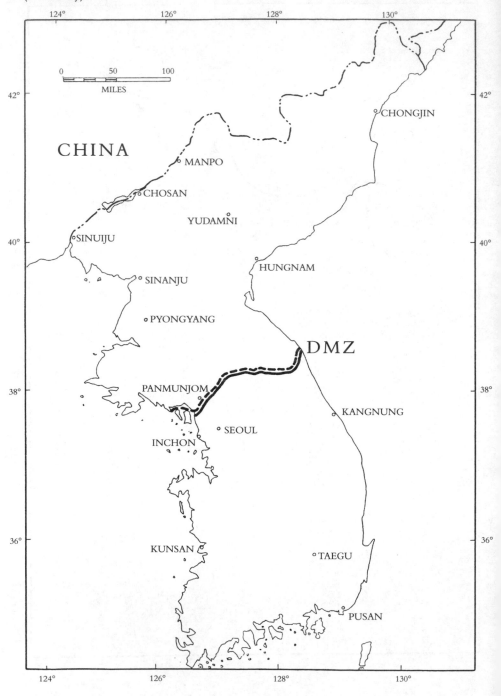

Chapter One

Introduction

An outpouring of books, articles and film in the last decade as well as an impressive memorial on Washington, DC's Mall have demonstrated that the Korean War (1950–53) is no longer quite "The Forgotten War", "The Unknown War", or "The War Before Vietnam". But this conflict has never assumed the mythic character of, say, the American Civil War or the Second World War. Coming as it did after the clear-cut victory of the Allies over the unarguable evil of the Axis in the Second World War, the localized Korean War, with its *status quo* armistice, hardly seems an inspiring conflict to study. But it would be practically impossible to understand the Cold War (*c.* 1946–91) without some knowledge of the Korean War.

As noted, a number of worthwhile studies of the Korean War have appeared in recent years, and several earlier accounts can be justly termed "classics", particularly the US Army's official and definitive first volume history of the war.[1] But there remains a need for a single-volume, concise history of the Korean War of modest length (and modest price!), which this work attempts to fulfill. It has been written for the student, researcher or general reader who may not be particularly interested in the exploits of the 999th Field Artillery Battalion or of the 334th Regiment of the Chinese People's Volunteers, but who wishes to know what brought them to Korea in the first place. Finally, I make no apology for the military emphasis that pervades this work. "The new military history" (unoriginal term that it is) of the last several decades has concentrated on what were admittedly some neglected and significant aspects of warfare, such as women, minorities, economics, technology, the fine arts, and so on. As such, these studies were a welcome addition to the traditional "battle and king" form of military history. But, that said, the course of the Korean War was, hardly surprisingly, more affected by events on the battlefield than by any other factor. The racial integration of the US Army, the social backgrounds of ROK or US Army or Chinese People's Volunteer officers, the comings and goings of the leaders and diplomats of the UN coalition, were all dependant on the military course of the war. Had the UN Command been thrown off the Korean peninsula in the summer of 1950, quite obviously there would have been little more than academic interest in, say, the class structure of the Korean People's Army or the racial composition of the US Army at the time. On the other hand, this study will not neglect such topics as the UN debates on the war, racial questions, the weapons of the war, or reflections of popular culture of the war (at least in the West), but almost always in the larger context of the course of the war itself. The one exception will be in the question of the forcible repatriation of prisoners of war. That unresolved, unmilitary question caused the war to drag on for more than a year after all other significant issues between the UN coalition and the Communist side had been resolved and the battlefield had hardened into a stalemate.

If anyone in the spring of 1950 had drawn up a list of possible sites for the world's next significant war (and, obviously, there were such persons, in the world's foreign ministries and ministries of defence, as well as in the US State and Defense Departments), Korea would have been towards the bottom in any such compilation. The US military, the Central Intelligence Agency and the Truman administration were mildly concerned about the possibility of further armed conflict between the Democratic People's Republic of [North] Korea and the Republic of [South] Korea, which had been conducting mutual border raids for more than a year. But most US military planners had concluded (in the little time that they had spent on the subject) that the ROK was indefensible. At any rate, Washington's eyes were on Western Europe; the North Atlantic Treaty Organization had been founded in 1949, a year that had also seen the termination of the Berlin Airlift and the explosion of the first Soviet nuclear weapon. A Soviet thrust into Western Europe seemed a far more threatening contingency than a possible dust-up between two unattractive regimes in a bleak former Japanese colony that most Americans could not (then or now) find on a map. But Americans, much against their will, would become very well acquainted with Korea in a war that would turn out to be the third bloodiest in their history, which would enormously increase the international prestige of the new People's Republic of China (at a cost to that regime of 360,000 casualties), and which for the Koreans themselves would prove the greatest catastrophe in their national history.

In looking back over history before 1945 it would be difficult to imagine a more homogeneous and united nation than Korea. Whatever Koreans' differences in caste or class, they are of the same culture (with minor north–south variations) throughout the peninsula, and the Korean language – Hangul – is universal. Korean cultural homogeneity can be illustrated in its place names, a source of confusion for non-Korean UN personnel throughout the war: Inchon/Ichon, Masan/Musan, Paengnyong/Pyongyang/Pyonggang Pyongchang, Kasan/Kaesong/Kaechon, Taejon/Taechon, Pukchong/Pukchang, Sunuiju/ Sinanju (the last two not that far apart geographically), to take a few at random. Americans complained that "every other Korean is named Kim!" (And seemingly the other was named Lee.) Then there were the two North Korean leaders, Kim Il Sung and Kim. Il. All of this was also a tribute to the simplicity of Hangul and was reflected in the considerably higher rates of literacy discovered among North Korean POWs of the UN, compared to their Chinese comrades.

To make matters even more simple, Korea, unlike even Japan, has no dispossessed minorities and its borders have been fixed for centuries; there is no question as to where China or Russia ends and Korea begins and none of these bordering nations harbour irredentist factions or longings for "lost territories".

Thus it was one of the great ironies of fate that two obscure US officials would casually segment this almost uniquely unified nation on the eve of Korea's liberation from a hateful state of colonial vassalage. This cruel division, still in effect after half a century, was hardened by a bloody and destructive three-year war. And it is the final irony of Korean history that this conflict would be termed by some scholars a "civil war".

The Korean War (25 June 1950 to 27 July 1953) emphatically marked the end of the post-Second World War era. The Sovietization of Eastern Europe, the Greek civil war, the Czech coup, and the Berlin Airlift, not to mention the "loss" of China to the communists, had all served to erode what had remained of the wartime "Grand Alliance" between the United States, Great Britain and the Soviet Union that had persisted through the war and to the establishment of the United Nations. But with American, British, French, Dutch, Canadian, Australian, New Zealand, South African, Greek, Turkish, Filipino and Thai troops actually engaged in combat with Communist forces, the Cold War seemed obviously to have taken on a new and far more bitter dimension, and indeed, might no longer even merit the term "Cold War". In the words of one scholar, "Without the Cold War there would have been no Korean War."[2] In fact, the entry of China into the conflict in late 1950 unleashed apocalyptic imaginings of a Third World War, particularly amongst Americans. Even after the Armistice concluding the Korean War, the Cold War would continue for more than four decades.

Despite the fact that a small segment of the Soviet Union actually bordered North Korea and although the Korean War was a reflection of the global Soviet–US confrontation, both super-powers punctiliously avoided direct combat with each other. The only shooting between military forces of the US and the Soviet Union were the one-sided downings of about one dozen American military aircraft around the periphery of the USSR. So far as is known, no Soviet aircraft were ever shot down by the US Air Force outside of Korea itself and its surrounding waters; intruders were merely "shouldered aside" even though they regularly violated the airspace of the United States and its allies.

At the time, the war was viewed in the West, with few exceptions, as an act of sheer aggression by North Korea against South Korea, an aggression plotted and sustained by the Soviet Union. Western leaders remained convinced throughout the war that Korea was a mere diversion, a "side-show" to distract attention from the real target of Soviet ambition: Western Europe. The first part of this conclusion was valid enough: Kim Il Sung did plot to invade and overthrow the Republic of Korea, and he was eventually aided and abetted in this aggression by Stalin and Mao, as more recently uncovered and released documents convincingly demonstrate. But there is no evidence whatsoever that this aggression was plotted with the object of diverting the democracies from the defence of Western Europe, which is not to say that Stalin, for one, did not welcome the diversion of men and weapons to Korea that might have gone to Western Europe.

The war had a strong, but not lasting effect on Western Europe. From 1950 on, the major diplomatic and economic efforts in the US and Western Europe shifted from post-war reconstruction to rearmament and the containment of potential Soviet aggression. Paradoxically, the bulk of this Korea-induced rearmament was directed not towards repelling Communism in Korea or in Asia, but towards blunting any Soviet incursion into Western Europe. Just as the Western allies adopted a "Europe First" strategy in the Second World War, so these same allies now gave first priority to Europe. In the words of the chief of Great Britain's Civil Service, Lord Franks, "there was a massive rearmament programme both in the United Kingdom and in the United States and France, and, of course, it was about Western Europe."[3] Although the cost of rearmament may have hindered economic recovery, particularly in Great Britain, increased military spending and military-linked financial aid from the United States, as well as the free-spending habits of overseas American servicemen, to some extent made up the difference. Certainly by the mid-1950s, Second World War bomb damage sites were more likely to be occupied by parked automobiles than by the ruins themselves.

In the United States, which along with the Koreas and China bore the brunt of the battle, Korea put an end to President Truman's "Fair Deal" and to a Democrat political hegemony that extended back two decades. Although it was a Democrat President who made the initially popular decision to send American troops to Korea and who had even earlier instituted a loyalty oath for federal employees, nonetheless the Republicans tarred their Democratic opponents as "soft on Communism" for not giving General MacArthur his head in a more aggressive pursuit of "victory" in Korea. The Democrats lost the 1952 elections badly to the Republicans under General Eisenhower – who then settled for a *status quo* armistice as a "substitute for victory". By then only the extreme right-wing of the Republican Party cared much one way or another about the outcome of this now deeply resented conflict. The war had gone on far too long for most Americans, who sullenly accepted the armistice agreement, when they even thought about it.

American military officers bitterly complained about having to "fight with one arm tied behind our backs". US Air Force jet pilots could see the dust trails kicked up by enemy MiG fighters as they took off unmolested from airfields in their Manchurian "sanctuaries". They could bomb only the Korean side of the Yalu border bridges, nuclear weapons were never used, and, of course, they could not drive once again, all-out for the Yalu and victory in Korea.

Yet these strong feelings overlooked the fact that the Communists also did not throw their full weight into the Korean War, a fact that more thoughtful observers readily acknowledged. UN truck convoys could head for the battle-fields, filled with munitions and supplies, with headlights blazing; the Communists never sent anything more than heckling warplanes south of "MiG Alley". UN ships could approach the South Korean coast and unload at the vital port of Pusan absolutely unmolested by enemy air power or submarines. In fact, Communist submarine attacks on slow-moving, unconvoyed UN ships heading for Pusan during the most critical days of the Pusan Perimeter battles would in all likelihood have finished off US and ROK forces barely hanging on along that battleline. Both sides held off committing their full military assets for precisely the same reason: fear of igniting a major war, perhaps even the Third World War.

In the same way, war-weariness on both sides, a disgust with a seemingly endless conflict with no side gaining anything more than local advantage, led, after the death of Josef Stalin, to the signing of a long-term cease-fire.

But the armistice did not bring about the usual pell-mell disarmament that had characterized all of America's previous post-war months. Military spending remained high, conscription was retained by all the major belligerents, and tens of thousands of American troops remained in Western Europe as well as two divisions in Korea. In fact, fiscal year 1953 saw the peak of American peacetime military spending as a percentage of gross national product. Not even the Vietnam or Reagan military run-ups surpassed this level of spending.

Certainly this conflict did not have as strong and as baleful an effect on the United States as did the Vietnam War. American troops "served their time" and went home, not to welcoming parades, true, but also not to contempt and controversy, and soon enough melded into civil life, where most carved out respectable careers. Even in Korea itself, after a conflict that had cost the lives of about one million Koreans, the border between North and South Korea remained basically unchanged and mutual antagonism continued to fester at least as much as before the eruption of this catastrophic conflict.

This was a war with only one hero: for many Americans General Douglas MacArthur's reputation soared well above that of the merely heroic; his removal by President Truman added a crown of martyrdom that the aging warrior was not loath to assume. But MacArthur stood alone. The resolutely plebeian Harry Truman was hardly cast in heroic mould; North Korea's premier Kim Il Sung was a remote figure given to Stalinist exhortations that bore little relation to battlefield realities, and South Korean President Syngman Rhee was an elderly patriot who, although personally symbolizing a decades-long struggle against brutal Japanese colonial exploitation, had few evidently engaging human qualities. On the battlefields in the opening months, Eighth Army Commander Lieutenant General Walton Walker proved to be a respected, scrappy fighter more often than not at the front, but nonetheless seemed to lack something of that inspiring spark. His successors, Generals Ridgway, Van Fleet, Clark and Taylor, were then and now considered excellent soldiers, and Ridgway will always receive justified credit for rebuilding a defeated Eighth Army. But none ignited public adulation, nor indeed did they make any such attempt.

Down the line, of course, there were heroes aplenty, beginning with those valiant South Korean soldiers who strapped explosives to their bodies and threw themselves under enemy tanks in the hopeless opening days of the war. There was US Army Engineer Sergeant George D. Libby, who in the retreat from the lost battle to hold Taejon kept his body between the wounded soldiers he was evacuating by artillery tractor and intense enemy fire, bringing his charges out but dying in the end. And there was the stand of the First Battalion of the British Gloucestershire Regiment – the "Immortal Glosters" – who held their ground in the face of what for once really were overwhelming enemy forces and suffered what may well have been the highest casualties to any one unit of that level or above during the entire war. In fact, the Glosters were the only particular unit of the Korean War to achieve public acclaim. The US Marine Corps as a whole added to their well-publicized laurels, with their landing at Inchon and their fighting retreat from the Changin Reservoir. Undoubtedly there were quite similar acts of individual and unit heroism on the Communist side, acts that will unfortunately and

6

unfairly remain unknown until the opening of files in Pyongyang and Beijing. Of course, officially, *all* North Korean and Chinese soldiers were heroes. This sentiment may be considered something more than mere propaganda, in view of the awesome rain of explosives, napalm and ever-burning white phosphorous that UN forces rained wholesale upon them throughout the war.

Korea has sometimes been termed "America's first ideological war". But the Soviet Union of Josef Stalin bore a considerably closer resemblance to that of Ivan the Terrible than to anything in Karl Marx's dreams, and the United States had been moving away from pure capitalism for decades. Korea did not unleash great surges of marital or patriotic sentiment in the United States, or in any of the other UN participants for that matter, except for South Korea. The Rhee administration was notorious for its "spontaneous" demonstrations that could rival anything even the Communists might lay on. For most Americans the Communist leaders were as remote and as incomprehensible and their regimes as repulsive as the Nazis or Japanese of the Second World War. In America itself there were literally tens of thousands of refugees from Communism who could vividly testify as to its bloody and "un-American" character, its atheism, its immorality. They in truth needed no Senator Joseph McCarthy (R–Wisconsin) to elucidate the dangers posed by "the Reds", foreign or domestic. Americans before Pearl Harbor could vigorously debate whether Hitler truly posed a threat to the Western Hemisphere. But there seemed no argument that a Soviet Union, led by a Josef Stalin, armed with nuclear bombs given away by British and American traitors and deliverable by copy-cat American B-29 strategic bombers was very definitely an immediate and mortal danger. And when a mere 22 misguided American POWs refused repatriation at the end of the war the worst fears of Americans seemed realized. Insidious Communist doctrines could be literally implanted in the brains even of American soldiers ("brainwashing"), something unheard of in that nation's previous wars.

The Communists were possessed of their own ideology, that saw the South Koreans as "puppets" of the United States, whose "ruling class" was the centre of world reaction to the inevitable victory of utopian communism, particularly of the variety practiced and preached by the Chinese Communists. In addition, the North Koreans were fighting for the unity of their cruelly amputated nation; they held the inestimable advantage of knowing that if they won, their nation would be reunited. Thus the Americans were doubly accursed for selfishly opposing the historic march of socialism/Communism and for perversely resisting the righteous cause of Korean reunification.

An ideologically divisive aspect of this war could be seen in the mass flight of refugees. In most cases they fled towards UN lines; the most egregious example was the evacuation of nearly 100,000 North Korean civilians along

7

with UN forces from the east coast port of Hungnam during the great retreat in the face of Chinese entry into the war. "Progressive" writers argued that such refugees were simply fleeing the fighting. (But why almost always to the south, that is, to UN forces?) Or they asserted that these civilians had nowhere else to go because insensate UN bombing and shelling had destroyed all shelter. (But why such flocks of refugees in the balmy summer of 1950?) It is still difficult to explain why so many workers and peasants would flee from the workers' and peasants' armies, which would presumably soon render them succour, unless they really believed that the UN forces could do more for them.

Peace in Korea was delayed for almost two years by the very ideological question of the disposition of Communist POWs who refused repatriation. The basic formula for a *status quo* cease-fire had been worked out in a matter of months in 1951, as both sides realized that victory in Korea could be achieved only at a cost they were not willing to pay. But the actual signing of an armistice was delayed until 27 July 1953 when the Communist side finally accepted the fact that more than 22,000 of their fellows bitterly opposed returning to their socialist motherlands. The 325 UN non-repatriates were in comparison small comfort indeed.

Like most modern wars, the Korean War was unanticipated in its outbreak, its course, its character and its conclusion. As Eighth Army commander Matthew B. Ridgway wrote 13 years after the conclusion of the war, "Before Korea, all our military planning envisioned a war that would involve the world."[4] Confounding military planners and Sunday supplement seers alike, no stratospheric bombers would overfly the polar regions to unleash nuclear weapons in enemy heartlands, no great tank phalanxes would clash on frozen plains, no airborne armies would descend on strategic points. Rather, relatively small numbers of soldiers on both sides of the Korean War found themselves in fetid rice paddies or clambering about rocky hills where the seemingly eternal battle truths of leadership, training, morale and small unit cohesion, as well as individual stamina, could make the difference between life and death, victory and defeat, as much as when Roman fought Carthaginian. Although the savage post Second World War military budget cuts were primarily responsible for the poor showing of US Army units early in the war, the US military establishment was also culpable for neglecting basic military principles in its fascination with technology, nuclear weapons and their delivery systems; as always, the individual US infantryman would pay a high price early in war for the mistakes of his political and military superiors.

In one very important aspect, however, technology did make a difference in the outcome of the Korean War: without Allied air power over the battlefield and control of the sea lanes there can be little question that US and Republic of Korea forces would have been driven off the peninsula by September 1950. As it was, up to and just beyond the very day of the Inchon landings behind enemy lines, UN forces, although enjoying numerical supremacy and total control of the air, could still have lost the war. Air power made the difference, but even here, it was not a particularly futuristic air power. Aside from the jet-to-jet air combat, the first in history, over "MiG Alley", both sides employed air power technology that was hardly changed from the last years of the Second World War. And at sea, almost all vessels employed by the UN were of Second World War vintage and employed the blockade and strike operations of that previous conflict.

The war rested much more easily on the United States, for as in the Second World War the homeland was spared its ravages. Military conscription took her sons, but most of them went to Europe, although more than 30,000 would lose their lives in Korea. But there was no rationing, no censorship, not even a reduction in automobile production. In fact, the war produced an economic boom that more than paid for the increased wartime taxes, although accompanied for the first year by inflation until the imposition of wage and price controls. Opposition to this war in the United States was limited to the "hard" left for whom the Soviet Union could do no wrong, and to the political right, who felt that their nation was "just wasting time" in Korea and should "win or get out", even if victory mandated the use of nuclear weapons. The vast majority of Americans simply accepted the war, after the initial burst of patriotic fervour in the summer of 1950, as one further consequence of global leadership in the fight against Communist aggression. The most important consequence of this conflict, apart from the loss of lives, was the beginning of what was by far the most sustained and greatest peacetime military mobilization and rearmament in American history, with conscription, for example, retained for the next 20 years.

Also as a consequence of the Korean War, foreign affairs would dominate national political debate in the United States, again for the next two decades. The fulminations of Senator Joseph McCarthy against suspected domestic Communists or fellow travellers, were all about their ties to foreign (i.e. Communist) powers.

Wildly overreacting, many otherwise sober Americans unhistorically concluded, along with President Truman (who, of course, detested McCarthy), that America stood at something like the greatest crisis in its history. And if it took the atom bomb to save America and the Free World from "Godless, atheistic Communism", well, that weapon had ended the Second World War quickly enough. President Truman, the only American Chief Executive to preside over two major US wars, should also be remembered for his decision *not* to "drop the bomb".

And Truman was not alone. His successor, Dwight Eisenhower, after almost casually letting it be known that he considered a nuclear device as just another sort of weapon and that he might indeed authorize, say, one or two on the Korean battlefield, did no such thing and went on to approve the armistice ending the war. Eisenhower's earliest and greatest accomplishment was his lowering of the collective temperature of the political debate in Washington. No one could believably accuse "Ike" of being "soft on Communism" (although Senator McCarthy tried), and thus he could finesse attacks from the Neanderthal Republican right.

America's UN allies, aside from the South Koreans, reacted with considerably less fervour, even though most of them were on a much shorter bombing run from Moscow than was America. The thought of the "immature" United States igniting a nuclear war terrified them. Many Europeans tended to view at least their own Communists more as "liberals in a hurry" than as agents of Moscow, dedicated to the overthrow of their countries. Nonetheless, there were staunch anti-Communists among them, particularly among those of the left, such as British trades union leader and Labour Foreign Secretary Ernest Bevin, whose hatred of domestic Communists went back to his battles with them in the docklands. But few, if any, of America's UN allies could be convinced that winning the Korean War was worth a nuclear exchange. This unequal commitment would complicate relations between the United States and its UN allies throughout the war.

The obvious exception to such "moderation" was the Republic of Korea under its irascible, violently anti-Communist and authoritarian President Syngman Rhee. The old patriot understandably could not push aside his dream of a united Korea merely for an armed truce, and almost to the last moment did his best to wreck the negotiations towards that truce. According to all the evidence, Kim Il Sung was as fervent a believer in Korean unity as was Rhee. But he was obviously more amenable to the advice of his own allies and suppliers that such a truce was all he could hope for at the time, and after truce talks began he never called publicly for any "drive south" as a counter to Rhee's "On to the North!"

The Peoples' Republic of China could be said to have emerged as the one undisputed gainer from this war. Mao Tse-tung had stirringly proclaimed that "China has stood up!" to the assembled masses in Beijing's Tien an Min Square after the total victory of the Chinese Communists in 1949. But in the eyes of the rest of the world, China truly "stood up" when her delegates met as equals with the global super-power, the United States, at the first Korean armistice talks in the summer of 1951. Her major cost had been the battlefield human losses (including a son of Mao Tse-tung) which, although very heavy, could be quickly replaced.

10

Less than two decades earlier, this timeless and proud land had been trampled by the Japanese army, and other foreigners held humiliating long-term slices of Chinese territory. Yet it had now humiliated the United States by expelling the technologically vastly superior American forces, led by the conqueror of Japan, the renowned Douglas MacArthur, from its North Korea buffer state. Further, although a major combatant, China had suffered no destruction on its soil, and could be said to have called the bluff of those Americans demanding blockade or even strategic and tactical nuclear strikes against her territory. Never again could Chinese military or political power in the world arena be ignored, patronized, or disparaged.

In the war itself, it would be difficult to imagine what surprised the United States most, the locale of the war or the initial performance of its troops in the field. US forces had been withdrawn from the Republic of Korea the year before and Secretary of State Dean Acheson had specifically ruled Korea out of the sphere of US commitments in his notorious speech early in 1950. Those Americans who were concerned with foreign affairs fixed on the newly founded North Atlantic Treaty Organization (NATO) and the struggle for European rearmament, European economic recovery, the Marshall Plan (again for Europe), and to a much lesser extent, Communist insurgency in the Philippines and Malaya, and the military occupation of Japan.

But, whatever Americans' unfamiliarity with Korea or lack thereof, the US Army's Chief of Staff at the time, General J. Lawton Collins, was close enough to the truth when he pointed out "how fortunate it was for us that the Soviets picked or this venture the one area in the world where the United States military forces of all arms were well-positioned if we should decide to intervene".[5] Whatever the quality of the occupational Eighth Army, its four skeletal divisions were just across the Tshushima Strait from South Korea. The US Navy, with its excellent Japanese bases and ports, was in a far better strategic position to fight a war than it had been on the eve of the Second World War. US Air Force jet fighter pilots could eat breakfast with their families, fly their missions over South Korea, and return in time for a domestic lunch. One can only conclude that Kim Il Sung, Mao, and Josef Stalin seriously underestimated America's advantages in any war in Korea, or, more likely, discounted the possibility of US intervention altogether.

These advantages were hardly apparent at the time. Americans were startled when their troops, the victors of Tarawa, Iwo Jima and Okinawa, were steadily pushed back to the Pusan Perimeter. Stories began to filter back to an incredulous home front of American troops breaking and running before the enemy. Of course, American troops had been defeated before, and not so long ago, at Bataan, at Kasserine Pass, in the early stages of the "Battle of the Bulge". But at Bataan they had held off the enemy for months, and the

Kasserine and the opening of the Bulge were over in a matter of days and the enemy rolled back. This retreat went on for several months and hardly seemed to slow down the enemy until overwhelming material and numerical superiority was achieved at the Pusan Perimeter. And just when this stain seemed to have been erased in the quick conquest of much of North Korea, Chinese Communist intervention surprised the American military and led to the longest retreat in US military history.

Much of this questionable troop conduct was attributed at the time and later to the supposedly overwhelming numerical superiority of the enemy. After all, "life is cheap in the Orient" and the North Koreans would not hesitate to sacrifice any number of their troops to gain an advantage. Some have been quick to see "racism" in all of this, as in so many aspects of US life. But this interpretation seems overwrought. Americans remembered well enough their early defeats at the hands of the Japanese and that enemy's skilful and tenacious fight-to-the-death defence of one island after another on the way to Tokyo Bay. Many US NCOs and officers were survivors of just those battles, and were hardly likely to underestimate the fighting powers of orientals. If US troops were outnumbered, America's complete air superiority and overwhelming armour artillery advantage should have compensated for numerical inferiority. It was certainly not reported at the time, but by August 1950 combined UN forces actually considerably outnumbered the North Koreans.

If there was any American racism in this conflict, it might have been found among US attitudes towards the Chinese. The Chinese Nationalists had been pushed around by numerically inferior but modern Japanese forces from 1937 to 1945, and practically all Americans who had the misfortune to deal with the Nationalist government were agreed on its venality and incompetence. Thus, the US military would not have been particularly impressed by the Communist victory over the Nationalists and would tend to discount the latter's threat to UN forces in North Korea.

And while one is throwing around the term "racist", it could be argued that Chinese leadership attitudes towards the American soldier could perhaps also fall into that over-worked category. An early Chinese "lessons learned" pamphlet for their troops denigrated individual American courage:

> Their infantrymen are weak, afraid to die, and haven't the courage to attack or defend. . . . They will cringe when, if on the advance, they hear firing. . . . Without the use of their mortars, they become completely lost . . . they become dazed and completely demoralized.[6]

This quotation has been frequently repeated, particularly by those with an interest in denigrating the American soldier. But it first gained circulation in, of all places, an official US Army history of the Korean War. Conversely, a similar US Army volume quoted from an Eighth Army evaluation of the Chinese so laudatory that the caveat had to be entered: "The Chinese soldier is not a superman."[7] And little, if any, effort has been expended on trying to determine why the North Korean Army stampeded northward after the UN seizure of Seoul in September 1950. The reader can determine which side was the more afflicted by "racism".

Whatever the American soldier's fighting ability and spirit at the time, the war did come close to being lost at the Pusan Perimeter, as well as later, after the Chinese intervention. The fact was that the initial US troop levies had been shipped over directly from the softest duty known to any soldier, the occupation of a docile Japan. In addition, budgetary and terrain constraints had severely limited realistic training in the Japanese home islands. Those budget cuts had also deprived Eighth Army units of personnel and equipment; many radios and shells had simply deteriorated in the intervening five years of peace. Finally, it should be noted that the American military, unlike its opponents, was not preparing for war in Korea, nor was it ready for conflict anywhere else, for that matter. On the other hand, the record is now clear that Kim Il Sung had been planning to "liberate" his suffering brethren in the Republic of Korea for more than a year. In addition, the Chinese People's Liberation Army had just completed something like five years of arduous and victorious warfare against the Chinese Nationalists.

This was a war without heroes, although, of course, individual troopers on all sides won their countries' highest awards for valour. The only heroism that made any lasting impression on the UN side was the stand of the Gloucesters at the Imjim River, a stand that was unstintingly praised by the American military and journalists alike. The Turkish Brigade also was consistently lauded for its courage and toughness and many a GI returned Stateside with tales of imaginative Turkish methods of night fighting. But, in contrast to earlier wars, the American people had no Sergeant York or Audie Murphy to laud.

In fact, the one mythic American military figure, General Douglas Mac-Arthur, was eventually "cut down to size". MacArthur, a Medal of Honor winner, had emerged from the Second World War in the Pacific larger than life, and his outstandingly successful military government of Japan only added lustre to his laurels. Probably an overwhelming majority of Americans firmly believed that with "Mac" on the scene, the irritating conflict in Korea would soon be triumphantly concluded. Even the retreat to the Pusan Perimeter was not held against him. There was a sufficiency of reasons for that surprising retrograde operation that at the time seemed to have little to do with MacArthur, and he could hardly be held responsible for the great run-down of the US military after 1945. But his blind romp towards the Chinese border, his two armies, the Eighth and X Corps totally separated by a nearly impassable mountain range, his fatuous raising of hopes of the boys being "home by Christmas", eroded his demi–divine status, although this erosion was not immediately apparent. Although there was a frenzied outpouring of adulation for the returning "Old Soldier" after his dismissal by President Truman, his star began to fade almost immediately and his inevitable run for the presidency in 1952 yielded nothing more than embarrassment for all concerned.

Although the more outlandish tales of wholesale slaughter of cowardly UN "mercenaries" and their "puppets" by unflinching Communist troops can safely be discounted, and although its propagandists insisted that *every* North Korean and Chinese soldier was a hero, there were undoubtedly genuine battlefield heroes on the Communist side. But it seems almost fitting that this most unpopular of wars should produce so few inspirational battlefield figures.

Not only was this a war without heroes, it was a war without victors. The Chinese Communists came out of the war with greatly increased international prestige, but still no victory; for all their initial success in throwing the "imperialists" out of North Korea, they too had failed to reunify Korea. The war actually harmed Sino–Soviet relations, with the Chinese remaining embittered over Stalin's refusal to commit his air power to the battlefield when it might have tipped the balance against the UN.

Even the end of the war itself was not clean–cut. The armistice agreement of 27 July 1953, simply an in–place cease–fire, seemed to either side a poor substitute for victory. No peace treaty has ever been signed.

Ignoring the War of 1812, Americans could bemoan the fact that this was America's first war that did not end with a victory parade down Pennsylvania Avenue. This feeling of lost victory simply intensified the domestic anti-Communist crusade that still goes by the patronymic of "McCarthyism". If America had not emerged once again victorious on the battlefield, it must have been betrayed, if not by actual Communists and spies in key domestic and Allied places, then by their "agents of influence", by liberals, one-worlders, weak-kneed do-gooders and other generally "Un-American" types.[8]

But the true losers, of course, were the Koreans. Both north and south, there remains an immeasurable and palpable sense of loss, something like one million of their kin, and the near-destruction of their nation, and the loss, again on both sides, of any hope of reunification at any time in the foreseeable future. The Korean people suffered personal and property losses roughly comparable to those of the Soviet people in the Second World War. All that either regime could show for such sacrifice at the end of the war was the reestablishment, more firmly and more intransigently than ever, of their respective regimes over almost exactly the same amount of territory that

14

they had controlled in 1950. The only area untouched by the fighting was the segment around the vital port of Pusan known as the Pusan Perimeter, where UN forces made their last-ditch stand. The rest of the Korean peninsula became a battlefield for the first year of the war, with the capital of South Korea, Seoul, changing hands no fewer than four times, while North Korea's capital was taken and lost by UN forces and then pounded to rubble from the air.

Almost all of the carnage wrought by the ground war was inflicted only in the first year of the war and primarily on South Korea. By the spring of 1951 the war had hardened into fixed battle lines that closely resembled the Western Front of the First World War and from which the civilian population had long since fled. From then to the end of the war, destruction would come from the air at the hands of UN air power and only over the North. In fact, North Korea was pounded far more heavily in the last two years of the war than in the first. South Korea, on the other hand, could begin to rebuild as early as the summer of 1951.

America's UN allies were glad enough to be rid of a conflict that had delayed their recovery from the Second World War, and they could look to the United States once again in its foreign affairs focusing upon Europe and NATO. They were also relieved that the threats of nuclear Armageddon from the more vocal of American military and political leaders would apparently lessen. (This hope was dashed when in the year following the Korean War's armistice, US Secretary of State John Foster Dulles lugubriously opined that his nation might have to go "to the brink" to show an enemy that it meant business and when loose talk circulated in Washington as the French garrison at Dien Bien Phu in Indo-China faced annihilation. And the most frightening nuclear confrontation of the entire Cold War era, the Cuban Missile Crisis, was well into the future.

In the following decades North Korea seemed to recover well from the war's destruction, to the extent that some "progressive" opinion in the West even asserted that here was one place where, at least in comparison to South Korea, Communism was indeed delivering the goods. But the South, in its long struggle to achieve economic recovery with sizeable US aid, had by the 1970s forged well ahead of its northern rival. The Republic of Korea became an almost charter member of the "Asian Tigers" economic powerhouses and by the late 1980s had indeed achieved as large a measure of democracy as any nation whose capital lies less than 30 miles from an enemy publicly dedicated to its destruction. The Democratic People's Republic, on the other hand, fell increasingly behind the South by every indicator of wellbeing. It desperately resorted to such acts of terror as aircraft bombing, the blowing up of prominent South Korean officials in Rangoon, and the sending of assassination squads across the Armistice Line, not to mention the digging of a vast complex of tunnels under the Demilitarized Zone, obviously in preparation for an invasion of the South. The literal worship of Kim Il Sung reached depths of public adulation that might have made even a hardened Stalinist blush. In fact North Korea could be fairly accurately characterized as "more of a cult than a country", a cult that was thrown into some disarray with the death of its seemingly immortal leader in 1994. Even before Kim's departure, clandestine reports from the land that had once seriously proclaimed itself as a literal paradise spoke of severe food shortages and even of starvation. In fact, in May 1995, the North Korean authorities had to take the humiliating step of actually appealing to the hated Japanese, as well as South Korea, for rice. North Korea, like the late Soviet Union, blamed "bad weather" for its agricultural shortfalls. (The weather seemed just fine south of the 38th Parallel.)

By the mid-1990s North Korea and Cuba remained the only two nations of the once-challenging Communist bloc whose leaders still seemed to make any thorough attempt to apply the nineteenth-century legends of Marxism/Leninism to the governing of a contemporary society. Only North Korea's nuclear potential and its enormous conventional military establishment brought it some measure of world attention. But aside from that serious consideration, the Democratic People's Republic of Korea plays a modest role in world affairs, certainly in comparison to the Republic of Korea. It is hard to imagine a time when its invasion of its southern rival impelled the greatest peacetime mobilization in American history and ignited fears of the coming of the Third World War.

Chapter Two

History and background

On 25 June 1950, President Harry Truman, having opened the new Baltimore
–Washington airport in one of the more meaningless routines inflicted on
heads of state, was flying to Missouri for a weekend with his family. His
recorded thoughts at the time were of domestic matters. In fact, in that halcyon
month most prospects would seem to please the once much-underrated
Middle America politician who less than two years earlier had pulled the
political upset of the century, confounding the experts by winning a second
political term in his own right. Those elections had also returned a Democratic majority in Congress. The President could now push ahead with the
Fair Deal, his not-very-original title for a package of programmes to provide
health insurance for all Americans. The nation had also weathered the recession of 1949 and moved into a new period of economic prosperity without
significant inflation.

Abroad, the situation admittedly was more clouded. The Soviets had
exploded their first atomic bomb that August and the Chinese Nationalists
had collapsed and fled to the offshore island of Formosa (Taiwan) after the
United States had poured several billions of dollars into that hopeless cause.
Received opinion was that the Nationalists would soon enough be ejected
from this last refuge. Further, Communist-led insurgencies were worrisome
in Indo-China, Malaya and the Philippines. The Japanese recovery from war's
devastation was lagging and Secretary of State Dean Acheson had publicly
delineated the fledgling Republic of (South) Korea as being outside America's
defence perimeter.

On the other hand, European recovery was proceeding nicely. The Western
Zone of Germany, after the currency reform of 1948, was already becoming
an economic powerhouse, had regained its sovereignty in 1949 as the Federal
German Republic and presented an illustrative contrast to the dwarf, depressed

17

and depressing rival Communist German Democratic Republic in the East. The Soviets had been compelled to end their blockade of Berlin that same year after a round-the-clock Allied airlift had kept the city so well supplied that it was actually exporting its industrial products to the outside world. The French and British economies were also recovering, particularly as a result of Marshall Plan aid. Just as importantly for America's political leaders, the nations of Western Europe, at the initiative of Canada and the US, had banded to form the North Atlantic Treaty Organization (NATO) which declared that an attack on one would be viewed as aggression against all. Thus was put into effect the supposed great "lesson" of the 1930s: that a concerted, binding, timely, public stand against the aggressors before the war might well have prevented the Second World War.

There is a hoary American saying that "All politics is local." "Local" politics continued to dominate the US scene even in the post-war era when the nation had supposedly "come of age" as a global power. European recovery and defence, however, commanded most of the attention of those relatively few Americans concerned with international relations.

President Truman had settled in for the night at the family's comfortable home in Independence, Missouri when he received the telephone call from Secretary Acheson informing him of the North Korean invasion. Even the President's most prescient advisers could not have told him that he would be facing his nation's fourth most costly war, and one that would, in addition to its awful human and economic cost to all concerned, savage his presidency and his party for the next decade.

History of Korea to 1950

It is something of an irony of history that a branch of the same tribes people who came to populate what was eventually termed Korea also began to people what came to be known as North America and the United States at roughly the same time, 30,000 to 20,000 BCE. Korea was able to develop and retain its culture and its independence through the ensuing centuries by its "special relationship" with China, to which she was usually tributary. But until the nineteenth century there would be no connection between Korea and the United States. Even Commodore Matthew C. Perry's opening of Japan to the outside world in 1854 provoked no interest in Korea. Korea itself, the legendary "Hermit Kingdom", was even less interested in outside contacts. When a US trading schooner, the *General Sherman*, ran aground in

18

the Taedong River downstream from Pyongyang in 1866, the vessel was burned to the waterline and the crew massacred to a man.

Five years later, the American Minister to China, Frederick F. Low, proceeded with a naval flotilla to Korea to negotiate a treaty for the return of shipwrecked seamen and made contact with local officials. But four US Navy steam launches were fired upon soon after by Korean shore batteries at the mouth of the Han River leading to the Korean capital, Seoul. The American vessels silenced the batteries, then sailors, fighting their way from fort to fort, captured five of the strong points and killed 250 Koreans. Notwithstanding this show of force, the Korean king still refused to make any treaty with the outsiders.

But in 1876 a Japanese flotilla, emulating Commodore Perry, sailed menacingly along Korea's west coast. This time the cowed Korean government signed the Treaty of Kanghwa (named after the island the Japanese had occupied), which provided for normal diplomatic and economic relations between the two nations. Five years later, a US Naval commodore, Robert W. Shufeldt, was able to negotiate with the Chinese viceroy in Beijing a treaty that would bind the United States and Korea. The Korean court itself agreed to the treaty and signed the instrument while meeting with Commodore Shufeldt on a hillside near Chemulpo in May 1882. The first American minister to Korea, Lucius M. Foot, arrived in Seoul the following year. The energetic Foot arranged for a delegation of Koreans to travel to the United States where they were welcomed with marked hospitality and were received by President Chester A. Arthur. Foot also arranged for Thomas Edison to secure an exclusive light and telephone system for the nation and for American missionaries to minister throughout the country in spite of specific Korean laws to the contrary. In fact, the first such missionary, Horace N. Allen, became US minister to Korea from 1897 until 1905. Thus the foundations were laid for what could be termed, at least in regard to South Korea, the third most committed Christian nation in the world, after the Vatican and the United States. As did Foot, Allen worked to secure American economic concessions in such fields as electric power, railroads and gold mining.

In the meantime, the Sino–Japanese War of 1894 had removed China as overlord and protector of Korea. A decade later, Japan and Russia clashed in full-scale war over control of the Korean peninsula. Japan emerged victorious, to the world's astonishment, and tightened its grip on Korea. Russia thus had lost its own opportunity to subjugate Korea to the status of a colony. But the Russians would be back. The United States, far from opposing foreign control of a nation to whom it was bound by treaty, actually encouraged Japanese domination of Korea. President Theodore Roosevelt admired the Japanese (while at the same time publicly fearing "The Yellow Peril")

19

but for some reason held the Koreans in utter contempt. Roosevelt's Secretary of State, William Howard Taft, actually proposed to the Japanese Prime Minister in July 1905 that Japan establish its suzerainty over Korea. Two young Koreans, one of whom was Rhee Syngman (Yi Sung-Man), futilely petitioned Roosevelt at the President's Oyster Bay, New York estate to abide by its treaty commitments to their nation. Roosevelt was too busy negotiating the Treaty of Portsmouth ending the Russo–Japanese War to have any time for such peripheral matters. In fact, one clause of the treaty provided that the Russian government "not interfere or place obstacles in the way of any measure of direction, protection, and supervision which the Imperial government of Japan may deem necessary to adopt in Korea". Basically the unwritten understanding was that the US would acquiesce in Japan's control of Korea in exchange for Nippon's performing a similar favour for the Americans in the Philippines.

In November 1905, Japan pressured the Korean King/Emperor, Kojong, into accepting a treaty by which his nation in all but name became a Japanese colony. Once again, President Roosevelt was petitioned, this time by the Korean monarch himself, to act in accord with the instrument of 1882, and once again the President refused even to consider living up to his nation's treaty obligations. The United States acquiesced further in Korea's subjection in the Root–Takahira agreement, by which the United States recognized Japanese supremacy in Korea and Manchuria. When Japan ended the charade of an independent Korea in 1910 by outright annexation, the United States looked on with tacit approval. So much for the Treaty of Chemulpo. Here was "power politics" at its most cynical. The annexation was all the harder for Korean patriots to accept, in that most of them regarded the Japanese as "barbarians", products of an inferior culture. Korean nationalists may have gained some measure of satisfaction in 1908 when two of their number assassinated an American employee of the Japanese government at a San Francisco railroad station.

Those nationalists could have been forgiven for believing in 1918 that President Woodrow Wilson, supposedly the champion of the liberties of oppressed peoples everywhere, would, in the wake of the First World War, prove more sympathetic. But Wilson, like his rival Theodore Roosevelt, simply ignored the petitioners (one of whom was, again, Syngman Rhee), and when the memorialists sought to make a personal appeal to Wilson, who was busily redrawing the map of Europe at the Paris Peace Conference, insult was added to injury when the State Department denied Rhee a passport on the grounds that he was now a Japanese subject! Rhee was not the only Asian or African (or African-American, for that matter) to discover that Woodrow Wilson's concern for the oppressed was fairly well confined to Europe.

Undaunted, Korean nationalists in the United States held a congress in Philadelphia to publicize Japan's misrule of their native land. In Shanghai another congress proclaimed a provisional government for an independent Korea and elected Rhee its first president (in exile, of course). In that same year, Korean nationalists in Korea itself ignited the famous Mansei Revolution, a mostly peaceful pro-Korean series of demonstrations throughout the land. The Japanese authorities put down this "revolution" with their usual brutality. Rhee tried again during the 1921–22 Washington Conference but with the same lack of success; the major maritime powers concerned themselves with warship tonnage limitations and Pacific island fortifications, not the woes of an obscure land that Japan seemed to have well in hand. Korea continued to be exploited by the Japanese in a manner generally more ruthless than anything endured by the colonies of the Western imperialists. The nation's very title was changed to "Chosin" and major cities had their names "Japanized": Pyongyang became "Heijo", Wonsan "Gen-zan", and Seoul "Keijo". The land itself was raped as Japanese colonialists denuded the Korean hillsides of their forest cover for the lumber, causing destructive erosion and flooding.

It was at about this time that the close relationship between Korean and Chinese Communism began. Some Koreans saw in Communism the hope for an end to their misery, and many Korean Communist exiles later fought alongside Mao Tse-tung against the Chinese Nationalists and the Japanese invaders.

During this time and for the following two decades, the only Americans who took any interest in things Korean were those church people who toiled in the Korean vineyard and their supporters in the United States. Rhee's 1941 book, *Japan Inside Out*, in which he warned that Japanese aggression threatened world peace, was practically ignored.

The Japanese attack on Pearl Harbor on 7 December 1941 matched the Korean nationalists and their moment. Both (by now Dr) Rhee and Kim Ku, leader of the Korean nationalists in Chungking, China, pledged their support to the Allies, and Rhee lobbied in Washington for American recognition of his movement as the government-in-exile of Korea. (It is indicative of the place of the scholar in Korean society that both Rhee and Kim Ku held legitimate doctorates.) Once again, Rhee was disappointed by the Americans. Although the State Department agreed that Rhee was indeed no longer a Japanese subject, it now felt that it would be unfair to fasten an unelected and out-of-touch government-in-exile on the Korean people. Further, and once again, big power politics played a significant role. The US State Department was well aware of historic Russian/Soviet interests in Northeast Asia, as well as of the desire of Korean Communists for post-war dominance in their land.

It was the Chinese Nationalists who came to the rescue of the non-Communist Korean nationalists. Generalissimo Chiang Kai-shek, staunchly anti-Communist and fearing post-war Soviet designs on Korea, prevailed on President Franklin D. Roosevelt and British Prime Minister Winston Churchill to join with him in proclaiming Allied support for Korean independence. A pledge at the end of the communiqué issued after the Cairo Conference in the autumn of 1943 stated that the contracting parties "mindful of the enslavement of the people of Korea, are determined that *in due course* Korea shall become free and independent" (emphasis added). The Soviet Union later agreed to the sentiment of the communiqué. The "in due course" phrase, of course, seemed to postpone what "free and independent" had given, to the outrage of Rhee, Kim Ku, and other Korean nationalists.

President Roosevelt later patronizingly proposed a four-power trusteeship for Korea's post-war reconstruction, a suggestion hardly more acceptable for a proud, united nation that had been brutally colonized by the mutual Japanese enemy. FDR and his advisers thought that it might take some 20 to 30 years of trusteeship before Korea would be fit for independence, that is, when they thought about Korea at all. (Privately FDR thought that Korea had become politically "emaciated" through lack of exercise in self-government.) It is indicative of the importance of Korea in the councils of the mighty that Winston Churchill later claimed "never to have heard of the place" before the Korean War erupted, even though the topic had, obviously, been discussed at the Cairo and Yalta conferences.

In July 1945, with US forces poised for the invasion of the Japanese Home Islands, General Douglas MacArthur was directed by the War Department to prepare for the occupation of Korea as well as of Japan. Two days after the Soviet declaration of war against Japan on 8 August 1945, two American Army Colonels, C. H. Bonesteel and Dean Rusk (later a US Secretary of State), were ordered to fix a line in Korea north of which Soviet forces would receive the surrender of Japanese forces in Korea and south of which the Americans would do the same. The line was drawn quickly, and on a map it appeared to segment Korea into two roughly equal parts. But, of course, this line was merely an administrative convenience, taking into account nothing of the geography, terrain, or economy of the peninsula and leaving the Japanese-built mighty hydro-electric complex and the major industrial plants in the north separated from the agrarian south, which relied on that power and on that industry. In sum, it can be said that North Korea got the industry and the resources while South Korea got the population.

But far more important than the provision for the surrender arrangements was the stipulation that this border would also delimit two military occupation zones. No one inquired as to the feelings of the Koreans on that supposedly temporary dividing of their nation. But, to be fair, no one at the time imagined that this line would become a permanent international border. (Actually, Japan in 1896 had rejected a Russian proposal to partition Korea into two spheres of influence along just that line.) On 15 August Premier Stalin accepted these arrangements. Truman has been much criticized for the division of Korea, but he was well aware of what was happening in Eastern Europe as the Red Army moved in on the heels of the retreating Nazis and established its own satellites. Soviet troops had already "liberated" Manchuria, dismantling its industrial plants and shipping them to the Soviet Union without a shred of justification in that China, of course, was an ally and a victim of the Japanese. Truman had probably forestalled a Soviet takeover of the entire Korean peninsula. Koreans received "half a loaf". South Korea would gain its independence and, eventually, by its own efforts, achieve democracy and great economic power. But all this would come at the cost of the division of the nation. (Things could have been worse: the eminent State Department official, George Kennan, actually thought that the US should basically keep order in South Korea until Japan could quietly resume its overlordship!)

The Soviet XXVth Army moved into Korea north of the 38th Parallel, and in its train came a "Committee of Liberation" and an embryonic Korean army composed of Korean expatriates, trained and presumably indoctrinated by the Soviets. The Soviets were far better acquainted with the situation in Korea, as was to be expected, considering that the USSR actually shared a short borderline with Korea.

Both the Americans and the Soviet occupiers began to erect roadblocks at crossings of the 38th Parallel, originally simply to regulate population movement. But soon enough the Soviets reverted to their own unique pattern of fencing in their own peoples. Later they cut communications with the south and fortified the frontier. The Americans tried to keep the border as open as possible, if for no other reason than that the south had to rely on the hydro-electric generating plants far to the north and on the fertilizer and industrial production of the Soviet zone.

On 8 February 1946, the Soviet occupation authorities established the Provisional People's Committee, headed by Kim Il Sung. The Committee held elections in November of that year for representatives who would establish a government for the north. The resultant Congress of People's Committees created a permanent People's Assembly which then functioned as the government of North Korea, under Kim Il Sung.

Kim had been born Kim Song-jun near Pyongyang to a peasant family sometime in 1912, soon after the imposition of Japanese rule. (Always something of a figure of mystery, Kim's exact birth date is unknown.) He attended school in both northern Korea and in Manchuria, but his formal schooling ended in 1929 when he was expelled from middle school and imprisoned by the Japanese for his nationalist activities. Upon his release, Kim joined guerrilla bands organized to fight the Japanese, who had occupied Manchuria in 1931. It was then that Kim followed the example of so many Communist leaders and adopted a *nom de guerre*. He would be known as Kim Il Sung the rest of his life. It is an indication of the shadowy nature of Kim's life that some doubt has even been raised that Kim the guerrilla of the 1930s and Kim the leader of North Korea were one and the same, but most scholars accept that they were. By 1938 Kim headed a joint band of Chinese and Korean guerrillas, and two years later this band defeated Japanese police forces near Kapsun, Manchuria. The inevitable Japanese counter-offensive drove Kim into exile in the Soviet Maritime Province by 1941. So far as is known, whatever Kim's military accomplishments against the Japanese invaders, they never took place on Korean soil.

Kim was recruited in 1942 by Soviet intelligence into the Special Independent Sniper Brigade. This 600-man, multi-racial (Korean, Chinese, Soviet) unit's mission was to gather military information on Japanese occupation in Manchuria and Korea. (There is no truth to the claim that Kim fought with the Red Army at Stalingrad.) Kim was also fortunate to have somehow escaped Stalin's several purges of Korean Communists, perhaps because of his unswerving loyalty.

After the Soviet military sweep through Japanese-occupied Manchuria and northern Korea, Kim returned to the land of his birth, along with Soviet occupation troops, in September 1945. Initial Soviet occupation policy was to work with a number of non-Communist "progressive" Korean nationalists as well as Communists, under Cho Man-sic, a staunch anti-Japanese Christian nationalist. But the Soviets, as in Eastern Europe, gradually drew northern Korea into their orbit, and essentially succeeded where Czar Nicholas had failed, in securing a Russian colony in Korea. In fact, North Pyongyang province had been virtually ceded to the Soviets as a special preserve with lucrative concessions. They had even given the province their own name, "Changjing".

The new quasi-government, under strict Soviet control, put Cho Man-sic under house arrest, silenced any opposition journals, established a Communist Party structure, and formed the Korean People's Army. All of this was very much in the pattern of the "People's Democracies" created under the Red Army's firm control in Eastern Europe. The Committee also instituted a number of economic and political reforms, including the expropriation of land and its free redistribution, the nationalization of all large-scale industry, transport, communications and banking. They also mandated an eight-hour day and proclaimed sexual equality. But unlike the situation in Eastern Europe, these standard Communist measures did engender some popular support, even in the south, where economic inequities were hardly being addressed. For all this northern "progress", however, a secret US Army intelligence report would note that no fewer than 2,187,015 North Koreans had *legally* emigrated to the south by the end of 1948.[1]

By this time the Chinese civil war was coming to its conclusion with the complete defeat of the Kuomingtang and its physical expulsion from the Asian mainland. Communist-led Korean troops had played a significant role in that victory. In fact, going back to the latter years of the war against Japan as well as the Chinese civil war, three of the best divisions in the (Chinese Communist) People's Liberation Army (PLA) were composed mainly of hardy Korean–Chinese troops. During the later conflict, Communist North Korea served as a convenient base for PLA forces in northeast China, which had become the decisive theatre of that war in the immediate post–Second World War years. North Korea was also a convenient transit point for Soviet supplies destined for the PLA; it supplied that army with no less than 2,000 railway cars of surrendered Japanese equipment, mostly *gratis.*

Still following the Stalinist satellite pattern, Kim proceeded to use Soviet power to purge the two factions that stood between his own group, the "Kapsan Ban", and complete control. (Kim's faction was named after that minor victory, noted above, over Japanese troops near the town of Kapsan, Manchuria.)

The first faction that stood in Kim's way was composed of indigenous Communist Koreans, one of whose leaders was soon assassinated. The remaining leader, Pak Hong-yong, a key organizer of leftist and Communist groups south of the 38th Parallel, returned North (one of the very few Koreans to do so) after liberation in 1945. Kim was further aided in supplanting the indigenous Korean Communist faction by the way in which so many of these fervent evangelical Communists headed South to spread the good news, leaving Kim with few rivals.

The second faction that Kim eliminated was sometimes known as the Yenan Group, which consisted of returned revolutionaries from China, led by Kim Tu Bong, who founded the New Democratic Party. But when the New Democratic Party and the North and South Korean Workers Parties were merged in 1949, Kim Il Sung, rather than Kim Tu Bong, became its head. Still, Kim Il Sung maintained an alliance with the Yenan faction. Kim Tu Bong did not fall completely from grace and power, for he did serve as one of the leaders of the Democratic Front for the Unification of the Fatherland.

Although supposedly harbouring suspicions towards the Soviets (at least in the view of his apologists) and seeking self-reliance, Kim Il Sung's public utterances made him a Stalinist of the Stalinists. Kim declared that "All the most precious and best things in the life of the Korean people are related to the name of Stalin", not a sentiment one would expect from a supposed staunch Korean nationalist. Even the buttons on new DPRK Army uniforms incorporated the Soviet hammer-and-sickle device, not the more generic Communist red star. Yet the North always pictured itself as the very model of independence in contrast to the "puppet" South, the "lick-spittle lackeys" of Washington and Wall Street. Kim himself was to go even beyond the semi-deification of Stalin and his "Cult of Personality", as hack party-line scriveners later solemnly proclaimed that the trees on mountain tops would bow in respect as Kim's airplane passed overhead. Later, a gold-coated, 60-foot statue of Kim was erected – facing South.

Kim and Stalin had to hold the United Nations and the United States at arm's length while unilaterally establishing their Korean state. The Soviet–American Joint Commission to reunify Korea (a forlorn hope if ever there was one) hardly functioned, and Stalin further rejected an American plan for a four-power conference that would determine the means for Korean unification and economic recovery. The Soviets insisted on a trusteeship for all Korea, as agreed at the Moscow Conference of December 1945, something bitterly opposed by all political groupings in the South – except for the Communists, who were following Moscow's "line". Soviet authorities in Korea refused to deal with any political groupings that opposed the trusteeship. The Soviets themselves were less concerned with the Korean question itself than with the precedent of the breaking of wartime agreements, such as those made concerning post-war Germany. The Western Allies then might have had a precedent for any agreement-breaking that they might have contemplated, not a remote contingency in Stalin's suspicious mentality. Considering the breadth and depth of feeling in the South against the trusteeship, it is surprising that the Communists there had the support they did. The Americans were caught in the middle, facing implacable South Korean opposition to the trusteeship plan which, as the Soviets reminded the Americans, had been drawn up by the Big Three wartime allies in 1943. Koreans had every reason to believe that, once again, their country would be sacrificed to international power politics. Their belief would have been reinforced had they seen a US Army Military Government brief of early 1946 which stated that "Since the primary objective of the US is to prevent Russian domination of Korea, and *since Korean independence is a secondary objective*, it is not believed to be in the US interest to form a Korean government which could be granted complete independence within the next few years."[2]

President Truman then referred the Korean question to the United Nations. Over Soviet protests, the UN General Assembly in November 1947 called for all-Korean elections under the auspices of the UN Temporary Commission on Korea (UNTCOK; later the "Temporary" was dropped), a body still in existence. The Soviets refused even to allow UNTCOK into its territory. (Apologists for the Soviet vetoing of Korea-wide elections have noted that South Korea held twice the population of the North, as though the possibility of losing an election justified cancelling it.) The United States then successfully pressured UNTCOK at least to supervise its elections in the South. These elections were duly held on 10 May 1948 and resulted in the election of a National Assembly, which then elected Syngman Rhee to the presidency of the newly-formed Republic of Korea (ROK). The elections were certified by UNTCOK to have been reasonably fair and representative, the second such in Korean history. (The first reasonably free elections in Korea were those established by US Army Military Government in the South in October 1946. See below.) No matter: within a few months, the Pyongyang regime was reported as vowing that "We will crush down the puppet government of South Korea and we will win final victory."

In place of UN-supervised elections in the North, Kim Il Sung called a Communist-sponsored unification conference in Pyongyang with Kim Tu-Bong as chairman. A large proportion of the delegates were moderate leftists or indigenous Communists, but they voted to continue the nationalization of industries and the collectivization of agriculture. On 9 September 1948, Kim Il Sung proclaimed the establishment of the Democratic People's Republic of Korea (DPRK). (Actually, the official title was the Democratic Republic of Chosen, harking back to the 500-year-old name. But the title is always translated as DPRK.)

The northern regime was almost totally dependent economically on the Soviet Union. With the collapse of the Japanese mainland empire, the North had been cut off from one of its natural trading partners. Also, the hydroelectric complex in the far North had few customers after Soviet troops had finished stripping Manchuria of its industrial plant. The Soviet Union emerged as North Korea's almost sole market and supplier of raw and finished materials as well as of technical expertise. As a result, whatever Kim Il Sung's nationalist impulses, he could make few if any decisions against the wishes of his "Beloved Comrade", Joseph Stalin.

During late 1946 the Soviets had established and supervised officers' training schools for a fledgling army and internal security forces, first as border and railroad constabularies, then as regular military forces. The officers were almost exclusively Kapsan Ban members. The core of this new military was the veteran cadre of the Korean Volunteer Army, which had been formed from Korean deserters from the Japanese Army and who would eventually fight with the Chinese Communists during the Second World War. Needless to

27

say, training, doctrine and equipment were of Soviet origin. The Korean People's Army (KPA, often written in the West as NKPA, or North Korean People's Army. But the DPRK authorities would never concede that there was anything but a single legitimate Korean government or army, one sentiment that was shared with the South) – the KPA, or *Inmin Gun* – was officially activated in February 1948. The high command of this force, after Kim, consisted of one army and two corps headquarters.

The Korean People's Air Force actually predated the KPA, having been founded as early as August–September at Sinuiju, as the Korean Aviation Society. Originally a unit of aviation enthusiasts, it had at first no particular connection with the Communist regime. But in the following month Soviet advisers as well as Koreans of undetermined political coloration had assumed the training and in 1946 the unit was given military status. In 1948 the KPAF became the Air Regiment. The even smaller Korean People's Navy grew out of, again, a Soviet-sponsored coast defence force organized shortly after the end of the Second World War and was elevated to navy status in 1948. The mission of all three military arms of the Democratic People's Republic of Korea was to protect the state from any incursions from the South, to maintain internal security – and to "liberate" the South.

Now-public documents from the archives of the former Soviet Union demonstrate clearly that Kim Il Sung early planned to "liberate" by military force his southern brethren groaning under the reactionary Rhee yoke. Kim's first raising of this possibility with Stalin, at a dinner or reception in Moscow in March 1949, was rebuffed by the latter. The canny Stalin realized that the North's military was as yet underdeveloped for any offensive operations and that the Chinese civil war, although going well, was still undecided, and (a point that seems to have escaped Kim) American troops were still in South Korea. In fact, Stalin's policy from the time of his establishment of the Soviet presence in the North, was a continuation of that of the Tsars of Russia, that is, the maintaining of a balance of power in the peninsula, and if this meant the continuing division of Korea, so be it.

Five months later, with the American occupation forces gone, Kim again pressed for permission, this time through Soviet diplomats in Pyongyang, to "liberate" the South, which he claimed was preparing to attack the North. However, the Soviets still felt that, even with the Americans gone, the balance of military forces did not decisively favour the North. A prolonged civil war could ensue, as in China. Kim was advised to devote his energies to strengthening the partisans in the South. The documents also show that, far from being simply a grouping of exasperated, downtrodden southern peasants, the partisans were strongly reinforced from the North in both weapons and troops. Kim, in fact, reported to the Soviet Ambassador that some 800 such reinforcements had recently been sent South. Yet Kim himself realized that partisans alone would not topple the Rhee regime. ("The people of the Southern portion of Korea trust me and rely on our armed might. Partisans will not decide the question.") By October 1949, Northern forces had mounted at least one heavy assault on ROK positions just below the Parallel on the Ongjin Peninsula, although such major action was against Stalin's specific orders.

At a January 1950 Pyongyang reception, Kim admitted, apparently with some disappointment, that "Rhee Syngmann is still not instigating an attack". Pressing for an invitation to Moscow to secure Stalin's permission for an invasion, Kim grovellingly asserted that he could "not begin an attack, because he is a Communist, a disciplined person[,] and for him the order of Comrade Stalin is law". (The Soviet Ambassador's record of this incident indicates that Kim "was in a mood of some intoxication".) But in that same month, Stalin wired his ambassador in Pyongyang that "I am ready to help him in this matter", and then "requested" a yearly minimum of 25,000 tons of lead.[3]

In March, Kim, "in order to strengthen the people's army and to fully equip it with arms, ammunition and technical equipment", requested 120 to 150 million rubles worth of "military-technical equipment", to be paid for that year with "9 tons of gold . . . 40 tons of silver . . . 15,000 tons of monazite concentrate", the latter, significantly, useful for the making of thorium nuclear bombs.[4] On the 11th of that month, according to two defectors from the North, a secret meeting between the top members of the DPRK Political Committee and Soviet advisers actually determined on an invasion of the ROK, but did not yet fix a date.

The Communist victory in China seems in large measure to have finally brought around Stalin's permission for an invasion. The Americans, despite their emotional ties to non-Communist China, had not intervened in the Chinese civil war, contenting themselves simply with supplying the Nationalists. In fact a post-Chinese civil war US State Department "White Paper" blamed primarily the Nationalists themselves for their defeat. At any rate, the Americans had modest remaining ties to Korea after withdrawing their occupation forces, basically the 482-man Korean Military Advisory Group (KMAG) and a sizeable civilian Economic Cooperation Mission (ECA). They had never unduly concerned themselves with the country anyway (as witness the Treaty of Chemulpo). So it was a logical assumption that, with their troops basically gone, any US reaction to an invasion from the North would be confined to strong protests at the United Nations. Of course, just the opposite construction could be put on this course of events: with the Chinese Nationalist government down, that left only the Republic of Korea as an American "client" state on the Asian mainland. The Americans might thus feel that they had to

29

fight all the harder to save this remaining regime. However, there is no evidence that such an argument was ever used.

The Soviet dictator gave tentative approval for the invasion during Kim's visit to Moscow in April 1950, contingent upon Mao's concurrent approval. "If you should get kicked in the teeth, I shall not lift a finger to help you. You have to ask Mao for all the help."[5] According to the report of Kim's translator on the Moscow trip, Kim made four points to convince Stalin that the Americans would not intervene to save the Rhee regime: (1) It would be an overwhelming surprise attack and over in three days. (2) 200,000 Communist Party members in the South would rise up as one to support the KPA. (3) The guerrillas in the South would also throw themselves into the struggle. And (4) The United States would not have time to respond. Of course, Kim was wrong, absolutely or in degree, on each of his points.

In May 1950, Kim flew to Beijing only to find a skeptical Mao, deeply involved in his own plans for an invasion of Taiwan. But the Chinese leader was negotiating for Stalin's support for this enterprise and could hardly hold back his own aid to another "fraternal socialist state". Kim presented Stalin as being enthusiastic about the invasion and in the end secured Mao's endorsement for the invasion of South Korea. Kim then notified Stalin that Mao was also now heartily in favour of the North Korean attack, thus managing to misrepresent both Mao and Stalin to each other!

The North accelerated its preparations for the invasion of the Republic of Korea. Chinese People's Liberation Army divisions of ethnic Koreans began deploying back to the Korean motherland. In that May, the Soviet advisers to the DPRK drew up a draft plan, revealingly entitled "Preemptive Strike Operational Plan", for the invasion of the Republic of Korea. A 1966 Soviet study of the Korean War showed just how well the invasion was planned:

> The correlation of forces between South and North Korea [on the eve of battle] was as follows: in number of troops, 1:2; number of guns, 1:2; machine guns: 1:7, submachine guns, 1:13; tanks, 1:6.5 [actually the South Koreans had no tanks, just armoured cars], planes 1:6. The operational plan of the KPA envisioned that [North] Korean troops would advance 15–20 kilometers per day and would in the main complete military activity within 22–27 days.[6]

The actual Soviet plan for the invasion of South Korea may have found its way into American hands. The US Far East Command Intelligence Section uncovered a Russian language "Intelligence Plan" for an attack by the North Korean Army, presumably drawn up by Red Army planners and confirmed by the Chief of the General Staff of the North Korean Army. The plan was divided into three "stages":

1st Stage: Breakthrough of the Defense Lines and Annihilation of the Enemy Forces. . . . 2nd Stage: Development of the Attack in South Korea and Annihilation of the Reserve of the Enemy. . . . 3rd Stage: The Mopping up Operation in South Korea and Arrival on the South shore of the Peninsula.

This was no contingency study for a riposte to some incursion from the ROK, certainly not in its frequent and frank use of such terms as "attack", "defense lines" of the ROK, and "arrival on the south shore of the Peninsula". Specific towns and cities are cited, with the days for their anticipated capture: Taejon, Seoul, Osan, Kwangju, Taegu – and with Pusan, the end of the war. The plan even called for "aerial reconnaissance" of the anticipated battle sectors as well as the receiving of intelligence from agents. It actually specifies on its last page the day of the invasion:

22 June? From the departure to the jump-off point. 15 to 25 June, 1950.[7]

Except for "aerial reconnaissance", this was indeed the cold-blooded scenario for North Korea's invasion of South Korea and the misery that was to follow.

The post-Second World War history of South Korea is considerably more chaotic than that of the North. United States Army forces began landing in Southern Korea during the first weeks of September 1945 at roughly the same time that their compatriots were disembarking in Japan to establish a military occupation of that defeated enemy nation. But Korea had been anything but an enemy nation, and many Koreans who had gladly welcomed the Americans as liberators from the hated Japanese soon enough began to wonder why their land was being occupied by another foreign military power. The Americans were given the useless information that they would be entering a land in which "some of the populace is Japanese, some Chinese, the people may be hostile to newcomers; you can expect all kinds of weather and the women are strange". To which one perceptive GI replied "Hell, it could be California".

The Americans, under Lieutenant General John R. Hodge, were not themselves sure of their mission. In October, General Hodge did receive a directive that the "ultimate objective" of Korean military government was the restoration of Korean independence. But in the meantime the occupation by the Soviet Union and the United States would continue, to be followed by a trusteeship, composed of the two current occupying powers, plus China and Great Britain. Restoration of Korean independence seemed impossibly far in the future for Syngman Rhee and Kim Ku, who had both returned to the South. Quite justifiably, they could not understand why their nation should have to endure partition (however "temporary"), alien military government and trusteeship. Further, there is no Hangul literal translation for the word "trusteeship"; its closest equivalent is a word that connotes the same type of oppressive supervision and control exercised by the detested Japanese, hardly a promising beginning for newly liberated Korea.

Certainly the economy had been damaged by the war and the nation was in political chaos, but the same could be said of many other nations immediately after the Second World War, including China, Italy, or France. No one was proposing a trusteeship for, say, France. Korean patriots could be forgiven for the suspicion that such expedients were solely for peoples of colour, perhaps simply a more subtle form of colonialism. In one of their last joint endeavours, the two occupying powers drew up an agreement for a five-year trusteeship. Thousands of urban Koreans took to the streets in tumultuous demonstrations in the American zone. No such outbursts were permitted to the North, of course, although it is highly unlikely that the proposal was any more popular there.

Communist propaganda would make much of the Americans' "collaboration" with the Japanese imperialists. And indeed, the first political movement or quasi-government of any kind in the South, the Chosun Keun Kook Chun Bi Hwei ("Preparatory Committee for Korean Rehabilitation"), was initiated and sponsored for several weeks by the Japanese High Command in the days before the arrival of American occupying troops. But this organization, under Lyuh Woon Hyung, rapidly filled with Communists or near-Communists. Two days before the American landings, it ambitiously retitled itself "The Korean People's Republic". The presidency and vice-presidency were then offered to Syngman Rhee and Kim Ku, both of whom refused. Both were soon after "expelled" from a movement that neither had ever joined! As this "government" moved into the chaotic Korean countryside, it also attracted some non-Communist membership. The "People's Republic" leaders presented themselves at XXIV Corps headquarters on 8 September 1945, but General Hodge would not meet officially with them because of their Communist support. He was also worried over seeming to favour one political faction over another. Hodge was apparently unaware of the People's Republic's Japanese beginnings. The general was dealing with a people that had known almost no political or individual freedom under 35 years of Japanese rule. The long Japanese occupation had left Korean politics for the most part raw, immature and extremist.

One month after the US landings, the Military Governor appointed a "Unification Committee for Political Party Activities" composed of a Communist, a nationalist, and a radical to lay the groundwork for reunification and the beginnings of political life. This admittedly naïve effort, doomed from the start, does at least reveal the American military in a somewhat less inflexible anti–Communist mode than might be supposed. Hodges' military government quite soon, however, began to favour non or anti–Communist elements of the southern Korean politically aware population. Hodge himself was a poor choice for military governor. He lacked any military government or Asian civil experience. He appeared to be a small-bore MacArthur, with what his own troops called his "Doug-Junior" sunglasses and his militantly mid-American approach to the problems of his exotic new responsibility.

Any popularity enjoyed by the American military occupation was early eroded by a statement that General Hodge never made: "To me Japanese and Koreans are the same breed of cat." Although no proof was ever adduced for this outlandish purported statement, Hodge's strictly temporary expedient of keeping former Japanese colonial officials in their offices added credence to the rumour. Hodge later explained that he had simply referred to the old Japanese/Korean police force he had inherited in 1945: whatever the nationality of its members, to the Koreans themselves they were indeed "the same breed of cat". Actually, the Japanese/Korean police force was almost immediately disbanded by the Americans, but 85 per cent of their replacements lacked any law enforcement experience. They tended to use Japanese methods and worked under the assumption that anyone taken into custody was probably guilty, otherwise he wouldn't have been arrested in the first place. Although the reconstituted police were forbidden to beat suspects, they now simply turned that function over to the fire department. The Japanese legacies of top-to-bottom graft and endemic violence were also almost impossible to suppress. One Japanese police legacy that was indeed abolished, and immediately, was that of the infamous Thought Police. There was some progress.

Several hundred registered political parties, many with the most obscure commitments, soon besieged General Hodge. Both right and left resorted to violence; the left's was more widespread, but the right's better organized. Even the Boy Scouts were perverted into right-wing strong-arm squads. In a foul temper, Hodge wired General MacArthur that

> The Korean people are the most difficult of all peoples I have ever encountered. They have only one common idea – independence. Independence means that all should be freed from any form of work and from any and all restraints on actions or words. With few exceptions, they are highly contentious among themselves, can cooperate to the extent that each individual can have his own way, have small conception of patriotism on a national basis, are highly volatile and unpredictable, can easily be bought, have low individual integrity, have low capacity for citizenship, are pro-self and anti-almost anything else. Although they

33

know we are trying to help them, they are suspicious of any controls and blame all their national ills on anyone handy who is not Korean.[8]

Addressing American troops at the Yongdongpo replacement depot in November 1947 General Hodge was reported to have ill-advisedly been even more blunt: "There are only three things the troops in Japan are afraid of. They're gonorrhea, diarrhea, and Korea."[9]

Yet it should be remembered that American Military Government of Korea did sponsor the first free elections in Korean history, in October 1946. These were marred by leftist boycott and rightist irregularities, but their results did reflect the conservatism to be expected of a peasant economy. Still, they did much to polarize right and left. (A questionnaire distributed at the time by US Military Government found that "rightists" outnumbered "leftists" by almost two-to-one, but that there were almost twice as many Koreans terming themselves "neutrals" than the two polarities combined, and that an overwhelming majority favoured "socialism" [70 per cent] over either "capitalism" [13 per cent] or "communism" [10 per cent].)

Rhee and his followers continued to rail against the trusteeship proposal while agitators, right and left, kept street demonstrations going. In the first two years US Military Government in Korea remained divided by the US State Department's continuing desire to establish a united Korea (albeit under the UN trusteeship) and the military's own ingrained suspicion of Communism and Communists.

In May 1946, the American and Soviet military delegates met again for the final time on the Korean question. It was soon obvious that they would reach no agreement. The Soviets were holding out for a satellite-type solution and the Americans for open elections that they believed would bring a democratic, pro-American government to power. Espionage and sabotage directed from the North were increasing; General Hodge ruefully maintained in 1946 that the Communists had his command well "cased".

In 1947 Kim Ku and Kim Kiu-sik made a forlorn final attempt to open the way for reunification by attending a North–South leaders' conference in Pyongyang. But the bulk even of the Southern delegates were Communist or pro-Communist. The high point of the conference was the "summit" meeting of the four major Korean leaders, Kim Il Sung, Kim Tu Bong, Kim Kiu-sik, and Kim Ku, which issued a communiqué calling for the immediate withdrawal of all foreign forces from the peninsula. The leading delegates from both North and South promised that they would engage in no civil war after the foreign troops had left and would hold a democratic general election for a representative assembly that would establish a national government. The four Kims agreed neither to acknowledge nor support any government established through a separate election in the South. Syngman Rhee denounced the conference, its delegates, and its communiqué. But it might be remembered that it was the American Military Government, supposedly committed to the most reactionary elements in Korean society, that permitted open Communists to work within its jurisdiction, to attend this conference, and to return to continue to agitate in South Korea.

By 1947, the Cold War gripped both super-powers. The Truman administration was beginning to adopt the policy of the "containment" of Communism. Accordingly, the United States shipped military aid, advisers, and financial aid to Greece for its civil war with Communist guerrillas, provided military and financial aid for Turkey, and announced the Marshall Plan to rescue war-devastated Europe from the threat of a Communist takeover. And the Soviet–American Joint Commission met for the last time in August of that year.

But for all that, the American government was not prepared to hold the line in South Korea. The US Joint Chiefs of Staff ranked various nations in that year according to their strategic importance to the United States. Korea and the Philippines were at the bottom of the list. In the autumn of 1947 both the State Department and the military Joint Chiefs of Staff agreed that the 45,000 American troops and their bases in Korea contributed little of strategic value and might actually be a liability. The Chiefs particularly worried that "violent disorders" in the South could force the Americans into a humiliating withdrawal. George Kennan again wrote off Korea in his "Résumé of World Situation" for Secretary of State Dean Acheson, asserting that Korea was "not of decisive strategic importance to us".

Both State and the Pentagon wished to cut their losses and evacuate the South under the best conditions, leaving the problem for the United Nations. The Joint Chiefs in February 1948 concluded that "eventual domination of Korea by the USSR will have to be accepted as a probability if US troops are withdrawn", but nonetheless planned for that withdrawal "at the earliest practicable date". American financial and military aid would be provided, but basically once again the United States was about to wash its hands of Korea. America's enduring foreign policy focus would remain that of Western Europe. By 1948 Washington was concerned with the Communist coup in once-democratic Czechoslovakia, the Soviet blockade of Berlin, the Italian national elections and the Greek civil war, all of which were seen as threats to the security and rehabilitation of Western Europe.

President Truman's Secretary of Defense, the irascible, ambitious Louis Johnson, had been rewarded with the post for his successful financing of the "lost cause" election of Harry Truman in 1948. Secretary Johnson took to economizing with a vengeance, closing military installations, mothballing ships, and cutting back on training. What military funding survived the relentless economizing of the post-war and the Johnson years was earmarked for such high-technology weapons as the giant B-36 intercontinental bomber. Voluminous military plans focused on repelling a Soviet thrust into Western Europe and the strategic nuclear bombing of the Soviet Union. Further, American military planners and political leaders were enmeshed in the great debates over universal military training, the aircraft carrier vs. the B-36 bomber, armed service unification, the founding of NATO and the proper American response to the Soviet explosion of a nuclear device in 1949 or the Berlin Blockade, not what might happen in Korea.

The most publicized and most rancorous military controversy of the 1948–9 period in the United States by a very public battle of words and statistics between the US Air Force and the US Navy as to the comparative value of the giant B-36 intercontinental bomber versus the super-aircraft carrier, as well as the wartime roles of the Army, Navy and Marine Corps. The controversy became so intense that it broke the spirit of the first US Secretary of Defense, James Forrestal, who resigned and soon after committed suicide. Charges of collusion between favoured government contractors and high Air Force officers, "leaked" documents and Congressional investigations spiced the debate. In the end, more from considerations of economy than of military strategy or effectiveness, the Truman administration came down in favour of the B-36, thus tying itself in large measure to what was later known as "massive deterrence" of the Soviets by the threat of air-borne nuclear annihilation.

Then there were the influential military experts and the popular journalists who regaled the readers of mass-circulation magazines and newspapers with fanciful tales of "push-button war" that had about as much resonance with reality as the contemporary breathless previews of "a helicopter/airplane in every carport". None of this controversy or this futuristic imagining did anything to prepare the United States for a nasty land war on the rim of the Asian mainland. In 1950 of the ten combat divisions in the United States Army, only one, the 82nd Airborne, was considered combat-ready. (It was never committed to Korea.)

Certainly events in Korea impinged little on American military planning and prognostication; political leaders in the South increasingly felt isolated from the United States. As noted, UN-sponsored elections in the South had resulted in the formation of a National Assembly, which in July 1948 drafted a constitution for a Republic of Korea (ROK), which, in theory, included the North, just as the Democratic Republic of Korea included the South. The Assembly, as noted, then elected Syngman Rhee as the first ROK President in elections that were, again, more or less free and under UN supervision.

However, a pall had been cast over those elections by the assassination of Kim Ku on 26 June of that year by a ROK Army officer. Feeling that the 1948 elections would perpetuate the division between the two Koreas, Ku had consistently opposed them. He had returned to the South, disillusioned by the determination of North Korea to control the conference and push for unification on the North's terms. Again, the left had stupidly boycotted the elections.

Rhee and the Republic of Korea itself were inaugurated on 15 August 1948, three years to the day after Japan had surrendered. In contrast to the North, the ROK dropped the traditional "Chosun" name. General MacArthur, Far East Command Supreme Commander, was the principal speaker, quite overshadowing Rhee. MacArthur declared that the "artificial barrier" of the 38th Parallel "must and will be torn down", thus reinforcing Rhee's dreams of absorbing the North. The Assembly held 100 seats for nonexistent representatives from the North, underlining the fiction that the ROK was the only legislative assembly for all of Korea.

Domestically, like the DPRK, the National Assembly passed abundant reforming legislation, including citizens' rights, social welfare, economic planning and even some redistribution of land. The high officials of the regime enjoyed good nationalist credentials, but at the lower military and police levels, former employees under the Japanese occupation predominated. The chief of staff for the ROK armed forces, for example, was a graduate of the Japanese Military Academy and had served during the Second World War with the Imperial Japanese Army, rising to the rank of major. In early June 1948 another prominent officer, who had commanded a special detachment of Koreans in the Japanese Army to suppress Kim Il Sung's guerrillas in Manchuria, led 2,500 of his goose-stepping veterans through the streets of Seoul. A new National Traitor Law, passed in September 1948, drew the rueful comment at a XXIV US Army Corps staff conference that were this law fully enforced, "South Korea will have to have many, many more prisons".[10]

Three months before the elections, the island of Cheju-do was racked by a Communist-led rebellion that would last for more than a year. Although the American Military Governor, General William Dean, insisted that the rebellion be settled with a minimum of force, when the newly established ROK government sent in its troops, the island was laid waste and 60,000 inhabitants became casualties. The brutal suppression of the rebellion received widespread and unfavourable publicity overseas.

The ROK government had hardly been in office for two months when the army's 14th Regiment rebelled at the port city of Yosu while under orders to help suppress the continuing Cheju-do rebellion. Rebellious officers seized the city, joined with Communist cadres, killed some 900 rightists and police, and decamped to the city of Sunchon. Both cities were retaken by loyal ROK forces, who brutalized and shot captured rebels, but many insurgents fled into the nearby Chiri mountains to fight on as guerrillas for several years. The US Army daily, *Stars and Stripes*, provided surprisingly frank accounts of the brutality of ROK forces in crushing this uprising, of popular support for the rebels, as well as of the rebels' industrial-scale massacres. It was indicative of ROK military brutality that one rebel leader was beheaded and his head put on display, another was hung on a cross in front of the Cheju City administration building and mutilated with bamboo spears, while in the so-called "human flesh distribution incident" scores of prisoners executed by vengeful police had their remains dumped on the doorsteps of prominent civilians. It is fairly obvious that something like civil war raged intermittently in South Korea since 1946, erupting into bloody insurrection in 1948–9. Authoritative estimates put the death toll at about 100,000.

From their bases in the Chiri massif, the guerrillas attempted to rally the indigenous population against the authoritarian Rhee regime. The more promising guerrillas were trained at the innocuously titled Kandong Political Institute, near Pyongyang. The Communist guerrillas saw 1949 as their year of victory. They then mounted a major offensive with some 3,000 fighters (aided by between 10,000 and 15,000 Southern supporters) in conjunction with numerous incursions across the 38th Parallel from the North. At their peak, these Southern guerrillas numbered some 27,000. But they were too scattered, could maintain only tenuous radio contact with the North, failed to rally the rural population, and faced a determined enemy unincumbered by much in the way of battlefield humanitarian scruples.

The Rhee regime mounted a counter-guerrilla campaign in October 1949, in the wake of the Yosu rebellion. Troops and police blocked key routes around known guerrilla base areas, removed the civilian populations to secure areas and established "free-fire zones" in the emptied areas. ROK forces then conducted sweeps through the base areas, killing or capturing most of the insurgents. But Seoul did not rely exclusively on force (at least in this matter). Its amnesty programmes netted no fewer than 40,000 of the disaffected in a five-week period. Undoubtedly the Rhee regime was authoritarian, but most ROK civilians would take considerably more convincing that the Communists had much to offer in its place. It helped that the government was at the same time carrying out a programme of land reform, in which small plots of land were made available, freehold, to tenant farmers. These new small proprietors may have sensed that the best the Communists could offer them was a place in a collective farm owned by the state, hardly a fulfillment of the Leninist slogan of "Land to the Tiller". Communist guerrillas in the South suffered a heavy blow with the capture of their two leaders Lee Chu Ha and Kim San Yong, in March 1950. Disheartened, surviving guerrilla leaders made their way back to the North, leaving the "liberation" of the South to an overt, full-scale invasion.

The revolts showed that the Rhee government was certainly not as popular as it made itself out to be, but the aftermath of those revolts, the absence of a widespread sympathetic popular rising, demonstrated that neither were the Communists. Also, the uprisings and their successful repression confirmed the ROK Army in its internal security role. Many patriotic Koreans were alienated from the new government in the South and its authoritarian leader. For some, it seemed that the Northern regime had made a clean break with the past and was more directly addressing Korean economic and social inequities. Nonetheless, this violence betrayed a certain desperation among the Southern Communists. Their ranks were about as fissured by faction as those of the non-Communists, and Stalin more or less openly disdained them.

Somewhat embarrassingly for the Americans and Rhee, the Soviets withdrew their troops from the North by the end of 1948, well before US forces, who stayed on until June 1949. A reporter for the *Chicago Daily News* wrote that "An atmosphere of defeatism and frustration grips Americans in this dreary, dusty capital as they prepare to withdraw after three years that many of them feel have been wasted".[11] For most US occupation troops, duty in this hardscrabble land made even bombed-out Japan look good. In retrospect, it would have been better for the US to have left behind a few small combat units (in addition to the limited KMAG organization) as an inexpensive "tripwire" to deter aggression. Kim Il Sung might not have been deterred, but the ever-cautious Stalin would not have given his blessing for an invasion that would draw in US troops.

Perhaps even more significantly, the Department of Defense had by the autumn of 1948 begun to redirect much of its Far East air power – roughly one-half of its medium bombers (the now ageing B-29) and large segments of its fighter, reconnaissance, and troop carrier units – to support the Berlin Airlift, over MacArthur's strong objections. This redeployment could not have been lost upon the North Korean authorities.

But MacArthur, at least in this instance, concurred with the Joint Chiefs, agreeing that the South Koreans could not defeat an invasion from the North and that US troops should not be introduced to save the day. The main American interest in Asia must remain Japan and the control of the Western Pacific and its island bases. Realizing the precarious state of his nation, Rhee appealed to the United States for support in the event of an invasion by the North but was rebuffed. In fact, the US Army drew up a thoroughly dispiriting plan which specifically ruled out the reintroduction of US troops to

Korea in case of an invasion from the North. Rather, the United States would simply evacuate its nationals and submit the matter to the UN Security Council. If the Soviets did not exercise their veto (unlikely), it might be possible for the UN to dispatch a task force that could include US troops to restore order in South Korea in what was actually termed a "police action". The study's authors admitted that "This course of action is unsound militarily" and could not be undertaken without the "complete cooperation and full participation by other member nations". It is not difficult to conclude that this was a mere paper exercise, simply to demonstrate that the Army had at least considered the possibilities. Such scuttle-and-run conclusions were never revealed to ROK officials. In the light of the American reluctance to defend his fledgling state, Rhee appealed to President Truman to demand from Congress at least American arms and munitions to give his army a fighting chance. Fearing that such equipment might be used by Rhee to "drive North", Truman refused.

War could have erupted in 1949 over a series of border clashes between the two Koreas, that at times rivalled in their intensity the nearly simultaneous internal revolts in the ROK. Both sides mounted major raids and probes of varying intensities and duration. Rhee was as often as not the aggressor. In October he vaingloriously and ludicrously boasted in an interview with a top US journalist that "I am sure that we could take Pyongyang . . . in three days. An all-Korean border with Manchuria would be easier to defend than the 38th Parallel".[12] The ROK Army initially did well in these border clashes, many indeed initiated by the South after US forces withdrew. In June a small group of ROK guerrillas was captured on a deep penetration raid into the DPRK. The following month, ROK warships brazenly bombarded shore installations at the mouth of the Taedong River (port for Pyongyang) and sank most of the DPRK's west coast fleet. But the aroused North then sent in regular Korean People's Army (KPA) units for the first time, and, in fierce fighting, recaptured ROK positions that were actually north of the Parallel. In September heavy artillery duels erupted between North and South, with the North demonstrating a decided superiority in heavy artillery, a portent of things to come. These clashes and their generally unfavourable results for the South weakened American goodwill towards the ROK and gave the Truman administration even less of a reason to forward to Rhee the heavy weapons he was demanding supposedly to repel any invasion from the North. On the other hand, there is no evidence of any Soviet or Chinese discouragement of these incursions from the DPRK. Casualties seem to have been fairly evenly divided and heavy. Intelligence sources reported North Korean trains steaming northward crowded with wounded and a KMAG observer noted South Korean dead "stacked in a tent like cordwood" after such clashes.

KMAG was caught in the middle of these clashes, attempting to train and equip the ROK Army but trying at the same time to restrain its aggressiveness. The KMAG head, Brigadier General William Roberts, disgustedly reported to Washington in August 1949 that "Both North and South are at fault", but added that "No attacks by the North have ever been in serious proportions".[13]

Perhaps in consequence of Rhee's aggressive policies, Korea in 1949 must have been one time and one place where there was more desertion to the Communists from non-Communist territory than vice-versa. On 5 May 1949, two whole ROK battalions with their weapons defected. One week later a US-built ROK minesweeper, one of the ROK Navy's largest warships, sailed into the North's Wonsan harbour. To make matters even more galling for Rhee, only 12 days later came yet another defection, as the US-flag freighter, *Kimball R. Smith*, on loan to the ROK, surrendered at Chinnampo, with two chagrined US Economic Cooperation Administration officials aboard (later released). These most embarrassing incidents were only partially retrieved by the southward crossing of a North Korean airman on 28 April and the 24 September defection of a North Korean pilot who brought his plane, an enlisted man and valuable intelligence over to the South.

The US Central Intelligence Agency provided a bleak assessment of the Korean situation in July 1949: the "inefficiency and shortsighted authoritarianism" of the ROK authorities would likely induce "a public reaction favoring Communism". The assessment held some hope that US training of the ROK's military forces and economic aid, anti-Communist psychological measures, and the fostering of traditional Korean values might just stave off the evil day, but "it is not expected that these factors can prevent ultimate Communist control of the whole of Korea". The report, oddly, concluded with an assessment of a highly improbable *Soviet* invasion of the ROK: in that case, understandably, "the life expectancy of South Korea would be, at best, only a few days".[14]

The very fact that the US withdrew its forces at a time when many felt that only those forces and US aid kept the Rhee regime alive was an indication that the US would hardly go to war to prevent the Rhee government's fall. But the bellicose and embattled ROK leader did possess one advantage that would prove of inestimable value a few years later. Although the Soviet Union vetoed the ROK's admission to the UN, that body did recognize South Korea as the legitimate government for all of Korea and permitted it to send delegates to its deliberations.

Rhee's anxieties were hardly allayed early in 1950 by a series of American official statements that brought out into the open ideas regarding Korea that had been circulating through Washington for at least two years. The first such statement was Secretary of State Dean Acheson's notorious speech to the National Press Club in Washington, DC. Acheson sketched America's Far East defence line, drawing it from the Aleutian Islands in the Northern Pacific, through Japan, to the Ryukyus (Okinawa), and to the Philippines. Should an attack be launched on a nation outside this perimeter, the inhabitants would have to rely at first on their own resources and then call in the UN – "the entire civilized world", as Acheson grandly put it. The Secretary chose not to deal with the possibility that the victim could not hold back the aggressor and that the UN might not mobilize a response.

The speech certainly set off alarm bells in Seoul. Acheson backtracked somewhat by publicly stressing "very substantial" American economic and military aid and the eagerness of the United States to preserve South Korean independence. But still the South Koreans could get no definite commitment that the United States would come to South Korea's rescue in the event of an invasion from the North.

Acheson's speech was no aberration. Republican Congressman Walter Judd deplored what he termed the plugging of "isolated rat holes around the Red Sphere in Asia if China is lost". The same figure of speech was used by other members of Congress at about this time. It was an indication of the Truman administration's strategic priorities that although Acheson had travelled to Europe in the past year no fewer than 11 times (when even by air each trip would take some 13 hours each way), he had not once bothered to look in on affairs anywhere in Asia.

The State Department *Bulletin* of March 1950 declared that there was good reason to believe that South Korea would survive and prosper, but "This, of course, cannot be guaranteed". Two months later, the powerful chairman of the Senate Foreign Relations Committee, Tom Connolly, replied to a reporter's question as to the fate of the Republic of Korea, "I'm afraid it's going to happen, that is, the abandonment of South Korea, whether we want it to or not". Queried further if South Korea were essential to America's security, Connally bluntly replied "No".

There is some evidence that all of this, plus the earlier redeployment of a considerable number of Far East Air Force aircraft to Europe, encouraged aggressive thoughts in Pyongyang, which already had its own plans well underway. In 1992, a retired KPA general reminisced that Acheson's speech did produce "a certain influence on Kim Il Sung".[15]

The Republic of Korea could take more comfort in the fact that Rhee had put down internal disturbances and the economy was finally beginning to prosper. In fact, in cotton textiles, coal and electricity (incredibly, in light of the North's total blockade of its hydro-electricity), the ROK economy was surpassing pre-war standards. Land reform had finally produced a nation of smallholders, albeit struggling to survive. Some have even argued that it was this progress in the South that made Kim Il Sung all the more determined to attack in 1950 rather than to wait until his enemy became even stronger. National elections in May 1950 had reduced Rhee's delegates to 49 out of 210 seats in the legislature. If nothing else, this development showed that at least at the time, Rhee was something less than the absolute dictator of his opponents' charges.

Although it is generally believed that General MacArthur's Intelligence section did not anticipate an invasion from the North, this is not the case. Far East Command G-2 (Intelligence) as early as 30 December 1949 reported that Pyongyang had set March or April of 1950 for its D-Day, and progressively warned in the intervening months that the military buildup in the North had to be for offensive purposes. A report of 8 March concluded that

> airfield construction has been initiated or completed in at least five different locations. These five fields give North Korea a line of airfields from coast to coast, and four of them are within a few miles of the 38th Parallel. The location of these fields is by no means logical if they are designed as bases for defensive air action. They are, however, so located as to place North Korean aircraft in decidedly advantageous positions for offensive air action against South Korea.[16]

One report, in March 1950, even predicted an attack in June 1950 but was ignored by MacArthur. But what could Far East Command do in response to these warnings? On the ground in Korea, US Ambassador John Muccio conceded that the North would probably win because of its superiority in tanks, aircraft and heavy guns. The chief of the US Army's KMAG, whose 482 officers and men would be caught up in any such invasion, was more concerned with the results of such an invasion than with when it might occur. General Roberts in March 1950 recorded his belief that the South Korean people would go with a winner and that the ROK "would be gobbled up to be added to the rest of Red Asia". Equally gloomy was the intelligence assessment of the US Far East Air Force: the Northern regime had the ability to undertake a war against the South, and South Korea would fall in the wake of any North Korean invasion. But a few months later something seemed to have changed General Roberts' earlier assessment of the ROK army. By the spring of 1950, facing retirement on 20 June, he mounted a publicity campaign portraying that army as a truly formidable military arm. In a statement that he would never live down, General Roberts

1. The age-old Korean agrarian cycle goes on despite the war, except now the women do the work. *National Archives*

asserted in *Time* magazine on 5 June that the ROK Army was the "best doggone shooting army outside the United States". (It remains unclear if the unfortunate general actually meant that the ROK army was the superior of even US forces outside the United States – which is one way his statement could be read.) Significantly, General Roberts' replacement was a Colonel who nonetheless repeated these sentiments in cables sent to Washington. But KMAG's right hand did not seem to know the doings of its left hand. In mid-June its classified semi-annual report warned that South Korea faced a "disaster" similar to that which had befallen Nationalist China. The ROK Army was so poorly supplied, it warned, that it could not sustain defensive operations for more than 13 days. And on 20 June, the US Central Intelligence Agency gave a mixed assessment of the ability of the ROK army to resist any invasion from the North. It claimed that South Korea would lose its northern reaches, including Seoul, but that without Chinese Communist intervention there was no certainty that what would be left of the South could be conquered. Yet on the same day, Assistant Secretary of State for the Far East, Dean Rusk, stated before the House Foreign Affairs Committee that "We see no present indication that the people across the border have any intention of fighting a major war". Even so, he concluded the ROK army "could meet most credibly the kind of force which the North Koreans established".[17]

The ROK Army in 1950 remained not much more than a rather effective internal security constabulary, with no heavy weapons of any kind and no armour. It had been organized by the Americans from eight internal security constabulary regiments which dated to 1946. Its legacy was thus one of main-taining internal security. Its officers were undertrained in regular (as opposed to guerrilla) warfare and the higher ranks were often political appointees. In all, the ROK Army consisted of 98,000 men in eight divisions: the 1st, 2nd, 3rd, 5th, 8th, and Capital. Half were deployed along the border with the North and half in reserve. The higher command was weak and deeply involved in political manoeuvring. ROK Army Chief of Staff Chae Pyong Duk ("Fat Chae") at 300 pounds was an easily recognized feature on the Seoul party circuit. Rhee henchman, Kim Chong Won was more militarily able, but also far more ruthless. A former Japanese Army "special volunteer", and known as "Tiger", he was notorious for his cruelties in the suppression of the Yosu-Sunch'on revolt and in the operations against the Chiri-san guerrillas in 1948–9, as well as for brutality towards his own troops. Kim Chong Won's influence on Rhee and the top ROK Army command was out of all pro-portion to his rank of Colonel, and his future brutalities would prove a source of continuous embarrassment to the ROK Army command and government.

The ROK Air Force consisted of a handful of light aircraft. Its armour numbered 26 armoured cars with small-bore 36mm popgun cannon, useful primarily for the breaking up of demonstrations. Only at sea was the ROK superior, having one frigate to match against the miscellaneous small craft of the North.

By contrast, in June 1950, the Korean People's Army could deploy more than 135,000 troops organized into ten regular infantry divisions, one armoured brigade (equipped with the excellent T-34/85 1944 model Soviet tank), five border constabulary brigades, as well as all necessary combat service support and combat support elements. In fact, the KPA was considerably better sup-plied than the Chinese People's Liberation Army. The high command was able, loyal, brave and tough. As for the troops, some one-third were veterans of the Chinese civil war and many had fought against the Japanese. It should also be remembered that Kim Il Sung himself was a military veteran with years of combat experience, as were his top comrades. By contrast, Syngman Rhee was a scholar-politician, his chief commanders more often than not political officers.

The *Inmin Gun* expected that most of the fighting would be over within 22 to 27 days, well within Kim Il Sung's grand goal of a reunified Korea by 15 August 1950, the fifth anniversary of Korea's liberation from the Japanese yoke. Yet it is an indication of the ferocity of the conflict that did develop and of the unforeseeable nature of war itself that, for all the differences between the two armies, the KPA and the ROK Army Chiefs of Staff would each bravely die within a few months of each other on the battlefield.

Chapter Three

Invasion and retreat

In the rain-soaked early hours of Sunday, 25 June 1950 (Korean time), tank-led North Korean troops, preceded by a heavy artillery bombardment and supported by air power, launched a full-scale invasion of the Republic of Korea. To be fair, the DPRK interpretation should be given: "Using the Syngman Rhee puppet army in a frontal attack, US imperialism opened up, by deliberate provocation, a piratic aggressive war against the Korean people."[1]

The invasion should have come as no real surprise to South Koreans or to the handful of Americans who followed Korean matters. But they were nonetheless caught completely off-guard, as Americans indeed had been at Pearl Harbor less than a decade earlier. Throughout the first day or so there was some question as to whether this attack was an actual full-scale invasion. That question was settled soon enough, as the Korean People's Army moved across a broad front, heading swiftly for Seoul.

It would seem that there could be little dispute of the basic fact that the Korean People's Army of the Democratic Republic of Korea invaded the Republic of Korea. But as early as 1952 the "independent" journalist, I. F. Stone, claimed that the accepted version was really all wrong, that South Korea had actually invaded the North, or at the least, that the North Korean invasion was an exasperated response to southern provocation and cross-border attacks.[2]

But we have seen that Kim Il Sung was urging support for an invasion of South Korea by 1949, that Stalin and Mao Tse-tung eventually agreed to support him in this venture, that armour, heavy artillery, and aircraft were flowing into the DPRK from the Soviet Union, that Kim and the Red Army staff had completed a detailed plan for an invasion for June 1950, and that the attack indeed was launched on 25 June.

We know that the United States authorities refused to deliver heavy artillery or significant air power to the ROK, specifically to dampen anyone in the South from taking the "On to the North" rhetoric seriously enough to do something about it. To believe that in spite of all of this, the South, inferior militarily in almost every way to the North, did indeed initiate some form of attack on the North, would require a near suspension of belief in probability. It also requires that one dismiss North Korea's plans and preparations as being designed merely as a riposte to South Korean aggression. At the same time one would need to see in the bombast of the ROK and in any unexplained South Korean action or any coincidence, sure evidence of planned aggression from the South.

Most convincing, then and now, was the report of the two Royal Australian Air Force UNCOK observers. Based on a series of reconnaissances of the 38th Parallel area between 9 and 23 June and actually filed one day before the eruption of the war, this report concluded that the ROK Army was a lightly armed constabulary force, incapable of any serious or sustained thrust northward but which was maintaining an attitude of "vigilant defense". (Considering that fully one-half of the ROK Army was on leave that Sunday of 25 June 1950, this characterization was something of an exaggeration.) As for the North, the two officers could engage in what could only be termed "long-range reconnaissance"; they were forbidden passage to the northern side of the Parallel. But they did note that units of the KPA had established salients in a number of areas actually south of the Parallel. The Australian chairman of UNCOK, the strong-minded Arthur R. Jamieson, anything but an apologist for the South or under the thumb of the United States and who was to remain a stout critic of Syngman Rhee's authoritarian government, was under no illusions as to the instigator of this invasion.

But Communist records themselves can prove even more explicitly their side's war guilt. It is indeed a pity that the US Far East Command did not see fit to release the Soviet plan for North Korea's invasion of South Korea. Note also the secret report on the preparations for war and the progress of the first day of that conflict that was dispatched to Moscow by the Soviet Ambassador in Pyongyang, T. Shtykov:

> The concentration of the People's Army in the region near the 38th parallel began on June 12 and was concluded on June 23, *as was prescribed in the plan of the General Staff.* The redeployment of troops took place in an orderly fashion, without incident. (emphasis added)

The report does add that "The political order of the Minister of Defense was read to the troops, which explained that the South Korean Army had provoked a military attack by violating the 38th parallel and that the government of the DPRK had given an order to the Korean People's Army to go over to the counterattack." But that line of reasoning was inadvertently quite undermined a few lines later when the ambassador admits that "The attack of the People's Army took the enemy completely by surprise."[3] A veteran North Korean general decades later noted that although even the most secret sections of the *Inmin Gun*'s operational orders employed the term "counterattack", he boldly added, "It was a fake", "disinformation to cover ourselves", as well as to "cover" the role of the Soviet Union in that invasion's preparation.[4]

In all reason, the success of this large-scale, efficiently controlled and co-ordinated, logistically well supported land, sea and air attack should in itself practically negate the argument that this was a mere riposte, a justified counterattack, or simply a grab for the Ongjin Peninsula or the rest of Kaesong city. Even the excellent KPA could hardly have mounted so professional an operation on such short notice. Those who still forward this argument display their ignorance of military matters. Here is one historical event for which the most straightforward explanation, an invasion from the North, is the most logical and verifiable.

The North had certainly prepared well for its blitzkrieg. Full-scale deceptive instructions were beamed from Pyongyang Radio to guerrilla bands in the South at a time when the ROK Army still had strong memories of the Cheju-Sunchon uprisings and other recent guerrilla actions. At about the same time, the Communist Korean League in Japan proclaimed that "we will engage in guerrilla activities directed at the destruction of imperialistic industry. Our operations are scheduled, until further notice, for August."[5] At the same time, Pyongyang now carefully refrained from further border incursions, thus strengthening the impression that the major threat was from within the ROK. The DPRK premier also had his Democratic Front for the Unification of the Fatherland (DFUF) organization send agents south of the border to make contact with "progressive" elements in the ROK. These agents were picked up almost immediately by ROK security forces and (perhaps minus a few fingernails) were soon making pro-Rhee broadcasts over Radio Seoul. All of this Northern activity, whether intentional or not, did serve further to distract ROK officials in the critical days just before the invasion.

But there was nothing obscure or subtle about the North Korean invasion itself. A heavy bombardment, followed two hours later by a spearhead of some 150 Soviet-built T-34-85 late-model medium tanks, and 110 warplanes, paved the way for the bulk of the Korean People's Army to surge across the Parallel in the most blatant − and one-sided − cross-border invasion since German panzers had rolled into the Balkans in 1941. Within a few hours the KPA had seized Kaesong and Uibongju in its main, four-division, armoured thrust.

Still, the ROK command was not alerted to an impending full-scale assault; because of previous engagements and artillery duels across the Parallel, this attack at first was generally seen as just another probe or exercise in belligerence. (Just a week earlier 20 South Korean civilians had been killed by shellfire from the North.) The troops at the immediate front knew quickly enough what they were facing, but communication was not one of the strengths of the ROK Army. Not that prompt information would have made much of a difference. The ROK Army was anything but prepared to meet full-scale invasion. Five of its eight divisions were positioned several miles south of the Parallel. The Kaesong corridor, a wide, geographically featureless valley leading straight to Seoul without any natural barriers except for the Imjin River, was guarded by only one ROK division. The Uibongju corridor, also leading to Seoul, was, also, protected by a lone ROK division. As noted, half of the ROK Army was on leave, and numerous ROK civilian leaders were out of the country, mostly in the United States. And it was a Sunday.

The US military attaché received news of some sort of military incursion from the North at about 6.30am. After receiving confirmation from a KMAG officer, he contacted the American Embassy, where the news was dismissed as just another rumour or another border rumble. Not until 9.30 did the embassy staff inform Ambassador John J. Muccio, and he did not cable the news to Washington until an hour later. In Washington, Secretary of Defence Johnson, who had just returned from a Far East tour along with the Chairman of the Joint Chiefs of Staff, General Omar Bradley, delegated authority to General MacArthur to handle what he believed were "rumours" of fighting in Korea and went to bed.

Some critics of America's involvement in the Korean War have seen something sinister in Johnson's and Bradley's presence in Tokyo as well as that of the prominent Republican foreign policy expert, John Foster Dulles, who proceeded up to the 38th Parallel itself on the very eve of the war's eruption. Just the opposite could more logically be argued. Why would these "imperialists" have undertaken a well publicized visit to the venue of their machinations?

The ROK Army and government had frequently and shrilly been warning of attack and magnifying local incursions from the North into full-scale invasion. They had cried "wolf" before. By 1950, however, ROK military and government leaders no longer boasted of any "drive north". Now it was the threat of overwhelming assault *from* the North, backed by Chinese and, possibly, Soviet power. Just days before the invasion, Rhee had pleaded with Dulles that "more positive action must be taken" as he predicted an imminent "hot war" on the peninsula.[6] The casual American response and the very disposition of ROK Army forces should at least weaken imaginings of an initial provocation from the South.

The ROK Army Chief of Staff, Chae Pyong Duk, made his initial blunders in these early days of the war. He directed the 2nd Division to move no less than 120 miles from Kaesong to the east of Uijongbu for a co-ordinated counterattack with the 7th Division. The 2nd never came near the manoeuvre area. The 7th had to attack alone and was defeated, its men scattered, its equipment abandoned. On the other hand, there are authenticated cases of ROK soldiers strapping explosives to their bodies and attacking KPA tanks. The ROK 1st Division fought well, but its mere 15 105mm howitzers, while inflicting heavy casualties on the *Inmin Gun*'s infantry, could do little against his tanks. Seoul was now open to seizure. But the standard tales of total South Korean panic and disintegration may well be exaggerated. The Soviet ambassador to Pyongyang reported that "The enemy is putting up resistance and while fighting is retreating into the territory of South Korea, mass taking of prisoners from the South Korean Army has not been noted." (Note that the Ambassador did not even refer to any "mass taking" of *defectors* from the South.) The ambassador already was criticizing the North Korean command. They "organize the battle poorly, they use artillery and tanks in battle badly and lost communications", but he did note "great enthusiasm" in the ranks.[7]

But General Chae could not take advantage of his enemy's failings. He compounded his initial operational error by ordering his troops to hold fast everywhere in the belief that American intervention was imminent. These forces were either overwhelmed or they extricated themselves to flock southward, demoralized, although the 1st ROK Division held its lines along the Parallel for several days. President Rhee then left Seoul, but not before leaving behind a recorded broadcast on South Korea's sole station calling for total resistance to the Communist invaders.

In the last hours before its capture, the capital was the scene of a catastrophe that almost cost the ROK the war. On the night before the city's fall, 27 June, while filled with retreating ROK troops and their transport, the Han River highway bridge was prematurely blown up by ROK Army engineers. Thousands may have died in that thunderous explosion. Tens of thousands more ROK soldiers, along with their equipment, were now stranded on the wrong side of the Han. It may have been the worst single disaster for the ROK of the Korean War. The chief engineer of the ROK Army was executed for this blunder. Seoul fell, and the Communists filmed the piles of abandoned American-supplied ROK Army equipment and forlorn lines of vehicles, to display, gloatingly, world-wide.

Nonetheless, many ROK Army units continued to fight stoutly, and the KPA did not breach the ROK's main defensive line until 3 July. North Korean units unsupported by tanks suffered particularly heavy casualties. As early as 4 July the Soviet ambassador cabled Stalin about what he twice termed the "complicated situation" at the front. Furthermore, and this must have proved particularly disheartening to the invaders, there was no reported mass uprising against the embattled Rhee regime. Apparently there was not even much guerrilla activity, although Communist irregulars would remain a serious problem for the next two years. In fact, Rhee's government was able, when it stayed in one place long enough, as at Taejon, to arm civilians for the defence of the ROK. It could also kill out of hand other civilians suspected of "Communist sympathies", which might explain to some extent the absence of any uprising. If South Korea were to be conquered, it would have to be at the hands of the regular Army of the DPRK.

The Truman administration, although well aware of the tension and bellicosity along the 38th Parallel, was nonetheless surprised by the North Korean invasion. American leaders found it hard to credit that a full-scale invasion was underway across an internationally recognized border. Soon enough, however, the "Munich" analogy became fixed in the minds of Washington policy-planners. Secretary of State Acheson (he of the "Korea is outside our Asian defense perimeter" speech of a few months previous) proclaimed that it was just such aggression against small nations that, unchecked by the democracies, had encouraged Hitler to embark on the Second World War. The invasion of the Republic of Korea must be stopped, even if it took a small war to forestall a much greater conflict: "No more Munichs!" (Although never one to admit a mistake, Acheson might have felt some guilt feelings about his notorious speech.)

Once the Truman administration was finally convinced that this was truly a full-scale invasion, it acted quickly and decisively. Less than 24 hours after the commencement of the invasion of the South, the President called a meeting of his highest advisers to determine a response to the crisis. The conference was held at the Blair House, across the street from the White House, then undergoing total rebuilding. Acheson came well prepared by his State Department advisers, and called for the US 7th Fleet to patrol the Straits of Taiwan to keep the Chinese Nationalists and Communists apart in what could be the opening phase of a general Far East war. The conviction that the invasion was part of a global Soviet conspiracy dominated these informal talks. President Truman even told his Secretary of the Air Force to prepare for the destruction of all Soviet air and naval bases in the area. More moderately, the presidential advisers recommended the dispatch of US naval and air forces to aid the South and to protect the evacuation of American citizens from the Seoul area, but held back on the commitment of American ground troops. All agreed that these measures should be announced in the context of an international response to outlaw aggression.

With the battlefield situation deteriorating hourly, the President called a second Blair House meeting the following day. Acheson then called for the unlimited use of US naval and air forces against the North Koreans, at least to the 38th Parallel. Army Chief of Staff, J. Lawton Collins, pictured the ROK defenders as being on the verge of collapse, but the usually bellicose Louis Johnson was now strangely passive, claiming that the United States, for the moment, had done all that it could. The consensus was that South Korea could defend itself if aided by US air and naval forces. Significantly, no member of Congress was present at either Blair House meeting.

On the 27th, the President did meet with 14 Congressional leaders from both parties and both Houses of Congress, as well as, again, the Secretary of State, the Secretary of Defense, the US Ambassador to the UN, the Joint Chiefs of Staff, and the armed services secretaries. This was undoubtedly the most important American governmental meeting of the entire war, for it determined and ratified the limited US, UN-sanctioned, prosecution of that war. These leaders perceived that this was in all likelihood part of a general Soviet-backed offensive in Asia and that NATO allies would help as they could. After the meeting, Old Guard Republican Senator Styles Bridges of New Hampshire told the press that what had just transpired was "damned good action". These meetings were more to ratify what the President had already done than to seek approval for any future actions. Later that day the President denounced the Communist invasion in the same terms he had used in his meeting earlier. He called for accelerated military aid to the Philippines and to the French and Indo-Chinese forces, all of which were fighting Communist-led insurgencies. He also declared the neutralization of Taiwan (or Formosa as it was then more often termed.)

When the President's statement was read to the House of Representatives that afternoon by House Majority Leader John McCormack, it received a standing ovation from all but one Congressman. (That individual, Vito Marcantonio (Democrat, New York City), an unabashed apologist for the Stalin regime, could be considered the closest the American political system ever came to electing a full-fledged Communist to the United States Congress.) The House then overwhelmingly voted to extend Selective Service (military conscription) for one year and gave the President authority to mobilize the individual states' National Guard units. The only other dissonant note came the following day when another Old Guard Republican, Senator Robert Taft, charged the President with "a complete usurpation . . . of authority", although he still voted to approve the President's actions. But President

Truman neither asked for nor received a Congressional resolution of approval, leaving himself all the more vulnerable later in the war to the partisan jibe of "Truman's War", with its echoes of "Mr Madison's War" of 1812. The State Department afterward thoughtfully produced a list of no fewer than 85 instances in which the President had undertaken military action without Congressional ratification.

Also on the 27th (Tokyo Time), General MacArthur, acting at the behest of the President, sent Major General John H. Church with a small survey team to aid in directing the US effort in Korea and to encourage the South Koreans to resist. He was to assure them that they would not be abandoned. Following Church's discouraging reports radioed back to Tokyo in the wake of the fall of Seoul, MacArthur himself flew to Korea on the morning of the 29th. He was escorted to the Han River south bank front and saw for himself the disintegration of the ROK Army. By the 30th, back in Tokyo and in receipt of even more depressing combat intelligence from General Church, MacArthur requested the commitment of US ground forces.

This was the background for President Truman's momentous authorization on 30 June of the immediate commitment of US ground forces to the aid of South Korea in addition to the US air and naval contingents already in battle. Truman, again, acted without Congressional authorization. He also continued to act without a Congressional declaration of war. The President had called in Senator Connally to ask whether such a declaration would be necessary if American troops were sent to Korea. Connally replied in words that accurately summarized the interpretation most of the nation gave to the war's outbreak and the responsibility for that outbreak (as well as giving a true Texan touch): "If a burglar breaks into your house, you can shoot him without going down to the police station and getting permission." This "crime control" analogy set the stage for the entry of the United States into the Korean War.

By this time, the only good news to come out of Korea was the successful evacuation of American civilians, without a single casualty, from the Seoul area in accordance with previous plans. Yak fighter aircraft of the Korean People's Air Force (KPAF) that tried to interfere with the evacuation on 27 June were shot out of the sky by F-82 twin Mustang night-fighters of the USAF Far East Air Force (FEAF). The KPAF, eluding FEAF fighters, continued to mount ground attacks for the next month, but afterwards was conspicuous by its total absence over South Korean skies.

Armed with the President's authorization, MacArthur ordered the commander of Eighth US Army, Lieutenant General Walton Walker, to get his 24th Infantry Division ready for action in Korea. In response, General Walker loaded a spearhead infantry battalion (1st Battalion, 21st Infantry Regiment)

2. General Walton Walker, 8th Army Commander, meets with one of his subordinates, July 1950. The war is not going well. *National Archives*

of the 24th Infantry Division into the only six C-54 heavy transport aircraft available in the Far East and dispatched them to South Korea. Thus began the cautionary saga of Task Force Smith, named for its commander, Lieutenant Colonel Charles B. Smith (a veteran of the Pearl Harbor attack). The remainder of the 24th would follow by sea.

Prevailing US Army opinion at the time was that US ground forces would soon take charge and wind up the war. Task Force Smith numbered 406 officers and men. Its combat arm consisted of two under-strength rifle companies, a communications section, a recoilless rifle platoon, and two mortar platoons. Its weapons, in addition to personal pieces, were two 75mm recoilless rifles, two 4.1in and four 60mm mortars, and six 2.36 "bazooka" rocket launchers. Most of these soldiers were 20 years old or less, and only one-sixth had seen combat in the Second World War. This was considered the best that Eighth Army could field on short notice. The 24th Division commander,

Major General William Dean, ordered Smith to block the main road south to Pusan as far north as possible. With this order Dean showed his realization that the port of Pusan was the goal of the KPA's invasion after the fall of Seoul. If Pusan were to be taken, there would be practically no other port for the unloading of troops and equipment; the war would likely be lost.

After landing at an airstrip near Pusan, the troops, attended by cheering crowds, embarked by train for Taejon. The head of US field headquarters at Taejon, General Church, had already exceeded even the earlier fatuous military appraisals of General Roberts when he asserted belligerently to reporters that "We will hurl back the North Koreans, and if the Russkies intervene we will hurl them back too." Generals Church and Roberts and, most unfortunately, Task Force Smith, were in for a rude awakening almost on the order of Pearl Harbor.

Colonel Smith, quietly spying out the land for himself, spotted a good blocking point about three miles north of Osan. This position was a line of low rolling hills which commanded the main railroad to the east, giving a clear view to Suwon, about eight miles to the north.

On 4 July Task Force Smith was reinforced by elements of the 52nd Field Artillery Battalion with its six 105mm howitzers, 73 vehicles, and 108 men under the command of Lieutenant Colonel Miller O. Perry. At 3am the following day, the combined force, drenched by a cold rain, moved into position, dug foxholes, and opened their C-rations. Their positions straddled the Osan–Suwon road for about one mile. Four howitzers were placed in a concealed position some 2,000 metres to the south of the infantry positions, while one howitzer was sited halfway between the battery and the infantry positions so as to enfilade the road and serve as an anti-tank weapon. Artillery volunteers manned four .50-calibre machine guns, and four bazooka teams reinforced the infantry positions. The vehicles were concealed just north of Osan. There were no reserves. And there would be no close-air support; the weather was too poor and earlier disastrous strafings of ROK forces had resulted in UN ground-attack strikes being confined to north of Suwon.

At dawn on the 5th, after registration firing, the force detected movement to the north. This was eight tanks of the 107th tank regiment, 105th Armored Division. At 08.16h the first American ground fire of the Korean War was on its way toward the KPA armour – to no effect. The US high-explosive (HE) rounds simply bounced off the T-34s' excellent sloped armour. The Americans had only six high-explosive anti-tank (HEAT) rounds, but these were allotted to the forward howitzer. It is probable that most of these rounds of Second World War vintage had deteriorated over the years. Even old anti-tank mines would have probably stopped the tanks, but Task Force

Smith had none. In desperation, Colonel Smith ordered his men to with-hold the fire of their last heavy weapon, the recoilless rifles, until the *Inmin Gun* tanks were within a 700-yard range. When that range was closed the crews' aim was good, scoring direct hits, but again to no apparent effect. Once more, the culprit here may have been the age of the rounds; these rifles were good weapons and would later score against North Korean armour. As the North Korean tanks opened their fire, the bazooka teams continued to blast away at close range, especially at the tanks' more vulnerable rears, once more to little effect. The forward howitzer fired off its HEAT rounds, finally with some result. The two lead tanks were hit and disabled. One flamed up. Two crewmen exited with their hands up, but a third fired a Soviet-built "burp gun" at an American machine gun position. Before being gunned down himself, he had killed an assistant gunner, the (unnamed) first Amer-ican fatality of the war. The third tank destroyed the forward howitzer, and the rest of the KPA tanks swept through the pass, as the remaining howitzer crews continued to fire ineffectual HE rounds at them. One other tank was later disabled from unknown causes and abandoned.

Now more tanks shot their way through the breach in the American positions. These new tanks unnerved some of the gunners, who abandoned their pieces, but as steadier officers and NCOs took their places, the jumpy artillerymen returned to their posts. One more tank was disabled by a hit in the track, but by 10.15h no less than 33 T-34s had passed through the American positions, killing or wounding some 20 Americans by their machine gun fire. Most of the vehicles in the American park were also destroyed by tank fire, but, unable to locate the American battery, the KPA armoured force simply clanked on its way south to Osan.

In the steady rain, the battered, shaken Americans used a one-hour lull to improve their positions. At about 11.00h three more tanks were spotted, again advancing from the north, followed by the sobering spectacle of a column of trucks and several miles of infantrymen of the 16th and 18th regiments of the 4th Division, one of the *Inmin Gun*'s best. As the long col-umn reached a point about 1,000 yards from the American position, Smith again gave the order to open fire. American rifles, mortars, and machine guns swept the apparently unsuspecting KPA column, causing moderate casualties but not panicking the disciplined troops, who promptly deployed from their trucks into battle formations. The T-34s, also unfazed, advanced to within 300 yards and raked the American positions with their shell and machine gun fire. Smith could not communicate with his artillery battery because the earlier tank force had chewed up his communications wire. He also believed that the battery had been knocked out. With his men down to an average of 20 rounds of ammunition apiece, the KPA raining down machine gun and

3. Task Force Smith moves up – to unexpected defeat. July 1950.
National Archives

mortar fire and the Communist tanks already in the rear of his position, Smith could hold no longer and ordered retreat. The plan was for an orderly leap-frog fighting withdrawal, but now many of the men broke under the heavy *Inmin Gun* fire, abandoning equipment and weapons. They suffered their heaviest casualties in this retreat rather than in the battle itself. The artillerymen did redeem their earlier skittishness by carefully disabling the five remaining howitzers, walking to the outskirts of Osan, and recovering their vehicles. Sadly, the litter-borne wounded had to be abandoned, although one medic volunteered to stay behind with them. This self-sacrificing soldier was never heard from again.

The Americans were indeed fortunate that the *Inmin Gun* did not follow in close pursuit. As it was, all men of the forward observer liaison, machine gun and bazooka groups were lost. Some 150 US troops were casualties in this disastrous first American–North Korean clash of the Korean War. It was not an auspicious beginning for American intervention to save the Republic of Korea. But the dispersed, disheartened Americans may have accomplished more than they could have realized at the time. A later US Army investigation determined that this lost battle had delayed the North Korean 4th Division by at least five days, when every day counted – for both sides. The KPA division itself lost about 42 killed, including the division assistant commander, and 85 wounded.

If the soldierly qualities of some of these US troops were weak in these early days of the war, their equipment, almost all of which was of Second World War vintage and deteriorating, was also deficient. For example, at Chonan, on 8 July, an *Inmin Gun* tank force fought its way towards American positions over a dirt road that had been carefully mined the previous day. Not one mine detonated. The commander of the 24th's tank battalion was killed later for want of a starter solenoid on the unit's tank retriever. Radios failed when their aged batteries gave out. Many shells failed to detonate on or over KPA positions. Perhaps the worst equipment scandal of the entire war involved the American 2.6in rocket launcher, a weapon that was long known to be inferior to similar German weapons in the Second World War. The new 3.5in launcher was in leisurely production in the States, but none would reach the troops until the battle of Taejon, when it proved to be a most effective anti-tank weapon.

The bulk of the US 24th Infantry Division was arriving at Pusan at this time. It attempted to hold the *Inmin Gun* at Pyongtaek, Ansong, Chonan, Chonui, Chochiwon and Taejon, all in the end unsuccessfully, although the invading forces were delayed. In the forlorn holding action at Chonan, the commander of the 34th Regiment, who was acting as gunner with one of those obsolete 2.6 rocket launchers, was blown in half by a T-34 tank shell.

The Task Force Smith debacle had only been the beginning. Americans were beginning to hear terms that had not been used since the darkest days of the loss of the Philippines to the Japanese in 1941–2. Official reports told of American troops "pulling back to prepared positions", of a "fluid" battle-field, of UN troops' "planned withdrawal", and so on, weasel words that tried, without much success in the face of an uncensored Western press, to cover the unpalatable fact that *the American Army was retreating*. Considering that the tactics of large-scale retreat had not been taught at West Point or in the Infantry School at Fort Benning or at the Army's senior staff colleges, the US Army did about as well as could be expected in the long retreat to the Pusan Perimeter.

To make matters worse, ROK and US troops encountered the full brutality of the *Inmin Gun*. During a counter-attack at Chonui, US troops found the bodies of six US Army jeep drivers and mortar men of a Heavy Mortar Company, hands tied behind their backs, shot in the head. They would not be the last. The KPA's 7th Division was particularly noted for its shooting of

4. Executed US soldiers, their hands tied behind their backs, shot by North Korean troops during the retreat south. *National Archives*

captured Americans and mutilation of prisoners. Apologists for the Communist side have pointed to the *Inmin Gun*'s lack of procedures for dealing with POWs, expecting as it did the rapid "liberation" of the South. But this lack could hardly excuse the calculated cruelty practised by its soldiers in the field and, later, in the POW camps. Towards the end of July, the North Korean high command did issue an order making the murder of POWs a court-martial offence, except in cases of "attempted escape". This clause left the way open for the hoary euphemism so often used by totalitarian regimes – "Shot while trying to escape." Consequently, embittered Americans and ROKs became more reluctant to take prisoners, although UN troops, with the occasional exception of the South Koreans, rarely, if ever, resorted to the studied brutality of their enemies.

American troops captured by the North Koreans in those early days of the war suffered about every imaginable fate. The *Inmin Gun* seemed to take particularly brutal vengeance upon the "American imperialists", who were, in fact, making the war increasingly difficult for them. US POWs, usually survivors of a number of "death marches", were paraded through the streets of Pyongyang. Their haggard, emaciated forms were frequently photographed and those photographs were given global distribution. Thus the North Koreans documented their own barbarism. Those who survived the death marches and the shootings found themselves in camps in the far North with a continuing ordeal of beatings, near-starvation and unrelenting physical and mental pressure to turn "progressive" and broadcast or write messages back home denouncing American "aggression" in Korea.

Many, perhaps a majority, of ROK troops captured by the North Koreans were "persuaded" to enter the ranks of their former enemies, as "misled compatriots" who had now seen the light. Under the implacable discipline of the *Inmin Gun* they made quite adequate soldiers.

Meanwhile, on 7 July, the United Nations authorized a unified UN Command (UNC) to repulse aggression in Korea. From then on, the anti-Communist forces on the peninsula would fight under the blue-and-white flag of that global body, as well as under their own national emblems. The following day, President Truman announced that General Douglas MacArthur would head the UNC. One week later, President Rhee, in one of that old patriot's most astute moves, placed the armed forces of the ROK under General MacArthur's control, vastly simplifying the war at the strategic and operational levels. In the field, US Eighth Army would execute the decisions of the UN Command and deploy the armed forces of the ROK. Eventually, 16 nations would contribute to the defence of the Republic of Korea.

On 12 July, the Eighth Army Commander, Lieutenant General Walton Walker, established his headquarters in Taegu, a city that would soon be on the front lines although never taken by the Communists. He assumed command of US forces in Korea the following day, although he was not formally given charge of ROK forces until four days later.

By this time, the US, now becoming aware that this was not to be any easy conflict and certainly nothing like the pundits' "push-button war", was beginning a sustained military buildup. Two groups of B-29s, the bombers that had burned the heart out of Japan's cities, were on their way, as were 22 B-26s, excellent piston-engine ground-attack light bombers. In addition, the carrier *Boxer*, operating under forced-draft all the way, was rushing across the Pacific, loaded to capacity with F-51 Mustang fighters. All of these warplanes were Second World War-vintage piston-engined models, many showing their age. More discouraging to General MacArthur was the news that he would receive for now only 44 of the 164 jet F-80 fighters he had requested.

On the ground, the commander of the 24th Infantry, General Dean, mindful of the fate of Task Force Smith, put in an urgent request for speedy delivery of the new 3.5in rocket launcher as well as of high-explosive anti-tank 105mm shells for use against the rampaging T–34s. Advanced elements of the 25th Infantry Division were also arriving at Pusan by this time. The 25th was the second US division to be committed to the war. The third, the 1st Cavalry (actually an infantry division, with the "Cavalry" title retained for senti-mental reasons) would begin to land at Pohang-dong by 18 July. In addition, the 2nd Infantry Division was on its way from the US West Coast and would begin arriving on 29 July. The first Marine elements were scheduled to arrive by early August at Pusan – if the North Koreans did not get there first.

That the United States moved so slowly to bring its military power to bear when it had a supposed bastion about two hours' flying time from Korea in Japan speaks volumes as to just how much that military power had wasted away or been deliberately whittled down since the end of the Second World War. More directly pertinent to the infantry type of war that would be fought in Korea, however, was the state of 8th Army in Japan. Stationed there were the 7th, 24th, 25th Infantry Divisions and the 1st "Cavalry" Division, with their supporting elements. These units were seriously under-strength as a result of the cut-backs mandated from Washington. Each of the 12 regiments in the divisions were under "reduced strength" tables of organ-ization with two instead of the regular three battalions, with the exception of the all-black 24th Infantry of the 25th Division. Thus none of the divisions could go into battle in accordance with combat-tested doctrine that called for the initial commitment of two battalions with one held in reserve.

Each regiment's direct-support artillery battalions were also reduced to two firing batteries (again, except for those supporting the 24th Infantry). Instead of the wartime strength of a medium tank (Sherman) battalion and a light tank company in each regiment, as well as a cannon company, each 8th Army division deployed a single tank company, and those fielded only light tanks and half-tracks. (The latter, however, with quad .50- or .30-calibre machine guns mounted, could literally shred KPA infantry elements and were thus probably a more effective weapon than the light tank.) The United States Army certainly had many of its medium Shermans left over from the Second World War. As for anti-tank weapons, infantry units were supposed to be equipped with the post-war 3.5in rocker launcher, but Eighth Army had to make do with the feeble 2.6in model.

The total armed forces of the United States in 1950 numbered 1,460,000. Fortunately, the low point of 8th Army strength had been reached in April 1948, after which a slow rebuilding continued in the wake of the Berlin Airlift, the Czech coup, and the unveiling of the Soviet atomic bomb. Intensive recruiting drives, which did not, however, speak much to the possibility that the young recruit might be involved in combat, helped to build up the force.

The greater number of troops by far would be furnished by the reinstated Selective Service levies.

One foresighted action, "Operation Roll-Up", initiated by Far East Command in 1948, scavenged Second World War vehicles and other military equipment from the battlefields and depots of the Pacific and sent them to the Tokyo Ordnance Depot for refurbishing. If the Army could not expect any new equipment in the budget-cutting climate of the Truman administration, Second World War re-treads would have to do. In the desperate first two months of the Korean War, 4,000 such vehicles were processed and rushed to the front. A year later, the figure was ten times higher. Although some of the rebuilt vehicles had little more than their fresh paint and new rubber and canvas to hold them together, the more thoroughly rebuilt performed yeoman service in the early days of the war. Yet even in those days the US Army was lavishly supplied with vehicles. For example, the supporting units of the 24th Division alone (engineers, medical, ordnance, quartermaster, and so on) in July numbered 4,236; they brought with them 1,717 motor vehicles; in other words, every US soldier in Korea could ride into battle without even crowding.

As for the American troops themselves, they were a long way from home in a hard-scrabble land of fetid paddies and charmless cities that made even duty in bombed-out Japan seem lush in comparison. Many wondered how the loss of South Korea could pose any real threat to the United States. Their easy, even luxurious, occupation "duty" in Japan, during which many low-ranking troopers operated their own autos and had their boots and "hootches" (barracks) cleaned by native "mamma-sans", had been interrupted by this unexpected, incomprehensible war.

It is one of the myths of this war, however, that these men were physically out of shape. Not only had 8th Army been gradually rebuilding its equipment and manpower, it had embarked on a more vigorous training programme in the face of the reduction in such activities elsewhere in the US military. Certainly General Dean was an excellent officer who pushed his men even in peacetime and who subsequently would perform heroically (and with becoming modesty) in battle. But Japan was a crowded, mountainous land, and room for training manoeuvre was very limited. Most of the flat land was extensively cultivated in the post-war years simply to stave off starvation. It speaks well of the US occupation that such land was not simply expropriated for military use. (Then again, MacArthur could hardly "teach the Japanese people democracy" if the Japanese people were starving.)

Unfortunately, many American soldiers came to despise Korea and its people. Their customs were incomprehensible, their land stank of human faeces, and truth to tell, the methods of ROK law enforcement seemed little less brutal than what they heard of the "Reds". For example, one group of Americans later in the war watched in disgust as ROK police induced a group of suspects to "confess" to some minor theft – by breaking their fingers one at a time. Worse, some American military personnel witnessed brutalization and massacres of supposed Communists by ROK authorities and could do nothing. On the other hand, many Americans gave freely of their time, money, and energy to build orphanages, to help war widows and the war-maimed, with 8th Army chaplains performing particularly heroic work. American Civil Affairs units undoubtedly saved tens of thousands from death by starvation or freezing in the first year of the war and did much to rebuild the economy, all gratis. Still, it was difficult to inspire the average US soldier to die for the Republic of Korea.

There can be little doubt that in the first months of this war, the *Inmin Gun* held the edge in troop quality. Except for the ROKs, UN troops, particularly the conscript Americans, often wondered just why they were in Korea, far from home. Many US officers and non-commissioned officers had combat experience from the Second World War, but most of the rank and file did not. At any rate, such experience was old; not one US soldier had seen battle in almost five years. The United States had quickly ended conscription after the Second World War, and although it had been reinstated in 1948, draft calls were light, with many exemptions until after the outbreak of war in Korea.

As noted, the Army of the ROK had been held by its American suppliers to an anti-guerrilla, internal security configuration; anything more and, the Americans feared, that army might set off on its proclaimed "March North". The ROK troops, unlike the North Koreans repatriated from China, almost entirely lacked combat experience except for those veterans of the Imperial Japanese Army. In addition to the material weaknesses noted, the former suffered from another serious disadvantage in comparison to the KPA. The latter army was fighting to unify the nation, the ROK for the *status quo*. For many nationalist South Koreans, even those not particularly leftist in their politics, this was enough either to take the fight out of them or even, in some cases, to induce defections.

On the battlefield, the UN forces were steadily falling back. The main *Inmin Gun* drive centred on the vital Seoul–Pusan highway where the shaky 24th Division, holding the south bank of the Kum River, the first major obstacle south of the Han, faced North Korea's 3rd and 4th Divisions. Although US Army engineers blew the major Kum River bridge at Kongju, KPA elements crossed that river in barges with little opposition from the thinly stretched, discontinuous, 3rd Battalion line of resistance. Many artillerymen fled their positions as KPA mortar shells fell accurately on their battery; ten howitzers were lost, along with between 60 and 80 vehicles. General Dean had not expected to hold at Kongju indefinitely, but he had hoped for better than this. The 19th Regiment put up more of a fight at Taepyong-ni. Again, bridges over the Kum were blown, and again the *Inmin Gun* managed to cross, although they suffered losses from UN air strikes.

The KPA forces continued to follow their standard and quite effective manoeuvre of a frontal attack sufficient to pin down their enemy, followed by flanking movements to produce confusion and cut off escape routes. Communist forces established a roadblock on the regiment's left flank, a typical manoeuvre, and the Americans, exhausted, outnumbered and demoralized, proved unable or unwilling to climb the hills to take the KPA positions. In confused fighting the 19th lost heavily; even the regimental headquarters, originally well behind the lines, recorded 57 troops killed or missing out of its 191 men. And, again, there were heavy losses of artillery and equipment. This was not a good omen for the defence of the important city of Taejon.

General Dean, fully aware of the condition of his forces, planned only a delaying action at Taejon and an evacuation on 19 July. But General Walker wanted more time to get the 1st Cavalry Division on the line in strength south of Taejon. Each day's delay of the *Inmin Gun* meant that much more manpower and equipment would be coming on line from Pusan. Dean promised Walker that he would hold out for another 24 hours and bolstered his defences at Taejon for that extra time. The major US Army units blocking the North Koreans before Taejon were the 24th Infantry Division and the 19th and the 34th Infantry regiments.

The KPA opened the attack with an air strike by six Yak fighters on the morning of the 19th. They scored little damage, but did drop some of the first Communist propaganda leaflets of the war:

> Dear conscientious officers and sergeants. Do surrender as soon as possible with all the men under your command. Dear friends! Be relieved and surrender.

With memories of their comrades shot out of hand by the *Inmin Gun*, it is unlikely that any American soldiers gave these leaflets much thought. At any rate, this air strike represented the last gasp of the Korean People's Air Force over the ground battlefield. From that day to the end of the war, no UNC, North Korean or Chinese soldier saw a Communist aircraft over the battlefield. (The jet dogfights over "MIG Alley" were fought in the vicinity of the Yalu River, well away from the front.) On the opening day of the KPA attack, FEAF fighter-bombers bombed and burned with liquid fire napalm KPA units advancing on the city. US air power, however, was hampered by the lack of airfields that could hold up under the F-51 fighters and C-47 twin-engine transports. In addition to the Taejon airstrip, only K-2 and K-3 airstrips at Taegu and Yonil, respectively, could, more or less, handle such warplanes. Consequently, most USAF air strikes at this point in the war had to be flown directly from Japan.

The Americans faced two KPA infantry divisions, the 3rd and 4th, plus an armoured spearhead. They were thus outnumbered by about two-to-one and they still lacked medium tanks. The KPA's 4th Division enveloped the city from the west and south and imposed an effective roadblock to the east, while the 3rd, along with a regiment of the 4th, maintained frontal pressure against the Americans. These were by now stereotypical KPA tactics, but, once again, they worked well. By the afternoon of the first day the 3rd had infiltrated the city along with T-34s of the 107th and possibly the 203rd Tank regiments.

But for the first time, the Americans had been issued some of the new 3.5in rocket launchers hurriedly air-lifted to the fighting as recently as 12 July, and they scored their first "kills" against the feared T-34s. In fact, the first known use of the new weapon resulted in three *Inmin Gun* tanks in a row destroyed on the second day's fighting. But this was the only bright spot in a tale of otherwise unrelieved defeat. Dean had lost contact with two of his leading battalions and did not know of the course of the battle or the location of its flanks. Earlier the 24th's commander had attached his Reconnaissance Company to the 34th Regiment which was to be the anchor of the defence of Taejon. Dean later forthrightly admitted that losing this company was one of his most serious mistakes of the battle. But he atoned for any command errors by his personal bravery and example. Leading several tank-hunting teams that destroyed at least one KPA tank, he later modestly pointed out that he did not actually fire on North Korean armour, leaving that to the experts. His troops were indeed taking the measure of the T-34, inflicting heavy losses. In fact, Dean did not at the time feel that the battle was going that badly. Only in the withdrawal did the full measure of the disaster become obvious. The maze of blazing city streets and the North Korean road block at the eastern edge of the city threw the withdrawal into confusion. Although there were some scenes of panic, the 24th did manage to pull out of the city in some order. But many straggled, were separated from their officers, got lost, and were captured.

The loss of Taejon by an exclusively American force was particularly disheartening, one of the most thoroughgoing defeats in American military history. The aftermath of the fall of Taejon also saw the highest-ranking UN personnel loss of the Korean War, when General Dean was himself captured after several weeks in hiding. Total US losses at Taejon were frightful. Although a mere 48 were reported killed in action, 874 were reported as missing in action. Many turned up later in Communist prisoner of war camps. In addition, the Taejon defenders lost virtually all of their organic equipment: a quartermaster company lost 30 of its 34 trucks, a field artillery battalion, all five of its 155mm howitzers. In fact, Taejon was a particularly rich lode for the North Koreans to mine.

The *Inmin Gun* suffered significant loses as well, however, particularly in armour and heavy artillery. At least 15 tanks were destroyed and the 4th Division alone lost 15 76mm guns. Taejon marked the last major deployment of KPA armour as well as of its air power. Communist personnel losses are almost impossible to determine, but it is known that the KPA's 4th Division suffered the most.

Perhaps the greatest single cause of the disasters at the Kum River and Taejon was lack of communications; for some reason there was a shortage of communications wire. Radio batteries were out of date and lasted only a few hours. Ammunition was also in short supply. The Americans were also outnumbered and exhausted, and up to a fourth suffered from dysentery picked up in the fetid rice paddies. But the North Koreans had not exactly just been trucked in from rest camps either, and had, in fact, been in almost continuous battle for about two weeks longer than the Americans. The Americans were also increasingly dispirited by the continuous retreats and lack of success in an incomprehensible cause and country. There were few qualified officers to replace casualties. By the time of the fall of Taejon the 24th alone had lost enough equipment to supply an entire US Army division. The *Inmin Gun*, on the other hand, was doing well overall and saw the goal of a united Korea now within its grasp. This must have helped to instill in that force a fighting spirit that, when combined with its savage discipline, gave it an edge over the UNC forces on the ground.

All of this came as a great surprise to Americans. Such surprise is usually and too easily attributed to "racism". In fact, most Americans at the time had no problem remembering that another Asian enemy, the Imperial Japanese Army, less than a decade earlier, had inflicted the greatest defeat on the United States in its history when it had seized the Philippines. No American could denigrate Japanese fighting ability after Guadalcanal, Tarawa, or Iwo Jima. But the Koreans were an unknown quantity. Although individual Koreans and some Korean formations in the Japanese Army had found themselves in battle against the Americans, few of the latter even knew of their presence. Through simple ignorance, Americans were unaware that, if anything, the Koreans could be tougher than the Japanese. Eighth Army itself tried to spell out Korean fighting tenacity in an official orientation to Korea booklet. It quoted a veteran infantry sergeant who responded to the oft-asked question, "What do these people have to live for, anyway?": "You'll find they fight like no one you have ever heard of. I've seen them in combat and I don't know either what it is they got to fight for so hard – maybe it's those dirty-faced kids – I don't know; but whatever it is, they sure hung in there after plenty of the other people were yelling quit."[8]

A more particular problem began to make itself felt at the front; the performance of the all-black 24th Infantry Regiment of the 25th Division. On 22 July, the 2nd Battalion of the 24th, while moving along a dirt road, encountered fire from a KPA light mortar and several automatic weapons and rifles. The men of E and F companies withdrew ("bugged-out") in a state of near-panic. The following day, the 17th ROK Regiment enveloped the same North Korean position and captured about 70 out-of-uniform KPA troopers. Similar incidents of misbehaviour and even panic multiplied over the weeks. The situation deteriorated so badly that the 25th Division Commanding General, William Kean, recalled the 1st Battalion of the 35th Regiment and placed it in blocking positions behind the 24th. Later, Kean demanded the break-up of the 24th. Its men were to be sent as fillers to other units at a ratio of one-to-ten. Kean also has been accused of "racism" here, but the general had a war to fight, and his position was that the UN was losing this war and that he could spare neither the time nor the effort to bring marginal units up to the rather low standard of US Army performance at the time.

The 24th's troubles stemmed from lackadaisical (usually white) leadership and a feeling by the rank-and-file that this wasn't their war. It should also be remembered that, as noted, white units at this time also suffered from a dismaying number of "bug outs".

The Far East Command was painfully aware of its problems in the field. A team of high-ranking officers from the United States toured every US division and regiment in Korea soon after the Taejon disaster. The team determined that

> having been commited [sic] more or less piecemeal, after incomplete training, and at reduced strength, with much of their equipment of marginal serviceability. . . . Our troops were opposed by an enemy who vastly outnumbered them [not so], and who was well trained, well equipped, skillfully led and inspired by a fanatical determination to attack. . . . The frontages were enormous and precluded a continuous line of defense. This facilitated outflanking and penetrating operations by the enemy and forced a continuous withdrawal.

The team further noted that these US troops were less mature and of lower intelligence (at least as determined by Army IQ tests of the time) than their predecessors in the Second World War (perhaps due to the fact that Selective

Service in the Korean War exempted those engaged in higher education). They reported that US Army forces had been committed piecemeal and after incomplete training. Further, the troopers were led by infantry officers who, in accordance with the Army's perverse personnel policies, were the poorest prepared for combat, where they could do the maximum damage. The team forthrightly concluded that

> The absolute discipline and automatic obedience to command that is vital for control in combat is lacking. . . . Like all green troops, they magnified the strength of the enemy, and tended to become panicky and stampede when small hostile groups got in their rear. . . . Infantry troops were specifically deficient in . . . aggressiveness in counter-attack, steadiness under fire, [and] confidence in their own weapons. . . . Lack of leadership in regimental and subordinate echelons was often evident, in both field and company grades, and among the non-commissioned officers.[9]

The only hopeful sign on the immediate horizon was that the US Army itself would draw up such a damning bill of particulars in wartime, without any excuses or special pleading and was prepared to learn from it and similar critiques. Indeed, in the end it could be said that the United States entered the Korean War with a poor army and ended it with a fairly good one. But such long-range improvement was well in the future in the crisis summer of 1950, a time when it appeared quite likely that the UN forces would be bodily thrown off the Korean peninsula.

The KPA was not having things entirely its own way, however. Continuing his earlier criticism, the Soviet Ambassador was reporting to "Comrade Fyn-Si" (Stalin) that Kim Il Sung had admitted to him that his "troops are moving very slowly, especially in the Central direction. The troop crossing [Kum River?] was disorganized." The ambassador further noted "the seriousness of the situation at the front and in the liberated territories" and he twice referred to the "complicated situation", a euphemism employed by leaders or propagandists when things do not seem to be going all that well at the front.[10]

We now know that General Walker possessed an advantage over the North Koreans that was almost the equivalent of his vital air support. Having broken the *Inmin Gun*'s radio codes, he could read his enemy's wireless traffic almost as soon as it was transmitted. Knowing practically every major move of the KPA, Walker could transfer his units to trouble spots and yet keep a mobile reserve that could be rushed on short notice to any other threatened or actual North Korean breakthrough. In fact, the main reason that General Walker did not evacuate Taegu when the city's fall seemed imminent during the Pusan Perimeter battles was that he did not have time to evacuate his mobile communications system, the only such equipment in the Far East. The KPA command, in their ignorant contempt for their enemies, did not bother to change their codes.

The KPA's offensive continued to roll south and west, but Communist casualties were mounting steadily – and unexpectedly. Far East Command intelligence reported that the *Inmin Gun* had been forced to open induction centres as well as replacement and training depots throughout the occupied areas of the ROK, something that Kim Il Sung had not imagined necessary when he mounted his "liberation" of the South. In the induction centres the conscript was given a few days or less of training, then dispatched on foot, sometimes without uniform or weapon, to the maelstrom of the front. (Some of those "guerrillas" captured in civilian garb may simply have been groups of these hapless conscripts.)

With North Korean air power eliminated for all intents and purposes, the UN Command enjoyed unchallenged control of the skies. The KPA was forced to mount its major offensives under cover of darkness or bad weather. Furthermore, those *Inmin Gun* tanks and self-propelled guns that were not hit from the air were beginning to wear out or break down as they ground their way to Pusan. The KPA lacked an effective replenishment net as well as enough motor trucks to bring up supplies and spare parts. And what trucks they still had could travel only when the skies were dark. Thus, disabled KPA heavy weapons had to be left by the side of the road, easy targets for UN air strikes. The Communist forces did possess a Soviet-made mortar that would cause UN forces considerable trouble to the end of the war. It might have been better for the KPA to have been equipped with many more of these excellent weapons so suited to the rugged terrain of South Korea and to the tough constitutions of the KPA troopers than the more terrifying but short-lived T–34–85s.

UN air power was getting into its stride, making the KPA pay a heavy price for its gains. Improved communications with the ground troops made all the difference. US and Royal Navy air units, which had performed so well in just such missions in the Pacific in the Second World War, were soon heavily on the scene, usually flying exactly the same propeller-vintage ground-attack aircraft that they had used in the previous conflict. UN air power, in fact, rather than ground attack, destroyed the vast majority of the KPA's T–34 tanks.

All this said, the KPA hardly paused at Taejon and continued its drive on the central front. Several days after the fall of that city, the newly arrived 1st US Cavalry Division began to make its presence felt on the battlefield. On 23 July, in front of Yongdong, its First Battalion of the 8th Cavalry

Regiment reported that it had destroyed three tanks, and by decimating fire from quad .50 and artillery bombardment helped to grind up *Inmin Gun* attacks northwest of the town. By the 26th, having put up a stout resistance, the 1st Cavalry fell back from the city in fairly good order. However, the division's 71st Tank Platoon had to abandon no fewer than seven light tanks and all its heavy equipment in the retreat. Again, as at Taejon, the KPA suffered heavy casualties; the KPA's 3rd Division lost about 2,000, mostly from US artillery fire, and was now down to half-strength.

The 27th Regiment of the 25th Infantry Division first went into action at roughly this time, as its troopers attempted to block the North Korean 2nd Division entering the main Seoul–Pusan highway. The "Wolfhounds" introduction to the war was certainly auspicious: in its first engagement with these American forces, the *Inmin Gun*'s 2nd Division lost all but two of its eight tanks, although several were also lost to USAF F-80 jets. In fact, both of the contending divisions were meeting their enemy for the first time. The next day the North Koreans were surprised in the open and were decimated by US tanks, artillery, mortar and small arms fire. The 27th finally had to withdraw in the face of greatly superior opposing numbers. But in five days (23–28 July), at a loss of 53 killed in action, it had inflicted about 3,000 casualties on the KPA 2nd Division. And three days later, as the Communists pressed forward, air and ground fire destroyed 13 T-34s and set another six aflame. Much of the 27th's success was due to its commanding officer, Colonel Mike Michaelis, an officer who could get the maximum from his troops, and who was certainly one of the best US battlefield commanders of the war.

The KPA rolled on, shaking off its heavy casualties at Kimchon (29–30 July) and Sangju (21–31 July), and continuing to lose its tanks. The Americans were increasingly fighting alongside their ROK Army allies. Both forces were falling back on the upper Naktong River, and both reached that watercourse by the end of the month. ROK divisions remained on the UN Command's right flank and gave a much better account of themselves than has usually been credited. The ROK 1st Division and the 17th Regiment both mounted very successful ambushes, the former in coordination with the US 24th Regiment at the Kallyong Pass on 23 July. The Americans would not mount effective ambushes of their own until several months later.

By 23 July, air reconnaissance revealed that KPA forces had begun to swing south and east behind the left flank (such as it was) of Eighth Army. General Walker had only the eviscerated 24th Division which had enjoyed exactly one day's rest in reserve before being ordered into the southern battle. It would be reinforced by two battalions of the newly arrived 29th Independent Infantry Regiment originally stationed on Okinawa. "Newly arrived" was certainly the term for these battalions: instead of the planned six-weeks' battle training, they were to go into battle immediately, their rifles not zeroed, mortars not fired, new .50-calibre machine guns that had the cosmoline only hastily rubbed off. Already the *Inmin Gun* had reached Mokpo at the south-west end of the peninsula, its progress impeded only by local ROK police units. These must have been brave units indeed, but then, Korean police were always known for their toughness. The Americans first engaged this most threatening KPA southern thrust outside Hadong. It was during an initial misfired American ambush that the former Chief of Staff of the ROK Army lost his life. Accompanying the Americans as a mere adviser, General Chae Pyong Duk was killed instantly in an almost simultaneous North Korean ambush. One month later, Chae's counterpart, the Chief of Staff of the *Inmin Gun*, Lieutenant General Kang Kon (known to the Americans, of course, as "King Kong"), also died in battle, blown up by a land mine.

Once again the retreat of the outnumbered Americans became at times a rout with resultant heavy casualties. When the Hadong area was retaken by UN forces in late September, no fewer than 313 US dead were counted. The Hadong action, in fact, may have been the single worst loss of American lives in any one-day's battle of the war, even worse than that at Taejon. About 30 vehicles, all crew-served weapons, and even most of the 3rd battalion's individual weapons were lost, signs of a precipitous retreat. The situation was little better around Anui, where approximately half of the 215 men of B and D companies were either killed or listed as missing in action. Both ROK and US forces continued to retreat to the east now that the far south had been lost. Americans of the depleted 34th Regiment facing Kochang were again fairly easily routed by the KPA's 4th Division.

The Americans, now reinforced by the veteran 17th ROK Regiment, attempted another stand in the Chinju area. Poor communications and some inexplicable failures to use heavy weapons doomed the UN forces to yet another retreat. But at least this was an orderly withdrawal, although tedious, as civilian refugees intermingled with the troops.

Further south, the KPA's 6th Division struck for Masan, the last major town before Pusan itself. The first US Army unit to head south was the excellent 27th Regiment, which in staving off an attack on Chingdong-ni on 3 August killed or wounded some 600 KPA troops for a loss of only 13 killed and about 40 wounded.

This southward *Inmin Gun* movement nonetheless compelled General Walker to order a general withdrawal of UN forces to the east bank of the Naktong River. For the most part, the retreat was successful although one battalion of the 5th Cavalry Regiment was nearly lost. The ROK divisions were more closely engaged by the KPA than the Americans. The ROK 1st was heavily pressed north of the river, while the 16th Regiment of the 8th was even more heavily embattled north of Andong. Perhaps with the Seoul highway bridge disaster in mind, the commanding general of the 1st Cavalry, Major General Hobart Gay, guarded the most important bridges over the Naktong, at Waegwan. He gave orders that no one but himself, personally, could order the structures blown. But again, bridge destruction caused a heavy loss of life, in this case almost entirely civilian. Each time General Gay would order his rear guard to clear the bridges prior to their immediate destruction, hordes of refugees would follow hard on their heels. This manoeuvre was repeated several times. But if the refugees were pressing the American rear guard, the *Inmin Gun* was pressing the refugees. General Gay had no recourse but to order the bridges blown, refugees and all. Several hundred died. General Walker meanwhile continued to be concerned about the perhaps overly rapid pace of the UN withdrawal behind the Naktong, and had to issue no fewer than three directives to his division commanders to see to it that their troops kept the North Koreans engaged while retreating.

As early as the middle of July it was estimated that about 380,000 refugees were streaming into ROK territory and that their numbers were increasing by 25,000 each day. Later, when 8th Army could catch its breath, their care was established on a regular basis. Hundreds of thousands were saved from starvation, disease and the elements.

It is instructive that the refugee flow throughout the war was documented almost entirely one way – towards UN forces. Some have tried to explain this away by arguing that they were fleeing insensate UN air and artillery bombardment. But why would they flee *toward* their tormentors? Others have said that the refugees had nowhere else to go and knew that the UN, or at least the Americans, had plenteous supplies. But how did the refugees know that the UN would take care of them, especially in the early desperate months? And would these "unpolitical" refugees not have been more likely to stay in place in their home villages, even if their homes had been destroyed, usually by the "imperialists" or their "puppets", and await the Communists, with their land reform and the rebuilding of those villages, happily minus the landlord and the money lender? One "explanation" with even less respect for the facts, is that the refugees were primarily landlords, bankers, money lenders, businesspersons, and so on, which, if true and considering the numbers involved over the months, means that South Korea was a far more prosperous nation than had ever been imagined. The logical explanation is that given by the refugees themselves: the Communists were brutally imposing an alien system on their land and their lives, hard and unrewarding as that land and those lives might have been.

Even though UN troops, weapons and supplies were pouring into Pusan, it was still problematic that the UN Command could hold behind its Naktong moat. The resistance put up by UN forces earlier at the Han or the Kum rivers was not such as would give any objective analyst much confidence that the Naktong River front would hold any better. Those refugees might yet find themselves in a mob scene on the Pusan docks, fighting to board barges in a final UN "Dunkirk" evacuation to Japan, leaving all of Korea to Kim Il Sung's Democratic People's Republic of Korea. That this did not happen was due in large measure to UN air power and to the delaying actions fought by ROK and American troops in the earliest weeks of the war. These actions were usually lost by the UN forces but they did slow the North Koreans, allowing the US to bring to bear its increasing preponderance of air and naval power as well as troops. Osan, for example, was not just a skirmish in which US forces were "brushed aside", as legend would have it. The casualties of the opposing division would indicate quite otherwise. In the vicinity of that battle a few days later, US Army intelligence found in the diary of an *Inmin Gun* trooper killed in action the notation that "Near Osan there was a great battle".

Chapter Four

The Pusan Perimeter

From southwest to northeast, the US Army units and their KPA opponents along the Pusan Perimeter were as follows:

25th US Infantry Division   6th KPA Division – "Guards"
24th US Infantry Division   4th KPA – "Kim Chaek, Seoul Guards" Division
1st US Cavalry Division   3rd KPA – "Seoul Guards" Division

Each US division was responsible for a front of from 32 to 64 kilometres, much more than laid out in contemporary US Army manuals.

ROK Army divisions held the eastern half of the line, just above Waegwan.

1st ROK Infantry Division   KPA 15th and part of the 13th Division
6th ROK Infantry Division   Elements of the KPA 13th and 1st Divisions
8th ROK Infantry   KPA 8th Division
ROK Capital Division   KPA 12th Division – "Andong"
3rd ROK Infantry division   KPA 5th and 766th Independent Infantry Regiment
                            KPA 105th Armored Division supported KPA infantry units as needed

Total US ground units strength at this time stood at approximately 45,000 troops. The combat strength of the Army of the ROK at the same time numbered 47,000. The troop strength of the KPA probably stood then at no more than 70,000. This disparity does not take into account the UN Command's complete control of the air and the sea lanes by this time, nor of its greatly superior armour and artillery. These odds apparently did little to daunt the North Korean high command. Kim Il Sung let it be known that he expected Pusan to fall by 15 August, the fifth anniversary of the surrender of Japan and a date celebrated both North and South as the day of liberation from the Japanese yoke.

The combat troops on both sides were exhausted by almost six weeks of continuous fighting. But the UN's forces were being replenished by unimpeded sea and air routes. Their troops arrived rested, completely equipped and well-fed, although not always so well trained. *Inmin Gun* troops, on the other hand, by now mostly had to walk to battle, were subjected to air attack at any time during the day and were living off the land or on handfuls of rice. They were then thrown into the maelstrom of steel, flame and white phosphorous more or less precisely directed on them by the UN Command's plentiful artillery and air-delivered ordnance. Tribute must be paid to this army's near-incredible discipline in the face of such odds, although that discipline would eventually break. Much of this steadfastness was due to the fact that, at least at the beginning of the invasion, perhaps one-half of the KPA's troops had combat experience on the winning side of China's lengthy civil war, and some were veterans of the war against Japan. The KPA was also known for its brutal discipline, a reflection of the toughness of life in Korea generally as well as of the tradition of "war Communism", dating back to the Russian civil war, when War Commissar Trotsky was shooting waverers. And KPA troops also had the great advantage of knowing that if they won, the land would be united.

US troops, on the other hand, had considerable difficulty in understanding just how winning or losing this war could affect their own nation all that much. In an attempt to spell out the issues, or at least the battlefield realities, General Walker, on 29 July, even before the retreat to the Naktong had been completed, had issued his famous "Stand or Die" order/speech to his division chiefs:

> There will be no more retreating, withdrawal, or readjustment of the lines or any other term you choose. There is no line behind us to which we can retreat. . . . There will be no Dunkirk, no Bataan . . . , a retreat to Pusan would be one of the greatest butcheries in history. . . . Capture by these people is worse than death itself. . . . We are going to win.

The order was timely; only four days later the KPA had launched an all-out offensive against the perimeter in five different locations.

Those critical of Walker have pointed out that Eighth Army did indeed retreat after this order. But these retreats were relatively limited and usually in fairly good order. The Americans realized now, if they had not before, that a retreat to Pusan might indeed cost them their lives or at least their liberty. There could be no guarantee of an orderly evacuation. In fact, General Walker had chosen his words well: "Dunkirk", a successful evacuation whose repetition could not be guaranteed, and "Bataan", where US troops were finally trapped and captured by a victorious enemy. "Capture by these people is worse than death itself" reminded wavering troops of the fate of their captured comrades: a bullet in the back of the head or the routine brutalities of a Communist prison camp far from home, often after a forced propaganda parade through the streets of Pyongyang.

Although General Walker had committed his share of mistakes in the retreat south, by early August he had come into his own as a scrappy, tenacious fighter. A graduate of the US Military Academy Class of 1912, he had combat experience in both World Wars and had begun the rehabilitation of Eighth Army in the last months of its debilitating Japanese occupation duty. He expected no less from his commanders than from himself. Walker bluntly informed one division commanding general that he did not want to see that officer behind the front again unless he were in his Army-issue casket!

In retrospect, it can be seen that almost all of the tangible military advantages by this time rested with the UN Command. The troops were compressed into what for the first time was an almost continuous battle line with much shorter routes of supply to Pusan and equally shorter interdiction times for their air power and artillery. UN forces now outnumbered their enemies, their casualties could be replaced relatively easily, their wounded received fairly prompt medical care of excellent quality, and they were about as well fed as any foot soldier in battle could expect. General Walker, of course, continued to eavesdrop on KPA radio message traffic. All of these advantages were far more marked among the US forces than in their ROK allies. The commander of the ROK 1st Division has recorded his astonished gratitude at receiving from American officers his first three-colour military maps. On the other hand, the KPA still enjoyed its offensive momentum, and its T-34 tanks continued to terrify new troops.

Perhaps suffering by then from over-confidence, General Walker determined to mount the first extensive UN counter-attack of the war in the southernmost corridor of the battlefront, scene of earlier US severe defeats. An American offensive here would also probably serve to divert KPA troops from their pressure against Taegu to the north. Three regiments (including the First Provisional Marine Regiment) collectively named Task Force Kean after the commanding general of the 25th US Division, would mount the attack, seize the Chinju Pass and secure the line of the Nam River. The attack started off well enough with the 35th Infantry pushing the North Koreans back near Muchon-ni. They inflicted about 350 casualties on the North Koreans, destroyed two tanks, one self-propelled gun, and five anti-tank guns, and captured four truckloads of weapons and ammunition, plus several briefcases of documents. But Task Force Kean, unwittingly, was colliding with an all-out drive by the excellent North Korean 6th Division. Two field artillery battalions were mauled at Pogam-ni, causing other units, which lacked artillery support, to give way. When UN forces retook the area five weeks later, the bodies of 20 men of one of the artillery battalions were recovered; all had been shot through the head by *Inmin Gun* troops. The scene had been well-named: "Bloody Gulch".

The attack continued in blistering heat, which felled considerably more UN troops than it did the North Koreans. A smart victory developed when the 5th Marines inadvertently dropped shells on a group of camouflaged KPA vehicles. Thinking they had been uncovered, the North Korean force quickly deployed into about 200 trucks, jeeps and motorcycles, laden with ammunition and supplies. As their bad luck would have it, a routine reconnaissance flight of four Marine Corsair prop fighters flew over the scene and, totally unopposed in the air, shot up the length of the convoy. Two Corsairs were forced down by anti-aircraft fire, but just then another flight of Corsairs and USAF propeller F-51s arrived and completed the work of destruction. When the Marine ground-pounders reached the scene they found 31 trucks, 45 motorcycles and much ammunition and supplies destroyed or abandoned along the road, not to mention scores of burned and blasted corpses. Despite these successes, Task Force Kean by then had disappointingly been pushed back about where it had started five days earlier. By then crises on other sections of the Pusan Perimeter had led the UN Command to withdraw the Marine brigade, and on 16 August a radio message to General Kean dissolved Task Force Kean.

The KPA's 6th Division had taken heavy losses, but then so had the task force. The North Korean command did not have to withdraw a single squad from service in the southern sector of the Pusan Perimeter. About the most that could be said of this US counter-attack was that the important southern city of Masan, a target of the 6th KPA Division, had been saved.

It was at this time of mortal combat that Far East Command determined on a means to augment depleted US units, the Korean Augmentation of the US Army (KATUSA). Between 30,000 and 40,000 Korean "troops", many mere schoolboys swept from the streets of Pusan and Taegu, were assigned to the ravaged US 24th and 25th Divisions. The ROK would pay and administer these men, but they would draw US Army rations special service items, valuable "perks" indeed to the mostly impoverished Koreans. At first the KATUSAs made a bad name for themselves by panic flight in combat and generally not knowing what was going on, although they were acknowledged to have performed well in menial tasks. Many of their deficiencies may be put down to language barrier. The KATUSAs were to learn a few words of English from their Army "buddies", but the latter were not expected to gain any Hangul words or expressions from the association. Soon after the stabilization of the lines, however, the picture had changed as KATUSAs could by then be better trained. Their duties expanded to scouting, intelligence, the guarding of enemy POWs, and assisting refugees, where their interpreting skills proved invaluable. Eventually many US soldiers came to acknowledge that their KATUSA "buddies" were their equal on the battlefield. By 1952 even frontline troops were being replaced with KATUSAs. Eventually they came to number about 24,000 just before the armistice signing. The programme continues to this day. By 1953 only the ROK government itself had its doubts about the programme; it limited recruitment because KATUSA offered greater prestige and tangible benefits than anything available to enlisted troops in the Army of the ROK.

Almost simultaneously with Task Force Kean and undoubtedly spurred into even greater effort by Kim Il Sung's setting of 15 August as the date for final victory, elements of the KPA's 4th Division began crossing at the so-called Naktong River Bulge in the southwest segment of the Perimeter. They waded across the shoulder-deep water at Ohang or embarked on field-expedient rafts. These troops established a bridgehead on the east bank of the Naktong, despite strong US counter-attacks. By this time the KPA division had constructed an underwater bridge spanning the Naktong and thus could move heavy equipment over to the east bank. Then, on 11 August KPA troops surprised and killed a US squad guarding the bridge at Namji-ri, cutting the only vehicular link between the 24th and 25th US divisions. Once again the crack 27th "Wolfhounds" were called in, along with the 24th Division's headquarters and engineer troops. Both forces eliminated the dangerous KPA penetration south and east of Yongsan. In these actions, the 27th's troops took four KPA artillery pieces – two of which were captured US 105mm howitzers. It was a sad indication of the amount of equipment lost or abandoned by the Americans so far in this war that the *Inmin Gun* had enough captured US Army ammunition to keep this war booty in action.

By the penultimate date of 15 August General Walker was convinced that he was facing the worse crisis so far of the Korean War, although he might have taken some slight satisfaction in the knowledge that Kim Il Sung's target date for driving his forces from the peninsula had slipped badly. Walker called on his strongest reserve, the 1st Marine Provisional Brigade, attached it to the 24th Division, and ordered an attack on the KPA still east of the Naktong as soon as possible. The 24th's commander also planned for an Army–Marine counter-attack on the bulge. Severe battles saw the *Inmin Gun* gradually pushed back towards the river. A radio interception revealed that KPA troops in the bulge were short of ammunition and were requesting permission to withdraw across the Naktong, one of the first acknowledged

KPA retreats since the opening of the invasion. On the 19th, Army and Marine forces met at the Naktong, and the Battle of the Naktong Bulge was over, the greatest setback for the North Koreans so far in the war.

But the purple prose of Kim Il Sung's official biographer puts a somewhat differing interpretation on the battle:

> The Rakdong River ran red with blood. Everything spat fire. Space was filled with flying shells and bullets, and over their heads ranged the enemy's planes. But it was the high-spirited People's Army that won the battle and it was the US imperialist aggressors and their mercenaries that shuddered with fear and flinched from the battle.[1]

"Shuddering with fear", the 24th Division alone buried more than 1,200 "high-spirited" KPA dead soon after the battle. POW interrogations revealed that about one-third of the 4th Division's wounded at the Bulge had expired from lack of medical care. (Ironically, on the very day that the Naktong Bulge battle was ended, the *Inmin Gun*'s mangled 4th Division was named a "Guards Division" for its victory at Taejon just one month previous.)

By this time KPA troops, many of whom were press-ganged South Koreans, were suffering mass death and indescribable agonies at the hands of the UN forces. Allied air power rained high-explosives and napalm on them. Napalm generated a consuming fireball over an area up to 275 feet long by 100 feet wide. A "refinement" of standard napalm bombing was the spraying of the substance above targeted troops, then the ignition of the hellish mixture. US troops occasionally reported that they could hear the screams of napalmed Communist troops more than a mile distant. UN artillery supplemented its nearly unlimited high-explosive shells with the white phosphorus that could burn even more excruciatingly and persistently than the horrific napalm.

By now the KPA high command often seemed to have no more of a military plan than to throw its troops into the battle and take Pusan by Comrade Kim's 15 August deadline. About all that the exhausted, decimated KPA had going for it at this stage was the feeling that just one more offensive must carry it to final victory and the unification of Korea. That army continued its dogged attacks, coming close on several occasions to breaking through the UN cordon.

For all their increasing advantages, the Americans and the ROKs still had to fight hard across the perimeter. The combat seemed primarily vertical, up and down hills. American soldiers grimly claimed that Korea was actually the world's largest country: if all its hills and mountains were somehow hammered flat it would cover the globe! But there was also combat in the fetid flatland rice paddies during the steaming heat of that South Korean summer of 1950. Belts and shoes of infantrymen rotted away in the continuous fighting. One GI remembered vividly that in the faecal paddies, when the sun came out after a summer rain, the whole countryside "stank like a giant diaper pail". But both sides fought on without a break.

Shrugging off its losses, the North Korean high command at about this time mounted one of its most dangerous penetrations at the small port to the north of the perimeter, Pohang-dong, where KPA troops actually entered the city. This advance guard was driven out, but the ROK Third Division in the meantime had to be evacuated by sea. The nearby USAF strip at Yonil also had to be abandoned, and the area became a no-man's land. UN naval forces had to pound the KPA with heavy-calibre bombardment in addition to the ubiquitous air strikes before UN forces could reestablish their lines and close off this "back door" to the ROK temporary capital and road and rail centre of Taegu.

Even more threatening was the KPA thrust on the central front against Taegu by no fewer than five North Korean divisions and elements of the KPA's armoured division. The ROK national and provincial governments hastily evacuated the city when a few enemy mortar rounds landed in the refugee-clogged downtown between 18 and 20 August. But, as noted, General Walker's headquarters stayed in place. The Eighth Army commander was unwilling to risk his irreplaceable mobile communications gear that enabled 8th Army to keep track not only of its own command but also to some extent of the KPA. To save the city, US Far East Air Force (FEAF) warplanes had carried out a "carpet bombing" on 16 August against KPA forces supposedly on the west side of the Naktong. FEAF deployed 98 B-29 heavy bombers in a raid reminiscent of Second World War operations. The bombing, which had been ordered by General MacArthur and opposed by FEAF itself, created a moonscape along the Naktong. As in similar Second World War operations, the results were debatable. Such bombing was never repeated over the Korean battle fronts. At any rate, most of the North Korean units had moved just before the bombing. The North Koreans actually crossed the Naktong in places and overran some 1st Cavalry positions although the excellent 1st ROK Division held. The *Inmin Gun* thrust was thrown back after heavy casualties on both sides.

The staunch resistance of the 1st ROK Division was no fluke. Its chief, Paik Sun Yup, was undoubtedly the best of the ROK Army field commanders, and would eventually rise to the position of ROK Army Chief of Staff. Here is one indication that the ROK Army was not completely beset with favouritism and corruption.

By 19 August the 3rd KPA Division had practically ceased to exist. Taegu, one of the most embattled cities of the war, held. Even worse for the KPA, a straight stretch of road that led through a narrow valley some 13 miles northwest of Taegu became a scene of slaughter for KPA armoured forces. Beginning on the night of 18 August and continuing through the 27th, KPA armoured units and their vehicles pushed down the valley, but there they met the 23rd Infantry Regiment and the 27th's Wolfhounds and were stopped cold in the so-called "Bowling Alley", again with heavy losses that were mostly irreplaceable in the case of their armoured vehicles.

The North Koreans were not finished with Taegu, however. On 2 September, with the 27th and 23rd Regiments withdrawn to plug other critical points along the Pusan Perimeter, the KPA's 1st, 3rd, and 13th divisions, totalling 22,000 troops, hit hard north of Taegu, sending the 1st Cavalry once again reeling in disarray. The battered US division withdrew a few days later to positions about eight miles above Taegu where they finally held, barely. Counter-attacks retook the main KPA position at a very heavy cost on 12 September, and by the 15th, North Korean forces were preparing to pull back.

On 29 August the first contingent of UN troops, after the Americans, to come to the aid of the ROK disembarked at Pusan. These were the British Army's 1st Battalion of the famed Argyll and Sutherland Highlanders, the 1st Battalion of the Middlesex Regiment and the headquarters of the 27th Infantry Brigade; these were all infantry forces and sorely needed. They were also all regulars, professionals and tough fighters, and the Americans and ROKs in the field were very glad to have them. The British troops almost immediately packed into troop trains for the front.

On 5 September the "Brit's" 27th went into action for the first time, in the defence of Taegu. The following day, they received a taste of the nature of this war. An Argyll combat patrol, encountering a superior KPA force, had to retreat, leaving behind, on his own orders, an officer and his batman, both badly wounded. Neither were heard of again. A British company was so isolated in the fighting around Taegu that airdrops of ice had to replace the water cans that were usually carried uphill to their positions. But Taegu held, in no small measure, thanks to the timely British aid.

None of the battles of the Pusan Perimeter were fought in isolation. For example, on 3 September General Walker had to face no fewer than five dangerous threats to the UN line: a KPA penetration at Pohang, the cutting of the lateral corridor between Taegu and Pohang, *Inmin Gun* gains in the mountains north of Taegu, a threat by KPA forces attacking UN defences in the Bulge area, and hostile penetrations behind much of the 25th Division in the extreme south. And the 1st Cavalry was withdrawing closer to Taegu under NKPA pressure, while the 2nd and 25th US divisions were embattled in the south. Most of these threats were part of the KPA's final offensive. The DPRK had its agents inside Pusan, and they must have been sending out reports by one means or another of the steady build-up of UN forces, the troops and equipment pouring in unhindered through the port facilities. The KPA high command could not but compare this reported buildup of its enemy with their own dwindling forces at the end of an increasingly attenuated and embattled supply line.

A spirit of desperation seems to have entered the planning of the KPA operations by this time, particularly in light of the missed 15 August goal. "Comrade Fyn-Si" attempted to cheer up Kim Il Sung on the 28th by communicating to him through the Soviet Ambassador in Pyongyang that "Comrade Kim Il Sung should not be embarrassed by the fact that he does not have solid successes in the war against the interventionists, that the successes are sometimes interrupted by delays in the advance or even by some local set-backs", and pointed out that "the position of the Russians during the Anglo–French–American intervention in 1919 was several times worse than the position of the Korean comrades at the present time".[2]

Still, the KPA was now actually somewhat larger than when it had first crossed the 38th Parallel, although the quality of the troops was not nearly so good. That army had even received some 50 new T-34-85 tanks in time for the last offensive. But the final Communist onslaught could hardly be dignified by terming it a campaign; the KPA high command simply threw its troops onto all roads that led to Pusan. This was undoubtedly an unwise spreading of force in the face of an enemy with numerical, heavy weapons, and air superiority. A single, powerful strike accompanied by a diversion would have held a much greater chance of success. These were, after all, the tactics that had nearly driven the UN forces off the Korean peninsula.

This general KPA offensive lasted from late August to mid-September, apparently in the hope that somewhere the UN line might break. And, again, General Walker used the 27th along the line as his fire brigade. But even that excellent unit, plus well co-ordinated artillery, mortar, and tank barrages, and a perfectly timed air attack, which left hundreds of KPA dead strewn across the battlefield, could not force the North Koreans off the crest of Battle Mountain, lost earlier by ROK troops and Americans of the 24th Infantry. After more than a month of steady and heavy fighting, all the 27th and the reconstituted 24th could do was to contain the mountain crest behind barbed wire and mine fields, pre-register artillery and mortar fire on all KPA approaches to the mountain and blast away. The 24th Infantry soon after also lost Pil-bong, a mountain peak even higher than Battle Mountain.

The first overt armed clash between US and Soviet forces since the end of American intervention in the Russian civil war took place at roughly this time. A Red Air Force bomber/reconnaissance aircraft passed over screening warships and headed towards the centre of an UNC naval task force operating off the west coast of the peninsula at approximately the 38th Parallel and was shot down. The UNC claimed that the Red Air Force warplane had opened fire first, something that the Soviets naturally denied; their aircraft was merely on a "training mission", albeit rather far from home and in quite dangerous skies for so pacific a flight. But both sides had their hands full with the current fighting in Korea and were not eager to take on another enemy and the incident was defused at the United Nations in early October 1950.

On the ground in Korea, the UNC's combat troops were bone-weary from their rushing about to plug *Inmin Gun* penetrations along the Pusan Perimeter, but the KPA's troops were weary also. It was becoming obvious with each day's battle that the North Koreans' chances of a major breakthrough were steadily decreasing. The KPA leadership was now aware that not only was its time running out, but that its forces stood in increasing jeopardy themselves. The troops only knew that their gains were decreasing and their losses mounting in the terrible meat grinder of the perimeter battles. Yet they continued, raw conscripts as well as toughened surviving veterans, with dwindling equipment and hope, to batter against the UN lines and to score local successes. To the end, despite the UN Command's increasing superiority, the defence of the Pusan Perimeter was a precarious business. More US troops died in the first 15 days of September 1950 than in any other 15-day period of the entire war. The Duke of Wellington is supposed to have remarked after the Battle of Waterloo that "it was a damned close-run thing". The battle for the Pusan Perimeter was about as close, and despite the UN Command's vast superiority in logistics, medical care, armour, naval and air power, and manpower, perhaps even closer.

Chapter Five

Inchon landings and pursuit northward

General MacArthur had planned to put his 1st Cavalry Division ashore at Inchon well behind KPA lines as early as 22 July. Here he was certainly guilty of the most gross optimism or ignorance, for such planning had to be abandoned on 10 July as US and ROK forces continued to stream southward in defeat. But also on the 10th, an undaunted MacArthur met with the commander of the Pacific Fleet Marine Force, Major General Oliver P. Smith. With Joint Chiefs of Staff approval, General Smith promised that the entire 1st Marine Division, veteran of many Pacific War contested landings, could be in Korea within six weeks and in action by 15 September. (The "square" US Marine Divisions, with their four infantry regiments, were more "heavy" than their three-regiment Army counterparts.)

Planning for a landing behind North Korean lines resumed on 12 August and was completed in only one month. Operation Plan 100-B was code-named Operation CHROMITE (originally and weirdly termed BLUEHEARTS). Planning was carried out by Far East Command's Joint Strategic Plans and Operations Group, under the control of FEC's Operations Division. General MacArthur then divided his forces. On 26th August he established X Corps, composed of the 7th Infantry and the 1st Marine Divisions, with supporting field artillery and Combat Engineer units. The 7th was the last continental US Army division, along with the 82nd Airborne, not already committed to Korea and was seriously under strength until topped off with reinforcements, including KATUSAs. The Marine division, which was commanded by Major General Smith, was over-strength with the addition of the Marine Brigade (redesignated the 5th Marines). It numbered more than 25,000 troops, including some 2,700 Army personnel. To command X Corps MacArthur appointed his Chief of Staff, the prickly, hard-charging Major General Edward Almond. General Almond was an officer who in imperiousness and vanity could be said to have out-MacArthured MacArthur. On occasion, ignoring the chain of command, he would go out into the field and tell brigades and battalions how to do their work. In this one aspect he was different from MacArthur, who maintained his Olympian distance from the front. MacArthur now had two independent commands under himself, a decision that would later have disastrous consequences.

For MacArthur there was only one landing site: Inchon. This was the port for Seoul and deep in KPA-controlled territory. But the short thrust inland from Inchon would be a stiletto to the throat of the Communists occupying Seoul, and the capital's loss would be a propaganda body-blow for them.

Still, there were several "buts" about Inchon. Yes, Inchon was well behind enemy lines, but the North Koreans were close by in large numbers at Seoul and Inchon itself. The port was indeed close to Seoul, but it could lift only one-tenth the cargo of Pusan. A landing there would probably catch the KPA by surprise, but Inchon's approaches from the Yellow Sea were by two narrow, twisting, rocky passages which joined ten miles downriver from Inchon. Both channels could easily be mined, and one sunken ship could block either channel. Further, the normal harbour current at Inchon was a rapid two to three knots and sometimes eight knots. Just offshore the triangular island of Wolmi-do was known to be fortified. Several heights dominated the proposed landing area: Radio Hill (315 feet) overlooked the harbour while Cemetery Hill (102 feet) towered over the 800-yard-long causeway leading to Wolmi-do. Observatory Hill (238 feet) and British Consulate Hill dominated Inchon itself.

What made a landing at Inchon even more improbable was the sudden and dramatic tidal range of the channels; this could vary from an average of 23 feet to a maximum of 33 feet, and at ebb tide the harbour was turned into mud flats extending as far as three miles from the shoreline. This is the second greatest tidal range anywhere on earth. (Undoubtedly, were Seoul not so near, there would have been no port at Inchon in the first place.) Although most landing craft drew 23 feet of water, the Landing Ship Tanks (LSTs), vital for the landing of heavy equipment, dipped down at 29 feet. A daylight landing would only be possible on three or four days of maximum tide in any one month. MacArthur demanded a landing before October because Inchon's maximum high tides occurred in mid-September. MacArthur's planners had a mere two months, as compared to the more normal five, to lay out a major, opposed, amphibious landing. To complicate matters further, Japanese and US tide tables for Inchon did not agree. The proposed Inchon site was deemed so risky that MacArthur's own staff investigated alternative sites and prepared plans for a landing at Kunsan in case of a change of objective. There were also proposals for landings at Chinnampo (the port for inland

Pyongyang) or Posung-Myon, 30 miles south of Inchon. The first was rejected as too far north and the second because of its inadequate road net from the beaches.

The American Joint Chiefs of Staff and even most of MacArthur's usually deferential subordinate commanders had serious doubts about the Inchon landing proposal. MacArthur made his final, most dramatic presentation as late as 23 August in a tense conference at his Dai Ichi headquarters, Tokyo. Army Chief of Staff J. Lawton Collins, and Chief of Naval Operations Forrest P. Sherman, were in attendance specifically to record the Joint Chiefs' "grave reservations". Naval and Marine commanders, not subordinate to MacArthur, were also present and apparently all voiced their serious concerns.

MacArthur then made his masterful response. He conceded the hazards of Inchon but proclaimed his confidence in the Navy and Marines to overcome them. Simply to reinforce the Pusan Perimeter might well lead to a stalemate, and an envelopment from Kunsan would prove too narrow. MacArthur's main point was that the obstacles that so distracted his compatriots were real indeed, but they would all actually work in favour of the proposed UNC operation: the *Inmin Gun* was also fully aware of those obstacles and thus would be much less likely to anticipate a landing at Inchon: "The very arguments you have made as to the impracticabilities involved will tend to ensure for *me* the element of surprise. For the North Korean commander will reason that no one would be so brash as to make such an attempt." The Far East Commander concluded with the famous peroration:

> I can almost hear the ticking of the second hand of destiny. We must act now or we will die. . . . We shall land at Inchon, and *I* shall crush them.[1]

One might be forgiven for thinking that MacArthur imagined himself striding, fearless, once again across the beach head, chastising the enemy, accompanied only by a platoon of photographers, as in his well-publicized Second World War return to the Philippines. MacArthur's florid prose seems to have won the day although the commander of the Pacific Fleet Marine Force still held out for Posung-Myon where Navy frogmen had actually landed and found favourable beach conditions.

MacArthur received JCS approval for CHROMITE on 28 August, a bare two weeks before the landings were scheduled to take place. CHROMITE's plans were finalized on 4 September. The naval component, commanded by Vice Admiral A. D. Struble, was organized into Joint Task Force Seven. (In reality, the 230-ship armada should have been termed a *combined* task force in recognition of the contributions of the other UN nations involved.) In addition to the majority from the United States, the task force included vessels from Australia, Canada, New Zealand, France, the Netherlands and Great Britain. They were to transport, supply and protect more than 70,000 Allied personnel involved in the landings. There were seven sub-task forces under Joint Task Force Seven, whose command ship was USS *Mount McKinley*. The core of the task force was the 47 LSTs which carried most of the troops and their equipment. The vessels of one other nation were also represented, but only in great secrecy. It was an indication of the threadbare nature of the US military even this far into the war that 37 of these ex-US Navy LSTs had been hastily recalled from the budding Japanese merchant marine and were manned by Japanese crews. Second World War memories were still too bitter and the Communists would have enjoyed a propaganda triumph if the presence of the Japanese "imperialists" had been known.

Meanwhile, the Pusan Perimeter battles raged unabated, and General Walker was loath to lose the Marine Brigade, one of his prime "fire brigades" that he could depend on to stanch KPA penetrations. The brigade was to be released for the landings only at the last possible moment and a regiment of the 7th Division would be held in Pusan as a floating reserve against any perimeter emergency. There would be many such emergencies before the CHROMITE embarkation.

The Marines in some ways had the heaviest stake in the Inchon operation. Many in high places had questioned the corps' very existence in the "new age" of atomic bombs, super carriers and flying wings. Just the year previous, amidst the unseemly "Revolt of the Admirals", the Army Chief of Staff, General Omar Bradley, had opined that large-scale amphibious landings were things of the past. President Truman, the former First World War Missouri National Guard battery commander, was no friend to the Corps. He dismissed it as composed of "fancy Dans" and in an unguarded moment later slandered it as having "the world's second largest propaganda machine". Were Inchon, a predominantly Marine operation, to fail, it was a reasonable conclusion that the Corps might well revert to its ancient role of serving as shock troops and enforcers of discipline on the Navy's warships.

CHROMITE's diversionary operations included the bombardment of Chinnampo by a Royal Navy task force and a landing party put ashore from an RN frigate. Far East Air Force warplanes bombed bridges and the road net leading to the port of Kunsan, 105 miles south of Inchon, and RN cruisers and destroyers bombarded the port one day after shelling Inchon itself. Naval aircraft from HMS *Triumph* and USS *Bandoeng Strait* hit railways and bridges from Kunsan north to Pyongyang, while ROK navy small boat teams raided west coast North Korean strong points. Even B-29 strategic bombers struck at Kunsan. At the last minute before the Inchon invasion, HMS *Whitesand Bay* landed US Army Special Operations troops and Royal

Marine Commandos, who made sure that their presence was made known to the North Koreans. And on a Pusan dock Marine officers loudly briefed their men about the landing beaches at Kunsan, within earshot of numerous Korean port workers.

Obviously, preparations for a major amphibious landing could hardly be entirely hidden, and in fact some in the Japanese press referred to the impending enterprise as "Operation Common Knowledge". FEAF's worse fears were confirmed in early September when its counter-intelligence agents unmasked a North Korean–Japanese espionage ring whose leader had a copy of the CHROMITE operation plan on his person! To this day there is no evidence as to whether he had been able to forward its contents to Pyongyang. We do know, however, that Mao warned Stalin and Kim Il Sung of the possibility of a UN counter-offensive on the Korean west coast, probably at Inchon. He was ignored.

On-site reconnaissance for the landings had commenced as early as 19 August, when Canadian destroyer HMCS *Athabaskan* escorted a South Korean vessel to Yonghong-do, an island only 14 miles from Inchon. There a small ROK military team went ashore on 1 September. The US Far East Command then dispatched a US Navy team to the island of Taebu-do where, under the noses of North Korean military personnel, the unit gathered intelligence on the surrounding waterways. Intrepid Korean team members infiltrated Inchon, Kimpo air base, even Seoul itself, returning with valuable intelligence. But the bad news was that the tides were as fluctuating as predicted, the mud flats would hold no weight, the sea walls were higher than estimated, and Wolmi-do was heavily fortified and studded with numerous Soviet-built artillery pieces.

The North Koreans became aware of the team's presence on Taebu-do. But only on 7 September, after several RN warships had bombarded Inchon, did they rouse themselves to dispatch one motorized and three sailing sampans to the island. In a running naval battle the team's sole motorized sampan closed with the North Korean flotilla, raking two of the vessels with .50-calibre machine gun fire, sinking one and demolishing the other; the surviving North Korean boat fled the scene. A US destroyer then appeared and bombarded the island with five-inch rounds. But the indefatigable team refused a proffered rescue and landed on yet another island, Palmi-do, which contained a navigation beacon that had been extinguished earlier by *Athabaskan's* Canadians. The team leader was instructed to remain on the island and relight the beacon just after midnight on 15 September. The Communist commander at Inchon, now finally aroused, mounted a raid on Yonghong-do, overwhelmed its defenders and in reprisal executed more than 50 men, women and children. But their sacrifice would not be in vain;

the *Inmin Gun* forces had been diverted from the vital beacon on Palmi-do. For at midnight on the 15th, the beacon would be relighted and the UN naval Advance Attack Group would safely thread its way through the treacherous approaches to Inchon.

On 11 September, one day ahead of schedule, the main body of the amphibious task force put to sea from Japanese ports. This was tropical storm season, and the assembling armada had first been pounded by the 110-mile-an-hour winds of Hurricane Jane on 3 September and then, at sea, by the forces of Typhoon Kezia. General MacArthur and, fittingly, ten of his favourite journalists as well as General Almond, Lieutenant General Lemuel C. Shepherd, Commander Fleet Marine Force, Pacific and their staffs and various other flag-rank officers, boarded flagship *Mount McKinley* at Sasebo. On the 12th the Advance Attack Group stood out from Pusan with the 5th Marines, who had barely time to refit after the second Pusan Bulge battle. The landing troops were entirely American: 1st US Marine Division and 7th Infantry Division, 21 aircraft squadrons, and specialist amphibious engineer, logistics and underwater demolitions units.

Admiral Doyle enjoyed the support of Fast Carrier Task Force 77, which flew fighter cover, interdiction and ground attack missions. Covering Force (Task Force 91), patrolling off the west coast, carried out yet more pre-landing deception missions with naval gunfire and aerial strikes and shielded the landing force from any surface or air threats. Task Force 99's patrol squadrons and seaplane tenders provided air escort for the transports and surveyed the surrounding waters, while Task Force 79 rendered logistic support.

On the morning of the 13th the armada's gunfire support warships, consisting of US Navy destroyers *Mansfield*, *De Haven*, *Lyman K. Swenson*, *Collett*, *Gurke* and *Henderson*, followed by HMS *Jamaica* and *Kenya* and US cruisers *Rochester* and *Toledo* steamed up the narrow channel towards Inchon and entered the outer harbour, borne toward the coast by the day's first high tide. Sharpshooters exploded floating mines. A cache of Soviet mines later discovered ashore indicated that the North Koreans would in a few days have completely mined the Inchon water approaches. The warships then commenced a withering bombardment of the Inchon beaches, while propeller-driven Douglas Skyraider attack warplanes blasted Wolmi-do with bombs, rockets, and gunfire. An intercepted message from the local Communist commander to Pyongyang, in clear, assured his superiors that the enemy would be thrown back into the sea. Considering the disparity of forces and the weight of the bombardment, it is unlikely that this commander forwarded any further such messages to his superiors. North Korean resistance was indeed weak that first day. The one UNC fatality was USN Lieutenant (JG) David H. Swenson, killed by a Communist shell on USN destroyer

Lyman K. Swenson. By an incredible coincidence the unfortunate lieutenant was namesake Lyman K. Swenson's nephew.

The following morning the UN warships once again moved up Flying Fish Channel to continue the bombardment along with Marine and British Fleet Air Arm aerial attacks. One pilot reported that Wolmi-do now "looked like it had been shaved". This bombardment continued throughout the 14th.

Early on the morning of the 15th, guided by the relighted beacon on Palmi-do, the combined armada majestically made its way in an 18-ship column into Flying Fish Channel. And at 05.08h, *Mount McKinley* hoisted the laconic, traditional US navy signal, "Land the landing force."

Marines clambered down aboard their landing craft. Once again Wolmi-do was blasted by UN air bombardment, now joined by an ear-splitting barrage from US Navy rocket ships attacking the reverse side of the devastated island. Covered by a veritable cloud of steel, the Marines' landing craft bows touched down at 06.33h, and men of the 3rd Battalion, 5th Marine Regiment stormed ashore. They were soon joined in succeeding waves by ten M-26 tanks, including one equipped with a flame thrower and two more with bulldozer blades, grim precursors of the fate that would await many KPA survivors of the unrelenting bombardment of their positions. When, despite demands for surrender from a Marine interpreter, a group of North Korean troops fought on, they were indeed buried alive by one of the 'dozer tanks. By 08.00h fortified Wolmi-do had been taken. The outer harbour had been secured at a cost of 17 leathernecks wounded.

By this time the entire force had to await the next incoming tide although it did not wait idly. The Marines dug in while the air and naval units continued their relentless bombardment of the North Koreans on the mainland.

Even this early the Inchon landing was beginning to "pay off". North Korean headquarters in Seoul, thoroughly alarmed, frantically radioed both the newly raised 18th Division, then approaching the embattled Pusan Perimeter, and the 70th Regiment near Suwon to pivot and head back towards Inchon. These two sizeable KPA units would not be available to be thrown against the UN lines holding the perimeter. Nonetheless, the KPA headquarters, back in Pyongyang, still seemed to look upon Inchon as a feint and remained fixated on Kunsan until it was too late. The Allied deception units had done their work well. Matters were not helped for the Communists when a US Navy carrier warplane exploded so much *Inmin Gun* ammunition in a fortuitous strike near Suwon that ships were rocked at anchor in Inchon, miles away.

With the incoming tide the call of "Land the landing force" went out for a second time on the 15th and the Marines headed for Blue, Red and Green beaches and sea walls on the Inchon shore, again under a protective umbrella of Allied bombardment. Once again, despite a fierce naval and air bombardment, enough North Koreans remained to cut down landing troops. There were the usual foul-ups, as when two Marine companies came under intense "friendly fire" from several landing ships, and suffered one killed and 23 wounded, and when several landing ships off Red Beach, confused by smoke and dust, intermingled and touched down at the wrong sites. But compared to such bloody assaults as the Tarawa or Iwo Jima landings of the Second World War, this was a relatively trouble-free operation with light casualties – for the UNC. In fact, the casualties were wildly disparate, as might be expected considering the vast Allied preponderance in firepower. On the left flank of Blue Beach alone, 2nd Battalion, 1st Marines killed 50 KPA soldiers and captured another 15 at a cost of one Marine killed and 19 wounded.

The North Koreans quickly evacuated Inchon city as their high command finally realized that this was indeed the long-awaited UN counter-stroke and that Seoul itself was in real danger. Kim Il Sung's biographer later had an explanation for the disaster. "Seeing through this scheme of the enemy's at once, Comrade Kim Il Sung took a series of measures. . . . paid deep attention to the defense of Inchon and Seoul. . . . [But] the Li Seung Yup spy gang had wormed themselves into the leading posts of the District Military Committee" and betrayed the defenders.[2]

In all, the Marines lost 21 killed in action, one missing, and about 42 wounded at Inchon. The improvised operating room set up on *LST 898* also treated 32 injured Korean civilians. Two UN aircraft had been shot down, but both of their pilots were rescued. It was one of the most one-sided amphibious victories in modern warfare. The Task Force could now concentrate on an over-the-beach logistics build-up for the drive on to Seoul.

The traditional interpretation, beginning from the hour when it was clear that MacArthur would prevail at Inchon, has been that this was a "master stroke", a work of "daring", of "genius". And yet, with the perspective (hindsight?) of history, these characterizations can be challenged, while not detracting from MacArthur's insight or the bravery and professionalism of the UNC forces who fought their way over the inhospitable mud flats and sea walls of Inchon. Some historians have claimed with a certain amount of logic that Inchon was even unnecessary. Eighth Army had undergone an enormous expansion and strengthening and was poised to break out of its Pusan Perimeter constriction at about the time of the landings. If X Corps had been combined at the perimeter with Eighth Army it seems unlikely that the North Koreans could have contained UN forces for much longer. Furthermore, even had the KPA been forewarned of the landings, or had the working out of the tide tables gone awry, given UN absolute control of the air over the landing sites it is difficult to see how the North Koreans could have done much more than harass the landings. A beached UN armada on the Inchon mud flats would have been an embarrassment but hardly a disaster. It is also difficult to escape the conclusion that General MacArthur was fully aware of the limited risks he was taking and played upon the imponderables of the operation for dramatic effect. And he must be given credit for realizing that UN forces within the Pusan Perimeter were now strong enough not only to hold their own but to break out and link up with X Corps, something many of his commanders failed to grasp.

In truth, these conclusions do smack of perfect historical hindsight, but that consideration does not detract from their validity. The noted historian Alonzo Hamby has termed Inchon "perhaps the most overpraised military operation in history".[3] This is perhaps an unduly harsh verdict, but one with more than a grain of truth: a fitting description of more than one MacArthur operation.

Chapter Six

The UNC drive north

With UNC forces firmly ashore at Inchon, their next mission was to retake Seoul. The North Koreans did attempt a hesitant counter-stroke on 16 September 1950. A column of 16 T-34-85 tanks moved down the main road to Inchon to interdict UNC forces; all the tanks were destroyed, half by Marine Corsair air attacks and the remainder by well-directed fire from Marine Pershing tanks in one of the few tank-to-tank clashes of the war. Early the following morning the North Korean air arm made one of its rare appearances when two Yak fighters surprised the UNC armada. They caught USN cruiser *Rochester* off guard and also strafed HMS *Jamaica*, killing one RN seaman and wounding two more. Alert RN anti-aircraft gunners brought down one of the North Koreans. But even this daring raid showed a certain lack of skill, as the pilots ignored the vulnerable transports and cargo ships and attacked well-armed warships. The following day saw another North Korean armour attack in support of a KPA rifle platoon. The North Koreans made no reconnaissance of the UNC positions and moved into a trap as the 5th Marines destroyed another tank column. By this time the US Marines were reinforced by their ROK counterparts, who, enraged by accounts of North Korean atrocities against their kin, ruthlessly sought out and often killed "subversives".

The heaviest fighting took place at and around the Kimpo airfield complex. Despite HMS *Kenya*'s firing of 300 six-inch rounds in support, KPA gunners at Kimpo inflicted some 30 casualties on the attacking Americans. And the industrial suburb of Yongdungpo held out against the Marines for three days. The advance to Seoul itself, however, continued with little lost momentum against an *Inmin Gun* clearly caught off balance.

Marine LVTs crossed the Han River on 20 and 21 September and were reinforced by US and ROK Army units as well as the 7th Marine Regiment.

On the 21st, KPA forces attempted another counter-attack against ROK Marine positions northwest of Kimpo but were obliterated by naval gunfire.

On the 21st, Joint Task Force 7 was dissolved and operational control of UNC forces was turned over to General Almond as planned. Almond, about as concerned with publicity as MacArthur, was keen to capture Seoul by the 25th, three months to the day after the North Korean invasion. General Smith, Marine commander, was less optimistic, and tension grew between the two leaders.

Seoul itself was assaulted from the west on the 22nd by the US Marines, who ran into strong resistance as the KPA troops finally poured reinforcements into the city for a skilful last-ditch defence. The Marines suffered heavy casualties as they took the city street by street and house by house. Impatiently, General Almond moved the US 32nd and the 17th ROK infantry regiments across the Han to flanking positions. Just before midnight of the 25th he declared the city liberated. Disgusted leathernecks and soldiers knew that much of the city was still being contested by the North Koreans. Nonetheless, General MacArthur and President Rhee the following day presided over a liberation ceremony in the shell of the ruined capital. The premature ceremonies were incongruously closed with everyone reciting the Lord's Prayer, led by General MacArthur.

In the meantime, UNC forces along the Pusan Perimeter had broken out in a planned counter-offensive to fix the *Inmin Gun* in the south and drive northward. The US 1st Corps, consisting of the 1st Cavalry, the 24th Infantry, the 1st ROK Infantry Division, the 27th British Brigade, and the US 5th Regimental Combat Team would break out of the perimeter at Waegwan. They would then drive northward along the Taegu–Kumchon–Taejon–Suwon axis, there to join with X Corps before trapping the bulk of the NKPA in a military nutcracker and driving on to Seoul.

Hill 268 (its height in metres) was the critical feature in the Waegwan breakout. It dominated not only the Taegu highway and rail line but also the main highway running south along the east (UN-held) bank of the Naktong River. Hill 268 would have to be taken if the breakout were to succeed. The area was defended by three understrength KPA infantry divisions, one armoured regiment plus two infantry regiments and the 65th Regiment of the 105th Armored Division. By this time most of the tanks of the two North Korean armoured units had been destroyed by UNC air power, artillery, and the effective 3.5in "bazooka". Further east, covering the main highway out of Taegu, were the North Korean 1st and 13th Infantry Divisions.

Word of the UNC landings at Inchon reached these *Inmin Gun* units only several days after the event. Their orders, stereotypically, were to "hold at all costs". By then the UNC breakout had begun. Hill 268 was taken in a well co-ordinated assault by units of the 5th Regimental Combat Team on the 19th. The KPA took their orders seriously, more often than not fighting to the last man. Between 200 and 300 KPA corpses, including that of a full colonel, were counted on the hill at the end of the battle. The battle for Waegwan itself cost the *Inmin Gun* another 300 dead plus considerable military equipment. American casualties through the 19th numbered 148.

By this time the KPA seemed to be breaking and their resistance slackening. Against no resistance, UNC forces crossed the Naktong River on the night of the 20th over a pontoon bridge erected by Army Engineers in a mere 36 hours. With two battalions across by the next day, the KPA was showing increased confusion and loss of control. Meanwhile, on the 17th, the 5th Cavalry Regiment had moved over to the offensive along the Waegwan–Taegu road against stiff resistance. North Korean forces on Hill 203 knocked out no fewer than nine US tanks and one tank-dozer by mines and tank and anti-tank fire, while their skilful use of mortars caused heavy US troop losses. Nonetheless, by the late afternoon of the 21st these forces had linked with 8th Cavalry which was attacking north from Taegu. As the ring was reinforced, large elements of the *Inmin Gun*'s 1st, 3rd, and 13th Divisions were cut off.

ROK forces also fought effectively. ROK 6th Division, which had held out against the KPA's 8th Division for two weeks, now threw itself against the North Koreans and sent them fleeing, disorganized, northward. The KPA's excellent 12th Division, composed of veterans of the Chinese People's Liberation Army (PLA), held out for a week against ROK forces in the Kigye area, but then was practically destroyed. Both the ROKs and the North Koreans were exhausted by three months of continuous combat, but the former held a substantial numerical advantage, vastly superior logistics support, and air power.

Those who still denigrated the ROK troops' fighting ability might have considered the events of 18 September when some 144 were wounded by KPA machine gun fire while attempting to rush a bridge over the Hyongsangang River south of Pohang-dong. In a final desperate attempt, 31 ROK troops volunteered to die if necessary to cross the bridge. UNC aircraft diverted the KPA's attention with dummy air strikes on other opposing positions. Of the intrepid 31, 19 fell in the attempt but the bridge was forced. Among the North Korean positions, the surviving ROKs found dead gunners tied to their weapons. On the other hand, an evacuation operation of 725 ROKs from a failed guerrilla mission had to leave behind 32 South Koreans who had refused to brave KPA gunfire to reach rescuing ships.

Eighth Army's breakout was no foregone event. As late as the 22nd, Eighth Army Intelligence saw no signs of a large-scale KPA withdrawal.

Aerial reconnaissance revealed about as many large *Inmin Gun* forces moving south as north, although both north and south movements were in some confusion. General MacArthur had been considering activating plans for another UNC landing at Kunsan to take more pressure off General Walker's forces. But, also on the 22nd, MacArthur's Deputy Chief of Staff pencilled "file" on the Kunsan plan, and it became history. By the 23rd there was no Pusan Perimeter.

The KPA was rapidly degenerating into something like a fleeing mob. Demoralization set in as the rigid control from Seoul or Pyongyang snapped. On one occasion, hundreds of KPA troops surrendered to a US psychological warfare aircraft. They dutifully piled into their trucks and headed south to captivity. By now, ROK and US troops more often than not simply waved surrendering *Inmin Gun* troops to the south, hardly pausing in their drive on Seoul. With his enemies largely cut off in a classic envelopment manoeuvre, this was MacArthur's most glorious hour. It was also sweet revenge for Osan and Taejon. Some 24th Division troopers had chalked on their vehicles' sides "We Remember Taejon".

As if Taejon were not of sufficiently evil memory, the advancing Americans uncovered irrefutable evidence of large-scale North Korean atrocities during their occupation of the city. The bodies of some 500 ROK troops, their hands tied behind their backs, were unearthed near the city's airstrip. In all, some 5,000 to 7,000 Koreans and Americans are estimated to have been murdered in that city by the North Koreans.

Now it was the Americans who threw up roadblocks and cut off retreating opposing forces. At such a barricade near Hyopchon the 38th Infantry Regiment killed some 300 *Inmin Gun* troops. A flight of F-51s caught the survivors in the open and almost completed the slaughter. It has been estimated that no more than 25,000 to 30,000 North Korean troops ever reached their homeland from the Pusan Perimeter. A substantial number of disorganized KPA personnel did slip into the rugged Chiri-san fastness to engage in guerrilla warfare. But over the next two years these guerrillas were to a large extent rooted out and certainly did little to impede the Republic of Korea's overall functioning or its military effectiveness.

At the same time, the British contingent was engaged in full battle. But UNC solidarity was sorely, if temporarily, strained, and the "Yanks" justly and roundly cursed on 23 September when the Argyll's position on Hill 282, during the drive on to Taejon, was napalmed and machine-gunned by a flight of errant USAF P-51s. Survivors plunged down 200 feet to escape a sea of flame. But the stout-hearted second-in-command, Major Kenneth Muir, was mortally wounded as he led a scratch team up to retake the hill.

He was posthumously awarded the Victoria Cross, Great Britain's highest decoration for valour. The hill had to be temporarily abandoned to the North Koreans. A count the next day showed 2 officers and 13 Argylls killed, 70 wounded, and two missing; 60 of these casualties had been inflicted by the misguided American air strike. To be fair, it should be noted that the North Koreans had displayed white recognition panels similar to those used by the Argylls, and the Britons could not raise the American pilots by radio to correct their approach. The Argylls were not to be the last Commonwealth unit to be mistakenly blitzed by their US comrades. In April of the following year a Marine Corsair ground-attack warplane napalmed D Company of the Royal Australian Regiment. This incident was the more galling, in that Marine air had a well-deserved reputation for placing its ordnance on the right target with something like pin-point accuracy. (Commonwealth units were not the first UN contingents mistakenly attacked from the air. As noted above, Australian warplanes themselves had, in fact, shot-up at least one ROK motor convoy in the earliest days of the war. Undoubtedly the long-suffering ROKs endured more, unpublicized, "fratricide" incidents throughout the war.)

The question of the crossing of the 38th Parallel did not weigh unduly on General MacArthur's mind as he approached that artificial line. The US Joint Chiefs of Staff informed him that his first objective was the destruction of all North Korean forces in South Korea. He was also to unite all of Korea, if possible, under the Rhee regime, but this latter mission was subject to his determining the extent of any Chinese or Soviet intervention. Non-Korean ground forces were not to be used in the area along the Manchurian or Soviet borders. And all of MacArthur's plans for operating north of the Parallel were to be submitted to the US Joint Chiefs. The UNC Commander immediately asked for a free hand in North Korea, a request Secretary of Defense George C. Marshall granted.

Marshall had succeeded Louis Johnson, on whom had fallen most of the blame for the unprepared state of US forces on the eve of the war. Johnson's too-obvious ambition, arrogance and unstable manner had made him no friends in Washington. Even then, an exasperated President Truman had to demand his weeping Secretary's resignation. It was a pathetic end for someone who had actually dreamed the American Presidential dream without much to recommend him except age and citizenship.

MacArthur issued a demand on 1 October for the surrender of all North Korean forces and another, "for the last time", on 9 October, ultimatums that were, of course, rejected by Kim Il Sung. Kim's allies, the Chinese, warned that they would not tolerate any invasion of their neighbour by the "imperialists". The Soviet delegate to the UN meanwhile proposed a cease-fire and the withdrawal of all foreign troops from Korea. These Communist reactions were, of course, ignored by the victorious UNC.

The US ignoring of the warning by China's Foreign Minister, Chou En-lai, to the Indian Ambassador, K. V. Panikkar, on 2 October, that China would enter the war if UN forces crossed the Parallel is considered especially reckless. The Chinese Foreign Minister had summoned Ambassador Panikkar at midnight, thus emphasizing the seriousness of the matter. Panikkar, as expected, passed on this warning through diplomatic channels to Washington, to no avail. President Truman distrusted Panikkar, believing that he was simply replaying a variation of the old Indian game of publicly denouncing the West while privately assuring Western leaders that it was firmly on the side of the democracies. The US Ambassador to Nationalist China forwarded an accurate report from Nationalist military intelligence strongly indicating that the Chinese Communists planned "to throw the book at United Nations forces in Korea". The report was also dismissed as wishful thinking on the part of the Nationalists, who realized that only a major war between the United States and China would see the liberation of the mainland.

But even the Chinese Communist messages were not all that unequivocal. Two weeks after Panikkar's message, the British minister to Peking was called to the PRC Foreign Ministry. There, the Chinese seemed "to back away" from their earlier warning, a "message" soon validated again by Ambassador Panikkar. On the other hand, and contrary to common opinion, the Americans did not simply ignore Chinese interests. They had the Indian Government pass on assurances that the US had no desire for war or even the establishment of a US military regime in North Korea. Such messages were dismissed by the Chinese leadership.

At any rate, it would have taken truly heroic restraint to hold back UNC forces on the eve of what seemed total victory after the bitter defeats of the summer. In fact, Secretary of Defense Marshall had encouraged MacArthur with his 29 September message that "We want you to feel unhampered strategically and tactically to proceed north of the 38th parallel". The Joint Chiefs of Staff authorized MacArthur to take on any Chinese forces found in North Korea if such action would offer "a reasonable chance of success", rather obscure guidelines.

Certainly Syngman Rhee had no doubts about crossing the Parallel and heading for the Yalu. Speaking before a massed, cheering crowd at Pusan four days after the Inchon landings, the ROK President proclaimed "We have to advance as far as the Manchurian border until not a single enemy soldier is left in our country". "Our country" was obviously now nothing less than the entire Korean peninsula.

It was actually under the orders from their US Army adviser that the first ROK forces, elements of the 3rd Division, crossed the Parallel on 30 September in the Kangnung area. They were soon averaging some 15 miles per day in their northern advance towards the port of Wonsan. There the KPA showed it still had some fight left. About ten self-propelled anti-tank guns penetrated to shoot up the airfield, burning out most of the hangers and buildings. In the Kumchon area to the east the North Koreans threw in their remaining armour. A number of KPA ambushes also caught UNC forces flat-footed and inflicted severe casualties. Nonetheless, the KPA now seemed to have shot its last bolt.

On the Communist side, newly released documents show discord and dissention now supplanting the euphoria of only a month or so earlier. Stalin was furious at the fall of Seoul and at Kim Il Sung for ignoring his considered advice to transfer four of his divisions from the Pusan Perimeter battle lines to the far more threatening Inchon front. The Soviet Politburo blamed the new turn in the war to a series of grave mistakes made by the *Inmin Gun*'s front line command and on up to the highest military authorities. The Soviet military advisers did not escape censure either, being blamed as much as Premier Kim for the failure to transfer promptly those four KPA divisions. The most rudimentary intelligence appraisal would have noted the great size of the UNC armada off Inchon. If news of such an armada could not have reached Pyongyang in a timely manner, then KPA communications must have been even more rudimentary than its intelligence. Soviet Ambassador Shtykov felt Stalin's particular sting for having fatuously recommended that a *Pravda* writer who did take the Inchon landings seriously should have been arrested and tried for panic-mongering. In Stalin's words:

> [Soviet advisers] failed to grasp the strategic importance of the enemy's assault landing at Inchon, denied the gravity of redeploying troops from the South toward Seoul. At the same time they procrastinated over the redeployment and slowed it down considerably, thereby losing a week to the enemy's enjoyment [deployment?].[1]

Stalin's criticisms were not entirely justified. Soviet advisers were strictly forbidden to work south of the 38th Parallel even when the KPA was on the offensive, and they were thus out of close touch with battlefield realities. Furthermore, it was one thing to advise the transfer of four KPA divisions, quite another actually to move them some 200 miles towards Seoul. Four divisions and their impedimenta could have travelled with reasonable dispatch and cohesion only by rail, and the rail lines of South Korea were constantly being hammered by UNC air power. It is hard to imagine that these divisions would ever have reached the vicinity of Seoul in time as fighting units.

Much of this censure may have been for the record; no Soviet advisers in Korea were transferred out and none are known to have been "purged".

Kim unconvincingly blamed poor KPA discipline and a failure to obey orders. He grovelled before "Deeply respected Iosif Vissarionovich Stalin. ... to You, the liberator of the Korean people and the leader of the working peoples of the entire world", begging him to supply "special assistance" or "assist us by forming international volunteer units in China and other countries of people's democracy for rendering military assistance to our struggle". Kim was here evoking the ghost of the Spanish Civil War's International Brigades (albeit not their fate of being on the losing side). He confessed to Stalin that

> under the air cover of hundreds of airplanes the motorized units of the enemy engage us in combat at their free will and inflict great losses to our manpower. ... the units of the People's Army that are still fighting in the southern part of Korea have been cut off from the northern part of Korea, they are torn to pieces.

But Kim unwittingly put his finger on one of the main causes of the disaster when he informed Stalin that "the adversary has a real opportunity to take over the city of Seoul completely".[2] Seoul had *already* fallen to UNC forces some three days earlier. Obviously the DPRK leadership was in some ignorance of conditions at the front. Ambassador Shtykov reported that Kim and his lieutenants were now "confused, lost, hopeless, and desperate", and thus in no condition to manage an orderly withdrawal northward. Kim did call for a "protracted guerrilla war" against the "imperialists", but this was an unlikely strategy in view of the peninsula's lack of heavy cover and the apathy of the population, none of whom seemed to have lifted a finger against the "imperialist invaders". Stalin replied by suggesting that KPA troops retreat cohesively and deliberately from one defensive position to another, rather remote advice when every move of the Communists seemed to be observed and blasted by the ubiquitous UNC air power. The meetings of the high Communist leaders were marked by mutual finger-pointing as disaster loomed. Through it all, Kim pleaded for Soviet and Chinese aid to save his regime from complete disaster.[3] Later, the DPRK put a considerably different cast on these matters, of course, terming the retreat north "an outstanding strategy", although admitting that "The temporary strategy was a sore trial for the people and the People's Army".[4]

The Soviet Politburo meeting on 30 September 1950 discussed options still available for rescuing the DPRK. Significantly, it also focused its debates on the need to avoid a direct military confrontation between the Soviet

Union and the United States, the mirror image of the main agenda of the Truman administration's Cabinet meetings at the time.

On 13 October Stalin actually ordered the abandonment of all of North Korea and the evacuation of Kim and the remnants of the KPA to Northeast China and the Soviet Far East. Twenty-four hours later he reversed his edict; the Chinese had agreed to enter the war.

UN units by then were embarked on a race to be the first to enter Pyongyang. The roads were often marked by groups of hungry and haggard KPA troops, their trucks strewn about, fuel tanks empty. Often they would wave UNC forces the way to their capital. The Australian 3rd Battalion captured no less than 1,982 KPA troops north of Yongyu when the Aussie commander mounted a tank and called out to KPA troops that they were surrounded and that their only hope lay in surrender. The opposing unit took him at his word and dropped their arms.

There were also cases of mutual misidentification between the fast-moving UNC forces and KPA units still possessed of some fight. A cut-off Australian officer made his way through North Korean troops by mumbling "Rusky", "Rusky", and receiving fraternal pats on the back. On another occasion a group of North Korean troops greeted a platoon of the Argylls with shouts of "comrade" and the offer of cigarettes. The official history of the US Army in Korea dryly concluded that "The ensuing fight was at very close quarters." Surprisingly, the British lost only one soldier.

Much ink has been spilled on what was "wrong" with the US Army forces committed early to the Korean War, often with considerable justification. But little enough has been detailed as to why the "highly-motivated" North Korean Army retreated north in even greater disarray, almost falling apart after Inchon. Some answers are obvious, always beginning with the UNC absolute control of the air. Yet this was the same Korean People's Army that had endured a hellish baptism of fire and steel along the Pusan Perimeter and had still nearly driven the UNC forces into the sea. But this army's discipline, tough and brutal as it was, had a brittleness about it that could not survive the death or disappearance of its officers. Matters were not helped, at least among *Inmin Gun* commanders, when they were themselves blamed for the defeat of their forces after Inchon. Inchon itself was a demoralizing development; the average KPA trooper knew only that something catastrophic had taken place well behind his lines of supply and that retreat was seemingly cut off. In fact, the KPA never truly recovered its original combat power to the end of the war. It may well be that as the "cowardly imperialists" and their "puppets" and "lackeys" suddenly showed up in the KPA rear, the individual *Inmun Gun* soldier felt betrayed, became confused and thought only of escape. Many had already become disillusioned as they faced UNC air power and increasingly stubborn resistance along the perimeter. Pusan seemed as far away as ever, despite Communist trumpeting of continuous victories that should long since have brought them to the city's waterfront. Comparison between the Communists' self-defeating denigration of the UNC forces and General Walker's stark "Stand or Die" order is instructive. US and ROK troops by then were fully aware of what they were up against, and indeed, had to be reminded (until Inchon) that the KPA was not composed of supermen. No UNC soldiers between July and September 1950 thought this war would be a walkover, and were thus psychologically better prepared for the horrors of a protracted war.

The honour of being the first UNC unit to enter Pyongyang fell to elements of F Company, 2nd Battalion, 5th Cavalry Regiment on 19 October, to the intense disgust of accompanying ROK troops of the spearhead 1st Division led by Paik Sun Yup, a former native of the DPRK capital city. The North Koreans did make something of a fight for their capital, although nothing like their defence of Seoul. In one last engagement just outside the city, advancing tanks of the US 6th Tank Battalion physically crushed KPA soldiers and equipment under their treads, killing an estimated 300 defenders.

The UNC Command set up civil government in the newly taken capital. Counter-intelligence troops seized a considerable amount of *Inmin Gun* classified material that would serve them well in the coming months. Twenty US prisoners were rescued in the capture of Pyongyang, but unfortunately these were just a lucky few, escapees from a far larger group of US POWs who had been moved north a few days before the fall of the city. Survivors would not see freedom until the end of the war, if then. A reminder of what the earliest US forces had endured in the war's opening months of retreat came in a touching ceremony at the Pyongyang airfield on 21 October. General MacArthur reviewed F Company, 5th Cavalry. The UNC Commander then asked all men who had landed with the unit in Korea 96 days earlier (and who had endured the worst fighting of the Pusan Perimeter battles), to step forward. Only five of the original 200 did so and three of them had been wounded.

The UNC proceeded to establish the only military government of a captured Communist capital until the US taking of Georgetown, Grenada, three decades later. The notorious "Tiger", Kim Chong Won, who had already beheaded some 50 KPA POWs, was, not unexpectedly, put in charge of the capital's military police. He was hardly the man to halt any settling of old scores by ROK troops. These unsavoury activities do not seem to have been widespread, if for no other reason than the presence of large numbers of UNC servicemen not possessed by the same hatreds that had riven the Korean peninsula. Most UNC soldiers simply took the opportunity to rest briefly and to enjoy the Army-sponsored entertainment provided by the likes of Al Jolson (who died a few days later) and Bob Hope. For the ROK forces and the inhabitants of the city there was President Rhee, who addressed a mass rally where he was enthusiastically received. Rhee moved on to Wonsan in a tour of what everyone presumed would be a part of the ROK in the very near future.

Earlier, while Eighth Army was plunging northward, X Corps had reembarked at Inchon, causing immense confusion. General Almond put his men ashore in North Korea in an unopposed landing at the major North Korean port and industrial complex of Wonsan – but not immediately. General MacArthur had hoped to replicate his Inchon master stroke at Wonsan, but ROK forces spoiled his triumph by capturing the port by landing a full week before the planned amphibious landing. To make matters worse, X Corps's flotilla was interminably delayed until 25 October by some 2,000 magnetic and contact Soviet naval mines sown liberally throughout the harbour. Several UNC ships were destroyed by the mines before the harbour could be swept. The cramped X Corps troops landed in a distinctly anti-climactic operation.

The mishaps at Wonsan, however, were of little consequence compared to the tragedy that had been built into the UNC Command's strategy to conquer North Korea. X Corps had been a hasty thrown-together affair. It was also a uniquely multi-racial force in what was still basically a racially segregated US Army. Under a commander on record as doubting the abilities of black American troops, the corps consisted of Koreans, as well as Puerto Rican, black, and white Americans. Oddly, Almond retained his job as MacArthur's Chief of Staff.

X Corps was to operate practically independently of Eighth Army in North Korea. The two armies would be separated by some 200 miles of mountainous terrain. Even radio communication had to go laboriously through Far East Command Headquarters in Tokyo, an almost impossible arrangement. General Walker was concerned about this disposition, which seemed to violate one of the basic principles of war: concentration in the face of an enemy. A loyal subordinate, Walker never put his doubts on paper, but he did write rather plaintively to MacArthur asking that he be informed of X Corps' plans and progress so that he could prepare better for its eventual juncture with Eighth Army.

Eighth Army's continuing drive north in October saw the first and only mass parachute drop of the Korean War. On 20 October the 187th Airborne Regiment made a mass drop at Sunchon and Sukchon in an attempt to cut off North Korean troops and political leaders and perhaps to rescue US

POWs as well. The well-executed drop from C–119 "Flying Boxcar" transports met with little opposition. Approximately 4,000 troops and 600 tons of equipment, including 105mm howitzers, 39 jeeps, four ¾-ton trucks, and 584 tons of ammunition were parachuted. MacArthur and assorted USAF and Army "brass" flew from Japan to witness the drop. It all made good journalistic copy and newsreel footage, but through no fault of its planners or the troops, the operation failed in all of its objectives, other than to keep the pressure on the dissolving KPA. Soon after, American ground troops did find additional US POWs, but unfortunately most had been killed by their North Korean guards as the pursuing UNC forces advanced. In a railroad tunnel and the surrounding area 74 murdered American troops were located, most shot down while they awaited their evening bowl of rice. The Americans also found 24 former POWs who had escaped the massacre.

On the 22nd the troops of C Company of the Australian 3rd Battalion further distinguished themselves in a wild hand-to-hand mêlée in which rifle, grenade and bayonet accounted for some 270 North Koreans killed and more than 200 captured. Incredibly, the Aussies suffered only about seven men wounded. At about the same time, 3rd Battalion of the 187th Airborne reported killing 805 and capturing 681 *Inmin Gun*. Even in their great retreat of the previous summer, UNC forces had not suffered anything like such heavy casualties.

Not surprisingly, North Korean resistance continued to weaken in the face of such losses. Further indication of the disarray of the KPA was found at Kujang-dong where the ROK 6th Division captured 50 railroad boxcars loaded with ammunition. An even more spectacular prize awaited the same division at Huichon where it captured 20 T-34 tanks needing only minor repairs.

The UNC had moved the front northwards more than 300 miles in less than six weeks. In the process it had nearly destroyed the KPA. But UNC forces were also being drawn ever more deeply into the forbidding terrain of North Korea, with absolutely no liaison between the two main UNC ground forces.

At about this time ROK troops made one of the more portentous but at the time completely unreported discoveries of the Korean War. At Konan, near the port of Hungnam, they discovered a vast "underground complex" which included a large uranium processing facility. During the Second World War the Japanese carefully sited the plant to take advantage of the ore and other necessary materials available nearby. This complex could also utilize the output of the hydroelectric generating plants in the far north, which produced more power than all the generating plants in Japan combined. Konan itself was the site of a massive industrial complex that produced heavy water and synthetic fuel. All of this was to produce Japan's own atomic bomb. It was indicative of the importance of the Konan facility that Japanese troops held out at Konan for a full two weeks after the official Japanese surrender. And soon after the Soviet occupation of the area, a USAAF B-29 flying near Konan and plainly marked with the national insignia and "POW Supplies" under one wing, was shot down by a Red Air Force fighter. The survivors were machine-gunned in the water, but, fortunately, only one crewman was killed in the incident, which the Soviets claimed was simply a "misunderstanding", and the mysterious affair was closed. The Konan facility's capture and its disposition by UNC forces have not been officially revealed to this day.

As UNC forces entered North Korea, the UN Interim Committee on Korea declared that it would recognize no government as having "legal and effective control" over all Korea, a reflection of the UN's dissatisfaction with the authoritarian nature of the Rhee government. President Rhee delivered an angry protest to General MacArthur, most improbably accusing the UNC of wishing to revive and protect the Communists in North Korea. He defiantly added that the ROK government was "taking over the civilian administration [of North Korea] whenever hostilities cease". Rhee was better than his word. Well before any anticipated end of hostilities, his agents and governors were spreading through the North in the wake of the UNC armies.

Washington and the UNC Command, not entirely displeased with the ROK's intention to control North Korea, forwarded US and ROK Army city and provincial Military Government teams. Although they also had health and welfare concerns, the teams discovered that the primary need was for the reestablishment of civil law enforcement and for the rehabilitation of the North's bombed industries.

Overall, the US Joint Chiefs of Staff ordered General MacArthur to "facilitate public order, economic rehabilitation and the democratic mode of life . . . and to prepare the way for unification of a free and independent Korea". The steps to this fine goal were: (1) a military occupation which the UNC Commander would administer, subject to the control of the UNC and the United States until order and stability had been established, (2) Korea-wide elections, after which MacArthur would step aside, and (3) all non-Korean forces would withdraw from Korea.

MacArthur was not to establish a central government for the North, but was to administer the area through existing or *de facto* authorities although the Communist Party was proscribed. He was to change as little as possible "the fundamental structure" of the former DPRK, and was, in fact, to retain even "land reform measures, nationalization and socialization of industries".

United Nations Civil Assistance Command Korea (UNCACK) Civil Information and Education Section, with the approval of the UNC Command,
drew up a fairly detailed plan to

> assist the people of North Korea in establishing and developing an
> educational system designed, in accordance with their own native cul-
> ture, economy, social and psychological patterns, to serve as a potent,
> influential, and continuing force for acceleration of the rehabilitation
> and unification of Korea and for restoring Korea to her rightful place
> among the family of peace-loving and democratic nations of the world.[5]

The schools were to remain closed until UNCACK could be assured that
they were "free from any taint of communism or ultra-nationalism" and would
remain under close supervision. Social studies textbooks were, understandably,
to "be completely re-written". As for North Korea's newspapers and radio
stations, the UNCACK team called for "a free flow of information, to see
that no foreign power shall utilize the information media to further their own
national interests". This was to be accomplished by a rather "Big Brother"
process of "closing, screening, and licensing information media", supervised
by "appropriate United Nations personnel".[6]

However, Eighth Army/UNCACK field teams had hardly embarked
on these programmes when Chinese intervention late in the year drastically
changed their mission to one of refugee evacuation and relief. UNC Military
Government of the North lasted only for a little more than three months,
from the crossing of the 38th Parallel in October 1950 to the expulsion of
UNC forces by December of that year. Undoubtedly of more lasting value
was the large-scale refugee relief that UNCACK and the US Army Civil
Affairs/Military Government teams carried out in the evacuation from
North Korea.

Kim Il Sung and his government had already fled to their temporary
capital, the Yalu River city of Sinuiju. Sinuiju's key bridges made the city
that much more of a prime target, and the USAF spent a good deal of effort
throughout the war in trying to burn the place to the ground. From there
Kim breathed out defiance and exhortation. But his power was by then sharply
diminished in proportion to the fate of his army, on paper an impressive 30
divisions, in reality containing only one division and two brigades in battle
order, plus some moderately effective guerrilla bands. The Chinese had the
controlling hand.

Stalin, ever cautious and reluctant to engage directly in conflict with the
United States, was pressuring the Chinese to enter the war. At the same time,
and in something of a panic, he authorized his representative at the UNC to
sound out the US State Department on its terms for peace. Newly released

documents from the Russian Presidential Archive suggest that the Communist leaders, Chou En-lai and Lin Pao, resisted Stalin's exhortations, citing to the Soviet dictator their lack of resources, the danger of reactionary forces still in China and the possibility of a US declaration of war. When the Chinese continued to resist intervention in the Korean War, and with the North Koreans nearly finished as a fighting force, Stalin, according to Nikita Khrushchev, became privately resigned to the Americans on his border:

> So what? Let the United States of America be our neighbors in the Far East. They will come there, but we shall not fight them *now*. We are not ready to fight. (emphasis added)[7]

But to the Chinese, Stalin then made a diametrically opposed argument, indicating a shift in Soviet policy: "If war is inevitable, let it be waged now, and not in a few years when Japanese imperialism will be restored as a US ally and when the US and Japan will have a ready-made bridgehead on the continent in the form of all Korea run by Syngman Rhee."[8] He further argued that even a limited number of Chinese "volunteers" (he seems to have coined the term) in Korea would compel the United States to conclude peace terms that would prevent them from occupying the entire peninsula and would even force them to give up Taiwan. Stalin backed off from any direct Soviet military confrontation with the USA on the grounds that his nation was still recovering from the Great Patriotic War (the Second World War), conveniently ignoring the fact that China was also recovering from that catastrophe, not to mention four subsequent years of a civil war just ended. It is difficult to know just how seriously Stalin took his own arguments. (Stalin a few days later, as noted, also suggested that Kim's government and army retreat into Manchuria, there to prepare themselves for reentry one day into their native land.) Along with these suggestions and entreaties, Stalin promised air cover for the Chinese in Korea. But basically, until the Chinese did agree to send in their "Volunteers", Stalin, in some disgust, had given up on Kim and his regime.

However, in the early morning of 14 October, Joseph Stalin received welcome news from Comrade Mao; the Chinese Communist Party Central Committee informed him by telegram that "our leading comrades believe that if the US troops advance up to the border of China, then Korea will become a dark spot for us and the Northeast [Manchuria] will be faced with constant danger". The Chinese, relying on Soviet air support, would intervene. One of Mao's particular arguments may have carried the day. This was that if the PRC waited for three to five years before intervening, "by then revolutionary movements in other Western European nations would probably be suppressed and the [world] revolutionary strength would be reduced".

In other words, Mao, like his American enemies, was looking to Western Europe.[9] We thus now know that the decision to enter the Korean War was strongly debated among the Chinese Communist leaders and was hardly a foregone conclusion.

It is most difficult to document the causes of both Stalin's and the PRC leadership's shift on the question of Chinese intervention. But we can be fairly sure that he did know that the United States was determined not to provoke China, that all targets in China were off-limits to American air power, and that the USAF was even interdicted, at least in theory, from hot pursuit of Communist aircraft across the Yalu. Of course, the Americans had already informed the Chinese as much through Mr Panikkar. Stalin, however, had a much better source than the obliging Indian diplomat. In the Joint Secretary of the Combined Policy Committee (which co-ordinated British, US and Canadian atomic policy), the UK Foreign Office official, Donald MacLean, the Soviet dictator had a dedicated agent deep in the enemy's camp. MacLean, who made a spectacular defection to the USSR in 1951, was privy to most of America's military and nuclear secrets, having access to security information denied to most US Congressmen, Members of Parliament, and Cabinet officers of both the US and the UK. MacLean, despite a well known and most venomous hatred for almost all things American (except his wife), was one of the very few persons, and perhaps the only foreigner, with an escort-free pass into the innermost recesses of the US Atomic Energy Commission. This despite his known and almost uncontrollable temper when drunk (to which state he was becoming increasingly habituated).

MacLean was actually tipped to become a future head of the Foreign Office itself. Incredibly, this drunken, anti-American diplomat undoubtedly knew the greatest military secret of the time. This was not the secret of the atomic bomb itself or how to manufacture one; Russian scientific genius and the British and American atomic spies had unravelled that one by 1948. Rather, the greatest secret of the post-war period was that of just how few tactical atomic bombs the US could actually drop. For several years after the expenditure of the last remaining assembled US nuclear bombs in the Bikini tests in 1946, the United States had no complete nuclear weapons, just their bits and pieces. The skilled crews needed to assemble the components were also critically short in numbers and the B-29s to carry them were bogged down in the Operation Silverplate conversion programme. At best, as late as 1949, the US would need some two weeks to assemble one atomic bomb. The "nuclear blackmail" so excoriated by "progressives" at the time rested on little more than bluff. Even though the US could muster some 200 atomic bombs in 1951, almost all were of the strategic type. The USAF did not even begin to test the tactical version until early 1951.

This dismal story could not have been a secret to His Majesty's Minister Plenipotentiary, Donald MacLean. There is certainly no question that MacLean was dedicated to the service of Stalin's Soviet empire. After all, he did defect to the Soviet Union. Thus it is difficult to understand why some writers on the Korean War have deprecated MacLean's espionage. What was a Soviet spy to have done in 1950–51, if not to pass on to the Soviet Union all that he could about the main enemy, the United States, and its plans for prosecuting that war?

MacLean's comrade (in the quite literal sense), Guy Burgess, was Second Secretary of the UK embassy in Washington and, like MacLean, a drunken anti-American and devoted admirer of Stalin, who fled to the Soviet Union with MacLean. A "Third Man" was Harold Adrian Russell "Kim" Philby, another well-born alcoholic who nonetheless served in Washington as the UK's Secret Intelligence Service (SIS) liaison with the American Central Intelligence Agency (CIA), and who also fled to the USSR several decades after his two comrades. With almost two decades in service to Stalin's intelligence apparatus, Philby was undoubtedly one of the Soviet's most productive agents ever. With this unlikely trio ensconced in the very heart of Washington's intelligence and nuclear establishment, it is difficult to imagine what critical information about America's war effort and policy would *not* have been forwarded to Moscow. The one institution closed to the three was the FBI, whose crusty Director, J. Edgar Hoover, somehow remained immune to the reputed "brilliance" and "charm" of Philby/Burgess/MacLean.

Thus Stalin and Mao would have known that America's threat of nuclear attack was mostly bluff. Hence, US Secretary of State Dean Acheson's despairing, unfeigned reaction when first apprised of MacLean's defection: "My God, that sonofabitch knew everything!"[10]

Thus the Chinese decision to enter the war was not quite so awesome as they themselves have made it out to be, not that they made light of taking on the United States. Whatever its self-imposed limitations, the United States was rearming, the supply of atomic bombs would surely increase, and the nation was embarked on something of a global anti-Communist crusade. And those limitations might not last for long. The PLA Chief of Staff is supposed to have exclaimed to the Indian Ambassador, "After all, China lives on farms. What can atom bombs do there?"[11] This statement was made in the full realization that Ambassador Panikkar would again do the PRC's work in passing on the message to the Americans that China feared not the bomb and thus might further induce the Americans to stay clear of the Yalu. The Chinese leadership, if not the Chinese people, had little to fear of USAF B-36 intercontinental bombers dropping atomic bombs, vaporizing their cities.

In the meantime MacArthur's fatally divided forces were advancing towards an unknown threat. Even at the time, UNC intelligence had positively identified some 24 Chinese divisions near Yalu River crossing points, and another 14 were reported as somewhere in Manchuria. These forces alone were more than the personnel strength of the entire UNC Command. But the US civilian Central Intelligence Agency (CIA) cautiously downplayed the possibility of Chinese Communist intervention. In an October appreciation, the agency concluded that "While full-scale Chinese Communist intervention in Korea must be regarded as a continuing possibility, a consideration of all known factors leads to the conclusion that barring a Soviet decision for global war, such action is not probable in 1950."[12] The muted Soviet reaction to the USAF strafing of a Soviet airfield on 8 October and the lack of any response to UNC reconnaissance flights near Siberia also helped to convince the UNC that Soviet or PRC large-scale intervention was unlikely.

At his brief, informal, almost slap-dash meeting with President Truman at Wake Island in the Pacific on 15 October, MacArthur assured Truman that "if the Chinese tried to get down to Pyongyang, there would be the greatest slaughter". Just before his meeting with the President, MacArthur had also assured the US Army Chief of Staff, General Omar Bradley, that the Eighth Army would be back in Japan by Christmas. The phrase was widely repeated, and the supposed final UNC thrust north was usually termed the "Home by Christmas" offensive.

On 24 October, MacArthur ordered his Eighth Army and X Corps, still completely separated, to proceed with all available forces to the Yalu. The Joint Chiefs questioned this violation of their direct order to have no non-Korean forces at the Yalu, but did not have the temerity to countermand it. After all, MacArthur was winning the war. Before the end of the month, small UNC units, including US troops, did reach the Yalu. UNC forces everywhere now began to encounter stout resistance. Contrary to MacArthur's breezy assurances, these were indeed Chinese troops and they were massing for an all-out offensive. General Walker now practically overruled his commander and began to regroup his western forces, fearing that they might be cut off. Walker's troops, at any rate, were suffering from supply difficulties caused by their rapid advance into the north as well as by the tying-up of his supply port of Inchon through X Corps' ill-advised Wonsan operation. Rail lines needed rehabilitation, and his motor trucks were rapidly wearing out.

Estimates of Communist forces poised in Manchuria were cut by MacArthur's intelligence chief, Major General Charles Willoughby (who had also failed to foresee the North Korean invasion) to a mere five divisions, and the Joint Chiefs speculated that these troops were probably only trying to protect the great hydroelectric generating plants along the Yalu. Although

5. General MacArthur and President Truman at the Wake Island Conference. All is outward cordiality, but the President did not appreciate the UN Commander's "greasy" cap. *National Archives*

some elements of the US intelligence community had warned of the North Korean invasion of June 1950, the UNC was not nearly so well served less than six months later. In fairness, it should be noted that UN aerial reconnaissance was, at least officially, restricted to the Korean side of the Yalu River, and thus might be excused for missing the Chinese buildup in China itself. The overlooking of masses of Chinese troops in North Korea, however, is more difficult to understand.

By this time, on the eastern front, the US 7th Division had reached the Yalu at Hyesanjin, and General Almond blithely planned a westward movement to cut off the KPA facing Eighth Army. Undoubtedly with the benefit of hindsight, MacArthur's successor, General Matthew B. Ridgway, in privately commenting decades later on the manuscript of the pertinent volume of the Army's official history of the Korean War asserted:

> I find it amazing that highly trained professionals with extensive combat experience could have approved and tried to execute the tactical plan of operations for the X Corps in northeast Korea in November 1950. It appears like a pure Map Exercise put on by amateurs, appealing in theory, but utterly ignoring the reality of a huge mountainous terrain, largely devoid of terrestrial communications, and ordered for execution in the face of a fast approaching, sub Arctic winter.[13]

Now facing Eighth Army and X Corps (MG Willoughby to the contrary notwithstanding) were no fewer than two Chinese army groups, the XIII, consisting of the 38th, 39th, 40th, 42nd, 50th, and 66th armies; and the IX, composed of the 20th, 26th, and 27th armies, for a total of above 300,000 men. And these included some of the best of the battle-tested Chinese People's Liberation Army, such as Lin Piao's 4th Field Army. Most troops were veterans of the victorious civil war, and almost all of the officers had fought the Japanese during the Second World War.

At roughly the same time, the UNC command numbered some 553,000 personnel, of whom 423,313 were ground troops. ROK ground forces numbered 223,950, US ground troops and Marines 178,464, United Kingdom 11,186, and Australians 1,002. Thus, persistent general opinion to the contrary, UNC ground forces alone *still* well outnumbered that of the Chinese and the North Koreans combined!

UNC aerial reconnaissance, such as it was, continued to report little or no sign of major Communist formations. Actually, Far East Air Force had no aircraft dedicated to visual aerial reconnaissance, and most photo reconnaissance aircraft were deployed in support of the bridge bombing campaigns along the Yalu. Reflecting the UNC's the Second World War mentality, its limited photo reconnaissance was concentrated on main roads, and few sorties were flown at night. The Chinese forces, in one of the most masterful deception operations in modern military history, moved under cover of darkness and used secondary roads and trails under the strictest of discipline. Troops were to stand fast at the approach of UNC aircraft; those who broke this discipline were to be shot on the spot.

Even those Chinese captured by UNC forces who correctly identified their units were disbelieved by their interrogators. On 23 November, Far East Command Intelligence, finally moving closer to reality, identified 12 Chinese divisions in Korea; in truth, on that date there were nine armies composed of 30 infantry divisions.

But the PVA/CPV was also self-deceived, looking back on its easy victory over the Chinese Nationalists and its supposed triumph over the Japanese, and fancied that it could prevail over a modern military force, in the vein of the Japanese Army of the Second World War which persisted to the end in the conviction that "our spirit will prevail over their steel". The fact that the US had defeated the Germans twice, as well as the British and the Japanese, meant nothing more than that the US could marshal resources superior to its enemies. The PRC leadership also believed, equally erroneously, that the Soviets, in their four-*day* campaign had played the decisive role in defeating the Japanese. So much for Guadalcanal, Iwo Jima and Okinawa. (The atomic bombings of Hiroshima and Nagasaki were dismissed as merely genocidal, racist blows against a people already more than willing to surrender.) Thus the US military's victory in the Pacific War gave the PVA leaders, in their ignorance, little pause. For them "the man behind the gun" was more crucial than the gun.

The Chinese People's Liberation Army maintained the fiction that their troops in Korea were truly volunteers (as per Stalin's suggestion), fervent to succour a fellow socialist state and to repulse the wicked designs of the "imperialists" on the integrity of the motherland. To the contrary, all evidence indicates that the Chinese People's Volunteers were conscripted in about equal measure as their comrades in the PLA, although there were undoubtedly volunteers, as in every army.

These CPV troops were above all a light infantry force, handicapped by their lack of air power, but also of armour, of artillery, transport, communication and logistical support. Their small arms were a hodge-podge of Japanese rifles captured in Manchuria, American Thompson sub-machine guns (once favoured by Chicago gangsters, but in this instance captured from the Chinese Nationalists), and Soviet makes of varying calibres. The unnerving bugle calls preparatory to a Chinese night attack were not the clever psychological ploy device imagined by jumpy UNC troops and gullible journalists, but simply makeshift substitutes for missing radio communication nets. The troops were clad in cotton-quilt uniforms much praised by some Western commentators for their warmth but which were very difficult to dry if soaked in the field. No identification tags were issued to the Volunteers, although some, pathetically, wrote their names on scraps of paper kept under the left inside of their blouses to provide some possibility of identification if killed in action. Their cloth, laceless, low-cut shoes proved a poor substitute for combat boots. If they had the time, Chinese troops would usually strip the combat boots from captured or dead UNC troops. The troops usually subsisted on a mixture of parched wheat, soybean and peanut flour, flavoured with salt and packed into a sock. (Numerous PVA troops got into trouble for hoarding and gorging themselves on canned UNC rations found in recaptured Pyongyang.)

The CPVs had high morale at first and more recent experience on their side, although the spirit of the press-ganged former Nationalist troops was problematical. Later, as CPV troops faced unremitting UN bombardment, that morale declined appreciably. The CPV leadership undoubtedly made a serious mistake in extolling their army's superior spirit and denigrating their enemies. The troops found out soon enough on the battlefield that it was not going to be all that easy, that "spirit" might in the end win over "steel", but that winning was a long time in coming, and in the meantime, casualties were mounting. In fact, one authority, not unsympathetic to the CPV, writes of the generally "low morale" of the CPV after early 1951.[14] Discipline was strict, but moderated by "re-education" or "criticism and self-criticism" policies that enabled the offender to reintegrate himself into his unit by honestly confessing his sins of the mind or spirit. Even deserters in wartime were usually not shot but let off with their pledge that they would not do it again. (The latter policy may have been a good indication of just how serious was the problem, again particularly among former Nationalist soldiers.) CPV troops were strictly enjoined to behave themselves among the Korean civil population. Special awards were established for those who saved Korean lives and the CPV raised large sums of money among its troops for famine relief in the wake of disastrous floods in the summer of 1951.

Although all members of the PVA were officially "heroes", the army leadership did establish special awards and recognition for particular acts of bravery. But there was a major and instructive difference between the Chinese awards and those of the Western forces in the UNC. The PVA awarded medals and scrolls to its troops who killed or captured numbers of enemy troops ("those who are good at annihilating the enemy forces with light infantry weapons at no or small cost . . . or who are always in its van to advance and in the rear to retreat"[15]). There seemed to be no equivalent to the Western awards (such as the US Army's Medal of Honor) more often than not awarded to those who risked or sacrificed their lives to save their comrades.

For all its weaknesses, the CPV was a tough, battle-wise force, led by highly experienced commanders against an almost fatally over-confident enemy. But its deficiencies would cost its soldiers dearly in the months ahead on the battlefields to the south.

Chapter Seven

China's intervention and the second great UN retreat

As the US Army liaison light aircraft dipped low over the wind-swept, snow-clad wastes of wintertime North Korea, relief suddenly became palpable in the cockpit. The long-overdue Army convoy had been spotted. It was easy enough to see, with its olive-drab trucks in startling contrast to the whiteness all about. Finally, it had broken out of the Chinese encirclement and was apparently now very slowly grinding its way along the rough trail to a safe haven. Perhaps too slowly. In fact, the convoy actually did not seem to be moving at all. And the snow, oddly enough, even lay on the vehicles' engine hoods. Then it became obvious: the convoy was not going anywhere, the snow on the hoods a sure indication that the engines beneath were stone-cold – long stopped. Passing just above the immobile vehicles, the observer could now see that this was in reality a convoy of the dead. Stiffened figures could be seen slumped behind bullet-shattered windshields, or stacked several deep in the truck beds, often in grotesque frozen postures. Truck cab doors flopped open forlornly in the bitter winds while yet other khaki-clad figures were sprawled along the trail's frozen gravel, mute evidence of drivers desperately and futilely attempting to dodge their way on foot past the Chinese ambush. These dead American soldiers were simply more victims of the massive Chinese intervention into the Korean War – and of the unconscionable disregard of some elementary military principles by their commander, General Douglas MacArthur.

The CPV forces entered the war cautiously and tentatively, but their first clash with UN forces, on 25 October, was certainly an indication that a new, formidable foe had entered the war. The 3rd Battalion, 2nd Regiment of the ROK 6th Division was practically destroyed as a unit when it fell into a Chinese trap eight miles east of Onjong. Its US Army KMAG adviser was captured and later died in a POW camp. The Chinese followed this success

117

with other equally effective attacks on ROK forces. US troops first clashed with the Chinese on the same day near Unsan, and netted the first Chinese POW of the Korean War. He told a chilling and quite accurate tale: there were 20,000 Chinese Communist troops in the vicinity. Other reports began to flow in to headquarters of POWs who understood neither Korean nor Japanese and of dead troops who looked Chinese. The commander of the ROK 1st Division (Paik Sun Yup) who had fought with the Japanese in Manchuria and knew his Chinese, reported to the US 1st Corps commander that there were "many, many Chinese" in his area of operations. And the weather was getting much colder.

General Walker was by this time sufficiently concerned to begin to discount the official line that there were only what amounted to "stray" Chinese in the North. He transferred his entire 1st Cavalry Division from security duty in Pyongyang to Unsan. But General J. Lawton Collins, US Army Chief of Staff, opined on 31 October that Chinese troop movements might well be a form of "face saving", in that Chou En-lai had publicly stated that China would not stand idly by to see their Korean comrades go down in defeat. (There was considerable talk at the time, particularly among those who professed, like General MacArthur and his entourage, to "understand the oriental mind", of the concept of "face" in the Orient. At times it seemed that such occidentals used the concept more than orientals themselves.) Another myth of the Orient was begun at about this time as the commander of the 1st Battalion of the 8th Cavalry Regiment, Major John Millikin, viewed through his field glasses hillsides seemingly alive with Chinese soldiers moving against the ROK lines. Major Millikin's observations were accurate enough, but other UN troops began to report, often with excited exaggeration, their own "human waves" of Chinese attackers. Such "human wave attacks" would become in the following weeks and months a convenient means of explaining UN defeats at the hands of the Chinese. Nonetheless, the PVA did attack on occasion in mass waves of troops.

Probably emboldened by the Chinese intervention, North Korean forces occasionally could still put up spirited resistance. Near Pakchon on 27 October the Middlesex's 1st Battalion routed the North Koreans in a fierce battle that saw some ten *Inmin Gun* tanks and two self-propelled guns knocked out. The following evening the Australian bazooka teams from the 3rd Battalion destroyed three KPA tanks, while US Army tank fire broke up the Communist attack. (Unfortunately, the Australian battalion commander was mortally wounded by a stray shell splinter the following evening.) Those KPA forces still unsubdued were then pulverized by an attack mounted by the US 2nd Battalion of the 21st Infantry Regiment, which, passing through the British lines, tackled the Communist forces above Chongju. Brushing aside an attempted Communist night ambush, the regimental and battalion commanders directed the battle from their radio jeeps while calmly observing the orange balls of *Inmin Gun* tank fire bounce off their own tanks, in probably the last armour clash of the war. A few days later the US 5th Regimental Combat Team killed some 300–400 NKPA troops at a road junction a few miles north of Kusong. But by then, General Walker had already begun to order the withdrawal of his outlying units in the face of the looming Chinese presence.

UN forces had their first large-scale, disastrous clash with the CPV at the town of Unsan on Eighth Army's front in the west. Here the 8th Cavalry Regiment of the 1st Cavalry Division was badly mauled and the ROK 15th Regiment virtually destroyed. The withdrawal of the US 1st and 2nd Battalions, 8th Cavalry Regiment, was accompanied with some confusion and even panic as the Chinese ambushed troops and their vehicles fighting their way southward, leaving a shambles of abandoned, blazing and wrecked equipment behind. Those who could, fled over the hills on foot. In some stretches of road the wreckage was so tangled that even tanks could not get through and had to be abandoned, although at least in this instance the crews destroyed their equipment first. The 3rd Battalion made a better fight of it when its headquarters was overrun. Hand-to-hand fighting killed many Chinese attackers, who were driven off. One island of resistance at the ramp to the battalion command post saw three men who manned a machine gun there killed in succession by Chinese grenades. American troopers fired bazooka rounds into their own vehicles, igniting them and providing sufficient illumination to shoot down their attackers in greater numbers. Six times the Chinese charged the embattled perimeter and six times they were beaten off. Eventually, most of the US troops were captured or killed as the few able-bodied survivors attempted to infiltrate back to UN lines. The battalion surgeon and the battalion chaplain both ministered heroically to their charges; the former volunteered to stay behind with the wounded and surrender them to the Chinese. In the end, troop losses for ROK and US Army units were about 600. In addition, the 15th ROK Regiment's loss of equipment was almost total, including five US Army liaison aircraft demolished on the ground. The 8th Regiment lost 12 howitzers and nine tanks and was considered for the time being to be inoperable.

Eighth Army did stabilize its lines along the Chongchon River after heavy fighting. Commonwealth troops, well supported by US artillery units, played a major part in perimeter defence. The Argylls' 1st Battalion was supported by intense fire from a US artillery company, one of whose howitzers fired some 1,400 rounds. After a fierce bayonet charge, the Australian 3rd Battalion retrieved some lost ground but had to withdraw subsequently to a defence perimeter astride the Pakchon Road. The Aussies killed some 300 of the Chinese attackers between 5 and 6 November, while air action had inflicted an additional 600 to 1,000 casualties in that one day and night of action. These actions were complicated by hordes of North Korean refugees fleeing to the south bank of the Chongchon, some 20,000 of them passing through checkpoints between 4 and 5 November.

The Chinese attack of 6 November would actually mark the conclusion of the first phase of the Chinese First Phase Offensive. Chinese forces then seemed to melt back into the desolate countryside.

After Unsan, the Chinese Army issued its well-known pamphlet which warned the Chinese soldier of the great fire power of the US Army but denigrated the individual American soldier's courage. When cut off from the rear, they

> abandon all their heavy weapons, leaving them all over the place, and play opossum. . . . Their infantrymen are weak, afraid to die, and haven't the courage to attack or defend. . . . They will cringe when, if on the advance, they hear firing. . . . At Unsan they were surrounded for several days yet they did nothing.[1]

The quotation has received wide publicity in subsequent years, but it first gained circulation in, of all places, an official US Army history of the Korean War. Much of this may have been true enough for the action around Unsan, but the writer of this text, for whatever reason, had obviously ignored the heroic stand of the 3rd Battalion, or the fierce firing of the 61st Field Artillery Battalion, 1st Cavalry Division. This writer might also have noted the US 1st Marine Division, which had, between 2 and 7 November destroyed the Chinese 124th Division, killing some 700 Communists at a cost of 314 total casualties themselves. Chinese soldiers who took this pamphlet's moonshine seriously might later find themselves dead. And the commander of the CPV himself would later, privately, make a considerably more positive evaluation of the American soldier. At any rate, the thousands of Chinese deserters to UN lines (at a time when they were winning) compared to the precisely zero number of known US or Allied defectors (at a time when they were losing), should give some indication of the relative morale of the two armies. It is also significant that such an indictment of the American soldier would be quoted with some approbation in American official accounts of the war. It is difficult to imagine the Chinese People's Liberation Army publishing any such enemy critique of its own "heroic volunteers". Finally, with their glorification of the guerrilla, the PRC leaders should have, but undoubtedly did not, note the fact that it was "soft" US Army soldiers who conducted stay-behind guerrilla operations, which enjoyed considerable success, against the Japanese during the Second World War, in the Philippine Islands.

To the east, the US Marines, still making their way north in the vicinity of the Chosin (Changjin) Reservoir, tackled the Chinese, rolled them back and destroyed their remaining armour. One combined air and ground action alone in this drive killed an estimated 700 Chinese troops; identification papers from the dead showed most of them to have been from the Chinese 124th Division. In this whole series of well-fought actions in early November the Marines had lost 46 killed.

But now the North Korean winter truly came upon the troops. During the evening of 10 November temperatures dropped by 40 degrees (F) to 8 degrees below zero (F), accompanied by a 30 to 35mph wind. Temperatures later would fall even lower, but the first shock of the winter was the most unforgettable. In the next two or three days, some 200 men of the tough 7th Marine Regiment collapsed from the cold and were hospitalized; stimulants had to be applied in many cases to revive depressed respiration. Water-soluble medicines froze and blood plasma could only be used after a 60 to 90-minute preparation in a warm tent. Contrary to another myth, the Chinese also suffered from the cold. They may have been hardy, but their equipment gave them much less protection from the elements. At about this time the PVA's 9th Army Corps suffered one-third of its troops out of action through frostbite over a four-week period.

The American Joint Chiefs by then were worried by the separation of Eighth Army and X Corps, as were Eighth Army and Marine commanders. But General MacArthur and General Almond remained resolutely complacent. MacArthur did expect liaison and communication between his two military arms. But the lateral "roads" (actually little more than trails) over the mountains had been cut by craters some 35 feet in diameter and 15 feet deep, blocked by boulders and destroyed bridges, all presumably the work of Communist guerrillas. Only once did patrols from either arm of the UN forces in the North meet. But, as noted, after 6 November Chinese forces seemed to withdraw and an eerie calm settled across the frozen hills of North Korea.

The US Joint Chiefs once again considered their future course in North Korea. General MacArthur argued against any change of mission: An advance would be necessary to obtain "an accurate measure of enemy strength", and he could defeat any Chinese forces known to be in North Korea. Still almost completely in the dark as to the magnitude of the Chinese intervention or of its aims, the Joint Chiefs could only acquiesce. MacArthur's drive to the North, his "Home by Christmas" offensive, would resume by Thanksgiving Day.

Unfortunately for the UN Commander and his troops, the Chinese would beat him to the punch. At the Battle of the Chongchon (25–28 November 1950), Eighth Army forces were badly mauled and the way opened for the longest retreat in US military history. Although many units made a good fight of it, there were also many cases of precipitous retreat, abandonment of equipment, and, again, some panic. Much of the latter can be attributed to the shock of having to halt the confident offensive against the North Koreans and to being attacked by seeming hordes of a mysterious, unknown enemy. The assault caused the virtual collapse of ROK II Corps, while Battery A, 61st Field Artillery Battalion, after its commander had been killed and all other battery officers wounded, abandoned both its guns (something artillerymen regard as shameful except in the direst of circumstances) as well as its vehicles. After suffering heavy casualties, the Chinese did call off their assault on the 38th US Regiment's line. Eighth Army intelligence continued to expound on the Chinese "conduct[ing] an active defense in depth along present line employing strong local counterattack". Far East Command Intelligence was no better: "should the enemy elect to fight in the interior valleys, a slowing down of the United Nations offensive may result".[2] Even General Walker, as late as 28 November, called for the renewal of the offensive drive to the Yalu. It should have been obvious that the UN forces were facing a massive assault by a fresh, undefeated army. Numerous Chinese POWs were not at all behindhand in revealing their units and their strengths. For once, MacArthur was more perceptive than his intelligence people. On the day after General Walker's call to his forces to prepare for a new offensive, the UN Commander informed the Chiefs of Staff that "We face an entirely new war", and that his plan for the immediate future "was to pass to the defensive".

To the east of the peninsula, X Corps, still separated from Eighth Army, faced a similar enemy, but with dissimilar results. X Corps intelligence unintelligently dismissed reports from civilians in the area of large bodies of Chinese around the Yudam-ni area. But Major General Smith (commander of the 1st Marine Division) had been suspicious of Chinese intentions for weeks and had incurred the wrath of the brash General Almond for his caution. On the day that MacArthur made his momentous pronouncement, General Almond flew to the battle area, awarded medals, and told Task Force MacLean, to general disbelief, that what X Corps faced now was no more than Chinese remnants fleeing north, and added "We're still attacking and we're going all the way to the Yalu. Don't let a bunch of Chinese laundrymen stop you", a statement in which the general's latent racism competed with his wilful misstatement to troops that within a few days would face disaster at the Changjin Reservoir. General Almond could not have entirely believed his own words; over the previous day and a half he had been informed by Marine commanders, including General Smith, that they faced strong Chinese units. General Smith's perceptiveness was in no small measure responsible for the Marines escaping from their trap in northeast Korea.

Thanks to X Corps depositions, the Marines had become in actuality a group of isolated garrisons which Smith had become convinced must be removed quickly from Korea's far north. Their exit was blocked by the Chinese 9th Army Group, consisting of ten divisions of 100,000 battle-experienced troops – a Chinese local numerical advantage of some five-to-one. As noted, the Chinese forces were grossly deficient in artillery, air power, communications and transport and many suffered from frost-bite. Still they were well supplied with small arms, machine guns and mortars. By 26 November, the 5th and 7th Marine Regiments were entrenched near Yudamni, a small town just to the west and south of the giant Changjin Reservoir. The remainder were strung out for 45 miles, guarding the main supply route to the south. On the following day the Marines moved out on a cautious offensive, as ordered by General Almond. But that night the Chinese struck back with overwhelming force as two PVA divisions attacked the 5th and 7th Regiments to an unnerving cacophony of bugles and whistles. Hundreds of Chinese dead piled up before the Marine perimeter, but survivors finally began to fight their way through. To the rear, the Marines found that the PVA 59th Division had severed their supply link. In desperate fighting amid sub-zero cold, the Marines managed to hold the Yudamni–Hagaru perimeter, including the Hagaru airstrip, carved by Marine engineers out of the frozen earth in only 12 days, and vital for the air evacuation of the wounded.

The commander of the 1st Marine Regiment sent forward a mixed relief force composed of British and US Army units and named Task Force Drysdale after the British Marine officer, Lieutenant-Colonel Douglas B. Drysdale, designated to lead the 900-man armoured-motorized thrust. At what Lieutenant Colonel Drysdale came to call "Hell Fire Pass", the relief column was almost totally destroyed in a hail of small arms and mortar fire from the high ground held by the Chinese.

After flurries of conflicting orders that saw some X Corps units receiving three conflicting missions within 72 hours, the command seemed to pull itself together, realistically if belatedly abandoned the drive to the Yalu and planned for complete evacuation from northeast Korea. But it was not until 9 December that General MacArthur gave formal orders for an evacuation by sea from the port of Hungnam. General Almond's operational orders called for the 1st Marine Division, I ROK Corps, and 7th and 3rd US Infantry

Divisions to embark in that order. The 3rd, as the last major army unit to arrive in the X Corps area of operations, and thus the freshest, was to bring up the rear.

Now even General Almond realized that the Marines had to be evacuated if they were to survive. Their farthest outpost, at Yudamni, was more than 78 miles from the coast along a narrow, winding, dirt road. Along that route some 100,000 Chinese troops were assembling to block the retreat of the 20,000 Marines and about to inflict what could have been one of the worst defeats in US military history.

On 1 December the Marines began their breakout attempt, usually moving by daylight to take full advantage of UN air power. USAF and Marine Air warplanes strafed and napalmed the Chinese on the ridges. Marine Air in particular came so close that trails of burning napalm occasionally trickled down into the column and expended gun shell casings bounced among the troops. Of course, the Marines could not let the Chinese hold the high ground, and friendly patrols kept the surrounding hills clear of the Chinese in a long series of short, sharp engagements in which they always emerged victorious. In one such engagement, that to hold the vital Fox Hill, a Marine relief battalion found that only 82 of the original 240 Marines could walk out of the positions that they had held against overwhelming odds for five days. Their wounded commander (who had won a Silver Star at Iwo Jima) directed the defence from a stretcher.

Although the Marines were in retreat, their morale held; there were no reported cases of panic or "freezing" in the face of Chinese fire. The Marine elite force emphasis upon training and discipline now paid off. In the dismal post-Second World War years of savage budget and personnel cuts and even attempts to dismantle the Corps altogether, the Marines did not lower their standards; Basic Training at Parris Island was essentially in 1950 what it had been in 1940 or 1930, something approximating Hell on Earth. Those who passed developed an enormous and belligerent pride, with which they condescended to the US Army in about equal measure as to an enemy. The Marines did tolerate the US Navy. (US Marines salute when the "Marine Corps Hymn" is played; the other US service personnel merely stand to attention. Also, it is a "hymn", not a "song".) Whatever their attitude towards the other US armed services, however, the Marines never under-estimated their enemy, as seen in General Smith's caution in the face of General Almond's impatience. The Marines' general attitude was perhaps best reflected at the time in the reply made by General Smith when some-one spoke of "retreat"; no, actually the Marines were simply "advancing in another direction". Not surprisingly, the Chinese suffered very heavy casual-ties in taking on such men.

But the long retreating column to the coast numbered US Army personnel as well as Marines. Army Task Force Dog gave valiant support, particularly in clearing a path through the town of Sudong. There an X Corps artillery commander and a Marine driver organized a two-man assault against the Chinese, although the artillery officer was killed in the action. Task Force Dog then mounted its own assault, which opened the way for the column.

Only the drivers and their wounded rode on this retreat; the rest walked the entire way out. The dead were buried as temperatures dropped to 16 degrees below zero (F) or were even trucked out. Unfortunately, civilian refugees followed the column, risking their lives to cross bridges before Marine engineers blew them up. The column moved out of Hagaru to Koto-ri, taking on the way East Hill, another dominating promontory where the 5th Marines killed an estimated 800 to 1,200 Chinese. Once again, the refugee stream followed, this time close on the tail of the Marine column evacuating Koto-ri. The Marines were fired upon by Chinese troops mingled with civilians. The last seven tanks, two tank crews, and three men from a reconnaissance platoon were lost, the only serious casualties of the retreat (or, as the Marines would have it, "attack in another direction").

Another serious situation faced the Marines between Koto-ri and Chimnhung-ni. A gap had been blown at the Funchilin Pass, directly in front of hydro-electric sluiceway control, blocking all further progress. The refugees made their way through the building, but the Marines and their vehicles, filled with the wounded, could not. In a unique joint operation that took only two days (6–7 December) from start to finish, a special Army parachute rigger team was flown over from Japan to supervise the air drop from eight USAF C-119 transport aircraft of eight 2,500lb steel treadway spans to bridge the gap. Four (the bare minimum needed) survived the drop and were picked up by two pre-positioned, special-purpose Army trucks and emplaced over the chasm by Marine engineers. The entire column, men and vehicles, then passed safely over the now-bridged gap.

In the final battle to clear the evacuation route, the 1st Battalion, with the indispensable aid of air and artillery support, had to drive the Chinese 6th Division from the heights of Hill 1081 in temperatures that now had descended to 25 degrees below zero (F). They counted some 530 Chinese dead. By now the constant air and artillery bombardment and the cold were beginning to be felt in the Chinese ranks as well, and many began to make their way to the Marine lines to surrender. By 11 December the last elements of the 1st Marine Division had arrived at the Hungnam coastal enclave on the east coast.

Most surprisingly, the Chinese made no serious efforts to interfere with the seaborne evacuation. They did probe on 16, 18 and 19 December, but nowhere with any success. These attacks may have netted the Chinese intelligence, but by the time that information could have been digested through the tenuous communications of the PVA, the UN forces had withdrawn to new lines. It is also likely that the 72,500 battle and non-battle casualties – some 60 per cent of the force – the Chinese had suffered at the hands of the Marines and their attached Army units had instilled a healthy caution in PVA commanders. Furthermore, as the defensive perimeters came closer to the coast, the massive bombardment of the naval Gunfire Support Group 90.8 could now be added to the already impressive artillery and air power of X Corps. Also, naval Task Force 77 could mount its air strikes more frequently at much closer range.

In contrast to X Corps' helter-skelter offensive drive north, its evacuation from Hungnam was a model of efficiency. Some 105,000 men, along with all of their 17,500 operable vehicles and 350,000 tons of supplies, had been removed in the face of advancing Chinese forces to be shipped south to fight again. As the bone-weary troops clambered aboard their sea transports, their boots split, their socks worn away to mere thin circles of elastic at the ankles, they entered a half-remembered paradise of hot showers and steam heat. Solicitous crewmen passed out sweet American candy bars; most of the Marines, after subsisting for weeks on frozen C-rations, promptly threw them up. Even captured Communist material, including lines of Soviet-made military trucks, neatly prepared, were shipped aboard.

As well, some 98,000 of those civilian refugees who had so dogged the steps of the Marines and Army units as they fought their way to the coast, were loaded into landing craft. Tragically, about an equal number had to be left behind because they failed to make their way to the port in time or due to a lack of shipping space. Their subsequent fate does not require much imagination; there was the example of the putrefying corpses of scores of "disloyal" North Korean civilians discovered at Hamhung, who, according to survivors, had been severely beaten by the North Korean authorities just before the town was abandoned to UN forces, then thrown, alive, down a mine shaft to die.

On 24 December the last rear guard units abandoned their final strong posts and made for landing craft with deliberate speed, still unopposed. Skilled demolitions experts had already placed charges in all important structures in the port area as well as in military equipment not considered worth moving. With the last of X Corps afloat, the port facilities were blown sky-high.

The evacuation from Hungnam was an achievement easily comparable to the Dunkirk operation or the mass exodus of approximately one million Eastern Germans from the advancing Red Army in early 1945. The Hungnam evacuation was unique, however, in that X Corps not only brought out all its troops, able-bodied or wounded, but also all US, Chinese, or North Korean equipment worth taking, plus nearly 100,000 civilians. The successful evacuation almost redeemed Generals MacArthur's and Almond's vain dreams of total victory. And at a cost of 342 dead, 78 missing, and 1,683 wounded, X Corps' Marines and Army troops had destroyed 77 combat-tested Chinese divisions, making the entire evacuation possible. The US, Allied, and ROK Army units of X Corps thus averted the large-scale disasters of the type that had rolled back in some disorder such Eighth Army units as the 2nd Division or the ROK II Crops at the Chongchon River.

But even Hungnam was no victory. One is put in mind of Churchill's famous dictum after Dunkirk: "Wars are not won by evacuations." The UNC had been severely defeated in North Korea.

Looking back, it is not really so astonishing that Generals Almond and MacArthur and others who presumably should have known better dismissed any serious Chinese threat. The easy explanation for such insouciance is the familiar one of "racism". Rather, it is in the light of what US and Western military authorities knew of Chinese armies that the UN race to the Yalu can best be understood. American generals of the time had known only of a China racked with warlordism and internal chaos, relatively easy prey for the rapacious Japanese, economically prostrate, its people on occasion literally starving to death, and which had just emerged the year previous from a debilitating civil war. Chinese armies, Communist or Nationalist, had been pushed around almost at will by the Japanese since 1937, and were generally considered something of a joke. (The term "Chinese fire drill" in contemporary America referred to any incompetent, disorganized, almost comical effort.) Few military observers were overly impressed by the Chinese Communist army's defeat of the Chinese Nationalist army. Nonetheless, the UN command in the last weeks of 1950 found itself in full retreat before this "bunch of Chinese laundrymen".

Chapter Eight

Chinese offensives and stabilization of the battlelines

To the west, Eighth Army, in considerably more disorder than X Corps in the northeast, retreated overland southward. On 5 December Pyongyang was evacuated and the city left in flames, but there is no evidence that the UNC deliberately fired the capital. Although the DPRK capital is an inland city, much of the evacuation was nonetheless waterborne, by way of the Taedong River. There were numerous parallels with the Hungnam evacuation. Tens of thousands of refugees followed the UN forces. Some 30,000 proceeded south by sailboat. Communist pressure was even less than at Hungnam; in fact, after 30 November no Eighth Army trooper had even sighted a Chinese soldier! Much of the equipment hurriedly destroyed at Pyongyang could have been saved had the evacuation been less precipitous. But the prime concern had become the preservation of the UNC troops, and for that goal North Korea and UN equipment there could be readily abandoned.

In the absence of Communist forces, the retreat became more orderly; by this time far more UN troops were dying in vehicle accidents than at the hands of their enemies. Considering the utmost speed which General Walker had always urged on his drivers, it was hardly surprising that he became one of those accident statistics in the midst of this retreat. On 23 December Walker was killed in a head-on collision with a civilian-driven army truck near Uijongbu. (The accident was eerily similar to the one that had ended the life of General Walker's mentor, General George Patton, whose sedan had also, at the end of the Second World War, fatally collided with a truck driven by a civilian.) The North Koreans later claimed that:

A monster called the Eighth US Army commander was beheaded. That was because Walker, fleeing Eighth Army field Commander,

together with his 80–odd aides–de–camp, was attacked by a reconnoiter-
ing party of the People's Army and all went down to the shades.[1]

At the urging of General MacArthur, Walker was succeeded by Lieutenant
General Matthew B. Ridgway, who was then deskbound in the Pentagon. But
Ridgway was every bit the combat soldier, the commander of an airborne
division and corps in the Second World War. From that time on, for some
reason, General MacArthur withdrew from the direct role he had taken in
planning and in conducting tactical operations. ("The Eighth Army is yours,
Matt. Do what you think best", were MacArthur's parting words to Ridgway.)
Ridgway, however, would faithfully keep the UN Commander informed of
all his significant decisions.

General Ridgway was distressed by what he found in Eighth Army in late
1950 and early 1951. That army's main headquarters were still at Taegu, far
to the rear, and tied down far too many staff officers. In his immediate recon-
noitering of the front lines, where Ridgway soon became famous for his
trademark hand grenade and first aid kit strapped one on each shoulder, he
found a general lack of spirit and a listlessness that forced him to abandon his
plans for an early counter-offensive. One young US Army officer wrote years
later that many of his men were so spiritless that they did not even bother to
come down out of the line for a traditional Christmas turkey dinner "with
all the trimmings"; they stayed on line, glumly eating cold C-rations and
facing combat. The officer decided to *order* the recalcitrants down, and most
of them later thanked him for the break.

Ridgway ordered that henceforth, "division commanders [were] to be up
with their forward battalions, and . . . corps commanders up with the regiment that was in the hottest action". The commander of the British Brigade
caught the new spirit. His order of New Year's Day 1951 outlined his
meticulously detailed plan for dealing with the Communist enemy: "knock
hell out of him with everything you have got". Further, the new Eighth
Army commander ordered aggressive patrolling to obtain intelligence. At
the time no one seemed to know what size or type of forces threatened
Eighth Army.

From the first, Ridgway had no intention of presiding over an evacuation
of the Korean peninsula, whatever options might be floating about in Washington, Taegu, or Tokyo. He showed his determination to remain and to
regain when he prohibited demolitions for demolitions' sake. From now on
such destruction "shall be such as to combine maximum hurt to the enemy
with minimum harm to the civilian population". Such destruction seemed
to indicate that the UNC was not planning to return soon. Not having got
the word, Army engineers three days later blew up Inchon's tidal gates

which then had to be rebuilt at great cost and delay when the UN retook the port several months later. But that was the last such mindless destruction by Eighth Army. There was to be no more "scorched earth" and there were to be no more "bug outs".

Not even Ridgway's exhortations and orders could save Seoul from the overwhelming Chinese pressure. However, this would be a much more orderly withdrawal than that of the previous June. Just before the evacuation of the ROK capital in early January 1951, all inmates of that city's prisons, most of the staff and patients of its hospitals, all ROK currency and money printing plates (essential to a government that papered over its deficits at whatever cost in rampant inflation), and the holdings of its archives, museums, and galleries had been shipped south. The majority of non-essential government employees and the families of government officials had previously been evacuated. The only major problem was, again, that of civilian refugees; about one-half of Seoul's population fled south, mostly on foot. Although the weather was indescribably worse than that during the city's abandonment six months earlier, this withdrawal for the most part went as expected, although some civilians did freeze to death along the route despite the best efforts of the US Army Civil Assistance teams.

The worst incident during the withdrawal came at the last moment. Company B and part of the heavy weapons company of the Royal Ulster Rifles, plus a dozen tanks, were cut off by a fast-moving force from the Chinese 39th Army. Local commanders, British and American, made no attempt to free the trapped units, although General Ridgway ordered that every effort be mounted. In the words of the British Brigade commander, the men would just have to "knock it out for themselves". Most failed to "knock it out", and between two and three hundred men and at least ten tanks were lost.

South of the Han River, Ridgway's troops finally encountered large-scale Communist forces when they were attacked along a narrow front in the east by remnants of the KPA. *Inmin Gun* troops mingled within refugee columns and thus achieved some surprise. One thrust actually drove almost as far south as the Naktong River of Pusan Perimeter memory. The dangerous penetration was contained, however, with the North Koreans suffering heavy losses. This was not the *Inmin Gun* of the summer of 1950.

Still, General Ridgway sensed a continuing lack of spirit in his command, a malaise worsened by the unresolved question of whether the UNC would stay in Korea, and if they did stay, whether they would be simply clinging to beach heads. In fact, last-ditch defensive lines were being constructed even inside the old Pusan Perimeter. Ridgway conducted a survey of morale and found that the US troops in particular repeatedly raised two questions: "Why are we here?" and "What are we fighting for?" If his army was ever to regain its fighting edge, these two basic questions posed by troops far from home had to be addressed. Ridgway's answer to the first question was brief because he was fully a product of the Anglo/American tradition of the subordination of the military to civilian control: "We are here because of the decisions of the properly constituted authorities of our respective governments." The second question warranted a more detailed response:

> Real estate is here incidental. . . . The real issues are whether the power of Western civilization . . . shall defy and defeat Communism; whether the rule of men who shoot their prisoners, enslave their citizens, and deride the dignity of man, shall displace the rule of those to whom the individual and his individual rights are sacred. . . . The sacrifices we have made, and those we shall yet support, are not offered vicariously for others, but in our own direct defense. In the final analysis, the issue now joined right here in Korea is whether communism or individual freedom shall prevail.[2]

These were inspiring words and did not do violence to the truth. To the end of the war, however, it would remain difficult for, say, a conscripted garage mechanic from Cairo, Illinois to sense a direct threat to his way of life in this out-of-the-way peninsula. The remaining non-ROK UNC forces for the most part needed little such encouragement; most of these volunteers were professionals doing what they were paid to do.

The new Eighth Army commander's determination was having its effect. On a visit to Korea in January, Army Chief of Staff, General J. Lawton Collins, was so inspired by Ridgway's attitude that he announced to correspondents "as of now, we are going to stay and fight". General MacArthur, who just a week earlier had termed the Eighth Army's situation "untenable", now agreed that the army could hold a beachhead in Korea indefinitely.

Already, Eighth Army patrols were ranging north of the last UNC lines – and making little contact. This lull in Communist military activity was hardly the result of any reconsideration of the war on the part of Beijing or Pyongyang. They still called for the expulsion of all "foreign imperialist" forces from the Korean peninsula. Rather, this pause pointed to the most significant flaw in the massive PVA and in the KPA: they could deliver heavy blows, but if their opponents retreated in good order while inflicting heavy casualties, pounding their supply lines and exchanging space for time, the Communist armies would soon enough outrun their primitive logistic support and grind to a halt. It is true that at the end of the war the PVA was even better equipped than it had been at the beginning, despite around-the-clock UN air strikes of its supply routes, but even its final offensives against various ROK forces inevitably sputtered to a close short of any major break-through. Basically the PVA/KPA could not sustain the offensive.

By early February 1951, the Great Retreat was over. The Chinese had outrun their supply lines and suffered enormous casualties. A few days fighting around Wonju in January, for example, cost the North Koreans more than 11,000 killed as a result of UN ground firepower and B-29 bomber strikes against their exposed positions; a single day of Chinese attacks against the 2nd Division's 3rd Battalion and the attached French battalion on 1 Febru-ary saw 1,300 Communist dead piled up outside their perimeter, victims of heavy artillery bombardments and more than 80 UN air strikes, as well as well-sited ground fire. In addition, the winter weather had stripped the ground of cover. The UN Command's supply lines, on the other hand, were again compressed and increasingly filling with new troops and supplies. Consequently, the Command ordered cautious probing northward and encountered practically no resistance. The Communists, perhaps, finally realized that they were up against a well-handled enemy, at least as far as the non-ROK forces were concerned. But ROK troops themselves could prove aggressive on occasion; on 10 February, in one of the few brushes with Communist forces at the time, a South Korean patrol moved across the Han River ice and into the lower edge of Seoul itself before being repelled by small arms fire. The same day Inchon was captured by US forces without resistance.

The Communists were merely licking their wounds, however, and, pre-sumably, digesting recent battlefield lessons. On 10 February, Eighth Army intelligence (G-2) came remarkably close to determining the particulars of the next CPV–KPA offensive, a tribute to General Ridgway's insistence on vigorous patrolling and probes across the lines. Ridgway believed that the Communists also enjoyed good intelligence; they had only to read the US Army's *Stars and Stripes* or listen to US Armed Forces Radio carelessly speculating about future UNC plans. But because of the Communists' tenuous communications, there was little they could do with this information in any short period of time. Ridgway's G-2 concluded that once the Communists' supply lines caught up with their combat forces they would renew the offens-ive, regardless of losses.

In fact, the next day the anticipated four CPV and two KPA division offensive against X Corps in the so-called Battle for Hoengsong practically destroyed the ROK 8th Division in the first hours. US Army supporting units were exposed and had themselves to withdraw through a tangle of abandoned ROK equipment, weapons and fleeing troops. Using battle-tested tactics, Communist forces worked their way behind UN units and along their main supply route, blocking an orderly withdrawal. US Army Support Team A, for example, lost two tanks, the tank platoon leader and nearly 150 men missing. Considering the general chaos surrounding the unit, this loss was understandable. Less excusable was Battery A, 503rd Field Artillery Battalion's saving of only one gun in its withdrawal, thereby presenting the advancing Chinese with a wealth of weapons, equipment and vehicles. That company lost two officers and about 110 men. The stout-hearted Dutch troopers again showed their mettle by their steady covering fire, which allowed several US units to escape with moderate losses. But the Dutch paid a price. Leading headquarters troops in a successful counter-attack to eliminate a Communist penetration, the battalion commander, Lieutenant Colonel M. A. P. A. den Ouden, was killed by a grenade.

Overall, a well-executed Communist offensive had pushed back a segment of X Corps lines about 13 miles amid some confusion, but, again, the offensive could not be followed up. UN losses totalled nearly 9,800 ROKs, 1,900 US, and 100 Dutch. Equipment losses of the ROK forces stood at 14 105mm howitzers and 901 other crew-served weapons, 390 radios, and 88 vehicles. US and Netherlands units lost 14 105mm and six 150mm howitzers, 277 other crew-served weapons, six tanks, and an incredible 280 vehicles.

A subsequent US Army investigation attributed most of the losses to the collapse of the ROK 8th Division. Although General Ridgway accepted these findings, he also warned his corps commanders that the "loss or abandonment to enemy of arms and equipment in usable condition is a grave offense against every member of this command". He promised to "deal severely" with any offenders.

After this inauspicious beginning, the Ridgway spirit did make itself felt in the ensuing weeks; a Chinese attack in overwhelming numbers against US and French positions at Chipyong-ni yielded them nothing at a cost of 648 dead counted around the wire after only one day's fighting. Overall, CPV dead was estimated at 3,200.

Operation KILLER (which term Army Chief of Staff Collins delicately and unsuccessfully protested, to Ridgway's disgust) and Operation RIPPER rolled the CPV and *Inmin Gun* back to the Han River and out of Seoul, encountering very little resistance, and eventually to the 38th Parallel.

The UNC's taking of Seoul for the second time, on 14 March, was accompanied by no such triumphal ceremony as that which had occasioned the city's first liberation from the Communists. This was the fourth time in eight months that the city had changed hands. Seoul was now nearly a dead city and the UN Command proposed to keep it that way, at least for the time being until the city could be made more livable. But Korean civilians, against orders, filtered back into their city which soon revived as a commercial, educational and political centre. This population movement was in distinct contrast to the mass flight of civilians from Pyongyang and from much of North Korea along with retreating UN troops.

Ironically, these offensives, billed as measures to kill Communist troops or at least keep them off balance with no particular territorial gains in mind, actually worked in reverse: the Communists for the most part pulled back intact before the UN offensives, but in doing so gave up substantial territory that put the battle lines back to roughly where they had been in June 1950. It was the *communists'* offensives that killed off so many of their own troops.

The blunting of the Chinese offensives, particularly that at Chipyong-ni in February 1951, demonstrated that Eighth Army, thanks in large measure to General Ridgway's rejuvenation of that force, had substantially regained the confidence and spirit it had lost during the long retreat from North Korea. Despite recommendations from his officers on the scene, General Ridgway had refused to give up Chipyong-ni. Catching the UN Commander's spirit, a senior US Army officer in the field told his unit commanders that although they would be surrounded by the Chinese, "We'll stay here and fight it out." The first Chinese attacks struck the French battalion's position. The imperturbable French responded to the Chinese bugles and whistles with their own hand-cranked siren, charged the Chinese in a grenade attack, and forced the large Chinese force to turn and run. US artillerymen initially refused to act as infantry to repel the Chinese attacks on their own defences, but most at least did not abandon their howitzers, which continued to pound the Chinese. The battle showed that UN forces could now give ground, consolidate, and then beat back Communist offensives.

Again the question arose of whether UN forces were to cross the Parallel, bringing the once-muted conflict between the UN Commander and President Truman into the open. Certainly personality clashes were involved here. The resolutely plebeian Truman could hardly stomach the lordly airs and fustian *pronunciamentos* of MacArthur. Furthermore, Captain Truman's military experience was limited to command of a battery of the Missouri National Guard in the First World War, and he remained suspicious of high-ranking "brass", with the notable exception for his Secretary of Defense, former General George C. Marshall. For Truman, MacArthur was a "failed" commander in the Philippines who should "have gone down with the ship" and a "dictator" in Japan. (MacArthur was certainly open to severe criticism for attempting to stop the Japanese on the beaches. On the other hand, he had been practically ordered out of the Philippines by President Roosevelt, and as Supreme Commander of the US occupation, he was *required* to be a dictator, just like Lucius Clay in Germany or Mark Clark in Austria.) Of course, MacArthur's barely concealed Republican political ambitions alienated the general and the President even further. Finally, there is good evidence that Truman anticipated a renewed Chinese offensive in the spring as well as possible air attacks on UNC units from Manchurian bases. The reaction of MacArthur (and the American right) to such an escalation of the war could well be imagined, and Truman was going to take no chances here.

On 1 December MacArthur, with his forces about to embark upon their long retreat, had argued in an interview with the American journal *U.S. News and World Report*, that Washington's refusal to allow him to *pursue* Chinese forces into Manchuria or to allow unlimited attacks on Chinese bases was "an enormous handicap, without precedent in military history", and implied that European allies were responsible for the hobbling of his war effort. Truman later wrote that he should have relieved MacArthur then and there, but such an action in the midst of the UNC's greatest crisis, with the very real possibility that tens of thousands of US troops would be trapped in North Korea, was out of the question, and it is likely that here the President was writing for the record. In the wake of the interview, Truman issued a Presidential Directive through the Joint Chiefs of Staff on 6 December, instructing US military officers not to comment publicly on sensitive issues.

There the contention more or less rested until UNC forces once again approached the 38th Parallel early in 1951. The President then drafted a carefully worded, non-threatening statement suggesting that the UN was willing to cease the fighting now that South Korea was close to being cleared of the Communists, and General MacArthur was so informed. But MacArthur had his own plans, and they did not include any olive branch. On 15 March 1951, he argued in a press interview that the UNC should not halt short of its true objective, "the unification of Korea". Further, on 24 March, MacArthur issued his communiqué in which he offered to confer with his hostile counterpart to arrange a cease-fire. In the opening of the message, MacArthur belittled Chinese military power (one would never have thought that his forces had recently been turfed out of North Korea in some disarray) and made statements that could have been interpreted as threatening an attack on China if it continued its "aggression". America's allies in Korea began to inquire if this UNC communiqué represented a shift in US policy from the one of simply driving the Communists from South Korea. Truman by then was determined to relieve his outspoken military commander, for his "open defiance of my orders as President and Commander-in-Chief that required all statements relating to national security to be cleared by Washington".

Then, on 5 April, MacArthur's old friend, US representative Joseph Martin, read on the House floor a letter in which the general agreed with the legislator's call for the deployment of Chinese Nationalist forces to Korea, which would probably have provoked an immediate widening of the war by China. MacArthur's letter concluded, in a phrase that came to epitomize the frustration felt at the time by the general and by so many Americans: "There is no substitute for victory." All of this was in direct violation of the Presidential/JCS Directive of 6 December. Truman then simply put into action his earlier determination and relieved his obstreperous general as of 11 April 1951.

Truman's action ignited a cyclone of criticism of the President in the United States, some verging on the hysterical. The "Old Soldier" returned to unprecedented, frenzied ticker-tape welcoming parades and became a rallying figure for all those discontented with the war, that is, those who wanted to "finish the job", "get it over with", "stop pussy-footing around", and so on. When MacArthur concluded his "Old Soldiers Never Die" valedictory address to a joint session of the US Congress, at least one Congressman seemed to imply that the voice of God had spoken. Although the general's plans for vigorously expanding the conflict stood practically no chance of execution short of a major mobilization of the nation, still they were discussed as serious alternatives to the current strategy employed by the Truman Democratic administration, which, according to most Republican partisans, was "soft on Communism". America's allies, on the other hand, with Truman sticking to his course of a limited war, heaved a sigh of relief; the Korean War would remain confined to Korea.

The debate went on into May and June of 1951 behind closed US Senate doors. The two most influential Senate committees, Armed Services and Foreign Relations, conducted hearings to deal with America's Far Eastern policy as well as with the MacArthur firing. Republican members of the committees used the hearings to arraign the Truman administration for its "blunders", "unpreparedness", or even worse, in the Far East. Witnesses ranged from the Olympian person of MacArthur himself to high Truman administration figures. The general, of course, denied that he had made any errors in Korea. For him, victory in that war would come from a drive to the Yalu along with the bombing and blockade of China. MacArthur dismissed any suggestions that such belligerent actions might unleash the Third World War.

Secretary of State Marshall, the Joint Chiefs, and Dean Acheson all gingerly avoided any attack on MacArthur personally. But they agreed that even if MacArthur's plans did not result in all-out war, they would most likely result in a much wider war involving the US and possibly its allies in what the Chief of Staff of the Army General Omar Bradley memorably termed "The wrong war, at the wrong place, at the wrong time, with the wrong enemy". The "right" war, presumably, was one that would be fought in Europe against the Soviet Union. (Remarkably, legend has General Bradley's quotation as referring to the Korean War itself rather than to a larger conflict with China!) Although initially attended by intense nationwide publicity, public interest waned as the hearings droned on. In the end, the American public, for all of its adulation of MacArthur, the hero of Bataan and Inchon, came to accept the administration contention that another World War in their lifetimes, or even simply a wider conflict, was too high a price to pay for a promised victory in Korea.

All of the excess and hysteria was not on one side, however. If right-wing American extremists could smell "treason", their liberal counterparts read into the Truman–MacArthur controversy a challenge to the lasting American principle of civilian supremacy over the military. Yet there is not a shred of evidence that MacArthur or any of his followers ever planned to challenge President Truman and the administration in any way other than through the political process.

These were all matters of high policy. Of considerably greater immediate interest to the US (and soon after, Commonwealth) troops in the line was the institution of a rotation plan devised by General Ridgway during his Pentagon tour of duty. The "Big R" provided that all troops, officers and enlisted men alike who accumulated 36 points could rotate home: a soldier earned four points for each month in the combat zone, three for serving between the line of emplaced artillery and regimental headquarters, and two for rear-echelon duty. The average surviving infantryman could thus expect to return to home delights within one year. Also, those who served six months with a division or other separate combat unit, or who had served one year at higher levels of command or with separate service units, or combinations of these (it could get complicated) would be eligible for rotation. The system was immensely popular with the troops, maintaining reasonably good troop morale in an increasingly stalemated and frustrating undeclared war fought over a far-off country about which most foreign UN troops knew little and cared less.

The Communists had something of their own "rotation system", although it was based on the more militarily sensible concept of rotating units rather than individual soldiers. No individual PVA or KPA soldier ever acquired the "right" to leave the battlefront. The 18 PVA armies were divided into two groups for rotation through the front lines every two to three months. The individual Communist trooper, however, did leave the line, and in vast numbers: killed, wounded, sick, captured or defected, although neither the PRC nor the DPRK have issued accurate figures. Three PVA groups of about 2.3 million men rotated in and out of Korea during the war, that is, about 66 per cent of the entire CPA field forces.

In sum, the UN programme strengthened individual soldier morale but at a cost in military effectiveness. Men who were approaching the magic "36" number were understandably cautious in the line, and individual rotation nearly destroyed unit cohesiveness. The UN system protected the individual at considerable cost to the unit. The Communists' system went strictly by the unit, with no concern for the individual in this matter. On the other hand, those Chinese troops who did survive the front were battle-hardened veterans, and unit cohesion was preserved.

Upon General Ridgway's elevation to Far East and UN Commander, command of Eighth Army devolved upon Lieutenant-General James Van Fleet, who was promoted to full general rank at the end of July 1951. Van Fleet was a graduate of the US Military Academy, class of 1915, with such classmates as Omar Bradley and Dwight Eisenhower. He was a proven quantity with outstanding service in the Second World War in Europe and with credit for guiding the Greek military to a complete victory over a Communist insurgency in the post-war years. It would be difficult to imagine a better choice. Van Fleet was a quiet, assured, excellent combat commander and a loyal soldier, but he would become increasingly frustrated with the Korean military stalemate. Immediately after his retirement he aroused controversy by claiming that political decisions in Washington had prevented him from driving on to total victory in 1951. Van Fleet's frustration over the course of the war was compounded by the loss of his son, a USAF pilot, over North Korea.

On the battlefield, the Chinese were gathering strength for their Spring Offensive, their last major advance of the war. CPV commanders informed their troops on 19 April that "this is the campaign that will determine the fate and length of the Korean War". In many ways it did, but not as the Chinese and the North Koreans had anticipated.

Again, as with the Battle for Hoengsong, the UN Command had a good inkling of what was to come. The general lack of cover on Korea's denuded hills and UN control of the air meant that the UNC would soon know of any major Communist preparations. In fact, when the 24th Division Commander notified I Corps that he expected to come under attack "in about two hours", he was proved correct almost to the minute. Despite this general foreknowledge, once again ROK forces fell back in disorder before the Chinese on 22 April, and once again US and Allied troops found their flanks peeled open and had to scramble to regroup in the opening days of the offensive. The US 24th Division and the Turkish brigade were penetrated, but they pulled back in relatively good order while the British 29th Brigade, the Belgian Battalion and the Filipino Combat Team all gave good accounts of themselves while falling back. Some officers on Van Fleet's staff had recommended more extensive withdrawals to better defensive positions, but he overruled them, replying that the enemy would have to "take all he gets".

Certainly the Chinese found no easy withdrawal when they encountered the gunners of the 92nd Armored Field Artillery Battalion along the Chichon-ni road. Within two hours the artillerymen, with the aid of Marine tanks sent forward as reinforcements, had completely destroyed a 2,000-man force from the Chinese 120th Division, at a cost of four dead and eleven wounded and were in marching order at the end of the clash. The following day some 400 soldiers of the *Inmin Gun's* 45th Division made the mistake of assembling in a steep-sided deep gully within full view of a US artillery forward observer. At the end of a battalion time-on-target barrage of 15 volleys using variable time fuses, an observer saw just two shocked North Koreans stumble out of the gully.

But the ROK 6th Division bolted for the rear, entangling the New Zealand artillery, the Middlesex Battalion and the US 213th Field Artillery Battalion, which had moved up to support the 6th. The three battalions retreated in good order with no loss of troops or equipment, except for one 213th howitzer which had to be run off the road to avoid smashing into a group of milling ROK soldiers. US Company B, 2nd Chemical Mortar Battalion staged a less successful retreat, its troops leaving behind 35 vehicles loaded with equipment. In addition, two American engineer companies which pulled out in confusion, abandoned tents, kitchens, several trucks and a just-installed water point. These lapses were somewhat redeemed by persistent American tankers who made several trips under intense fire to rescue Australian wounded. They then tidied up the battlefield by driving out the abandoned vehicles of the departed chemical mortarmen and retrieving the equipment shed by the engineers in their hurried retreat that morning.

Commonwealth forces continued to give a fine account of themselves, as the Kiwi artillerymen broke up a Communist force crossing the Kapyong River and Canadian mortarmen and machine gunners blasted back numerous Chinese assaults. The heaviest cost was to the Australians, who lost 31 killed and 58 wounded, while the Canadians suffered 10 killed and 23 wounded.

With the end of this Chinese offensive, the UNC pointedly investigated how two Commonwealth battalions and a US tank company could beat back attacks equivalent to those that had routed the ROK 6th Division. The UNC was angered that the 6th's precipitous retreat had caused its supporting US units to lose some 73 vehicles, 15 105mm howitzers and considerable equipment as they tried to push their way past overturned ROK vehicles and other abandoned impedimenta. The 6th's commander argued that his division's problems stemmed from a lack of training. But General Van Fleet rejected this explanation. He pointed out that the division had acquitted itself well in past actions. Echoing General Ridgway, Van Fleet emphasized the intangibles of military leadership, such as devotion to duty and physical and moral courage. The performance of the 6th certainly undermined President Rhee's continuing demands for a larger ROK army. Ridgway and Van Fleet pointed out the obvious: the ROK Army had far less need for more men than for more competent leadership. Such leadership was conspicuously absent, from the minister of defence down to the lowest platoon leader in the ROK ranks. Soon after, the UNC did order a much more professional and rigorous programme of training for ROK officers and NCOs. It should be emphasized again that the UN Command, acting on the orders of the US Joint Chiefs of Staff, had control of all forces fighting the Communists in Korea, and this command included the ROK Army, which certainly simplified such matters.

The Chinese Spring Offensive was also marked by the near-destruction of the British Gloucestershire Battalion – The Glosters – in the one great epic stand of this war. The Glosters were cut off south of the Imjin River and despite US, Filipino and ROK armoured thrusts to save them, suffered debilitating losses. The surviving ranking officer had given his remaining 100 men the choice of remaining behind to surrender or going with him to try to make their way to UN lines; not a man took the surrender option. A guardian angel USAF "Mosquito" liaison aircraft guided the group in the right direction and called in friendly fighter aircraft which shot up the Chinese-held ridges, but to little effect. Even the 40 survivors of this group might have been lost were it not for the ROK 1st Division commander who earlier forwarded a battalion and two US heavy tank platoons into the area. Although the force could not reach the Gloster positions, the American tankers penetrated closely enough to meet up with the retreating remnants. Trotting alongside or riding on the rear of the tanks which continually sprayed the surrounding hills with heavy machine gun fire, the pitiably small number of Glosters were finally brought to safety. Of 699 men on the rolls at the opening of the Chinese offensive, 530 were captured, of whom 153 had been wounded. Twenty-six would die in the rigours of Communist POW camps. But the sacrifice had not been in vain; intelligence information indicated that the Glosters' stand had helped to upset the attack schedule of the Chinese XIX Army Group. The Glosters' stand is memorable for the manner in which the troops acquitted themselves and for the fact that this was the one case in which the Chinese commander's strategy of destroying a non-ROK unit to take the heart out of foreign support for the war came close to success.

The "Epic Stand of the Glosters" received great publicity in Great Britain and the United States, and, if anything, the tributes were more fulsome in the latter than in the former. The Glosters received an American Presidential Unit Citation for "the most outstanding example of united bravery in modern warfare". This was something of a pardonable exaggeration, but General Van Fleet did assert that the Glosters' stand "saved Seoul and saved the Eighth Army". (After the war, General Ridgway privately criticized the Commonwealth Brigadier for not understanding that the Gloster commander, Lieutenant Colonel James P. Carne, was a man given to understatement, whose reports did not reflect the full seriousness of his battalion's situation. Ridgway concluded that "the Gloster battalion should not have been lost".)

Ridgway had continued his usual pattern of withdrawing in the face of Communist offensives until they petered out. The one exception came with the defence of Seoul. The UN Commander concluded that the loss of the city for a third time to the Communists "would ruin the spirit of the [ROK] nation". Artillery was set up in the very grounds of the Presidential Palace. This time the Communists would have to fight hard for Seoul. But by late April it was obvious that, once again, the CPV offensive was sputtering to a close. Chinese killed on the I Corps front were estimated to number some 45,000, approximately the strength of five Chinese divisions, and the Communists' supply situation was becoming critical. Total US divisional dead numbered 314 killed. And once again the Communists had melted back. It was an indication of the transformed spirit of Eighth Army that General Van Fleet replied to reports that five Chinese armies were massing for an attack in the west central section by saying, "I welcome his attack." Captured Chinese troops began to deprecate their army doctrine of "man over weapons", conceding that such theories worked only when their enemy's technological superiority was not too great.

General Van Fleet may have been prepared for and even welcomed the next Chinese offensive, but recent history was replayed when the attack did come along the Soyang River; the ROK 6th Division again collapsed and again entangled US forces, this time the US 2nd Division. That veteran unit, however, in spite of the confusion and their own appreciable losses, inflicted serious casualties on its opponents. The 23rd Infantry Regiment of the 2nd, for instance, suffered 72 troopers killed, 158 wounded and 190 missing. The regiment also abandoned more than 150 vehicles. But in return it had inflicted an estimated 2,200 killed and 1,400 wounded on the Chinese 31st, 35th, and 181st Divisions. The heavily outnumbered troops of Company K, 38th Infantry, cannily allowed the Chinese into their own lines. They stayed in their bunkers and called down a blanket of artillery fire on their own positions, which did little serious damage to the well-constructed bunkers. But upon emerging, the Americans counted no fewer than 800 Chinese bodies. Massive and precise bombing by formations of USAF B-29s also broke up impending major Communist attacks, a welcome change from the earlier obliteration of empty landscapes along the Pusan Perimeter.

Their units battered and bleeding, the Chinese command now ordered a rather rapid withdrawal, so rapid, in fact, that Van Fleet's inevitable counter-attack could not reach most of the Communist units. An exception was an incident in which Chinese troops were trapped below Chiami-ni. They had the added misfortune of attempting to break out against what would have seemed easy prey, a medical company perimeter. Yet Chinese losses at the hands of the hard-fighting medics totalled some 300 killed, 400 wounded, and 400 demoralized troops taken prisoner.

In fact, CPV troops were surrendering in large groups and totalled nearly 38,000 POWs just from the most recent contained offensive. The failure of the latest "human wave" Chinese offensive was palpable. The Netherlands Battalion on Hill 975 in May reported that attacking Chinese came on in waves, walking upright through an artillery bombardment, not even crouching as soldiers tend to when moving under heavy enemy fire. Those not hit simply stepped over their fallen comrades. Here was also evidence that, although the top Chinese command was capable enough and battle-hardened, lower-level leadership had learned little in their battles, and accordingly suffered casualties that were eventually insupportable even for the manpower-rich CPV. The reconstituted *Inmin Gun*, however, remained a relatively unknown entity, although it seemed to be fighting well at the time.

The Communist defeat in the fifth campaign/offensive forced the Beijing leaders, and in particular Mao, to reconsider their hopes for total victory. Even for the Beijing leadership, the butcher's bill was becoming too high. They argued that by throwing the UNC forces out of North Korea and by pushing them well away from China's borders they had achieved a large measure of success. Now was the time to extract the best terms they could from the UNC by "fighting while at the same time negotiating".

Obviously, Kim Il Sung would prove less than enchanted with this new interpretation of the Communists' war aims. He was invited to Beijing in early June to confer with the PRC leadership. As well as pointing out some military realities to Kim, the Beijing leadership argued more positively that negotiations could also cover such topics as the gradual withdrawal of foreign troops from Korea and the settlement of the Korean question itself. Kim, about as wrongheaded as he had been in June 1950, responded that the Communist armies still held the military advantage whatever their casualties and that, at the least, the Communist side could extract better terms by annihilating more UN forces. Kim's contentions were hardly based on any first-hand knowledge, as he was rarely seen near the front. He demanded of Mao and Chou En-lai an immediate offensive to restore the 38th Parallel. Although the CPV commander was amenable to Kim's demand, deputy CPV commander Deng Hua thought such action premature in the face of the now well-fortified UNC, and apparently so convinced Mao. By now the CPV was the major Communist force in Korea, and Kim had to yield to the new Chinese strategy.

Although the UN forces had emerged victorious on the battlefield, the US Joint Chiefs of Staff came to a remarkably similar conclusion about the war at about the same time as Beijing. On 1 May they issued orders restricting the depth of any Eighth Army advance. The UNC forces had not suffered anything like the losses of the CPV or the *Inmin Gun*, and there was strong sentiment in the US military to take advantage of the Communists' current disarray and advance at least to a Pyongyang–Wonsan line across the "waist" of Korea. But the US held back from this course partly because it would have required a major mobilization of US manpower and resources, but primarily because Washington was fairly well convinced that the main Communist threat remained in Europe and that the bulk of the Western defence effort must be concentrated on that continent. A US Central Intelligence estimate of "Probable Developments in the World Situation Through Mid-1953", drawn up in September 1951, devoted the bulk of its analysis to the Soviet Union and its threat to Western Europe.

> The Soviet bloc will probably by mid-1953 still be able to carry out almost all of the offensive operations of which they are presently considered capable, except in the unlikely event that the effectiveness of new weapons developed, produced and actually employed by the West should offset the present preponderance of Soviet military strength on the Eurasian continent.[3]

Thus, on 16 May the US National Security Council, acting with the advice of the Joint Chiefs and America's allies and with the subsequent approval of President Truman, officially declared that the United States would seek to conclude the fighting in Korea with a suitable armistice. Now the UN allies would indeed seek a "substitute for victory".

There was already considerable diplomatic activity, much of it unrecorded, in the lobbies and lounges of the United Nations as well as in Beijing. The eminent State Department official and scholar, George Kennan (who had previously dismissed Korean nationalist claims), met privately several times with the Soviet delegate to the UN, Jacob Malik, at the latter's summer home on Long Island, New York. (Note that Malik did not come to Kennan, a point that seemed to have escaped the latter.) On 22 June the US State Department's radio Voice of America obsequiously called on Malik to "say the one word the whole world is waiting for", again more the approach of a supplicant than of the voice of a military command that had defeated a string of Communist offensives. In fact, this ill-advised effort set the tone for the subsequent early armistice negotiations, in which the Communist side managed to make the UN Command look the defeated party suing for peace.

Jacob Malik did graciously "say the word" on 23 June 1951. The US and its allies joyously and quickly instructed General Ridgway to respond positively. Malik's statement came immediately after a Moscow meeting between Stalin, Kim Il Sung and Gao Gang, representing the PRC. Yet the evidence is strong that the Communist side was not prepared at the time to bargain in good faith for an end to the fighting. On 13 June Mao had advised Gao Gang that:

> we consider it advisable for Korea and China to advance this question [armistice negotiations] today, since in the next two months the Korean Army and Chinese volunteer troops must occupy a defensive position. . . . [But] in June and July preparations will be carried out intensively. In August we will carry out a stronger operation. . . . If the enemy does not send new reinforcements to Korea and does not make an amphibious landing, then in August we will be significantly stronger than now.[4]

On the same day, Mao cabled "Filippov" (another Stalin alias) the same message: "In July we will be stronger than in June and in August we will be even stronger. We will be ready in August to make a stronger blow to the enemy." Mao noted on 26 June that

> the government of the PRC intends to send fighter divisions armed with MiG-15s to Korea for participation in the military actions. It is therefore necessary in the course of one and a half to two months to retrain the 6th, 12th, and 14th fighter divisions, which are armed with MiG-9s, or MiG-15s, with a calculation of sending them to the front in September 1951. The government of the PRC asks you to give an order to the Soviet comrades in China to retrain the 6th, 12th and 14th fighter divisions on MiG-15s in the indicated periods.[5]

This statement came only three days after Jacob Malik spoke piously of "a sincere desire to put an end to the bloody fighting in Korea". And on the 28th, Stalin's military representative in Beijing reported to the Soviet leader that the MiG-9 fighter divisions would indeed be retrained on the much more advanced MiG-15. The period of retraining was established as one and a half to two months so that these air divisions could take part in the forthcoming operations in Korea.

Kim Il Sung, on the other hand, seems to have been out of the picture. He wired Mao as late as 29 June, "How should we relate to this? How should we answer, if Ridgway wants to conduct negotiations?"[6] Although Mao was more forceful and presented his own views, it was Stalin who now controlled the negotiations on the Communist side, and Stalin counselled delay.

There was heated debate in Washington over the public expressions of the Communists' desire for armistice talks. The "hawks" in the US government were later excoriated for their skepticism over these offers, for their "obsessive anti-Communism", which rendered them incapable of seizing a worthwhile opportunity for peace. Their views were summarized by USAF Chief of Staff Hoyt Vandenberg, who argued that the UNC was now hurting the Communists badly and any respite given them by an armistice would only give them a breathing space to build up and to start fighting again. In the end the arguments of Secretary of State Acheson prevailed and put the United States on the road to negotiations with the Communists. However, the historical record validates those who feared that the Communists, badly hurt on the Korean battlefields, were primarily playing for time.

Ridgway's first proposal that the negotiations take place aboard a Danish hospital ship in Wonsan harbour was rejected by the Communists, but both sides soon after agreed to meet at Kaesong, Korea's ancient capital, just below the 38th Parallel.

On 8 July 1951 the first UN negotiation liaison teams drove up for their first meeting at Kaesong in jeeps on which white flags were innocently mounted as had been helpfully suggested by the Communists "to avoid confusion". The image was flashed around the world by gloating leftist press/propaganda: the US was entering negotiations as a beaten supplicant. Nonetheless, the Chinese and the Americans, as well as the North Koreans, were meeting as military equals. (This was not the first time that KPA and US negotiators had met. There had been face-to-face negotiations near Kaesong in 1949 for the release of the two US officials captured in the defection of the *Kimbell R. Smith*.)

Some professed to see significance in the fact that these developments were taking place on the first anniversary of the outbreak of the war. In actuality, they were almost exclusively in response to the course of events on the battlefield and the fact that neither side was willing any longer to pay the price for victory. As it was, stalemate had cost the Communists close to 1 million casualties (UNC POW cages also bulged with some 163,000 captives). UNC losses themselves now approached 294,000; 215,000 ROK, 77,000 US and 4,500 other UN units. But on any objective balance sheet, the Communists had been hurt on the battlefield far more by this war than had the UN forces.

General Ridgway had meanwhile aroused some Joint Chiefs' interest in his plan for a major three-pronged offensive, commencing 1 September, to occupy a line across the waist of the peninsula, Pyongyang–Wonsan. Oddly, in light of General Van Fleet's later assertions that victory had been snatched from him at the time, it was Van Fleet who had counselled Ridgway that this offensive not be carried out unless there would be a major deterioration in Communist forces by 1 September. Ridgway instead would confine his command to strong patrolling and local attacks.

Overall, the UNC exaggerated the ability of the Communists to recover from its recent defeats. On the other hand, the UNC's unexpected retreat from North Korea, stemming from a gross underestimation of the Chinese military, had now given the command a more realistic respect for its adversary.

When the victorious Chinese Communist leader Mao Tse-tung had addressed hundreds of thousands of followers in Beijing at the proclamation of the Chinese People's Republic in 1949, he declared in a much-repeated phrase that "the Chinese people have finally stood up!" But Mao's victory over the bedraggled Nationalist armies did not particularly impress most foreign observers. Rather, it could more accurately be said that when the representatives of Mao's armies on 8 July 1951 met the Americans at Kaesong as military equals for the first time, China had indeed "stood up".

Chapter Nine

The United Nations' first war

The Korean War was the first and only protracted conflict conducted under the auspices of the UN. All other UN military ventures have been to separate belligerents and to maintain that separation. They have all been on a much smaller scale than the Korean conflict. In Korea the moral authority of the United Nations was employed to label the Democratic People's Republic of Korea the aggressor and to rally member states either to drive the aggressors from the Republic of Korea or at least to support that effort. That commitment would endure for three years.

The UN involvement with Korea goes back well before the beginning of the Korean War. In 1947 the Truman administration, in the wake of the failure of a mixed US/Soviet commission to agree upon the reunification of Korea and the Soviet Union's rejection of a US proposed four-power conference to discuss steps towards that reunification, placed the question before the UN General Assembly. The US resolution called for a nine-nation UN Temporary Commission on Korea (UNTCOK) and for elections no later than March of the following year. The resolution passed on 14 November by a wide margin and with little fanfare; the contemporaneous UN partition plan for Palestine, the Greek civil war and the question of the international control of atomic energy absorbed reporting on that international body's deliberations. When UNTCOK arrived in Korea the Soviet commander refused access to the North. This was the first of a series of Soviet and North Korean blunders that would eventually put these two states in the embarrassing position of being in opposition to the world body, and in the case of North Korea, eventually in armed opposition.

The United States then argued successfully that elections should be held at least in the South where UNTCOK could move relatively freely. These elections (May 1948) supervised by UNTCOK resulted in the establishment of an anti-Communist regime, the Republic of Korea (ROK). In August of that year, the old reactionary patriot Syngman Rhee took his place as ROK President. UNTCOK certified that the elections reflected the freely expressed will of the Korean people – in the South – and thus gave the ROK the stamp of international approval.

Nonetheless, Great Britain and Canada did not support the US position that the 1948 elections had established a national government for Korea, but they did agree that the ROK was the only legitimate regime on the peninsula, a fine distinction that was undoubtedly lost on many casual observers. On 6 December the UN Political and Security Committee voted to reject the DPRK's petition for legitimacy and instead invited the ROK to send delegates to the UN. Two days later it voted by a large majority to adopt a US-sponsored resolution calling for the withdrawal of all foreign troops from Korea, a position ratified by the General Assembly on 12 December, despite criticism from the Soviets; Moscow actually called for UNTCOK's disbandment. Instead, within 30 days UNTCOK would be working with the ROK for Korean reunification. All of this, of course, reflected the overwhelming power and influence that the United States held in the UN before the mass admissions of Asian and African states beginning in the later 1950s.

Undeterred, the DPRK as well as the ROK made application for UN membership. But when the UN Membership Committee recommended acceptance of the ROK, the Soviet Union effectively vetoed South Korea's admission. The sting of this refusal was somewhat removed by UNTCOK's remaining in the ROK and reporting on any progress towards reunification. UNTCOK iterated, however, that without Soviet–US co-operation Korea would never be reunited and would more than likely face a terrible civil war. Far from being a "tool" of the US, UNTCOK blamed both super powers about equally for Korea's persisting disunion. Somewhat to the disgust of the US State Department, it also criticized the authoritarian Rhee regime.

On the very eve of the Korean War it was two Royal Australian Air Force UNTCOK military observers who provided the earliest contemporary evidence of the lack of culpability of the ROK in initiating that conflict (see Chapter Three). The subsequent UNTCOK report was not suddenly produced in the wake of the opening of the Korean War to indict the DPRK. Rather, it was drafted in Seoul on 24 June, one day before the North's invasion. On 26 June UNTCOK cabled a précis to the UN Secretary General in New York. It was later reproduced as UN Security Council document S/1507. On the basis of this report, the Security Council determined that, in the absence of any evidence to the contrary, North Korea had indeed invaded South Korea.

Independently of any of this, on the day of the North Korean invasion, 25 June 1950 (New York time), the Security Council condemned that attack as "a breach of the peace" and called for the North "to withdraw forthwith". With the UNTCOK observers' précis in hand the next day, the Council felt that it need use no ambiguity or "even-handedness" here in determining the aggressor. And unlike previous military crises, as in Palestine in 1948–9, this aggression involved the crossing of a UN-recognized territorial border to attack a UN-supported (if not actual UN member) state.

The UN Secretary General, Trygve Lie, matched the United States in his determination to deal with the North's aggression. Both had very much in mind the disastrous results of pre-Second World War "appeasement" of the dictators. In New York, as in Washington, the single word "Munich" was much in use in those days as a shorthand expression of this feeling. Lie's only concession to the Communist side was his removal of the phrase "an unprovoked act of aggression" from the US draft of the resolution.

All of this would have been for naught had the Soviet delegate been present and voting. However, the Soviet delegation remained absent from the Security Council, continuing its boycott, begun in January 1950, to protest the representation there of Nationalist China. Thus the Soviets were forestalled from vetoing UN action in Korea. Such action could have been authorized by the much larger General Assembly, but by then the North Korean Army might well have been in Pusan.

Two days after branding the DPRK as the aggressor in Korea, the Council took the next logical step of calling for members to come to the aid of the embattled Republic of Korea. (Seoul would fall within a day.) All of this was a reaction to the United States' expressed determination to act as well as a new UNTCOK report that the DPRK was carrying out a "well-planned, concerted, and full-scale invasion of South Korea", an accurate enough description of the situation.

Under the sponsorship of Great Britain and France, the Security Council Resolution of 7 July 1950 established a unified command to control all UN forces in Korea, the United Nations Command (UNC), under the direct command of the US Army Far East Commander and Supreme Commander for the Allied Powers in Japan, Douglas MacArthur. MacArthur was authorized to operate under the United Nations flag, but no provision was made for UN supervision of his operations. One week later, all ROK forces were also placed under the UN Command. Thus all military forces fighting the North Korean invasion were officially under UN auspices but in reality under United States military command. This was an arrangement unique in modern military history; command of the Allied armies in the Second World War had remained with each national command structure, with co-ordination among equals at the higher levels, such as the Supreme Headquarters Allied Forces Europe (SHAEF), although even then the United States did increasingly dominate decisions simply by reason of its greater resources.

When the war turned in favour of the UNC, the UN authorized entry of its forces into the territory of the DPRK in October 1950 – after General MacArthur had already ordered his troops into North Korea and ROK troops had actually crossed the 38th Parallel. In other words, this momentous decision had already been taken out of the hands of the UN by the UN Command.

The UN did reassert itself when it resolved that it would recognize no current regime as having "legal and effective control" over all of Korea. To begin the process of establishing a Korea-wide government, the United Nations established the UN Commission for the Unification and Rehabilitation of Korea (UNCURK). In the meantime the UNC began to administer military government throughout the North. Basically the US and ROK armies would do the job. This concession hardly mollified Syngman Rhee, who angrily protested to the UNC Commander that his regime was the legitimate government for all of Korea and warned that he was already dispatching governors for five of the North's "liberated" provinces.

Even before the massive incursion of the Chinese People's Volunteers into Korea, the UN General Assembly invited representatives of the PRC, which was not, of course, a member at the time, to its temporary headquarters at Lake Success, New York to discuss the Korean question. The delegation arrived in New York on 24 November 1950, the very day that General MacArthur launched his abortive home-by-Christmas offensive. The delegation's head, Wu Hsui-ch'uan, addressed the General Assembly for two hours and uncompromisingly demanded the condemnation of the US "aggressors" and the withdrawal of its forces from Taiwan and Korea. Wu further denounced the Taiwan UN delegate for using English (which was, after all, a language of diplomacy) in the subsequent debate, thus supposedly confirming the latter's status as a lackey of the Americans. Wu's delegation returned soon after, but not before cleaning out numerous exclusive Manhattan shops of their bourgeois luxuries. The delegation had made clear its uncompromising position that any armistice must be linked to the status of Taiwan and the PRC's right to a UN seat. The feeling among most Asian and African leaders that the world's most populous nation was surely entitled to representation in the UN, was weakened by the PRC's continuing to reject out of hand the recommendations of the UN Cease-Fire Group. Thus the UN Political Committee could adopt a US resolution condemning China as an aggressor and calling for the consideration of additional anti-Beijing measures.

Almost surrealistically, with the military situation in Korea deteriorating daily, the UN approved a US-sponsored resolution on 1 December 1950 "providing for the relief and rehabilitation of Korea". The resolution created the UN Korean Reconstruction Agency, which, of course, could not function in the DPRK, and which at the time seemed unlikely to operate for long in the ROK, either. Eventually the UNKRA came to do good work in the rehabilitation of South Korea, despite obstructionist tactics by the Rhee regime. Along with the UNC's Civil Assistance Command Korea (UNCACK) and the American Economic Cooperation Administration, it can be said that UNKRA laid the foundations for South Korea's eventual emergence as an Asian economic super-power.

In reaction to the stunning, massive Chinese intervention into the war, the UN General Assembly passed a resolution on 12 December 1950 sponsored by 13 nations from the Asian–African group to determine from the Chinese on what basis they would accept a cease-fire. It forestalled an unhelpful Soviet resolution calling for the total withdrawal of all foreign forces from the peninsula. The UN also called for China to halt at the 38th Parallel. (A little later, a high-ranking PRC Foreign Ministry official pointedly inquired of Indian diplomats as to why those 13 nations had not proposed a cease-fire a few months earlier when UN forces had crossed the same sacrosanct parallel.) The United States reluctantly supported the proposal, having already made the decision to return to its original objectives in the war, that is, the clearing of the Republic of Korea of its invaders. The Soviets opposed the 13-power resolution and its implementation of a UN Cease-Fire Group, although just two months earlier, the same Soviet delegate had called for a cease-fire. But then the Communist side at that time was losing the war. (As with the 13-nation resolution, it obviously all depended on whose ox was being gored.)

On 21 December 1950, Mao specifically ordered Peng Dehuai, commander of the Chinese People's Volunteers, "to cross the 38th parallel". (Note, not just to clear the "imperialists" and their "puppets" from North Korea.) The next day Beijing formally rejected the 13-nation cease-fire resolution. But at least now the United States could show the world that it had made a good faith effort to halt the war on reasonable terms. At the same time the Truman administration could simultaneously stand up to its critics at home and point out that it was still very much in the fight against "international communist aggression".

By the middle of December the UN Cease-Fire Group had worked out terms acceptable to the UNC. But the Chinese considered the Group illegal because the PRC had taken no part in its establishment.

153

The US-sponsored UN Resolution of 1 February 1951 was that body's most tangible expression of its reaction to China's uncompromising position on the Korean question. By a vote of 47 to 7, with 9 abstentions, the General Assembly condemned the People's Republic as an aggressor in Korea and established yet another committee, the UN Additional Measures Committee, which with the UN Good Offices Committee (successor to the Cease-Fire Committee), took up the question of a resolution of the conflict. Many UN members were unenthusiastic about the resolution, fearing that it might exasperate the Chinese and bring Asia closer to general war. But then, failure to support the resolution might lead the United States to go it alone, unrestrained, with results possibly as dire.

In all truth, the Chinese in late 1950 and early 1951 were not particularly interested in any mediation by an international body from which they were excluded and which was dominated by its enemies in Korea. But more importantly, China was winning the Korean War and could see no benefit in any cease-fire or settlement that might enable the "imperialists" by diplomatic manoeuvring, to snatch a cease-fire from the jaws of defeat. Mao also seemed to be infected by the same "victory disease" that had blinded General MacArthur in his race to the North a scant two months earlier. Furthermore, Beijing had to stand by its North Korean ally. Kim Il Sung was certainly not about to end his dream of a united, Communist, utopian Korea at this moment of renewed victory. But the UN should be given some credit. Public debates served to release pent-up emotions on both sides, and delegates' private pressures on the United States may have deterred that nation from more precipitate action in the wake of Chinese intervention. Finally, China had hopes at the time of bargaining on the question of the status of Formosa/Taiwan, on its admission to the UN and on any Japanese peace treaty, and thus did not slam the door entirely on negotiations on Asian matters.

UN backing for the ROK was not confined to resolutions of support. Forty-nine nations went considerably further, contributing supplies, money and equipment. Four more, India, Norway, Sweden and Denmark, provided hospital units. Denmark also sent a valued hospital ship, while India deployed the largest non-US medical unit to Korea, the 60th Indian Field Ambulance and Surgical Unit. These latter nations, while proclaiming their neutrality in the conflict, nonetheless sent far less medical aid to North Korea. Even India, which publicly rarely passed up any opportunity to criticize the West, confined most of its highly regarded medical aid to the South. The Indian doctors and medics, each airborne-qualified and a veteran of the bitter fighting in Burma during the Second World War, provided such good service that troops from Allied units that had their own perfectly adequate medical support facilities would often attempt to obtain treatment from the 60th.

Fifteen UN member-states from every continent but Antarctica dispatched fighting units. These nations aided South Korea from a variety of motives, ranging from fear of Communism and of the consequences of unchecked aggression, to a desire to improve their international image or their relations with the USA.

The UN coalition that fought in Korea was hardly of the magnitude of the Allied forces in the Second World War. In fact, 11 years after the end of the Korean War, the US Joint Chiefs of Staff actually advised *against* relying on allies in the Vietnam War by asserting that the US had gained "no significant support in Korea. . . . The US did essentially all of the fighting, took all of the casualties [Fortunately, the South Koreans presumably did not get wind of this assertion.], and paid all of the bills."[1]

It would be difficult to imagine a more ignorant and uncharitable misreading of recent history. The USA did furnish 50.3 per cent of UNC ground forces, 85.9 per cent of the naval and 92.4 per cent of the air forces in the Korean War. The ROK provided 40.1 per cent of ground forces, 7.4 per cent of the naval and 5.6 per cent of the air forces to save their nation. But even from a tangible viewpoint (the only one that seemed to matter in the MacNamara era when that Army report was drawn up) it could have been noted that Allied contributions gave the UNC the equivalent of an additional two divisions and took 15,000 casualties that would have been borne by the US or the South Koreans. Intangibly, those contributions legitimized the conflict as an international struggle against aggression, rather than a mere civil war into which the US had intervened or blundered. By 1953 a respectable 15 per cent of the 155-mile Korean battle line was held by non-US/non-ROK ground forces. And the newly formed North Atlantic Treaty Organization (NATO), specifically organized in 1949 to rally resistance to Soviet expansion, basically fulfilled its mission; every NATO nation, with the exception of prickly Iceland, contributed land, sea and/or air forces to the UN cause. As will be noted below, several non-NATO nations, such as Colombia, the Philippines and Turkey, also dispatched troops to Korea. (Taiwan was actually the first nation to offer ground troops, but these were refused for political reasons – fear of China entering the conflict – and the feeling that the Guomindang had not done all that well against the Communists anyway, or they wouldn't have found themselves barricaded on Taiwan in the first place.)

After the South Koreans and the Americans, British Commonwealth forces (first entry into combat, 13 November 1950) represented the largest contribution of military manpower to the UNC and were the first, again after the US, to dispatch ground forces to Korea. The Labour government of Prime Minister Clement Attlee did seem more concerned with gaining leverage to prevent the Americans from embarking on some anti-Communist "crusade" against the People's Republic of China than in coming to the defence of a victim of aggression. In fact, the UK military service chiefs only reluctantly acquiesced in the Prime Minister's decision, feeling that Great Britain's armed forces were stretched too thinly as it was.

Australia's contribution in proportion to its population was greater than any other UNC ally, again except for that of the United States and the ROK. This commitment was understandable, considering Australia's relatively close proximity to the Korean peninsula, closer than any other UNC ally, except Thailand. The dominion also had strong memories of being actually bombed by the Japanese early in the Second World War; Korea and Japan are about equidistant from Australia. In the immediate post-war years Australia had reoriented its defence policy toward the United States and had begun to pay much more attention to Asia.

Royal Australian Air Force No. 77 Squadron, flying US-built, piston-engine P-51 Mustang fighters, was the first non-ROK, non-US unit to enter the Korean War. The unit had been based in Japan as part of the USAF's Fifth Air Force and thus was familiar with the Americans' air procedures. The Australian airmen went on to render valuable aid in the defence of the Pusan Perimeter and throughout the war. No. 77 Squadron served within 5th US Air Force, and, in fact, its official history is titled *Across the parallel: the Australian 77th Squadron in the United States Air Force in the Korean War* (G. Odgers, 1954).

Australia also sent an infantry battalion, the Third of the Royal Australian Regiment, which entered combat on 5 November 1950. The Third then acted as rear guard for retreating US and ROK forces from North Korea, and later advanced towards Seoul in the UN counter-offensives of early 1951. As part of the British 27th Brigade, and backed by the Canadian infantry battalion and the New Zealand artillery regiment, the Third defeated a Chinese division in a major action at Kapyong. As noted, the first commander of the Australian battalion, up front with his troops as usual, was killed by a stray shard of Chinese shell while in his tent, just after a clash.

As early as 29 June 1950, the Australian government authorized the deployment of frigate HMAS *Shoalhaven* and destroyer HMAS *Bataan* (the latter's name a nice touch, commemorating as it did the US last-ditch defence of the Philippine Bataan Peninsula in the early days of the Second World War in the Pacific). For the remainder of the war, Australia continuously maintained two destroyers or frigates in Korean waters. In October, aircraft carrier HMAS *Sidney* arrived off Korea, carrying two squadrons of piston-engine Sea Furies and one of Fireflies, all organized as 20th Carrier Air Group. *Sidney* was Australia's only aircraft carrier and the dominion's only combat deployment of carrier aviation.

The first British ground unit, 27th Brigade, helped defend the Pusan Perimeter. In all, nine British regiments served in Korea, one being the immortal Glosters. The Commonwealth forces were first attached as independent units to US Army divisions, then later unified as the 1st British Commonwealth Division (which included the Indian 60th Field Ambulance and Surgical Unit) and assigned as a unit to US 1st Corps. After the Pusan Perimeter battles, they advanced towards the Yalu, opened a gate for the retreating 2nd US Division running the gauntlet from Kunu-ri in the North, and fought the hard battles that halted the Chinese offensives in the first half of 1951. The general American opinion was that the British commander, General A. J. H. Cassels and the Canadian Brigadier, J. M. Rockingham, personified the best of the Commonwealth's military heritage. And, aside from their military virtues, both displayed exemplary tact and diplomacy in their integrated command.

There were appreciable differences in military doctrine and outlook between the British and the Americans. For one, the British believed in taking the high ground in defence whereas the Americans stressed holding the slopes to deliver the maximum of interlocking fire. (The latter may have had some history on their side: a British-commanded Tory force, ensconced on the summit of King's Mountain, South Carolina, during the War for American Independence, was almost annihilated by American "over the mountain men" making their murderous way up the slopes; the Tories consistently fired over the heads of the Americans.)

The Royal Navy's commitment was also made promptly. Within days of the UN Security Council's authorization of military assistance to the Republic of Korea, a fleet of RN vessels from the Far Eastern Squadron headed by light carrier *Triumph* was conducting military operations in Korean waters. As early as 2 July 1950 RN cruiser *Jamaica* and frigate *Black Swan* participated in the destruction of five DPRK torpedo and motor gunboats in the first and only fleet action of the war, albeit a quite one-sided clash. The following day, fleet aircraft from *Triumph*, stationed off the west coast, began to strike targets inland and to fly air and anti-submarine patrols over Anglo–American Task Force 77. It was also at about this time that the first hospital ship of the Korean War, HMHS *Maine*, entered the war zone.

Not surprisingly, the British naval contribution to the Korean War was exceeded only by that of the US Navy. No fewer than four Royal Navy aircraft carriers, *Glory, Theseus, Ocean* and *Triumph*, served in Korean waters, along with cruisers *Belfast, Jamaica, Birmingham, Kenya* and *Newcastle*, destroyers

Cossack, Consort, Cockade, Comus and *Charity* (obviously of the "C" class), and other RN warships. Close co-operation between USN and RN naval staffs recalled the similar co-ordination of the Second World War, which included a regular sharing of assets. In fact, the entire west coast of Korea, up to latitude 39/30, was under an RN admiral, Rear-Admiral William G. Andrewes, who commanded all Commonwealth and non-USN allied warships and most of those of other coalition naval forces. To improve liaison with the USN, Admiral Andrewes established RN theatre headquarters at Sasebo, the Japanese port which was also the site of US Navy fleet headquarters.

The RN was allotted its missions along the west coast because Great Britain recognized the People's Republic of China; any wanderings of Commonwealth vessels into PRC waters could thus be handled through established diplomatic channels. (The east coast naval group was under USN operational control and contained all the USN units.) British and US naval forces engaged in similar off-shore bombardment, blockade, raiding and naval air attack missions against their respective coastal areas.

Because of its dominance in Korea's western waters, RN ships, strongly represented in the Inchon landings, also conducted diversionary manoeuvres along the opposite coast. With the turn of the tide against the UN, a Commonwealth-led destroyer force boldly sailed up the Taedong River estuary in hazardous weather to evacuate personnel from Pyongyang. In another even more hazardous riverine operation, RN ships entered the Han River estuary under constant threat from the North Korean-held north shore to carry out soundings and place buoys in these shallow, tide-swept waters.

Further north, Commonwealth warships aided UNC-supported North Korean guerrillas in their operations from tiny islands off North Korea's west coast, but were unable to stem the Communist re-taking of the far northern island of Taewa-do in late November 1950. With the stalemate of the ground war, RN maritime duties also settled into the routine of blockade duties, commando operations, and shore bombardment. The RN and the Royal Australian Navy flew approximately 25,000 air sorties. Approximately 3,500 RN personnel served at any one time on some 34 warships in Korean waters during the course of the war. In all, Great Britain, Australia, Canada, New Zealand, Colombia, France and the Netherlands contributed the impressive total of five aircraft carriers, five cruisers, 17 destroyers, 17 frigates and numerous support ships to the UN cause in Korea. And to Canadian destroyer HMCS *Nootka* went the honour of capturing a North Korean mine-layer, the only Communist warship taken during the Korean War.

Lacking bases near Korea, the Royal Air Force's contribution was considerably more modest, but still much valued. It consisted of artillery spotter aircraft and three squadrons of large Sunderland maritime reconnaissance flying boats.

New Zealand provided an artillery regiment, which gave extremely accurate artillery fire at Kapyong (and elsewhere), despite suffering an accidental USAF napalm attack, and despite the fact that not a man had artillery experience when the unit initially landed in Korea. In the last phase of the war, the Kiwi gunners and an additional transport platoon continued to render valuable service to the end of the war.

Canada provided the three-battalion 25th infantry brigade, which entered combat on 21 April 1951. The first battalion forwarded was the Princess Patricia's Light Infantry; later, on yearly rotation, the "Princess Pat's" were replaced first by the 22nd (the traditionally French Canadian "Van Doos") and then by the Royal Canadian Regiment.

The hasty raising of this Canadian all-volunteer force produced some anomalies. Recruiting offices were swamped with volunteers. The harassed authorities gave the most perfunctory of interviews with volunteers – some 30 per cent of whom had to be weeded out later or who deserted (but only before leaving Canada). But those who made it to Korea formed a highly regarded force that proved itself in the battles for nondescript hills and ridges during the last two years of stalemated combat. The battalion was essentially a self-contained unit with its own engineers, medical and support troops. However, the Canadians were issued the US M4A3B8 model of the Sherman tank, which veterans remembered from the Second World War.

The Royal Canadian Air Force contributed Transport Squadron No. 426, equipped with Canadian-built North Star four-engine piston transports. These large aircraft regularly flew important long-range missions between McCord Air Force Base in Washington State and Japan's Haneda Airport. Canadian fighter pilots were attached to 5th US Air Force, where they shot down 20 Communist aircraft.

The Canadians and the British both dispatched units to put down open rebellion in the UNC POW camps. Both contingents were appalled by the laxity they found. Both also felt that the Americans were attempting to spread the blame for one of the UNC's most embarrassing failures of the war, and both commanders protested the failure of the UNC to consult with their governments before dispatching their troops on such a mission. Nonetheless, the troopers straightforwardly assumed their guard duties. (British former Prime Minister Clement Attlee later sniffed that had the camps been under British control there would have been no riots in the first place.) These relatively minor disagreements aside, British Commonwealth troops were consistently highly regarded by their US counterparts, even if the Americans did question the refusal of the "Brits" to wear helmets in action.

The Netherlands contributed an infantry battalion composed primarily of one-year contract soldiers, and attached to the US 38th Infantry Regiment. It first saw action at Wonju on 3 December 1950 and earned a Presidential Unit Citation for its "courageous four-day stand" there. The following month the Belgian–Luxembourg contribution, an all-volunteer, elite infantry battalion which first saw action on 6 March 1951, was also awarded a Presidential Unit Citation for its fierce fighting on the Imjin River in spring 1951.

The only South American nation to send ground troops to Korea was Colombia, its first action on foreign soil in 127 years. These soldiers, evenly divided between volunteers and veterans from the regular Colombian Army, first entered combat on or about 1 August 1951. They saw their heaviest fighting in 1953 on Old Baldy and at Pork Chop Hill.

The Ethiopian infantry battalion, another volunteer force, was raised from the Emperor Haile Selasse's bodyguard. They entered combat on 15 August 1951, attached to US 1st Cavalry Division, and remained the only ground fighting force from Africa in the Korean War. This was also the first occasion that Ethiopia had fought outside Africa in 13 centuries. Ethiopia was a special case; Mussolini's Fascist Italian invasion of that land had highlighted the League of Nations' impotence against armed aggression. The Ethiopian battalion was highly motivated and claimed that they did not lose a prisoner or leave a single man unaccounted for on the battlefield, a record even better than that of the fearsome Turks. The US Army Chief of Staff at the time wrote that "They returned as they went out – all together – whether they were living or wounded or dead."

Nonetheless, the Ethiopian battalion may have given the most problems. The officers were touchy about being categorized as "negro" (back in Ethiopia black Africans had been enslaved for generations). There was also a certain arrogance among the more highly born elite and some lack of co-operation with the UNC. That command quickly asserted its authority and sent home offending officers. There was no trouble with the rank-and-file, who were considered very good fighters indeed, although lacking in mechanical ability.

The only other military contribution from an African nation came from South Africa, in the form of one fighter squadron. South Africa, officially fervently anti-Communist, had already contributed to the Berlin Airlift, but argued that it did not have the resources to commit more than the one squadron to Korea. South Africa's Nationalist government had motives beyond just resistance to Communism. Joining a UN crusade against aggression might help restore some of its international reputation, now sadly tarnished by its official racial *apartheid* policy. Too small to be independent, the all-white South African Air Force Squadron No. 2 ("Flying Cheetahs") was attached to 5th US Air Force. Its earlier-model P-51 Mustangs were slower than those still used by the USAF, so Cheetah pilots concentrated on ground strafing missions, blowing klaxon horns as they enthusiastically dived to the attack.

Highly regarded by the USAF, No. 2 Squadron refused to become a part of the projected Commonwealth wing, preferring to remain with the Americans. Much to their delight, Cheetah pilots found themselves transitioning to the F-86 Sabre jet interceptor in 1952–3. Subsequently, they participated in the heavy Allied raids on Pyongyang. The South African air contribution was considerable: some 826 SAAF pilots flew with No. 2 Squadron, 34 died in the war, and nine were repatriated from Communist captivity.

The French infantry battalion (first combat early January 1951) was composed of professional troopers commanded by a highly decorated general who had been badly wounded in the First World War and who took a cut in rank to the level of lieutenant colonel to take the command in Korea. For some reason, he adopted a *nom de guerre*, "Ralph Monclar", in place of his real name, General de Corps d'Armee Magrin Vernerrey. The French, along with General Ridgway and the Turks, believed in the bayonet. (The very word "bayonette" comes from the French town of Bayonne.) They also developed their own unnerving "cold steel" tactics. Digging two parallel lines of ditches, the Frenchmen would allow the Communists to take the first ditch, then before their enemy could consolidate, the French troopers would leap from the second in a surprise mass thrust, skewering the Communists with their needle sharp bayonets. If the Chinese advanced with their bugles and horns, the French likewise charged the Communists with a howling hand-cranked siren. Not surprisingly, this force, described by bemused American observers as "half-wild Algerians", was awarded three Presidential Unit Citations for actions at Hill 543, Chipyong-ni and Hongchon, with General MacArthur personally presenting the first two awards. Its most famous accomplishment, for which, oddly, it did not receive a Presidential Unit Citation, was its major role in taking Heartbreak Ridge – again by bayonet charge. The French were also most adept in their use of armour support, primarily because the French liaison officer to the parent 23rd US Infantry Regiment was an armour expert and because the 23rd's tank company commander fortuitously spoke fluent French! Not surprisingly, the French considered themselves to be almost an integral part of the 23rd, which was delighted to have these fierce professionals, although expressing some reservations about their attitude towards the chain of command.

French losses during the war were the highest proportionally, save for the Americans and South Koreans, of any UNC contingent: 262 killed, 1,008 wounded, 9 missing in action, and 10 POWs. On the other hand, the condition of the French POWs was remarkably better than that of their fellow UN prisoners because the Chinese had shrewdly picked them to be the camp cooks! The French "rotation system" was also indicative of the nature of this unit. The men were all considered professional soldiers. Why should they leave Korea while there was a war on? A French trooper did not leave Korea unless he became *hors de combat*. Although comparisons are usually odious, it could be argued that the French provided the best UNC unit in Korea.

Greece dispatched an infantry battalion that eventually numbered 1,263 men, mostly conscripts, but strongly anti-Communist. It was particularly favoured by the UNC, in that most of its officers at least were veterans of the Greek civil war against the Communists, where they had employed mostly US weapons and had US Army advisers attached to the larger units; the officers were selected for their knowledge of English. The troops found the mountainous Korean terrain and the frigid Korean winters much like home. In their first major action, the Greeks repelled an attack on Hill 381 using grenades, rifle butts, bayonets and bare hands when their ammunition was exhausted. They held the hill, preventing the Chinese from surrounding nearby UNC troops. A Greek company also was dispatched later to help clear out POW resistance on Koje island. Because the Greeks had seen so many of their own children kidnapped by the Communists in their civil war, they were particularly kind to Korean children, feeding, sheltering and clothing orphans and the young destitute. The Royal Hellenic Air Force contributed intrepid Flight No. 13, equipped with ageing US-built C-47 transports. The flight was awarded a Presidential Unit Citation for its sterling service in air evacuation of wounded from northeast Korea in late 1950.

Implacably anti-Communist (or at least anti-Russian), Turkey also fielded an infantry battalion. Its almost 5,455 troops and the total of nearly 15,000 Turks who served in Korea made that nation the fourth largest contributor of soldiers to the UNC, after the ROK, the US, and the UK. Korea was also the scene of the first Turkish Army action since 1923.

The Turks' individual aggressiveness and ferocity contributed some of the few legends of the Korean War. One concerned a Turkish commander, incensed because a US officer had doubted the high number of Communist troops his men reported as having killed in a particular action. He then issued a bran sack to each of his men. The following day the officer reported back to the American, whereupon his men emptied their bran sacks – filled with Chinese ears – at the astonished US officer's feet. Laconically suggesting "divide by two", the Turk strode off. Then there was the Turkish night patrol which came upon a sleeping Chinese detachment. Silently beheading all but one in the freezing weather, they propped each victim upright with his severed head in his lap. The petrified Chinese survivor could be counted to spread far and wide this tale of Turkish horror. Such stories were neither proved nor disproved, but the point is that they were widely believed and retailed by US soldiers. Better documented were the Turks' personal modesty that frowned on communal showers and their religious scruples that forbade autopsies of their dead.

Like the French, the Turks were great fanciers of the bayonet. In fact, it was because of the Turks' successful bayonet charges in the battle to regain Seoul in January 1951 that General Ridgway decided that all UNC infantry rifles would affix bayonets to their rifles. The Turks, lacking the generous resources of many of their UNC allies, were also noted for their field improvisations. It was a matter of justifiable pride for the Turks that not one of their prisoners of the Communists died in captivity or was "turned" to Communism. This survival was due in large measure to the Turks being inured to hardship and to their practical ability to supplement meagre prison fare with such nutritious wild substitutes as dandelions, bark and bulbs. Their language was incomprehensible to the Chinese, who soon dropped their attempts to convert these prisoners to the rewards of "scientific Marxism". Turkish POWs treated their guards with aloof contempt; the poor fellows weren't even Turks!

UNC higher commanders were somewhat less enthralled with some other aspects of Turkish troops. They noted great language and identification problems that led rather frequently to their misunderstanding of orders or their failure to communicate vital information to nearby UNC units. On several occasions they fired on other UN troops or civilian refugees. In sum, it can be said that the Turks were individually ferocious, resourceful fighters but somewhat lacking in discipline and organization. Almost 750 Turkish troops died in Korea, 2,068 were wounded, 234 were captured, and 173 were listed as missing in action.

Finally, Thailand (which also provided transport aircraft) and the Philippines each sent infantry battalions to Korea. Each saw hard fighting, the former at Porkchop Hill where they repelled several mass Chinese attacks, the latter along the Imjin River front in spring 1951, where Filipino tanks and infantry made a forestalled attempt to rescue the Glosters. The Thais were attached to US IX Corps, where they were considered to be lacking somewhat in aggressiveness and mechanical ability but were still welcome.

The coming of the Philippine Combat Battalion in September showed the need for a reception centre to orient new units from different linguistic and cultural backgrounds. Accordingly, the following month the UN Reception Center (UNRC) opened at the once-embattled city of Taegu to "provide familiarization training with US Army weapons and equipment".

UNRC cadre did not confine themselves to the training facility. Many went to the front lines to analyse battle techniques and bring "lessons learned" back to Taegu.

The British Commonwealth forces, sharing (more or less) the same language with the Americans, posed no particular problems upon arrival in Korea. The UNC never had the nerve to suggest that Commonwealth contingents pass through the UNRC. These units were each evaluated as already highly trained and experienced. They had many Second World War reservist and regular veterans in their ranks, and were sufficiently familiar with US procedures that they could by-pass such training and orientation. Commonwealth forces later did set up their own reception and training centre, also at Taegu.

Each UN ground contingent was attached to a US Army unit: battalions to US regiments and brigades to US corps or divisions, and each was to be, at least in theory, used as any similarly attached unit in the US Army. The Philippine regimental combat team was attached to the US 65th Infantry Regiment, a mostly Spanish-speaking unit from Puerto Rico. But in the Philippines, English was the language of commerce and government whereas the rest of the archipelago's inhabitants shared some score of languages, of which Spanish lingered on in little more than place and personal names. Some ill will resulted from this avoidable mismatch. All but the US 7th and 24th Infantry Divisions had UN contingents attached to them by the spring of 1951. The US Army kept these two divisions separate in order to test and utilize new combat methods with purely US troops. Despite the added communication and supply burden that each UN contingent represented, there is no record of any receiving less than a cordial welcome from their US Army parent unit.

Each national contingent was different, and each took varying amounts of time to adjust to Korea. The Greeks and Turks, from a mountainous terrain that was severely cold in winter, easily acclimatized to Korea's similar environment. The Thais, from a flat, warm country, experienced more difficulty.

The US Army provided the bulk of the food rations, but with variations, of course, for national tastes. The Moslem Turks would eat no pork, the Hindu Indians no beef. The French, Dutch, and Belgian–Luxembourgeois wanted far more bread, potatoes and cheese than the Americans could supply, while the Thais and Filipinos demanded more rice and hot sauces. (The Thais were allotted a ration of the fierce Louisiana Cajun Tabasco sauce as the closest approximation to their own culinary dressings.) The British, Australian and New Zealand forces could eat either British or US rations. They detested American beer ("watery, gassy stuff") and supplied their own as the French (of course) did their wine. Neither would touch the over-refined, spongy American excuse for bread. The French, again, made their own. All UN

164

allies, except the Canadians, who all along preferred American rations, agreed that the ubiquitous American peanut (groundnut) butter was an acquired taste, but many did develop a lasting fondness for American ice cream. The Americans, in turn, came to appreciate British beer (suitably cooled to their accustomed near-freezing temperature), but never steak and kidney pie. The UNC also provided packaged rations for many UNC contingents. It canned, for example, Korea's national staple, kimchee, for the ROK troops. (The rumour was that the fiery cabbage blend ate the bottoms out of the cans until a plastic liner was added.) Yet, in all, the UNC's problems in meeting its allies' differing culinary tastes were minor. If, say, the Dutch wanted more bread or the Thais more rice, they got it from the UNC's ample larders.

The British and New Zealand units basically brought all of their own British-designed and manufactured equipment, including the 120mm gun British Centurion tank, probably the best of its kind in Korea. The Canadians used predominantly their own equipment, except for special items like US Army bazookas and a few other weapons, vehicles, boots and foul weather gear. (Considering that dominion's climate, it is surprising that the Canadians would have turned to the Americans for such.) But all equipment was paid for from Canadian funds. The Australians, Belgians, Thais, Turks, Dutch, Ethiopians, Filipinos and Colombians essentially employed US equipment. None of this equipment was given away. Reimbursement was officially voluntary, and an accounting system about as complex as the culinary demands of the Allies was devised; Great Britain posed difficulties about its reimbursement account with the Americans until as late as 1964.

In addition to artillery support, US Army units also had to provide transportation for many Allied contingents, some of whom either lacked road transport altogether or brought Second World War or even pre-war vehicles. Many Allied personnel, coming as they did from nations yet to enter the automobile age, were deemed mechanically inept by US standards. Consequently, the US Army provided most of the road transport in Korea. (One exception was the Colombians, who although coming from a non-motorized nation, nonetheless easily matched or even exceeded US Army motor maintenance standards.) Mainly because of this lack of vehicles in many UNC allied contingents, most medical evacuation was through the US Army system, although the ROK and Commonwealth forces had their own channels.

The brutal Korean winters posed a special Allied supply challenge, and here again the UN allies had to turn to the Americans. Few of the Ethiopians or the Australians had ever seen snow and the Canadians came prepared for a tropical country! Whatever their reservations about American bread, beer, or peanut butter, all seemed to agree that the American cold-weather gear was first-class.

6. US Army forces in the field. No shortage of motor vehicles. *National Archives*

Except for the French, as noted, the UNC allied contingents had their own troop rotation system: one year of service for the Belgians, six months for the Greeks, eight to ten months for the Dutch, and "one winter twelve months" for the Canadians, while the British units practised unit-by-unit rotation.

Although English was the official tongue of the UNC, language remained the greatest single obstacle to military efficiency. In a few extreme cases, some non-English-speaking UNC soldiers actually died from confusing fuel tablets with the food or salt versions.

The Allied contribution to the UN Command was remarkably free from friction, considering the great cultural, military and political differences among the nations involved, and the fact that, except for the ROKs, none were fighting for national survival. Much of this amity was simply because the United States so dominated the UNC through its resources and manpower. Those nations that wished to participate in the Korean War had to do so pretty much on US terms. But the US made a strong effort to preserve Allied unity by swallowing without retort the often ignorant denigration of its soldiers and downplaying its allies' own deficiencies. In fact, there has been so little written criticism of UNC Allied units then or later that one almost suspects something of a benign conspiracy of silence. Surely the Americans and South Koreans were not the only troops ever to flinch before the Communists in Korea.

It must be noted that some higher Commonwealth officers tended occasionally to a certain superciliousness towards their American "cousins" that bordered on outright denigration. The New Zealanders seemed the worse offenders, in this case down to the ranks. The American soldier was deemed too road-bound, softened by luxuries from their Army's ubiquitous Post Exchanges and lacking in spirit and discipline. US officers generally refrained from making any response, realizing that they could well find themselves in the interests of inter-Allied solidarity facing court-martial proceedings. Perhaps the British military attaché in Washington hit exactly the right note when he wryly remarked that naturally the British were doing rather well in withdrawing from the North; after all, the British Army had extensive experience in such "retrograde operations".

"Progressive" journalists, particularly in the UK, occasionally took up the theme, somewhat mangling their Marxist ideology. Instead of the politically correct depiction of enlisted American troopers as noble proletarians press-ganged into an imperialist war by their evil leaders, they instead followed the current "party line" that even the American common soldier was a Coke-swilling, "gook"-cursing, sadistic racist, who delighted in casually blasting Korean villages, raping the women and gunning down the men. British troops, on the other hand, were indeed seen as stout-hearted lads in a bad cause not of their making.

The US Army, particularly in 1950, suffered from some severe deficiencies, but deficiencies that the Army took some pains to correct. Further, in comparing the qualities of the various Allied units it should be remembered that most of the non-ROK, non-US forces were composed primarily or entirely of volunteers, who in many cases, like the Canadians, had volunteered specifically for Korea. The highest proportion of conscript soldiers in any British unit never surpassed 50 per cent and most were much lower. In US Eighth Army, on the other hand, most troops by far were conscripts, inducted into the Army involuntarily in large, impersonal units for a one-year tour of duty in a Korea they were ecstatic to leave. Any American military unit that was composed of more than one-half volunteers was regarded as elite; there is no recorded Allied criticism of the US Marines. Fortunately for the alliance, the condescending attitudes of America's major allies seemed to fade the closer one approached the battle front. Conversely, the American military rarely denigrated their enemy and *never* their allies. (The rough-and-ready relationship between US and Commonwealth troops could be seen in the story that

Nations which participated in UNC operations, in order of their commitment

Nation	Forces Contributed
Republic of Korea (not a UN member)	ground, air and naval
United States	ground, air and naval
Australia	ground, air and naval
United Kingdom	ground, air and naval
The Netherlands	ground and naval
New Zealand	ground and naval
Canada	ground, air and naval
France	ground and naval
Philippines	ground and air
Sweden	hospital
Turkey	ground
Thailand	ground
South Africa	air
India	field ambulance and surgical unit
Greece	ground and air
Belgium	ground
Luxembourg	ground
Denmark	hospital ship
Colombia	ground and naval
Ethiopia	ground
Norway	hospital
Italy (not UN member)	hospital

in 1952 or 1953 the US 2nd Division had painted rocks in front of its headquarters with the unit legend "Second to None". The Commonwealth Division promptly followed by painting on its own headquarters rocks "None".)

But perhaps the final word on the subject should come from the Chinese. Before their troops actually clashed with US forces, Chinese field commanders expressed the usual Marxist-chauvinistic clap-trap about the physical and moral inferiority of the decadent Americans compared to the battle-hardened, highly-motivated CPV. Considering that the official "line" was that the Soviet Union and the Chinese Communists had won the Second World War in Asia practically alone, it was natural that these commanders knew little, if anything, of Bataan or of the hard-fought American victories at Guadalcanal, Tarawa, or Iwo Jima. But by December 1950, even as Chinese armies were clearing those Americans and their allies from North Korea, the CPV commander, Peng Dehuai, expressed (privately) a markedly different opinion: "the US forces are good at fighting and that is why more American soldiers are killed than captured alive."[2] And Mao Tse-tung himself, six months later, had to acknowledge that his plan to undermine US morale by annihilating an American division or even a regiment was now impossible: "the American troops at the present time are still [filled] with strong desire to fight and are self-confident".[3]

In addition, UN members contributed large amounts of aid to the Unified Command Emergency Relief Program for Korea. A total of 46 nations provided economic assistance to the ROK, either through the UNC or to UNKRA. Such assistance included medical supplies, cleaning materials, food, fuel, school supplies, raw materials, clothing, blankets, livestock, tentage, baby food and clothing, medical books, newsprint, duplicating machines, plus large cash donations.

In sum, the United Nations provided the forum for mobilizing support for the embattled ROK. For all the undoubted and welcomed military value of the UN forces sent to Korea, their main contribution was to validate the UN effort as the response of the international community to armed cross-border aggression. Much to the frustration of the Communist side, the Korean War had indeed become a UN war.

Chapter Ten

The air and naval war

The air war in Korea was a juxtaposition of the old and the new. The latest models of jet fighter-interceptors clashed over the Yalu River, while over the land battlefields Second World War-design Mustang, Corsair, Skyraider, or Firefly propeller fighters shot up Communist trucks and bunkers. The US Air Force was almost completely unprepared for the anachronistic aspects of this conflict and had to re-learn its painfully acquired lessons of the last great war, lessons in close-air support, the impossibility of completely choking off enemy supplies, and the limited returns from the mass aerial bombing of cities.

The reason for the USAF's lack of preparedness for the air war that soon developed in Korea was simple: that service saw its primary mission as basically the nuclear bombing of Soviet industrial and political targets. It had fought bitter battles with the US Navy for the production of its ultra-heavy nuclear bomber, the B-36, to do just that. And its front-line jet fighter, the F-86, was intended as an interceptor of Soviet bombers trying to do to Washington, DC, what the USAF intended to do to Moscow. For a generation of airmen who had professionally matured under the slogan "Victory through Air Power" the stalemate of Korea was indeed a frustrating experience. Furthermore, the brutal budget cuts in the years just preceding war in Korea stripped the USAAF/USAF of so many of its conventional capabilities; what money there was had to go primarily to the big bombers. The Korean War did little or nothing to divert the USAF from what it perceived as its nuclear bombardment top priority. At the beginning of the Korean War the USAF had about 298 atomic bombs and 364 bombers capable of delivering those bombs. By the end of the war the USAF had some 1,161 atomic bombs that could be dropped by 762 bombers.

The US Marines' air service was an exception to this picture of doctrinal tunnel vision. That service still could envisage the need for close-support of its "ground pounders" and was thus far better prepared for such an even-tuality as Korea. During the Korean War one Marine ground commander exclaimed that he would rather have no air cover if he could not have the Marines overhead. The US Navy was deprived in 1949 of much of its nuclear bombardment mission with the cancellation of super-carrier USS *United States*. It still had a large inventory of piston and jet fighters and ground attack warplanes and the carriers to bring them into Korean waters. Still, only the USAF had the front-line jet fighters to deal with the MiG-15.

The aircraft

About as wide a variety of aircraft fought within the confines of the Korean War as in the global Second World War. The Korean People's Air Force opened the Korean War with ground attacks launched by Soviet-built YAK 3, 7, and 9 fighters as well as Iluyshin Il-10 "Sturmovik" ground attack light bombers. The latter was perhaps the best low-level attack aircraft of the Second World War, while the performance of the former approached that of the classic US F-51 Mustang. Thus the Korean People's Army (*Inmin Gun*) would briefly be well-served in the air.

The Republic of Korea Air Force, on the other hand, consisted of a handful of US-built Piper L-4 Cubs and similar light liaison and spotter aircraft. AT-6 Texans, used for advanced air training in the Second World War, represented the "heavy" aircraft in the ROK air inventory.

The first air clash of the Korean War involved those YAK fighters (310 to 359mph), and USAF F-82 heavy escort fighters (461mph). (The USAF before the Korean War had changed its designation from "P" for pursuit to "F" for fighter.) The F-82 was a rather bizarre aircraft, nicknamed "Twin Mustang" for its two fuselages which resembled twin P-51 Mustang fuselages connected side by side. The idea was that the two pilots could relieve each other of flying duties on long bombing escort runs to Japan, but the aircraft was deployed too late for the Pacific War. In the war's first aerial engage-ment, the F-82s promptly shot all three of the attacking YAKs out of the sky with no damage to themselves. Soon afterwards the F-82 was rewarded for its early fame by being withdrawn from combat because of a lack of spare parts.

The next USAF aircraft over the battlefields of Korea was the liquid-cooled piston-engine F-51 Mustang (450mph), the classic fighter of the Second World War. A majority of pilots from that previous conflict seemed to prefer this fighter over its sister, the P-47. Yet, it was a pity that the P-47 had been phased out of the USAF inventory, for its giant radial engine would have made it the better ground-attack aircraft. As it was, the Mustang, for all its virtues, could be brought down by the smallest hit in its liquid cooling system, and carried only 2,000lb of ordnance; the P-47 could carry 2,500lb. The USAF did bring back its very successful medium bomber from the Second World War, the B-26 Invader (330mph) (not to be confused with the Second World War Martin B-26 Marauder). Most models were fitted with a fearsome 18 .50 calibre machine gun armament in the nose, which could literally shred "soft" ground targets.

The first jet on either side to deploy to Korea, the F-80 Starfighter (600mph), designed as a high-altitude, high-speed interceptor, had a heavy fuel consumption and was so fragile that it could not be used on the unimproved airfields that predominated on the peninsula. It also carried no more ordnance than the Mustang. Presumably to the disgust of the "kerosene cowboys", no fewer than six USAF fighter squadrons in the summer of 1950 had to turn in their post-war jet F-80s for the piston-engine F-51. Even though more rugged, the F-51 suffered twice the loss rate of jet aircraft in ground attack missions. Consequently, the F-80 and the Republic F-84 Thunderjet (622mph) continued in ground-attack missions throughout the war.

The Marines showed that they were far better attuned than the USAF to an air war in a Third World country when they arrived in the summer of 1950 with their superb Corsair F-4U piston-engine fighters and fighter-bombers. The Corsair (395mph) was also one of the greatest aircraft of the Second World War. As late as 1952 improved versions of the Corsair were still being built, a record for any fighter aircraft. But its loss rate was about the same as that for the F-51. Where the Corsair truly excelled was in the weight of ordnance it could heft; more than 5,000lb of bombs and/or rockets as well as its four 20mm cannons. The design concept of the Corsair was carried to its monstrous conclusion with the giant Douglas AD Skyraider (a relatively slow 322mph). Here was another Second World War piston-engine design, which could carry 8,000lb of bombs, twice the load of a Second World War medium bomber. It could absorb more punishment than the Corsair and went on to gain near-legendary fame in Vietnam. The Skyraider was the largest single-seat warplane ever to go into production.

The main Navy and Marine jet fighters were the Grumman F9F-2 Panther (625mph) and McDonnell F2H2 Banshee (586mph). Both aircraft were inferior in speed to the MIG, but proved quite useful in the ground attack role that dominated the air war in Korea, and a few even shot down MIGs.

The earliest heavy/medium bomber to be used in Korea was the B-29 (358mph) of Pacific War fame. Two of these warplanes had dropped the first atomic bombs. (In light of the death tolls of the Tokyo fire raids, the two nuclear bombings, and of similar raids on Pyongyang and Sinuiju, the B-29 can be said to have killed more civilians than any other aircraft in history.) Throughout the interwar years the piston-engine B-29 had been the atomic first-line bomber of the USAAF/USAF Strategic Air Command, although an improved B-29, the B-50, was assuming that role, slowly, in the face of post-war military budget cuts. The B-29, with its 31,850-feet ceiling and ten-ton bomb load, was indeed a formidable bombardment aircraft, particularly against industrial and urban targets. But the Communists' MiG-15 could inflict unacceptably heavy losses on any unescorted B-29 daylight bomber missions.

The reliable twin-engine Douglas C-47 Skytrain (DC-3 in civilian life and "Dakota" in the RAF) cruised at 250mph and could carry 28 passengers, and far more if necessary. It has become an immortal aircraft that will undoubtedly fly in considerable numbers on into the twenty-first century. It was actually a mid-1930s design as a civilian air liner; before the Second World War it represented about 90 per cent of all major airlines' flying equipment. The C-47 military version of the Second World War flew in every war zone and home front from Stalingrad to Mandalay. It was revered for its reliability and its ability to absorb the grossest abuse and fly on. In Korea it flew troops and equipment in and out of battlefields from Pusan in the South to Hagaru-ri in the North. In both wars it could be termed the jeep of the air. (Sensing a financial opportunity, the Douglas Corporation came out in 1952 with its "Super-DC-3". Almost no one bought it; used DC-3s were doing fine and were a lot cheaper.)

The four-engine C-54 Skymaster (275mph) also performed yeoman service during the war and had double the carrying capacity and range of the older DC-3/C-47. It flew ill-fated Task Force Smith, for example, directly from Japan to Korea. Both of these transports had also been converted from civilian models.

The first two USAF transports designed specifically for military service saw considerable use in Korea. These were the twin-engine C-119 "Flying Boxcar", whose rear door greatly eased entrance and egress of troops and equipment, and the four-engine C-124, a transport giant of the time, which revolutionized cargo and personnel transport, carrying 200 troops and five times as much material as its predecessors. With the C-124 also dawned the age of air disaster mass casualties.

The fighters of "MiG Alley", the USAF's F-86 Sabre Jet and its opposing MiG-15, reflected the latest jet fighter technologies of their time and took most of the headlines of the air war in Korea. The F-86, the USAF's first swept-wing aircraft, had a top speed of 500 to 600mph, could climb to 48,300 feet and was armed with six machine guns. The Sabre's swept wing had not come easily. Although suggested in early studies that went back to the Second World War, the new wing design was not accepted until very tangible evidence of German success with the concept could no longer be denied.

The MiG, also swept-winged and also beholden to German aerodynamics, held a speed advantage over the F-86 at 670mph, and a slight edge in ceiling at 50,000 feet. It could climb faster, had far more range, and was armed with two 23mm and one 37mm cannons. But the MiG was even more derivative than the Sabre. In an act of gratuitous folly the British Labour Government in 1947 had sold to the Soviets the most advanced jet engines in the world: the Rolls Royce Nene (25 sold) and the Derwent (30 sold), along with working plans, presumably as part of its export drive. (A bemused Stalin was supposed to have wondered aloud "What fool will sell us his secret?") The MiG fighter project had actually stalled for lack of a good engine until the Attlee Government came to its rescue. Now the MiG project forged ahead with a fine VK-1 reverse-engineered engine based upon the Nene/Derwent; within a few years numerous UN aircrew would die at its hands.

Both fighters had been designed as interceptors against bombers, not as air supremacy or escort fighters. The latter was the role in which the F-86 found itself, although the MiG was indeed deployed as an interceptor over "MiG Alley" and did well against the B-29.

The MiG and the Sabre offer a cautionary tale against "going by the numbers". In most tangible measurements except diving speed, manoeuvreability, engine reliability and its electronic gunsight, the Sabre was inferior to the MiG-15. Yet the Sabre took and held the measure of the MiG throughout the air war over "MiG Alley". USAF pilots and analysts attributed the Sabre's edge to superior USAF pilot training and to electronic gear about a generation in advance of anything in Soviet jet fighters. The F-86 also was equipped with air brakes and a transonic tail plane, which made it much more manoeuvrable than the MiG. Finally, F-86 pilots alone were equipped with gravity suits, which greatly reduced the stresses of high-speed combat. In fact, Soviet–North Korean intelligence made the obtaining of a USAF gravity suit a high priority mission early in the jet air war. (The suit itself was a symbol for US "jet jockies" of their elite status.)

In the last year of the war the USAF and the US Marines introduced two all-weather jet night fighters. The Air Force's Lockheed F-94 Starfighter (585mph) provided escort protection for bombers while the Marines' Douglas F35-2M Skyknight (600mph) performed base protection as well as escort duty. Both straight-wing warplanes were powered by the same model twin-jet engines and packed with electronic gear. And both were credited with six MiG kills by the war's end.

Yet it was the decidedly low-tech Polikarpov PO-2 fabric-covered bi-plane, not the MiG, that came to make the night miserable for UN forces in the Seoul area. "Bed Check Charlie's" small and erratic bombs disturbed the sleep of personnel and occasionally even destroyed or damaged parked UN aircraft. The light construction of these "washing machines" baffled radar and evaded the human eye. UNC anti-aircraft batteries could rarely plot these pests and their smaller ordnance rounds often passed right through the aircrafts' light structure, as did an unknowing Navy jet night fighter; both aircraft were demolished. But the PO-2 did more than disturb sleep. In one raid over Pyongyang (while that city was in UNC hands) these biplanes destroyed more F-86s on the ground than had been lost to the Communists to date!

Several UN contingents brought their own air power to Korea: the Greeks, who loaned C-47 transports to a USAF transport squadron; the Australian 77th RAAF Squadron, and the South African 2nd SAAF Squadron. Both Commonwealth squadrons flew F-51s. But the latest aircraft flown by the RAAF at the time, the British Gloster Meteor 8 jet fighter, was also a mid-to-late Second World War design, obsolescent since the later 1940s. The RAAF also fielded No. 36 Transport Squadron, which flew C-47 Dakota transport aircraft, and No. 30 Communications Flight.

Only the Royal Canadian Air Force and the Royal Navy Fleet Air Arm brought indigenous aircraft to the war. The Canadians flew post-war Canadair four piston-engine North Star transports, although some Canadian fighter pilots also gained experience in the latest fighter jets by flying with the USAF Fifth Air Force. The Royal Navy's Fleet Air Arm's types were all obsolete models from the Second World War, but still proved effective in the ground attack role in the absence of Communist opposition in the air.

Finally, and most significantly as another example of the determination of both super-powers to keep this war limited, neither the US nor the Soviet Union deployed their first-line bombing aircraft to Korea. For the USAF's Strategic Air Command this was the giant ten-engined B-36 front-line nuclear bomber. It was not an aircraft that SAC wished to deploy on what it considered a diversion from its main mission, that of the nuclear incineration of the Soviet Union's population centres. SAC's other nuclear bomber, the B-50, also was not deployed to Korea. The trouble-plagued B-49 "Flying Wing" six-engine jet (originally piston) bomber was already being scrapped when the Korean War broke out.

For its part, the Soviet Air Force retained its front-line Tupolev TU-4 in the Motherland. This bomber, which, unlike its B-29 progenitor, may have been built from the start with a nuclear capacity, was a very close copy of the American B-29, duplicated from four such USAF bombers that had been forced to land in the then-neutral Soviet Union during the Pacific War. Stalin ordered these then "cutting-edge" heavy bombers reproduced after he found that he could not purchase the aircraft or any of its parts from the United States. The planes were reproduced down to the last countersunk rivet, with only minor differences, in perhaps the most thoroughgoing "reverse engineering" project in history. US authorities worried that the TU-4 could bomb American cities on one-way missions. (The B-29 had another odd foreign episode during the Korean War, when several squadrons-worth of the bomber were transferred to the RAF in 1951 to close that service's gap in heavy bombers until the advent of its own world-class jet "V-bombers". The loaned B-29s were termed with trans-Atlantic courtesy "Washingtons" and remained in RAF service until 1958.)

The Korean War also saw the first military use of helicopters on any scale. Two early, light models, the Bell H-13 and the Sikorsky H-5, were used primarily and successfully for combat medical evacuation but also for reconnaissance, resupply, and observation. The H-19 was a much larger aircraft, capable of carrying up to ten persons, and it pioneered the earliest helicopter-borne military assaults. The H-19 also inserted and evacuated intelligence agents and guerrillas into and out of North Korea. At least one was lost in these very dangerous missions.

Air war in Korea

The air war in Korea opened with the North Korean blitzkrieg, as YAKs and Schturmoviks led the way. Here was a forerunner of the major mission of air power in the Korean War – close air support. The minuscule, unarmed aircraft of the ROK Air Force could do little, if anything, in response, except to report on the Communists' swift advance.

On the second day of the invasion, now aware that this was more than just another probing attack from the North, the US Ambassador ordered the evacuation of all American civilian personnel from Korea. To cover their departure, General MacArthur ordered his Far East Air Force (FEAF) into action. FEAF directed the 8th Fighter-Bomber Wing to fly air cover over FEAF transport aircraft and the sea evacuation.

On 27 June, the 8th's F-82s crushed KPAF attempts to interfere in the mission. Later in the day another four YAKS were downed by the same type of aircraft. The North Korean Air Force seemed to have earned a healthy respect for FEAF after this, only venturing out on occasion, as during the battle for Taejon the following month. But after 1950 no ground soldier,

North Korean, Chinese, or UN, ever again saw the red star of a Communist aircraft over Korea's battlegrounds.

This total UN air supremacy over the front lines was possible not only because of the vast industrial superiority of the United States over its Communist opponents and the absence of Soviet air power over the Korean battlegrounds but also because of the proximity of Japan and its air bases. It was possible for a USAF pilot to have breakfast with his family, drive to his base, take off for a mission over Korea, and return, commuter-like, in time for his home-cooked dinner.

Even though many UNC pilots were Second World War veterans, they needed to re-learn the close air support lessons of that earlier war. As noted, Task Force Smith had to face its ordeal without air cover because of earlier strafing of ROK convoys by "friendly" aircraft.

But with the virtual elimination of the North Korean Air Force, FEAF could throw practically all of its aircraft into the battle for close air support of the retreating UN forces. Contrary to popular misconception, the *Inmin Gun* was not a light infantry force; rather it was heavily dependent on motor truck and rail transportation for its supplies, and in the first months of the war it even enjoyed armour superiority over its enemies. All of this presented good targets for UN air power and soon the limited road network of both South Korea and much of North Korea itself were littered with the burned-out hulks of KPA trucks and tanks. Railroad transport fared no better, with most main bridges dropped, usually temporarily, early in the war, and practically all rail lines cut at one place or another.

UN air interdiction efforts approached what the Western Allies had mounted in the Second World War. About one-quarter of all UN air combat sorties of the Korean War were devoted to interdiction. Operations STRANGLE I and II repeated the very names of the Second World War operations, and had a similar lack of lasting result. SATURATE and the "Air Pressure" concept all slowed the Communist logistic flow to the battlefield but they hardly "interdicted" (that is, halted) Communist logistics.

In June 1951, USAF Brigadier General Dare H. Alkide confessed that he would like to meet (after the war, that is) the Communist supply chief to find out how he did it. High and deserved tribute indeed, but the General literally had not seen the half of it. Six months later, an intelligence report noted that almost the entire offensive effort of TF 77, 60 per cent of that of 1st Marine Air Wing, and 95 per cent of that of Fifth Air Force was expended in the interdiction struggle. The result? The cost of the UN aircraft lost was higher than that of all the destroyed Communist vehicles, rolling stock and supplies! But then, wars are not often fought on a comparative cost basis.

General Alkide never had the opportunity to meet his Communist opposite number after the war, but if he had, Hong Xuezhi would presumably have been glad to give him the details. The Communists did it through ingenuity and energy: with an enormous expenditure of human labour dropped bridge spans were repaired time and again, temporary structures were removed by day, fords or hidden underwater crossings at the more shallow watercourses replaced the bridges themselves, trains and trucks travelled only at night and parked in tunnels or "farmhouses" during the day, bomb craters in the roads were quickly filled in, porters and animals were extensively conscripted and route and camouflage discipline remained strict. Long truck convoys ran after dusk, lights extinguished, their routes marked by civilian guides with hooded lights. Damaged trucks were spotted alongside the roads to divert UN aircraft attention, while operating vehicles sheltered during the day in camouflaged and isolated havens, usually invisible from the air. Trains sheltered in tunnels during the day and ran nightly over rails often relaid nocturnally. Air watchers stationed on hills called out or radioed warnings of approaching UNC warplanes.

Offensively, the Communists set up "flak traps" and deployed massive amounts of Soviet-manufactured anti-aircraft artillery along their supply routes. At their peak, the Communist anti-aircraft units numbered three anti-aircraft divisions, 4 AAA regiments, 23 AAA battalions, one searchlight regiment, and one radar company. Later in the war UN air power became more adept at attacking these night supply efforts, but the routes were never cut. The situation, like the battlefront after 1951, would hardly change to the end of the war.

But in the process much of North Korea was turned into something of a moonscape, as every likely village and even farmhouse was blasted as a possible hiding place for Communist trucks. The North Korean capital, Pyongyang, was burned and blasted level, its remaining inhabitants reduced to a troglodyte existence. One USAF tactical bombing raid must have come as the result of superb intelligence. This was the bombing run on CPV headquarters on 24 November 1950, which not only scored a direct hit on the main building, but killed a son of Mao Tse-tung as well as two staff officers. For security reasons not widely reported at the time, one undoubtedly successful CAS naval air mission relied on accurate intelligence to intrude on a major Communist meeting at Kansan in October 1951. Skyraiders from carriers *Essex* and *Antietam* killed an incredible 500 key North Korean cadre and reportedly destroyed all Party records.

Further, as basically a peasant-conscript army, the CPV lacked a cadre of technically adept support troops. For example, no fewer than 1,500 UNC trucks were captured at Somso-ri in the great UNC retreat out of North

Korea. But the PVA could not find enough drivers and mechanics for the vehicles; most sat immobile and soon all but 200 had been shot-up by UNC warplanes.

At the end of the war, after three years of intensive and unrelenting UN aerial bombardment (there were no bombing "halts" or "pauses" in this war), the Communist soldier was better fed than he had ever been (probably even better than in civilian life) and was furnished with about all the ammunition and supplies he needed, at least by the standards of his own army. Some Communist artillery shelling in the last months of the conflict actually rivalled the "carpet" preparatory bombardments laid down by UN forces. Whereas in 1951 a Communist offensive would run out of supplies within six days, by the end of the war well-fed Communist troops could mount offensives that extended for more than a month. In August 1951 Communist artillery ammunition expenditures were a mere 16,000 rounds; in July 1953 they were 375,000. By then, the Communist forces actually deployed more artillery "tubes" in Korea than the UNC, although they generally still fired far fewer rounds from smaller tubes than did their enemies.

Of course, it must also be remembered that the Communist soldier got by on far less food and comforts than his UN counterpart. Even in 1953 the former could not count on new boots or even rubber-soled sandals, when his old ones gave way, or hot rations brought up to the line on "A frames" carried by enduring civilian porters. But he had the basics in food and ammunition and weapons and with these he could inflict casualties that would deter any "end the war" UN offensive.

First jet-to-jet combat

The jet war over the far north of Korea, in "MiG Alley", was the one part of this grubby war that provoked any sort of glamour and continuing public attention, at least in the West. Here, as in the First and Second World Wars in the air, combat was clean and non-ideological. It pitted man against man, each mounted in the latest weapon, in the frigid skies over the Yalu River that marked the forbidden border with China. As with practically every other Communist development in this war, the beginnings of the jet air war caught the UN Command by surprise.

Jet-propelled aircraft had fought in the Second World War in Europe, as both the RAF, the *Luftwaffe* and (considerably later) the USAF, put jet fighters into the field. The war ended, however, before these pioneering warplanes could clash with each other, although RAF jet Meteors did tip German pilotless V-1 pulse-jet flying bombs away from London.

In Korea the UNC's unchallenged air control was challenged suddenly and unexpectedly on 1 November 1950 as UN forces were achieving their maximum penetration of North Korea. On that date a forward air control light aircraft and its F-51 Mustang escorts were jumped by six jets of a type that had never been seen in Korea – or anywhere else in public, for that matter. The skilled USAF pilots managed to elude their attackers – MiG-15s – the latest jet fighters in Stalin's air arsenal, and could count themselves as indeed lucky to do so. (The Soviets claimed that their MiGs shot down two USAF F-82s on that same day, but the claim is suspicious in that the F-82 had been withdrawn from FEAF inventory by then, and the USAF acknowledged no such loss.) This was but a curtain-raiser. History's first jet-to-jet battle came on 8 November when MiGs struck at a B-29 formation and its escort of F-80 jet fighters.

Surprisingly, an F-80, piloted by Lieutenant Russell Brown, shot down a MiG, and the rest departed. But Lieutenant Brown and his fellows had been fortunate; again, it was only superior pilot training that had saved their day. The F-80 represented later Second World War technology and was no match for the MiG-15.

We now know that these MiG pilots were Soviet. Chinese pilots required further training at the time and were not committed to battle until the spring of 1951. There were few enough North Korean aircrew survivors of the early piston-engine clashes with UN aircraft; their MiGs entered battle even later than their Chinese allies. Paradoxically, this serious Soviet intervention came just a month after the US National Security Council had concluded that Stalin would be unlikely to take such a risk. Also, the fiction would be maintained by both sides for decades to come that there was no proof of such Soviet aerial involvement. (Actually, USAF and Red Air Force fighters had clashed already, in November 1944, when YAKs and P-38s had tangled over Yugoslavia, in what was at first undoubtedly a case of mis-identity. But when it was all over, three YAKs had been shot down with two pilots killed and two P-38s, also with two pilots dead and one captured.)

The Soviet pilots showed some lack of skill at this early stage of the jet air war. Later, Red Air force veterans explained that their main mission had been to knock down the USAF bombers, not to tangle with the jet escorts, although the fact remains that in this first jet-to-jet encounter, the B-29s themselves emerged unscathed. In later battles, the bombers would not be so fortunate.

The USAF immediately recognized the danger and hurriedly shipped the 4th Interceptor Wing with its F-86 Sabre jets to Korea. A wing of F-84s was also dispatched to Korea, but this straight-wing jet fighter was so out-classed that it soon was relegated to ground support, in which mission it was very successful.

Only the F-86 stood between the MiGs and disaster over the Yalu. In October 1951 another wing exchanged its F-80s for F-86s, some of them the newer E model. The Chief of Staff of the USAF forwarded another 75 Sabres to Korea at about the same time while the 4th finally received its third squadron. The odds against the Sabre were now somewhat redressed. Maintenance problems plagued the squadrons, however, particularly because they operated from primitive airfields, aside from Kimpo/Seoul. But then, the airfield complexes across the Yalu were hardly world-class, either.

Whatever the challenge of the MiGs, the USAF continued its B-29 bombing missions into the hostile skies of MiG Alley. But the Soviet pilots were sharpening their skills in combat. By early 1951 they were inflicting heavy daylight losses on the B-29s. In April three of the bombers were shot down and ten others badly damaged by MiGs.

The Soviets steadily increased their fighter power over North Korea, moving into bases along the Chinese side of the Yalu. By June 1951, they could muster three air divisions comprising about 200 MiGs.

The worst USAF losses came in October 1951 during the so-called Battle of Namsi, the greatest air battle of the war. Earlier, daylight raids against North Korean airfields at Tachyon, Saamchon and Namsi stirred large-scale response. On 24 October no fewer than 150 MiGs broke through the 55 escorting and outclassed F-84s. They shot down four B-29s over Namsi and seriously damaged another four; only one bomber escaped relatively unscathed. Why the obsolete F-84s were still escorting B-29s this late in the air war in the face of the greatly superior MiG menace is difficult to explain. By the end of the week a total of five of the bombers had been downed by the MiGs and eight seriously damaged. The bomber losses since the beginning of the war had been doubled in one week. The USAF finally pulled the lumbering, piston-engine B-29s, with their gunsights too slow-tracking for the jet age, out of daylight bombing missions. But even night missions could not foil the MiGs, and the USAF turned to specialized jet night escort fighters, the F-94 and the US Navy's F9F-2. These escorts were straight-wing warplanes some 100mph slower than the MiGs but they carried exponentially superior electronics. The USAF evened the score on 30 November when, in a large-scale air battle, 31 Sabres tackled 50 MiGs escorting no fewer than 28 piston-engine Soviet medium bombers. Twelve Communist aircraft were shot down and the entire formation was disrupted without USAF loss.

By the end of the war, the B-29s had more than evened their own score. Recent figures show 16 B-29s lost to Communist fighters, but the well-trained bomber gunners shot down 34 fighters, 16 of which were MiGs, as well as 17 "probable" MiGs. Obscured in the publicity of MiG Alley was the fact that the bomber campaign reaped, overall, only marginal success. General MacArthur was determined to stanch the flow of Chinese troops and equipment transiting 11 international bridges across the Yalu, as well as to burn to the ground the temporary North Korean capital, Sinuiju. In a Second World War style mini-Dresden fire raid in November 1950, 70 B-29s burned out some 60 per cent of the two-mile-square target area of the river city. The bridges and their approaches on the south bank of the Yalu suffered varying degrees of damage, but all escaped total destruction and the flow of troops and equipment was slowed – again, hardly interdicted. Thus it would remain throughout the Korean War; the US mounting nighttime bomber raids on key North Korean facilities, with the MiGs challenging the bombers and the escorting fighters responding. But in the end, in the air, as on the ground, stalemate.

Both the Communists and the UN air powers claimed that they were fighting this air war with "one hand tied behind our backs". The Americans made their claims publicly and loudly. Their pilots could see the dust trails kicked up by the MiGs as they taxied, unmolested, onto runways in their "privileged sanctuaries" across the Yalu. The Sabre pilots had to wait until the MiGs had crossed the international border before they could make their attacks. Nor could enthusiastic "jet jockies" follow fleeing opponents back into Manchuria, even in "hot pursuit" – supposedly. In order to keep this "limited war" limited, the United States and its allies decreed that the air war ended at the Yalu River. There were also more tangible reasons for the Yalu borderline. Any F-86 over MiG Alley was near the end of its fuel endurance. As it was, more than one Sabrejet pilot practically had to glide back to the Seoul area.

The Communists had their own self-imposed restrictions, although, unlike the Americans, they rarely spoke of them. If the air war ended at the Yalu for the Americans, it ended at about Pyongyang for the Communists, thus leaving the entire ground battle area under the umbrella of UN air power. From the late summer of 1950 to the end of the war, Communist troops were bombed, strafed, rocketed, white phosphorized and napalmed without sighting one friendly warplane. And, most importantly, the Communists never attacked the fat freighters and troopships lumbering to Pusan, or the UN truck convoys that drove where they pleased, headlights blazing; serpentine trains carried soldiers and their equipment to the front around the clock, molested only by local guerrillas. Further, Moscow permitted no more than 40 MiGs to operate over North Korea at any one time, whereas the USAF dispatched as many Sabres as it could or as the situation required.

And UNC trans-border restrictions were not always respected. For example, on 8 October 1950, presumably in the flush of victory as UN forces began crossing the 38th Parallel into North Korea, two USAF F-80s penetrated some 60 miles into the USSR and leisurely shot up a Soviet airfield! It is difficult to determine who was the more embarrassed by the incident, the Soviets, whose "falcons'" inefficiency had permitted "imperialist" warplanes to penetrate deeply into the motherland's air space on a "blatantly aggressive" mission and to return unscathed; or the United States, determined to keep this war limited and forced to admit that the two errant pilots must have been abominable navigators. Ten days later, when the US apologized and offered restitution, the matter dropped from public view. And, of course, this was the second case of US hostile action against Soviet armed forces, coming only a little more than a month after the downing of the Soviet reconnaissance bomber at sea.

On occasion, Sabre pilots would throw cautionary orders to the winds and cross over into Manchuria in "hot pursuit" of a MiG. They always seemed to survive the experience and their superior's "wrath". UNC ground and naval forces remained exempt from Soviet attacks. The only known occasion when the other side violated this unwritten understanding on any scale took place in November 1952, when unmarked MiGs attacked UN naval Task Force 77 as its warplanes were making an attack close to the Soviet border. One MiG was downed by Navy Pantherjets with no US loss. On several occasions during the Korean War Soviet aircraft seemed intent on penetrating Japanese airspace. On 18 November 1952 an La-11 was "escorted" out of Japanese airspace. A more serious incident on 16 February 1953 saw two USAF F-84 jet fighters actually fire on two Soviet La-11 fighters over the northern Japanese island of Hokkaido. One Soviet warplane was seen smoking and losing altitude as it headed back to the Soviet-occupied Kurile Islands. Neither the Soviets nor the Americans publicly made anything of these episodes. In fact, every problem faced by one side had its duplicate or its equivalent on the other, a rather fitting development for this ultimately stalemated conflict. It seems a constant in most wars that each side believes firmly that it labours under the most debilitating of disadvantages that it imposes upon itself in the interests of decency, and prevails only by reason of its own superior morale and training.

The Soviets, operating out of Manchuria and North Korea, provided cover for the key industrial and administrative centres of northeastern China, including the great hydroelectric complexes along the Yalu, the railway bridges across that river near Antung and North Korean lines of communication down to Pyongyang. They flew in close co-operation with the fledgling North Korean and Chinese air arms. Recently opened Russian archives show in some detail that the Soviet air effort in Northern Korea was provided by the Red Air Force Detached 64th Fighter Aviation Corps, consisting of 13 fighter air divisions, each usually comprising three air regiments, two naval fighter regiments, two independent night fighter regiments, four anti-aircraft artillery divisions and assorted supply units. The corps was headquartered in the major industrial Manchurian city of Mukden (Shenyang), and the air formations were deployed at fields in Mukden, Anshan, and Antung. According to recent Soviet revelations, these were elite units, previously concentrated in the Moscow area. No fewer than 72,000 Soviet air personnel were rotated through eight to fourteen months Korean tours of duty in the course of their air war. Even the aircraft they flew carried the solid red star of the Red Air Force on their wings and fuselages rather than Chinese or North Korean markings, which should have been a dead giveaway as to the nationality of the pilots.

Soviet pilots were restricted from flying over UNC-controlled territory and the sea, had to wear Chinese uniforms and were required to refrain (in theory) from speaking their native language in radio transmissions. ("We wore reddish brown boots, cotton trousers, like workers used to wear, tucked into the boots, and green dress-jackets."[1]) If captured, they were to say that they were Chinese of Russian extraction. The Soviets were deadly serious about these matters. One Soviet pilot downed behind UN lines ejected safely, but then shot himself, presumably rather than face Stalin's wrath upon repatriation. In another case, a Red Air Force pilot who was shot down over the water was actually machine-gunned to death by his "fellow" fliers, despite UNC aircraft efforts to rescue him. Obviously, it could be argued that the Soviets operated under considerably more onerous "political restrictions" than anything laid on UNC pilots, who at the least could speak their own language, wear their own clothes, and did not have to fear death at the hands of their own fellows. Stalin seemed to have about as genuine a fear of the imminence of the Third World War at the time as did his UN adversaries. He was well aware that some 22 nations were arrayed with the other side in Korea and that the Americans were dropping bombs on the DPRK at a rate exceeding that of the Second World War. The Soviet dictator summarized to Mao his extreme caution in this air war:

> We can send a certain number of aircraft to offer air cover; however, our air force can only be used in [your] rear and front-line positions [the latter never happened]. In order to avoid any damaging effects to world opinion, our air force should not be employed behind the enemy's rear so as to guarantee that our aircraft will not be shot down and our pilots captured.[2]

Both sides felt it to be in their best interests to refrain from revealing the fact that Soviet pilots were flying most of the MiG missions. Even USAF pilots claimed to be unsure of this fact and wasted a lot of time in speculation as to the nationality of their opponents. The US government was quite sure from Central Intelligence Agency reports that the best MiG pilots were indeed Soviets, but this information was kept secret for some four decades, for fear that the far-right would then demand "tougher" measures that could well lead to a widening of the war. A CIA National Intelligence Estimate of 30 July 1952 flatly stated that "a de facto air war exists over North Korea between the UN and the USSR". But nothing was said publicly on the question. One of the few cases of an American soldier positively identifying Soviet troops in Korea and telling the tale was one Captain (Retired) Jack Gifford, US Army, who reports that as a POW:

> on the way to the POW camps I passed near a rest and recreation area for Soviet air defense soldiers. I met those Russians, in their Russian uniforms and riding in their Russian vehicles.[3]

There is no question that the American political leadership knew very well that Soviet pilots were flying those MiGs. The papers of Dwight Eisenhower contain at least four memoranda drawn up just before and soon after the armistice, whose conclusions were based on interviews with scores of returned former POWs. All documents pusillanimously agreed that no "unfavorable publicity concerning Soviet participation" be released.[4] The Soviet government also kept the secret. Apparently the US could bomb hell out of a fraternal socialist state just across the border from the Soviet Union, but if the Soviets were known to have fought openly in aid of that friendly power, that might be considered an unwarranted escalation of the war.

The Chinese themselves first entered the air war on 21 December 1950, flying their initial combat missions with the Soviets. The basic problem with the People's Liberation Army Air Force (PLAAF) was that from its beginnings, in 1949–50, it recruited more on the basis of political reliability than technical expertise. Not one PLAAF trainee had air combat qualifications, yet they were to go up against UNC pilots with a wealth of Second World War experience. The PRC military leadership actually believed that air combat was relatively simple, and that motivated pilots could pick up what they needed to know through hands-on training. Most unrealistically, Chinese military air leaders actually believed that they would prevail over the USAF. Further, the leadership emphasized that the PLAAF was indeed but a branch of the PLA, yet the PLAAF was never used in the role of ground support. The Soviet air advisers could do little to reverse this inauspicious beginning. Their role was advisory only, and, in fact, when the PLAAF entered its initial

combat against UNC air forces, those advisers had for the most part been withdrawn and the remainder played a negligible role in air operations.

In January the PLAAF did score its first kill, an obsolete straight-wing
USAF F-84 jet fighter. There were recurring problems with technically
incompetent fliers, however, including air-to-air collisions. In the early months
of combat one out of every 42.2 sorties resulted in a serious accident. For
example, on 10 and 12 February 1951 three accidents claimed three pilots
and four MiGs. Understandably, for the next six months air operations were
conducted solely by Soviet pilots. But a Chinese air regimental commander
was shot down the following June by defensive fire from a lumbering B-29
bomber. The PLAAF also had to give up plans for close air support of its ground
troops and did not even deploy any of its aircraft to bases inside North Korea.
PLAAF piston-engine bombers did so poorly in their missions that they
were withdrawn entirely from Korean combat. One such mission, against an
ROK-held island used as an intelligence-gathering station, resulted in four
Tu-2s and three La-11s lost to USAF Sabres. Most Chinese jet air victories
were scored against the older, straight-wing jet F-80s and F-84s.

The North Koreans entered their own air war, much later than their
allies, with one air division at the beginning of 1952 and another two by the
end of the year. They, however, do not seem to have seen much combat
because of their low state of readiness.

After early 1952 the Soviets apparently gave up their attempts to wrest
air supremacy from the UNC. Instead they seemed to use MiG Alley as a
"finishing school" for the advanced training of North Korean and Chinese
fighter pilots, as well as to give their own fliers a taste of combat.

The Soviets used this war to obtain as much information as possible on
the military aviation technology of the West. The North Koreans had proved
hopeless in their interrogations of downed fliers. More often than not, these
"air pirates" were simply beaten to death. Matters came to a head in December 1950, when MiGs downed near the Chinese border a senior Pentagon
intelligence colonel on a special mission in a brand-new jet light bomber in
what could have been the greatest intelligence prize of the war. But the
colonel's unco-operative attitude so angered a North Korean general that
the American was taken to a local village with the placard "War Criminal"
around his neck – and was beaten to death by villagers.

The Soviets then directly intervened with proper interrogations, tough,
even brutal at times, but certainly an improvement on that of the North
Koreans. (Throughout the war just about anyone, Soviet or Chinese, was
an improvement on the North Koreans.) Stalin and the Red Air Force were,
of course, particularly eager to obtain an intact F-86 as well as a late-model
USAF helicopter. A special squadron was even set up to force down a Sabre

jet intact, but the attempt failed disastrously, with two MiGs lost instead! By the end of 1951, however, one such F-86 was somehow obtained and shipped to the Soviet Union, where it was stripped down to the last rivet and detailed drawings were made up. Apparently a new "Soviet" F-86 was built from these drawings. A USAF helicopter was also obtained by being lured into a trap when the Soviet adviser to a North Korean intelligence team forced a captured USAF pilot to broadcast a phoney message on the rescue channel with his portable transmitter.

The Soviets' technology-gathering programme eventually paid off. The information obtained in "MiG Alley" enabled the Red Air Force to narrow the gap with the United States considerably in aviation technology. Further, the Chinese People's Liberation Army Air Force, as a direct result of the Korean War, grew from practically nothing to one of the world's largest air forces by the end of the war.

Some US pilot POWs were taken out of North Korea into China, where they faced intensive interrogation that over the months yielded not only technical data on aircraft and bases, organizational structures, flight patterns and battle tactics, but also information on crew members, from home addresses to professions, income of parents, and so on, even to the taste in whiskey of a certain squadron commander, or whether another preferred blondes or brunettes. The interrogators were Soviet air officers, posing as Chinese, or were Soviet ethnic Chinese, Mongols, or Koreans. Apparently some USAF commanders in the field, realizing what their aircrews might have to face, told them (informally) that they would probably have to give their captors more than the traditional "name, rank and serial number". Although the Communists managed to extract valuable intelligence from their USAF POWs, apparently none actually collaborated with their captors. Decades later a Soviet veteran of these interrogations in North Korea conceded that he could "not recall a single instance" in which a USAF pilot agreed to work for the Russians.[5] There is also evidence that some USAF pilots were taken to the Soviet Union itself, but none have ever returned to tell that tale. In all, 56 F-86 pilots were shot down, but the fate of 30 of them remains unknown.

Just like the Soviets, the United States also wanted to get its hands on their enemy's latest jet fighter, but went about it differently. "Operation Moolah" crassly offered $100,000 to the first MiG pilot to fly his intact aircraft to a UNC base and $50,000 to subsequent jet defectors. Although this gambit played into the Communists' stereotype of "capitalist corruption", several Communist pilots were depraved enough to try for this jackpot. None succeeded until a few weeks after the armistice. Then the first North Korean pilot to fly his MiG-BIS South somewhat spoiled the general rejoicing by claiming that he knew nothing about any monetary offer, although he did put in his claim. President Eisenhower, preferring a more purely ideological appeal, was not happy about such vulgar financial inducements. The $50,000 rewards were withdrawn, although at least one more North Korean pilot later also flew South. The first defected MiG was carefully examined and flown by USAF technical experts, but the Americans did not construct an "imperialist MiG" or copy any of its features.

The UNC Commander at the time of "Moolah", General Mark Clark, and the USAF official history of the Korean War agreed that one of the side-benefits of "Operation Moolah" was the considerable falling-off in the quality of MiG pilots, as fliers were dispatched into battle more on the basis of their loyalty than their air skills. There is also evidence that the Soviets withdrew their pilots from combat, for Stalin was still determined that none of his military personnel should fall into the hands of the UNC.

Although the Soviet MiG pilot rotation policy aimed to give Red Air Force jet fliers combat experience at about the time these pilots were really learning their job they were rotated out of the combat zone. This policy combined with an inferior training programme and a general way of life that discouraged individual initiative to give a sharp edge to the American fliers. For example, in the winter of 1952 the USAF reported that of 32 MiGs seen falling into a spin during air combat, only eight pilots had been observed to bail out or correct the spin.

Contrary to general opinion, however, Sabre pilots were not more experienced in jet aircraft than their opponents. Only the RAF and the *Luftwaffe* had flown jet aircraft combat missions in the Second World War (although, as noted, not against each other). If anything, Soviet pilots had a slight edge in modern jet combat experience. A Soviet air division was dispatched in early 1950 to the air defence of the Shanghai area where its MiG-15 pilots shot down eight Nationalist aircraft. By contrast, no USAF pilot was involved in any aerial combat, jet or piston, between the end of the Second World War and the opening of the Korean War. However, there is little doubt that the USAF could draw on more sophisticated equipment as well as on far more technically experienced ground maintenance enlisted cadre, who in their teenage years may well have torn down and rebuilt a series of "hot rod" automobiles. Most of the USAF's Korean War "aces" also were veterans of piston-engine aerial combat in the Second World War, but then so were most Soviet pilots.

At the time and for decades after, USAF pilots claimed to have shot down MiGs at the unprecedented ratio of 8 to 1. More recent data coming from the former Soviet Union tends to reduce the number of MiG kills from the 792 originally claimed to something under 400. According to these figures,

Sabre losses were slightly over 100, giving them an actual kill ratio of about 3.5 to 1, when victories by other aircraft (such as US Navy fighters and Allied aircraft) are factored into the ratio. Some recent sources, however, still claim a USAF kill rate superiority of some 7 to 1. There is nothing particularly mysterious or reprehensible about such conflicting aerial victory claims continuing so many years after a war. Battle of Britain comparative losses are still in dispute. Whatever the cause or the exact "kill score", the superiority of the Americans in "MiG Alley" sounded the one note of undoubted, sustained victory in this frustrating and stalemated conflict.

On the other hand, if one counts in the number of UNC aircraft lost to ground fire, or obsolete piston-engine warplanes, then there is no argument that the UN air forces in the Korean War lost far more aircraft than did their enemies. Although only 147 USAF aircraft were shot down in air-to-air combat, more than 816 were lost to ground fire. US Navy and Marine air lost approximately 600 aircraft – again, the overwhelming majority to ground fire. But then, far more aircraft have been lost to ground fire than to air combat in practically every air war.

The USAF was obviously successful in its missions of air reconnaissance, transport, medical evacuation (some 8,600 front-line UN troops evacuated) and Air Service Rescue. For example, all wounded from the retreat from the Changjin were air-evacuated to the rear. This was also the first war in which airmen downed in enemy territory stood a reasonable chance of rescue (some 996 airmen rescued), because of the helicopter (and UNC air control).

Finally, the USAF was by no means reconciled to a policy of no nuclear strikes in Korea. At the beginning of the war, Strategic Air Command chief, General Curtis LeMay, professed surprise that the United States did not immediately "nuke" North Korea. In early 1951 the USAF conducted the first tests of tactical nuclear weapons and then embarked on a programme to install these weapons into its tactical warplanes. The fitting of atomic bombs into the B–29 – "Project Saddletree" and "Project On Top" – had been ongoing since 1948. Both the Air Force and the Army high commands considered that if the armistice negotiations failed it might become necessary to resort to nuclear weapons to overcome the Communists' supposed enormous manpower advantage. The Joint Chiefs of Staff approved of the nuclear proposal but only in the event that Eighth Army faced annihilation.

In the end, the only USAF mission in Korea that was remotely nuclear was the strange Operation HUDSON HARBOR, in which dummy atomic bombs were actually dropped over North Korea. HUDSON HARBOR did demonstrate the requirement for an effective battlefield nuclear strike: the timely identification of masses of enemy troops in sufficient numbers, which was almost completely absent in Korea – something that UNC intelligence could have told the USAF in the first place. At any rate, had "The Bomb" indeed been dropped against some target in Korea, with predictably meagre results, the fear-inspired nuclear deterrent would have been largely dissipated. In actuality, the direst American nuclear threats were issued after the armistice and were calculated to see that the peace was not broken.

Such inconvenient considerations, however, did little to dampen the USAF's enthusiasm for cheap "push-button, nuclear warfare", and US military planners continued to insist that nuclear weapons were merely "just another type of battlefield ordnance". The Army, not to be outdone, developed plans for nuclear artillery shells for the "Pentatomic Divisions", plans that eventually brought forth the atomic cannon, a monstrous weapon that took hours to emplace and which must have been one of the most useless weapons of modern times.

It seems incredible that the United States, already labouring under something of a moral cloud since the nuclear bombings of Hiroshima and Nagasaki little more than five years earlier, would even consider the dropping once again of nuclear ordnance on Asians. Presumably, high US authorities eventually did take into account the global adverse propaganda "fall-out" that would have followed such a horrific action, although the record here is unclear. The US President had no intention of becoming the only man in history to order twice the dropping of an atomic bomb. For Harry Truman, once was quite enough.

Naval air war

During the Korean War, aircraft carriers were employed primarily as mobile airfields off the Korean coast in ground attack interdiction missions. In this conflict there would be no great carrier-to-carrier clashes over hundreds of square miles with hostile air fleets battling above the carriers, as took place in the Second World War in the Pacific. In fact, none of the USN's front-line, late-Second World War carriers, the *Midway* class, were ever deployed to Korean waters, another indication that the Pentagon and US political leaders viewed the Korean War as a "sideshow" compared to the main threat in Europe. UN carrier forces would enjoy near-complete freedom from Communist interference in their missions.

US and Commonwealth carriers gave the UNC an ability to penetrate deeply into North Korea with minimal fuel worries. (This war was fought for the most part in the pre-air-to-air refuelling days.) UN naval air power, hastily grouped into Anglo–American Task Force 77, consisted of RN carrier

7. US Navy pilot surveys his bomb load – everything including the kitchen sink.
National Archives

Triumph and USN carrier *Valley Forge*. TF 77's warplanes first struck ground targets on 3 July 1950, attacking Haeju Airfield and Pyongyang itself. They shot down two YAKs and destroyed another on the ground along with railroad rolling stock. Later, TF 77 fighters ranged even further into North Korea, devastating the Wonsan oil refinery, which could supply some 500 tons of petroleum products per day to the Communist forces.

With great accuracy, UNC naval air attacked Communist ground targets during the Pusan Perimeter battles. Here the slower but more rugged piston-engine fighters that still formed the bulk of the UN naval air fleet proved their worth, coming in low, slow, and accurately just ahead of UN positions. Any problems were not so much in the equipment but in the lack of effective radio communication between Air Force and Naval strike forces and their ground controllers. Fully 30 per cent of naval close air support (CAS) missions had to be "scrubbed" because of this single problem that persisted through the end of the war.

Both USAF and USN CAS methods had their merits, with the former emphasizing second-echelon air interdiction and the latter dealing with the

Communists down to the perimeter wire. To take an extreme example, at the Marine withdrawal from the Changin Reservoir, Marine/Naval air sometimes flew *under* mortar fire to deliver its ordnance. In brief, for the Navy and Marines CAS was a substitute for a lack of artillery, while for the USAF, CAS was an adjunct to long-range artillery. But the USAF doctrine and its application came under heavy criticism because its shortcomings were so obvious to the troops on the ground.

Naval air ranged up and down the Korean peninsula, following the fortunes of war. At any one time, TF 77s usually operated in the Sea of Japan off Korea's east coast, with three carriers on station, two conducting flight operations and one replenishing at sea. A fourth carrier would be enjoying port call in Japan, although on 12-hour recall status. Besides the United States, Great Britain and Australia were the only powers to deploy aircraft carriers to Korean waters.

The USN carriers launched piston-engine F4U Corsairs and AD Skyraiders, as well as jet F9F Panthers and F2H Banshee fighters and ground attack warplanes. RN and RAN carriers flew off obsolete Supermarine Seafire 47s, Hawker Sea Furies, and Fairy Fireflies. Nonetheless these latter were rugged aircraft and performed yeoman service in ground attack missions. (It might even be argued that the greatest contribution of the RN carriers at this time was in the application of their combat experience in perfecting the angled-flight deck, the enclosed bow, the lens mirror landing system and the steam catapult, all RN innovations that were later taken up by the US Navy.)

None of the USN, RN, or RAN naval air fighters could stand up to the MiGs and had to be escorted on their missions over North Korea by Sabres. Astonishingly, USN and Marine aircraft actually shot down more MiGs than were lost to the MiGs: 13 MiGs to 5 USN and Marine aircraft. As with the USAF, far more UN naval aircraft were shot down by Communist ground fire than in air combat. It was an indication of Soviet backwardness in electronics that the efficient Communist anti-aircraft barrage was directed by British and US fire control systems shipped to the USSR as a part of Second World War Lend-Lease. They also deployed one Japanese early warning system, possibly an ex-Nazi *Freya* radar, as well as Soviet models. Nonetheless, US Navy Electronic Counter-Measures (ECG) personnel reported that North Korean anti-aircraft equipment was effective and their crews well-disciplined in its use, a conclusion that UNC pilots would heartily reinforce.

UN naval air forces were not spared the frustrations that so characterized the Korean War. They shared daunting losses for modest discernible gain in the interdiction campaign. Due to their reputation for mounting accurate ground attacks, Navy and Marine pilots were especially used in attacks against bridges.

But the Communists knew that these were prime targets and were ready. Losses were heavy enough to affect morale, as was brought out by James Michener in his classic novel, *The Bridges at Toko-Ri*. Korea was the last war fought almost totally with what would later be termed "iron" or "dumb" bombs. In later conflicts, precision-guided missiles would make the mission of bridge dropping decreasingly hazardous.

By the end of the war the US Navy and Marines had lost 564 aircraft, about an average of one per day; 400 fighters, 140 attack aircraft. The remaining lost USAF aircraft were observation, patrol and utility types. Almost all were lost to Communist ground fire.

Naval surface warfare

On 25 June 1950 the US Naval Force's Far East Fleet (FE) was a modest force indeed, totalling one light cruiser, four destroyers, four amphibious ships, one submarine, ten minesweepers and an attached frigate from the Royal Australian Navy. (Not much of a force with which to start a war, even in Korea.) But this force became the nucleus of an expansion that would see 12 USN carriers serve in Korea. All four of the USN's *Iowa* class of battleships (the last class of battlewagons ever completed: *Iowa*, *New Jersey*, *Missouri* and *Wisconsin*) would eventually come on station, providing vital off-shore bombardment with their enormous 16in guns.

UN naval forces could cruise along the Korean peninsula's coastline, hitting Communist troop concentrations, supply caches and supply lines, unhindered except for mines and shore batteries. They destroyed hundreds of North Korean small craft. In return, Communist shore batteries damaged 84 UN warships, inflicting a small number of casualties but not sinking one. North Korean mines, on the other hand, cheap and plentiful, sank several South Korean and USN minesweepers. USN destroyer *Walke* suffered the highest UNC naval casualties of the war when it struck a mine off Hungnam on 12 June 1951, losing 26 seamen, although the ship remained afloat.

Primarily, UN naval power made it possible to bring to the peninsula the troops and equipment needed to save the Republic of Korea. The very strength of this armada undoubtedly discouraged the Communist powers from even attempting to challenge the bridge of ships and their escorts to Korea. President Truman had made it clear at the very opening of this war that any attempt by the Chinese Communists (and by implication, the Soviets) to interfere with UN forces deploying to Korea would be met with force. To make his point, he ordered the Seventh Fleet, consisting of carrier *Valley Forge*, heavy cruiser *Rochester*, eight destroyers, and three submarines, to manoeuvre along the Chinese and Korean coasts. Despite their strong protests about "provocative gestures" the Chinese and the Soviets apparently read Truman's message aright. By this single gesture President Truman probably avoided a wider war and saved the Republic of Korea. To the end of the war, freighters and loaded troopships lumbered their way to Pusan without hindrance, usually not even in convoy.

Second in importance only to its mission of securing the unhindered passage of troops and supplies to Korea, the UNC navies were able to blockade North Korea far more tightly than could air interdiction. Like all naval blockades, this one involved tedious work, rarely reported in the press, devoid of major clashes with the enemy, and with little sense of accomplishment. Blockaders can take pride only in what their enemy is *not* able to accomplish. The Communist forces were *not* able to resupply their troops through Wonsan or Hungnam. Had they been able to do so, the UN position, at least in the first months of the war or in early 1951, would have been even more precarious. As it was, the US Chief of Naval Operations could report that any "leakage" of the blockade amounted merely to a trickle of coastal small craft that could bring in only minute amounts of high-priority cargo at night. The highlight of the UN naval interdiction of North Korea was the blockade of the major port of Wonsan. From 16 February 1951 to the end of the war, Task Force 95 denied the North Koreans the use of this vital facility by off-shore bombardment and naval air strikes. It was the longest naval blockade of modern times and it is credited with diverting some 80,000 Communist troops from the battle lines to the south, awaiting a landing that never came.

Naval surface operations in the Korean War began in the opening hours of the invasion, late on the night of 25 June. An ROK patrol craft intercepted and sank a North Korean warship off the southwestern coast that was apparently coming to aid a Communist *coup de main* against Pusan. One week later, on 2 July, US cruiser *Juneau*, RN cruiser *Jamaica* and RN frigate *Black Swan* intercepted a North Korean naval force of torpedo boats and gunboats off the east coast as they moved towards Pusan. Five of the North Korean ships were destroyed. The only fleet action of the Korean War, this engagement may have forestalled another Communist attempt on Pusan. These small-scale and one-sided encounters had long-term effects, putting an end to any North Korean pretensions of a naval flanking of UNC positions. Of course, the North Koreans had their own version about the early days of the naval war in Korean waters:

The 2d Torpedo Boat Unit of the Navy sank a heavy cruiser of the US imperialist navy and damaged a light cruiser. This was a fact unparalleled in the history of naval battle.[6]

No such USN warship was ever sunk in this war. Had the US Navy been able to hide the sinking of one of its heavy cruisers for something like half a century it would indeed have been a "fact unparalleled"!

The greatest UN naval operation of the Korean War was, of course, that in support of the Inchon landings in September 1950. There 230 UN warships protected and disembarked the main components of X Corps without much hindrance from Communist air or naval forces and turned the tide of battle in favour of the UNC. General MacArthur's plans for another "master stroke", the landing at Wonsan on Korea's east coast, did not follow the script so closely, but instead degenerated into a major de-mining operation.

For the remainder of the conflict, UN naval forces blockaded North Korea, protected supply routes to the Korean peninsula, bombarded shore targets and landed special forces behind Communist lines. As with UN air power, UN sea power could not have won the war, but it is difficult to see how UN forces could have even maintained their hold in the South of Korea in the absence of either weapon. Several decades later, Admiral of the Fleet of the Soviet Union, Sergei G. Gorshkov, recognized that "Without the extensive active employment of the Navy, the interventionists would hardly have been able to avoid a military defeat in Korea."[7] High praise indeed from an unexpected source.

UNC naval losses were very moderate, a tribute to that command's near-complete control of the waters around the Korean peninsula. It is somehow indicative of this naval war, that more than 4,000 US Navy personnel died from injuries or disease, but only 458 in combat.

Air and naval superiority gave the edge to the UN Command, enabling it to fight the Communist forces to a stalemate. But a stalemate is not a satisfying conclusion to any war.

Chapter Eleven

Behind the lines

Civil affairs and military government

Among the most pressing problems behind the lines – and along them at times, for that matter – was that of civilian refugees. During the Second World War in Europe, the US and British Armies had developed an effective apparatus for taking care of these unfortunates. By the end of that war, some 25,000 US Army civil affairs personnel had been responsible for an incredible total of 80 million enemy and Allied civilians, either through the relief activities of what it termed civil affairs or through military government in the battle zone and in occupied enemy nations. Not one documented case is known of any overt resistance to Allied civil affairs/military government, a remarkable record considering that some of these people were armed, and that there was a war going on.

But this civil affairs/military government legacy had been sorely diminished with the end of the war. This loss would not prove crippling in the Korean War because US Army civil affairs would be operating in a land in which the overwhelming majority of the inhabitants were farmers, agricultural labourers, shopkeepers and craftsmen, where fertilizers and draft animals were more important than electricity supply or railway rehabilitation. The other UN contributors did not field civil affairs units in Korea.

The Japanese colonial economic legacy did leave a respectable rail and communications network, by far the most developed hydroelectric complex in Asia, a scattering of small to medium-sized factories and a surprisingly large class of professionals. But this legacy had been superimposed upon a society that had remained overwhelmingly agrarian and steeped in an ancient, proud and united culture.

In this war US Army civil affairs had to work with an internationally recognized government, which for all of its faults proved punctiliously insistent upon its sovereignty. Thus, the Korean War was also the first US conflict in which its Army became far more involved with civil affairs than with military government; that is, with the preservation and restoration of a nation, as opposed to its governance by an outside military power.

Further, in place of the Civil Affairs Division of the Second World War US Army, Civil Affairs now had to work through literally dozens of officially recognized organizations. Within Eighth Army alone seven different units had varying degrees of direct relationship with Republic of Korea authorities. There was the United Nations Commission for the Unification and Rehabilitation of Korea (UNCURK) and its executive agency, the UN Korean Reconstruction Agency (UNKRA). Then, in the first year of the war, Eighth Army established a special staff section titled the Civil Assistance Section, later raised to a command titled the UN Civil Assistance Command, Korea (UNCAK). Fortunately, this organizational complexity and the necessity for constant consultation with their Korean ally did not seem to inhibit US Army civil affairs units and personnel in the field from compiling an impressive record, particularly in refugee assistance and economic reconstruction.

Something like three million Koreans, North and South, were uprooted by this war and moved or had to be moved out of the way of combat operations. They also had to be fed, inoculated and at least temporarily housed, in accordance with international law. The refugee problem was exacerbated by North Korean troops' unnerving habit of changing into civilian garb and infiltrating behind the lines, at least in the first months of the war.

Because the government of the Republic of Korea was a functioning entity throughout the Korean War, the necessity for actual military government was limited to the areas of combat operations. The UNC's military government and civil affairs mandate was strictly limited and could not always exercise the control necessary to protect the civilian population from the UN Command's own troops. For example, the liberation of Pyongyang was marred by widespread looting. US civil affairs troops also witnessed some appalling civilian atrocities by ROK troops and police, including the execution of political prisoners, and could do little more than remonstrate and report on what they had seen.

More positively, US Army civil affairs programmes contributed substantially to the immediate rehabilitation of Korea's infrastructure, with UNCAK concentrating on restoring Korean manufacturing capacity, the railroads, communications and road networks, as well as importing unfinished and semi-finished materials, fertilizer and livestock.

Only in the Democratic People's Republic of Korea itself and then only briefly, did the UNC exercise military government. Stationed behind ornate desks, over which avuncular portraits of Stalin and Kim Il Sung gazed, US officers had the satisfaction of administering Pyongyang for some six weeks. Throughout the two-thirds of North Korea that was occupied, the UNC mandated a purge of Communists from positions of authority and influence but also planned for unimpeded elections for a united Korea. Of course, the intervention of the Chinese rendered all these preparations purely theoretical exercises. The one tangible accomplishment of UNC military government in North Korea was the successful evacuation of hundreds of thousands of Korean civilian refugees.

Aside from its refugee work, it is difficult to assess the more lasting contributions of UNC civil affairs to South Korea. Peasants returned to their farms with or without the blessing of civil affairs, military government, or ROK officials and picked up their timeless agrarian cycle. Furthermore, the US Army persisted in viewing its civil affairs as something akin to disaster relief, thus giving strong support, for example, to refugee relief but considerably less to longer-term work with the settled population. Civil affairs was also unable to prevail on the ROK national government to take strong measures to check the ravages of monetary inflation. But the Republic of Korea did not have the resources to fight an all-out modern war and still function as a nation. Therefore, the US Army had to step in to keep the rather primitive ROK economy functioning throughout the war.

The North Koreans themselves imposed a brief occupation on the Republic of Korea, except for the Pusan Perimeter, between July and September 1950. Of course, officially, this was no occupation at all but the "liberation" and "reunification" of the nation under the all-wise Kim Il Sung and the Korean Workers' Party. The Pyongyang regime found no dearth of South Koreans willing to collaborate with the "reconstruction" of southern life. Nearly 50 members of the old ROK Assembly who had remained to take their chances now declared their allegiance to the DPRK. A former ROK political leader who had fled North and become Minister of Justice, Yi Sung-yop, exploited anti-Rhee sentiment to form a Seoul People's Committee, under strict Communist control. He promised that there would be no purges of former rightists, that, indeed, all but the most refractory would flourish under the new order.

Despite Yi Sung-yop's kindly words, a reign of terror did take place in the South with old scores being settled, with landlords, police and political opponents shot. The hundreds of thousands of pre-war refugees from the North also had some explaining to do or went into hiding. The South's large

Christian population was particularly singled out for "correction", and many, again, went underground.

Some writers sympathetic to the Communists give the North's occupation credit for land redistribution and something of a social revolution. Yet well before the North's invasion, land reform had been under way as a result of US pressure on the Rhee regime during the American military government of the South, and would have been difficult to undo, even if Rhee's government had the will. Supposedly a majority of the workers and about one-half of the students in the Seoul area rallied to the new regime and many volunteered for service in the KPA to unify their country. As time went on, however, word of the battlefield "meat-grinder" to the south filtered northward and such volunteering dropped off markedly. Tenant farmers who had believed that henceforth they would live peacefully on the land of their deposed landlord now found themselves saddled with taxes at least the equal of their former rent payments and ROK taxes combined. Their sons who might earlier have eluded the ROK Army net were now being rounded up by the *Inmin Gun* press gangs which, unlike the Rhee minions, were less likely to look the other way in return for a bribe. In all, life in "liberated" Korea turned out to be more harsh than anything under the Rhee regime. (For his "moderation" during the KPA occupation of South Korea, Yi Sung-yop himself was arrested immediately after the end of hostilities, given a military trial and shot soon after as a "state enemy who colluded with the American imperialists" to overthrow Kim Il Sung's regime.)

PVA military government and civil affairs basically began with the Communist re-taking of Pyongyang and the establishment of a temporary regime that was by all available accounts orderly and untouched by the looting and settling of scores by ROK troops during the brief UNC occupation. This was understandable in that the PVA was liberating a friendly city and the anti-Communist elements had most likely fled *en masse*. The PVA occupation of Seoul and the northern reaches of South Korea also seems to have been fairly modest, although troop misbehaviour or heavy exactions would hardly have been publicized. In North Korea and occupied ROK territory, food requisitions for the PVA officially fell more heavily on "landlords and rich peasants", while the poor were more likely to be fed by the Chinese military. As peasants themselves for the most part, CPV troops were particularly useful in helping Korean farmers with their crops. The CPV also provided food, clothing and medical care to Korean civilians and even set up small shops where civilians could purchase basic consumer goods unobtainable from the devastated local economy. Here, as in their POW policy, the Chinese attempted to win over more by "re-education" than by force, although this was wartime and they were not to be trifled with. Certainly there were tensions between the North Koreans and their CPV rescuers as the latter came to dominate the anti-UNC war, but probably no more than those between the UNC and the Rhee regime in the South. Nonetheless, the PVA had nothing like the resources for any civil affairs programme like that mounted by the UNC throughout South Korea.

Ideology and psychological warfare

The fact that the end of the Korean War was delayed for about one year of arduous and acrimonious negotiations primarily over the very ideological issue of whether POWs should be repatriated against their will gives some indication of the passion of this conflict. The Communists were fighting for a united, utopian, Communist Korea; the Republic of Korea and its allies to halt "Communist aggression". In such a conflict psychological warfare would obviously be emphasized by both sides. There seems to be a perception that psychological warfare in Korea has been almost ignored, at least in the West, this may have something to do with the perception at the time and even today that the Communists were somehow "masters of propaganda". Of course, all the Communist propaganda that is available in the West, at least until the opening some day of the Pyongyang and Beijing archives, are some of the leaflets themselves and transcripts of Communist loudspeaker and radio broadcasts that have been preserved in the West. Western "psywar", on the other hand, is amply documented, although little used.

Less than 24 hours after President Truman's decision to commit US ground forces to the Korean War, the first psychological warfare leaflet was dropped over the battle zone. It urged South Korean troops and civilians to stand firm, and pledged that Free World forces would soon come to their aid and throw back the aggressor. This first US psywar effort, composed in typescript and with only the UN logo for illustration, was fairly primitive by Second World War standards or in comparison with what was to come in this war. But almost 12 million were printed and dropped, by far the largest one-day drop of the war. Of course, all of this was performed *ad hoc*, after hasty arrangements with the USAF Far East Air Force. For the remainder of that conflict, leaflets would serve, as they had in most twentieth-century wars, as the primary medium for psychological warfare.

Apparently all anti-Communist propaganda was in the hands of the UNC, which meant, for all practicable purposes, the United States Far East Command. But a competent corps of Korean and Chinese translators was able to write up psywar messages in language credible to the target audiences.

During the desperate Pusan Perimeter fighting, UNC leaflets defiantly stressed the growing might of the UN forces pouring into Korea. These leaflets at first showed the full faces of "happy POWs", a common theme throughout the war; later the subjects' eyes were blurred or blanked out in deference to fears that their families might be victimized. Later still, the visages had to be restored after Communist broadcasts claimed that they had been disfigured by poison gas experiments. These weeks also saw the first specific safe conduct/surrender leaflets, carrying a message in English that ordered UN soldiers to treat the bearer "as an honorable prisoner of war". Unfortunately, by war's end there were six different versions, which often confused possible defectors who might wonder which was the current valid version.

Through the summer of 1950 UNC psywar could claim little tangible success. This was understandable, considering the military situation. On the eve of the Inchon landings, Eighth Army had captured only a little more than 1,100 Communist troops. But with those landings, UNC psywar personnel could point to increasing numbers of Communist POWs as some evidence of the success of their efforts. In fact, it was at this time, September through November 1950, that the UN Command garnered by far its greatest number of POWs as the North Korean armies retreated northward. But Chinese intervention and the UN retreat back to South Korea ended this phase of the war.

By early 1951 some 160,000,000 leaflets of 100 different types had been dropped by the UNC in Korea, a figure that was still well below the numbers dropped just in the Philippines in the Second World War. As for the effectiveness of UNC psywar, US Army studies at the time indicated that about 30 per cent of Communist POWs claimed that they had been influenced by the product. Another survey attempted to avoid any pro-UNC bias in its conclusions by asking roughly 750 POWS more indirect questions in a "probing, conversational" framework. These prisoners claimed that the greatest obstacle to their surrender was their fear of being killed in the attempt. The promise of cigarettes and freedom from hard labour as well as safety from aerial attack were important to these captives, most of whom claimed that they believed the "happy POW" leaflets. Another group of 768 North Koreans and 238 Chinese prisoners gave roughly the same answers. This batch of prisoners also claimed that they had discussed the leaflets among themselves despite their officers' prophylactic and punitive measures, but that the messages had little influence on those officers or NCOs.

The most far-ranging of these studies at this time concluded that "The enemy has shown, by his own emphasis on psywar, by specific imitations of US methods so far as his resources permit, and by his strenuous countermeasures, that he takes psywar seriously."[1]

In late January 1951, Eighth Army established its own Psychological Warfare Division under the Assistant Chief of Staff for Operations (G-3). By that summer the unit had grown to more than 139 military, US civilian and indigenous personnel, and its title changed to the Psychological Warfare Section.

At corps level (two divisions), psywar was handled by one full-time officer, usually a major in G-3 (Operations), responsible for leaflet dissemination and loudspeaker operations. At the division level, one officer, usually a lieutenant or captain, also in G-3, was assigned "additional duties" in psywar of target selection and the facilitation of psywar originating at higher echelons. Yet to the end of the war, despite the undoubted success of UNC psychological warfare, "old army men" still doubted its effectiveness and, in fact, hardly understood what it was all about.

By the summer of 1951, with the war of movement stalled as the United Nations entered into armistice negotiations with the Communists, desertion became physically much more difficult. Practically every foot of no-man's land could be hit by artillery and small-arms fire from both sides. Under these conditions simply encouraging Communist troops to desert was not enough. In response, US psywar began to give detailed escape instructions. Now a typical message might use a well-drawn comic-strip to illustrate in a general way how a Communist soldier could escape to UN lines, there to receive a friendly welcome.

Dissemination of UNC leaflets showed no improvement over that in the Second World War. Due to the inaccurate nature of air drops, artillery remained the only means available in Korea for truly accurate delivery of printed propaganda to specific front-line Communist units, in theory. But the Commonwealth Division, with its 25-pounder guns, was the only UNC unit that could actually fire its artillery leaflets with reasonable accuracy. It was galling to the Americans that the Chinese/Soviet leaflet mortar shell was very simple, very accurate – and in front-line use.

Along the fixed battle lines, loudspeakers for both sides then came into their own. UNC/US Second World War loudspeaker equipment, all that was available until the last year of the war, was heavy and not particularly robust. As in the Second World War, some friendly units complained that loudspeaker units at least did a good job in attracting enemy fire. One report even claimed that in a few cases some of that "incoming" was, for whatever reason, coming in from "friendly" units! Judging from surviving loudspeaker scripts, US loudspeaker teams produced messages that were straightforward enough, certainly compared to those of their enemies in the field.

Like their leaflet counterparts, typical US loudspeaker messages avoided overt political themes. They usually simply offered a way out for the individual Communist soldier, for example:

Soon you will be committed to battle again to be sacrificed in the UN's sea of fire. Think of the thousands and thousands of your comrades who have already died for nothing in this foreign land. Friends, be wise, come to the UN lines, at the first opportunity; you are guaranteed good treatment.

Conversely, the loudspeaker broadcasts by the Communists proved to be something of a unique art form. Verbatim translations give some of the flavour of standard Communist loudspeaker scripts – or something was lost in translation: "United States soldiers, write and ask your families to sign a peace treaty that was drawn up in Philadelphia [?!] a couple of years ago." Another message, directed to the 40th Infantry Division, claimed:

> We have plenty of food, victuals, intercourse, and time off to play cards. Your artillery has broken our microphones. . . . We now must work at night and are required to yell.[2]

Communist leaflets ranged from the professional to the pathetic. Lacking air power, the Communists psywarriors employed farmers or even small boys, carrying their propaganda in nondescript sacks, although the excellent Communist mortar leaflet shells were occasionally employed for short-range delivery.

One Communist leaflet cleverly lifted a beer advertisement from a recent US magazine showing a pair of bathing beauties attended at pool side by two swim-suited young men. It labelled the loungers as a couple of soldiers' wives and their draft-dodging boyfriends back home, a theme that might have raised a twinge of doubt from a GI who perhaps had not heard from his wife for a while. Marxist jargon and mangled names, however, undermined any potential appeal of the leaflet proclaiming that "The real fact is that the American capitalists and their running dog – Truman Clerk [Clark?] turns [sic] your lives into cannon fodder". But another leaflet exhorted in perfectly respectable slang:

> Use your Head Soldier! If you Want to Keep It! Every GI That's Been in Battle knows the Score. Leave Korea to the Koreans.[3]

Probably the best of this mixed lot showed a beaming American soldier, dockside, Stateside, with an arm around his ecstatic wife, and simply said "Leave Korea to the Koreans!", a sentiment that would have been heartily endorsed by about 99 per cent of the non-Korean troops in Korea. Until Pyongyang's and Beijing's archives are opened, it will remain impossible to determine the qualitative disparity in Communist psywar. It is possible that later leaflets improved because of the input, voluntary or otherwise, of UN

POWs, but the leaflets were undated and such an explanation must remain in the realm of conjecture. However, the Americans were much more likely to collect and trade the leaflets than to be influenced by them. Both the Chiefs of the Eighth Army and of US Army psywar departments complained that GI souvenir hounds were complicating their efforts to obtain Communist leaflets. All non–ROK UNC troops were perfectly free to read, buy, sell, or exchange Communist propaganda whenever they wished.

In an effort to achieve some type of "scientific" basis for its psywar, Eighth Army psywar section established a more formal leaflet pre-screening panel composed of North Korean and Chinese POWs. This was a good idea but somewhat tricky in practice. Certain POWs tended to be used time and again, and the more literate, English-speaking, and assertive captives soon took informal leadership roles and told their interrogators what they wanted to hear.

UNC Army psywar efforts were also constantly hampered by rapid personnel turnover after the troop rotation policy was introduced in 1951. One corps with four divisions rotated out no fewer than eight different psywar officers in a single month, and one division ran through six psywar officers in one year. Some psywar officers also complained that their troops were "over-educated" for the work they were doing. They may have had a point; the enlisted men of the 1st Radio Broadcasting and Leaflet Company, for example, held between them more PhDs than there were officers in the group.

Some US leaflets began to show impressive imagination: one printed on flimsy paper stock solicitously noted "Perhaps your supply services are not providing you with cigarette paper. We know that you have been using leaflets to roll your cigarettes". The UN Command would now supply that need in the field by using flimsy paper leaflets, but how much better the fate of the soldier in a POW camp, with all the free cigarettes he could smoke. Another inquired of opposing troops, "Can you keep your feet warm and dry?" under photos depicting shoddy Communist footwear and graphically contrasting this trash with the fine white leather boots worn by "Old White Boots", Lieutenant General Nam Il, at the Panmunjom armistice negotiations. According to one source, for the next three months POWs gave wet, cold feet as a major reason for surrendering.

Eighth Army also offered a considerable number of messages that tried to splinter the "fraternal socialist unity" of the Chinese, the North Koreans and the Russians. Using a commendable knowledge of Communist culture and language, one such leaflet warned the Chinese that they were dupes of *Lao Mao Tzu*, a play on both the name of the "Great Leader" (Mao) and the traditional Chinese term for Russians, "the old hairy". Army psywarriors also targeted press-ganged Nationalist Chinese ("Your ability is being ignored") and South Korean troops in the Communist armies, as well as Communist guerrillas in the South.

Such leaflets also studiously avoided caricatures or denigration of the opposing forces:

> To the men of North Korea; who with doubtless bravery hurled their bodies against a solid wall of flaming steel. We honor you for your courage.

Other themes included emphasis upon the world-wide response to Communist aggression. UNC leaflets even honoured the Chinese icon, Sun Yat Sen, by contrasting his principles with those of China's Communist overlords. ("The Father of Modern China", "His principles must never die".) These leaflets emphasized that the struggle was not with the Chinese people but with their evil leaders, who had sold out to the "Great Hairy". Another effective US leaflet simply featured the Chinese Communist flag, along with some innocuous sentiments praising China and the Chinese people. The last two leaflets had the added advantage that any Communist trooper caught reading "these filthy enemy lies", could plead "But comrade commissar, I just saw our flag [or our beloved Sun Yat Sen] lying there in the mud, and so naturally . . .", and get away with it.

But the surrender leaflet was still the most used to the extent that many Communist soldiers came to believe that they *had* to have one to surrender unharmed. Accordingly, another campaign was mounted to show that all surrenders, with or without the pass, were certainly welcome. Probably the most read leaflet of this war was the newsletter *Free World Weekly Digest*. According to the UNC chief of psywar, POWs almost unanimously agreed that this was their principal source of information that was not egregiously biased.[4] Although the UNC did employ radio propaganda, the very limited access of Communist soldiers to receivers makes any evaluation of effectiveness problematical.

Several US Army or contract studies made near the end of the war indicated genuine success in the US psywar effort. Their conclusions, remarkably similar throughout, are that US Army battlefield psywar did make a difference, particularly when directed at the so-called "marginal man", the Communist soldier who was already discouraged, perhaps in trouble with his NCOs, homesick and worried. These conclusions must be given weight, even when discounted for interviewers' self-advertisement, or mission pride, or for their erstwhile unfamiliarity with their subjects' language and culture, and, of course, for the POWs' "camp-wise" attitudes.

Certainly the 22,000 Communist soldiers (compared to 359 UNC troops) who refused repatriation have over the decades been cited as the strongest proof of the efficacy of US psywar. But from what we know more recently about conditions in the UNC POW camps, that evaluation might be challenged to some extent. Further, US psywar evaluations and reports might be dismissed as self-serving. But it is difficult to argue with the evaluation of several Chinese authorities, writing decades after the war:

> the strongest challenge to the political control of the CPV was the US/ UN psychological warfare. . . . These propaganda measures had a great effect on the Chinese troops. CPV political personnel found out that many soldiers kept the US/UN "security passes" [safe conduct leaflets] in case they were captured. . . . Maintaining high morale among the CPV rank and file became a serious challenge.[5]

The Communists may have gained greater publicity, if not success, with their global "germ warfare" campaign than with their more overt psychological warfare. It is possible that the Communist side genuinely feared that the UNC was about to use bacteriological warfare in Korea when Radio Beijing and the Chinese *People's Daily* reported that Koreans had actually witnessed USAF aircraft drop insects that later caused cholera. The following month, Communist sources claimed that US artillery had shot typhus germs across to Communist positions along with infected animals.

In truth, the US Army had established experimental laboratories for research on such topics. (Evidence unearthed in the 1970s and later also indicates an almost criminally irresponsible attitude towards the safety and ecological dangers posed by such experimentation.) In an even more disreputable development, the US had given immunity to Japanese Army Lieutenant General Shiro Ishii, the commander of a bacteriological warfare centre in Manchuria that had experimented on human beings, in exchange for sharing his findings. This unsavoury bargain had become known to Communist sources, who then spread accounts that the US was working with Japanese war criminals in bacteriological warfare projects. The Communists could also point out that the US was, after all, the only power in the world to use nuclear weapons – against Asians.

In February 1951, Soviet Foreign Minister Malik varied the theme by charging that the US was employing poison gas. Again, Malik might have been reacting to the decision by US Secretary of State Marshall to permit the production of bacteriological weapons in the wake of Pentagon fears that the Communists themselves were probably developing such armament. And later that year, General Ridgway routinely warned US troop commanders to be prepared for possible Communist chemical, biological and radiological attacks. Former Secretary of Defense Louis Johnson conceded that the US did have biological weapons that could be used in Korea if necessary. But however genuine their fears, there is absolutely no evidence that such methods of warfare had actually been put to use in the war by either side.

The Communists soon enough realized that they had the US in something of a double bind. It is logically impossible to prove a negative; the absence of proof cannot count as proof. Furthermore, by denying the charges ("No, the United States has never engaged in bacteriological or chemical warfare in Korea"), the US simply helped along the Communist effort to disseminate those charges. Ignoring the charges would obviously "prove" that the United States had been found out and could not produce convincing proof to the contrary.

The Communists themselves were not immune from bacteriological warfare suspicions. UNC forces occupying Pyongyang in the fall of 1950 found germ cultures at Kim Il Sung Medical College. When the Eighth Army's chief of public health and welfare interrogated as many of the workers as he could at that and other medical facilities, he found suspicious discrepancies in their descriptions of bacteriological research being conducted in North Korea, but had to drop the matter in the absence of any tangible evidence.

It may be significant that the anti-US bacteriological warfare campaign began in early 1951, precisely at the time when the Communist armies were at the end of their tethers, suffering massive casualties as much a result of disease and malnutrition as of overwhelming UNC firepower. There was good UNC intelligence that the Communists were indeed suffering from something like a public health disaster. During the war, their medical services on the peninsula had nearly disintegrated. The movements of hundreds of thousands of troops and civilian refugees up and down the peninsula provided convenient means of spreading disease, while the fighting and bombing destroyed what rudimentary public health facilities and water supplies Korea had possessed prior to the war. The use of human waste as fertilizer exacerbated matters, as did the fact that only a minority of Koreans had been immunized against diseases. In February 1951, Premier Kim Il Sung issued an emergency decree calling on the army and other governmental institutions to initiate a systematic anti-epidemic programme. In each month, six randomly selected clean-up days were to be observed in which rats and flies were to be killed, privies cleaned out, and, portentously, raw food avoided and drinking water boiled. The Chinese people were also put on the alert to defend themselves against the devilish machinations of the Americans and, like their DPRK comrades, were exhorted and compelled to clean up the country, with, again, a campaign against rats and flies. These efforts were coupled with a "hate America" campaign in which most of the ills of the world were laid at the door of American "imperialism". (There were no corresponding "Hate China" or "Hate North Korea" campaigns in the UN countries. A distinction was always drawn between the evil Communist leaders and their decent but downtrodden subjects.) The North Koreans needed no such "Hate America" campaign. The general destruction inflicted by the continual bombing of the DPRK could certainly arouse hatred even from those citizens not particularly enamoured of the Pyongyang regime.

To lend credence to their charges of germ warfare, the Communists needed more proof than the confessions of downed "air pirates", who might be likely to tell their captors what they wished to hear. Thus in March 1952, the International Association of Democratic Lawyers, an ostensibly "impartial" organization, agreed to examine the evidence. In not one case did these non-scientists reject or even modify any Communist claim. Their finding of deep US culpability were given worldwide publicity by the Communist media. They were further publicized and buttressed by another Communist "front", the World Peace Council, which to no one's astonishment found the American military guilty of practically every war crime known to man. In May 1952, two USAF pilots "confessed" to waging germ warfare after having been threatened with trial as war criminals and with non-repatriation, as well as being subjected to the severe mental assault that came to be known as "brainwashing". Even then, the Communists had to edit severely their statements, rewording and taking phrases out of context and splicing recordings to arrive at suitable "confessions". Yet another Communist "front", the International Scientific Commission for the Investigation of the Facts Concerning Bacterial Warfare in Korea and China (which contained some Western scientists who should have known better) supposedly added the scientific weight that the "Democratic Lawyers" had lacked. In September 1952 the Commission issued a 700-page report – from Beijing – which agreed basically with each of the Communists' claims.

But the Communists lost considerable credibility when North Korea and China refused to allow either the International Red Cross or the UN World Health Organization to enter their territory to investigate the allegations. The Communists even rebuffed the International Red Cross' proposal that a team of experts, including Asians approved by North Korea or China, examine the evidence. The Communists' case was weakened still further when, in April 1953, they failed to respond to the UN General Assembly's delegation of a five-power commission to investigate the bacteriological warfare allegations. But by this late stage of the war, the Communists seemed to have lost interest in a campaign that had reaped only modest propaganda advantages in weakening the high moral ground that the US had taken in its stance against forcible repatriation of POWs.

The "germ warfare" campaign did divert attention from the very real public health crisis in North Korea and helped to drum up support in China for the war. It also resulted in a lasting improvement in the public health situation in both nations, as the anti-"plague" measures became a permanent part of the public health programmes of both countries.

The shrill and unforgiving nature of the "germ warfare" campaign makes an instructive contrast with the final US tactical psywar mission of the Korean War, the air dropping of a Chinese and Korean-language leaflet on the last night before the armistice was to go into effect on 27 July 1953. This last leaflet, written by General Clark personally, was almost poignant in its spirit of respect and humanity offered to his enemy at the close of a bitter, ideological war in which neither side could claim victory, and is worth quoting in full:

> With the signing of the armistice, peace and quiet returns [sic] to the hills and valleys of Korea. Over the war-crushed countryside, peace once again reigns. We are happy to know that the days of fear, hunger, cold and exhaustion are over for you. We hope that your leaders will now permit you to leave the service. With good fortune, you may now turn from the bloody waste of war to the achievement of a man's traditional right to rebuild his shattered homeland, till his fields, rear his sons – and given this good fortune, you may now do this. May you be permitted to return to your homes speedily, may you soon be reunited with your families, may we never meet again on the field of battle.[6]

The POW camps

Behind the lines on both sides, the prisoner of war issue festered, and neither side could take pride in the treatment of its captives. There could be no questioning the eagerness of the overwhelming majority of UNC prisoners of the Communists to return home. The US troops that had fallen into the hands of the *Inmin Gun* in the first months of the war were brutally treated. In fact, in the summer of 1950 KPA troops organized something of a "Death March" north for US POWs which easily rivalled anything meted out by the Japanese in the Second World War. Starvation rations, beatings and executions on the spot rapidly thinned out prisoner ranks. Those who survived to enter POW camps near the Yalu were hardly in any condition to endure the next round of brutalities. In the minds of the North Korean military, their ROK compatriots might be excused their being on the "wrong" side; they had most likely been led astray by their "puppet" leaders. But the Americans had no business in Korea in the first place and were responsible for the frustration of the North's well-planned "glorious liberation and unification" of Korea. Of course, one could argue that the average GI was also a relatively innocent victim of "warmongering circles" in the United States, but North Koreans who had seen so many of their comrades burned alive by napalm or white phosphorous strikes usually missed that point. Conditions improved somewhat when the Chinese military had taken control of the camps in late 1950. These new custodians had the experience of their "Lenient Treatment Policy" for POWs in the Second World War and the Chinese civil war. POWs were, in theory, to be well-treated and educated/indoctrinated as to the glories of Communism, then in some cases released to their compatriots to spread the word that life as a Communist POW was at least better than being killed on the losing side of the war. But the Chinese soon found that UNC captives, in most cases coming from nations enjoying far higher standards of living and greater political and personal freedoms, were relatively recalcitrant to the blandishments of the commissar.

The Communist cause was not helped by its practitioners' pathetic ignorance of life outside the Marxist prism. On one occasion a Chinese officer lectured a group of black GIs to the effect that in America "only the rich can afford an automobile". One GI raised his hand and politely reported he actually owned a car. "An obvious exception", the lecturer quickly retorted. But another captive offered the same disconcerting information. Soon practically all the prisoners ("exceptions") were wistfully describing their laid-up autos back in the States and the meeting was adjourned in some confusion. The vast majority of POWs in Communist hands were profoundly uninterested in a Marxist world view and simply wished to return to their capitalist hells as soon as possible.

After the fighting stalled in the wake of the opening of peace talks, the Chinese became more aware of the propaganda value of their captives. Prisoners were often physically divided into "reactionary" and "progressive" categories, with the latter receiving such benefits as better food, mail access, cigarettes, and so on. In return, they would broadcast or write about their fine treatment by the CPVs and denounce the "warmongering" American government and its allied "lackeys". The numbers and extent of such collaboration in the camps became a very vexed question in the United States soon after the war, with considerable spilling of ink on the subject of POW "brainwashing" and collaboration among US POWs. Repatriated UNC POWs from other nations were quickly either discharged back into civilian life or resumed their military careers. Although there had been undoubted collaboration among these other UNC POWs, the awkward matter was quietly shelved. Only in the more open American society has this question remained contentious and still unresolved.

211

In the camps, "uncooperative POWs" often found that if they resisted, they would be slapped around and reviled but then left alone as "hopeless reactionaries". But most UNC POWs seemed in agreement (perhaps somewhat tongue-in-cheek) that after the Chinese were put in charge of the camps the worst of all Communist "atrocities" were the interminable lectures (compulsory, of course), on the eternal principles of Marxism–Leninism. Harangues by an ignoramus of a lecturer on "The running dogs of Wall Street" or "Capitalist exploitation" could provide fleeting comedy relief from near-terminal prison camp boredom, but flesh and blood could take only so many hours of "the surplus value of labour". It could be argued with considerable justification that whatever barrack-room leftists went into the camps, few enough came out.

The situation in the UNC camps was in distinct and shameful contrast to the well-ordered POW compounds of the Western Allies in the Second World War, about which very few German or Japanese captives could justly complain. Although the early chaotic conditions in the initial camps on the Korean mainland were eased by the move to the island of Koje-do just off the southeast coast, basic problems remained that would lead to bloody insurrection and the worst propaganda "black-eye" for the UNC since the initial retreats of 1950.

There could be no question that something approaching pandemonium prevailed in the UNC POW camps. No effort had been made to separate the Communist and anti-Communist factions, and the militants from both sides battled it out in the camps under the bemused eyes of their guards. The Koje compounds themselves were makeshift affairs, flimsily constructed, over-crowded and far too close to a village that contained Communist sympathizers.

Once the question of repatriation was raised, Communist militants convened kangaroo courts inside their compounds that sentenced anti-Communists or even waverers to death, often by torture ("hard-core" recalcitrants had their testicles pulled out with pliers).

There is less evidence that anti-Communists systematically killed their enemies, but the Chinese Nationalist leaders did exert severe physical and psychological pressure in their compounds. In addition, the Seoul government also maintained some coercive influence in the camps. The chief UNC negotiator at the time, Vice Admiral C. Turner Joy, noted in his diary entry for 12 April 1952 that two US Army Chinese-American interpreter officers had informed him that in at least one Nationalist Chinese-dominated compound those indicating a wish to return to mainland China were "beaten black & blue or killed". The terrified POWs in those compounds would only murmur "Taiwan" over and over in answer to any questions. This was certainly bad enough and has been gleefully seized upon by apologists for the Communists ever since the diary's publication in 1978 as proof that the UNC side was about as much in the wrong as were the Communists. But these apologists fail to continue the entry quotation, where Admiral Joy promptly had the two interpreters repeat their story to General Ridgway, who was impressed enough to order that all compound leaders be removed and the POWs be placed in more manageable facilities of no more than 1,000 prisoners each. Admiral Joy himself was in no doubt as to which was the right side in this matter. His diary as well as his book *How communists negotiate* are fervent anti-Communist tracts. In fact, the whole point of both Joy's and Ridgway's concerns was to *increase* the number of voluntary repatriates to a figure that might be more acceptable to the Communist side and thus facilitate the signing of an armistice.

The UN Prisoner Command had inaugurated an ostensibly voluntary education and indoctrination programme that served to inculcate a positive view of Western democracy, but it was administered by some rather unsavoury Nationalist Chinese cadre from Taiwan. With the impasse in POW repatriation, the programme emphasis shifted to a concern with patriation to Taiwan. Much of this anti-Communist activity in the UNC POW camps was in violation of the Geneva Convention. (As noted, the programme was voluntary, but in the anti-Communist compounds, those who did not attend were marked men.) Both Communist and anti-Communist compounds basically ran their own affairs as the careless UNC Prisoner Command abdicated its responsibility in international law for its charges.

All of this took place under the noses of US and ROK guards who were mostly second-rate; first-class troops were needed for the combat zone. As far as ROK guards were concerned, the situation was not improved by the fact that at first the POWs received better rations than the guards. As for camp commanders, they were replaced at the incredible rate of about one per month in the first nine months after the camp's establishment.

Still, in comparison to the Communists' camps, conditions in most of the UNC compounds were more than bearable. There was sufficient food, clothing and medical attention, and a minimum of guard brutality, at least after the stabilization of the battle lines slowed the number of Communist POWs flocking into the camps. In fact, one category of detainee established by the UNC Prisoner Command was that of South Korean civilians who had sneaked *into* the camps for free food, and so on.

It was the impending move by the UNC to take back control of its camps from both Communist and anti-Communist forces that sparked the main Koje riot and kidnapping disaster of May 1952. Deeply worried about the UNC decision to screen its POWs to determine how many favoured repatriation, the Communist leaders within the Koje-do camp (and probably outside as well) determined to disrupt the process. In a well-planned operation, Communist POWs seized the Koje camp commander, Brigadier General Francis T. Dodd, on 7 May 1952. To secure Dodd's release, his second in command, Brigadier General Charles F. Colson, was forced to sign a humiliating "confession" admitting in fractured English that suggested it had been dictated by the mutinous POWs, "I do admit that there has [sic] been instances of bloodshed where many PW [sic] have been killed and wounded by UN forces". Ensuing negotiations by the captive Dodd and by Colson gave the POWs even more propaganda advantages. After Dodd's release, an Army investigating board, acting on the time-honoured military principle of looking after one's own, exculpated both generals. But the verdict and the whole bungling behaviour of the two generals outraged the Eighth Army and UNC Commanders, General James A. Van Fleet and General Mark W. Clark, respectively. A second board, undoubtedly more attuned to the high command's feeling in the matter, reversed the original findings. Generals Dodd and Colson soon afterwards found themselves colonels and soon after that retired from the US Army. It was not as though ex-generals Dodd and Colson had not been warned. Just three months earlier, a major clash between Communist POWs and guards had left 77 of the former dead and 140 wounded. Yet General Dodd had carelessly walked into a compound controlled by militant Communists for a "conference" when he was seized.

With full Department of the Army backing, Clark ordered the new Koje commander (the fifteenth!), Brigadier General Haydon L. ("Bull") Boatner, to clean out the Communist-controlled compounds. On 4 June Boatner's squads mounted a test-run by moving into two of the Communist compounds, tearing down political signs, bulldozing flagpoles and burning banners, with no casualties on either side. They also rescued 85 anti-Communist prisoners of the Communist prisoners, some bound and presumably awaiting execution. Six days later, crack paratroopers rousted the fiercely resisting militants out of the core Communist compound. Using flamethrowers (!) and tear gas, UN troops moved into the "iron triangle" of the Communist resistance. Thirty-one Communist POWs were killed, some by their fellow POWs, and 274 wounded at a cost of one US soldier speared to death. Six Patton tanks, their 90mm guns trained on the last hold-outs, put an end to the uprising. In another Communist-dominated compound, the bodies of 16 murdered POWs were found.

Serious damage had been done to the UNC and to the US principle of opposition to forcible repatriation. Worldwide, the Communist media trumpeted the story, and in Teheran, a leftist youth protest turned into a riot that left 12 dead and 250 wounded. The media focus also appeared to have sparked riots and strikes in several US prisons and even at Soviet forced labour camps.

Even these bloody repressions did little to quell the ardent spirits of the Communist militants. Immediately after General Boatner had moved the leaders of the June riot to neighbouring Cheju island, the POW leaders planned to defy the camp administration, continue their demonstrations, prepare for yet another uprising and this time kill the camp commandant. Their plot uncovered, they rose in open rebellion on 1 October 1952. In the ensuing fighting with their guards, 51 prisoners were killed and 90 wounded. But the UNC was finally and for the first time firmly in control, with the compounds broken up into much smaller facilities. The Communists were well separated from the anti- and non-Communist POWs.

Paradoxically, it was the civilian Communist internees on the small island of Pongami who, in December 1952, sparked the next and most bloody of all POW revolts. After a series of defiant acts which may have been planned by General Nam Il, the internees, in response to an order from the camp commandant to cease their drilling and commotion, linked arms and behind this human shield hurled rocks and debris at their South Korean guards. Ignoring warning shots, the demonstrators continued to rain missiles on the advancing guards, who finally opened direct fire into the defiant prisoners. The full blast was taken by the linked-arms front-line demonstrators. In all, 85 POWs were killed and 113 hospitalized; the guards suffered four wounded.

Even this violent revolt was not the end of the sorry story. On 7 March 1953, POWs on the island of Yoncho-do mounted an attack on the prison commandant and were only put down at a cost of 27 POWs killed and 60 wounded.

Although the general public in the Western democracies tended to lump all of the violence into the one Koje revolt, these bloody POW uprisings undercut the high moral ground that the UN had assumed on the principle of voluntary repatriation. That principle had resonated positively around much of the world: the UN was carrying on the battle in Korea to secure the free choice of the POWs on both sides to determine their destiny. Now those POWs were revolting and being killed in significant numbers.

It is impossible to say how much of the violence and the uprisings in the camps had been planned beforehand by the Communists, but it is obvious that they considered that their war by no means ended with capture. In fact, there is convincing evidence that Communist military authorities actually ordered numbers of their more committed cadre to be captured on the battle-field in order to enter the UNC POW compounds and there raise hell. Communist POWs were simply soldiers on a different battlefront. The UN cause paid a heavy price for its failure to understand this important aspect of the North Korean and Chinese Communist way of war.

Guerrilla and counter-guerrilla

Quite literally "behind the lines" in the Korean War, guerrilla, or partisan, operations proved a headache for both sides, but never came close to affecting the outcome of the conflict.

Apparently the ROK had given no thought to any guerrilla harassment of the Communist occupiers in the summer of 1950, although their partisan bands had engaged in raids north of the 38th Parallel in 1949. There is also no record of any spontaneous popular anti-Communist resistance. But that situation changed, at least locally, with the UN evacuation of North Korea at the end of the year. Many of the inhabitants of the North's Hwanghae province had close ties with Seoul and had collaborated with the UN occupying forces.

After the UN debacle to the North and undoubtedly bearing in mind the fate of similar collaborators at the hands of the Communists, some 6,000–10,000 North Koreans fled the returning North Koreans and the Chinese. Seizing fishing boats, they sought refuge on islands off the DPRK's west coast. The Eighth Army there provided them food, clothing and shelter, armed them with captured Soviet weapons and began to recruit and train the able-bodied for guerrilla operations against the west coast of North Korea.

The first offensive operations began in early 1951. Missions came to include raids against Communist lines of communication, headquarters and transport; intelligence gathering and guidance for UN naval bombardments; and the rescue of downed friendly aviators. These United Nations Partisan Infantry (UNPIK) forces, nicknamed "The Donkeys", also attempted, unsuccessfully, to establish guerrilla bases on the Northern mainland itself. This failure can be attributed to the brutally tight control that the Communist regime maintained over its territory, particularly in wartime. The "Donkeys" were, however, somewhat more successful in recruiting North Korean civilians to their ranks.

Although small-boat raids against the North Korean Hwanghae province coast enjoyed moderate success, UNPIK's best results came from their more mundane missions of shore bombardment fire control, erecting and maintaining aerial navigation equipment and the rescue of downed UN airmen. They plausibly claimed to have diverted large numbers of Communist troops from the front lines to the Hwanghae coast, but, then again, the North Koreans and the Chinese Communists were never short of manpower. Although UNC kept the operations of the "Donkeys" under cloak of secrecy, the North Koreans were obviously aware of who had been raiding their coastline, and had, in fact, taken back one of the "Donkey's" islands.

Parachute insertion of UNC saboteurs and guerrillas directly into the North failed almost uniformly. In fact, there was justifiable suspicion at the time that much of the programme had been compromised to the Communists. On one occasion, an agent, as he was parachuting from a USAF transport carrying him over North Korea, threw a hand grenade back into the aircraft. The resultant explosion wounded several crewmen, but they managed to fly the plane back to the nearest South Korean airstrip. Most agents, however, simply went missing or radioed back messages that were obviously being sent under duress. In view of the fact that of the 200 American CIA operatives in South Korea not one could speak Hangul, it is hardly surprising that such matters did not go well.

On the other hand, signals intelligence, SIGINT, was one of the UNC success stories, as noted. General Ridgway, like General Walker, was tipped for each Communist offensive. He was well prepared to "roll with the punch" and inflict maximum damage on the Communist forces because of such timely intelligence about his enemy's movements.

This conflict also saw the first use of colour aerial photography. Discoloured foliage could reveal recent Communist troop and vehicle movements across grass and through vegetation that might not have been evident on the ground or in black-and-white aerial photos.

While unable basically to affect the course of the war, Communist guerrilla forces operations did enjoy considerably more success than UNPIK. For the three years of the Korean War they tied down no less than one-third of UN forces committed to that conflict. North Korean guerrilla forces enjoyed the benefit of an impressive tradition of Communist partisan warfare dating from the period of the Russian civil war and extending through the large-scale Soviet partisan operations against the German invaders and Chinese/Korean unconventional warfare against the Japanese in the Second World War. In the just-concluded Chinese civil war much of the Communist armies by choice or necessity fought in guerrilla or near-guerrilla-style operations. Guerrilla or partisan warfare comported nicely with the Communist notion of "a people in arms" against their oppressors.

Communist guerrilla operations in Korea commenced well before the Korean War itself erupted. The ROK's brutal suppression of the Cheju-do uprising in April 1948 and the subsequent mutiny of the 14th Regiment (see Chapter Two) led the rebels to establish guerrilla bases in the Chiri Massif, located in the southwest of the peninsula, as noted.

With the North Korean invasion in June 1950, the scattered remnants rallied to the invaders, but the *Inmin Gun* seemed quite able to drive the UN forces off the peninsula by itself, and little was heard of Communist guerrillas that summer. The most effective Communist partisan warfare contribution came during the invasion of North Korea in the autumn of 1950. KPA troops were ordered to fight as guerrillas behind UN lines. An X Corps report in November of that year identified 62 different guerrilla organizations and noted 109 of their attacks on UN forces in that month.

In the autumn of 1950, the UNC determined that there were three general types of Communist guerrillas in their command: the "stay-behind" Communist forces in the South, those who found themselves trapped behind UN lines as they attempted to flee northward and ordinary bandits perennially operating in the more remote areas of the peninsula. Of course, these categories were not hard and fast; trapped KPA troops could be ordered to remain where they were and conduct raids against UNC forces, bandits could be recruited to join elements of the KPA and former KPA troops could turn to banditry for sheer survival.

With UN forces back in the South after the Chinese intervention, the Communist guerrilla remnants renewed their struggle. Such guerrilla units, however, of necessity exercised considerable independence. By 1951 there was more of an effort to co-ordinate Southern guerrilla operations under the command of the KPA's 526th Branch unit, with headquarters (presumably underground by this time) in Pyongyang. Under the direction of the 526th, guerrillas in the South were organized into three branches, the 3rd Branch Unit in the Taebaek Mountain region and the 4th Branch Unit in the central and southwestern mountains, and the 6th in the central mountains. Numerous bands also operated more-or-less independently. In addition, the depredations of bandits and the destitute, of which there was no lack, often made it difficult to distinguish between the "political" and "criminal" bands.

Mostly centred again in the Chiri region, these armed fighters ambushed UN convoys and patrols, fired on trains, cut communication lines and assaulted ROK police stations. With little success, two entire US Army divisions had to be diverted to their suppression. Finally, in December 1951, the ROK government declared martial law in southwest Korea. (Area residents might have been unable to discern the difference.) It mounted a once-and-for-all operation, sardonically dubbed Operation Rat Killer, to end the guerrilla threat. Two ROK divisions, the 8th and the crack Capital, pushed through the area, while national police, youth regiments and local security elements blocked escape routes. At the end of Operation Rat Killer, the UNC reported 9,789 Communist guerrillas killed and 9,383 captured. Guerrilla activities continued for several more years, although it became difficult to distinguish such partisan warfare from mere banditry. Certainly the guerrillas never again posed any great menace to the ROK. But they had diverted four UNC divisions, two at a time, from the battlefront. The Communist guerrillas failed to pose a serious threat to the ROK because of a lack of widespread support in the countryside, the absence of heavy vegetation to shield their movements, the difficulty of forwarding troops and supplies down from North Korea, their lack of air support and the ruthlessness of the Rhee regime.

UNPIK's record was one of even less obvious success. Eighth Army was never particularly keen on unconventional warfare, and the ROK military looked upon the "Donkeys" as a lot of draft-dodgers who worked for the Americans primarily for the better rations. The UNC never regarded its partisan units' operations as anything more than a sideshow. After the armistice, it wasted little time in disbanding these forces.

Medical treatment

The Korean War witnessed enormous advances in the medical treatment of military casualties, at least on the UNC side. Although the medical branch of the US Far East Command was about as unprepared as its non-medical counterparts, battalion medics were on duty with Task Force Smith in the first ground clash between the US Army and the *Inmin Gun* – and had to abandon their wounded to their enemies.

By the time of the Pusan Perimeter fighting, the first Mobile Army Surgical Hospital (MASH) had been established. These field hospitals had been designed late during the Second World War to provide emergency frontline surgery to stabilize the severely wounded for their evacuation to the rear. Instead, they developed during the war into small general-purpose hospitals. Although originally designed and equipped for a maximum of 60 patients, one would often hold hundreds during the Pusan Perimeter fighting. And although originally meant to support one division, Korean War MASHs served several, plus a growing number of Allied troops. In addition to MASHs, a few field hospitals and a single evacuation hospital also were ordered to Korea. These, too, were overwhelmed with casualties from the fighting along the perimeter that inflicted on the UNC the largest average daily toll of casualties for the entire war.

X Corps, Army and Marine personnel alike had to learn their work in the field on the job at the Inchon landings and immediately afterward. The Navy had assembled a casual staff of orthopaedists, surgeons and dentists, whereas Eighth Army medical personnel were already seasoned veterans. In the headlong advance into North Korea, US Army hospitals' main problem was that of keeping up with the swiftly moving UNC forces. But in the retreat from the Yalu, they were once again overwhelmed, and this time under far worse weather conditions. Lights and heating would fail as ice blocked fuel lines in the sub-zero cold, plasma froze in the operating rooms and patients' incisions emitted steam when exposed to the frigid air even in operating rooms. By the time the lines were stabilized in the spring of 1951, most UNC medical personnel had gained enormous valuable experience in the field, usually under combat conditions. On the other hand, the sufferings of wounded Communists, bereft of anything but sporadic first-aid in the field, hardly bear imagining.

Along with the MASH, another major medical advance of the Korean War, again for UNC troops alone, was that of medical evacuation. By the time of the stabilization of the battle lines, helicopters could pluck the most severely wounded from the battlefield, smoothly delivering them to a regimental or division clearing station and then on to a MASH or a hospital ship, thus saving them the agonies of a long, jouncing ambulance trip over dirt trails. Neurosurgical cases, spared that ride, particularly benefitted from helicopter evacuation. After stabilization, those wounded requiring further treatment would be airlifted to Japan or even to the United States. Yet, helicopters, expensive, few in number and mechanically still cranky, evacuated no more than some 4 per cent of UNC casualties throughout the war. The rest were still moved by motor ambulance or the Korean railways, much as in the Second World War. Nonetheless, it was the combination of the helicopter and the MASH that achieved fame several decades later in the popular novel *M*A*S*H* and the film and television series of the same title. In fact, the MASH became the only enduring image in the West of the Korean War.

From the late spring of 1951, the most serious and most baffling medical ailment that faced UNC medical personnel in Korea was the periodic outbreaks of viral haemorrhagic fever. Early mortality rates in some hard-hit UNC units reached 20 per cent among those affected. The best efforts of army laboratories and of a special haemorrhagic laboratory of the 8228th MASH brought the mortality rate down to 2 per cent, but they never found a cause or cure for the disease. Haemorrhagic fever cases were considered serious enough to rate automatically a helicopter evacuation. Communist sources are lacking for any documentation of this plague on the North side of the lines.

Overall, UNC health and treatment improved considerably with the battle lines fixed. Troops could bathe far more frequently, they could be vaccinated and inoculated regularly, change into clean clothing and socks, eat more hot food and revive themselves during the bitter winters in special warming tents. By this stage of the war, death rates among US hospital patients were about half of the Second World War rate of less than a decade earlier. Consultants could visit the forward areas and share with MASH and army hospital personnel the latest medical techniques. Specialized informal medical societies sprang up spontaneously with military medical personnel presenting and critiquing each other's professional papers. The Army and Navy's Surgeons General forwarded teams to explore the problems of wound treatment, cold injury and surgery. Out of these visits came unmistakable medical progress, most strikingly in cold injury treatment and prevention; the Army's "Mickey Mouse" cold-weather boot saved many a foot soldier's foot. This improved care showed up in the statistics: in the Korean War the ratio of deaths to wounds was far lower overall than in the Second World War. No soldiers to date had enjoyed such a near-lavish abundance of medical care than did the UNC soldiers in the later years of the Korean War.

The good care extended across the UNC spectrum: Navy hospital ships served as mobile hospitals along the coast, treating soldiers and airmen, both US and Allied, as well as USN personnel. Military hospitals in Japan and the USA shared their patients as needed, with little regard for branch of service. Neutral nation hospitals provided front-line treatment to all before they evacuated their patients to MASHs or rear-echelon hospitals. The Commonwealth forces had primarily their own chain of treatment and evacuation, but could also freely draw upon US Army medical facilities when needed. The ROK Army's medical service, about as poor as that of the *Inmin Gun* at war's beginning, gradually improved, eventually even opening a Korean-staffed neurological hospital. By the end of the conflict, ROK military medicine was judged by the US Army Surgeon General to be about on a level with that of the US Army's in the First World War. To the end of the war, ROK soldiers requiring complicated treatment were evacuated to US Army hospitals.

Earlier in the war there was a puzzling disparity between the ratio of one US Army soldier killed in action for every four wounded, compared to one US Marine killed in action for every six wounded. Reasons adduced for the disparity ranged from a lower Army *esprit de corps* to pre-war Army training that emphasized military over medical skills. Whatever the reasons, Army medical training at Fort Sam Houston, Texas was considerably tightened and the battlefield ratio narrowed. But the Navy's Hospital Corps remained more efficient in providing trained enlisted medics than did the Army's Medical Service, which was without a permanent career enlisted corps.

For all its efficiencies, the UNC medical system had its problems. The introduction of personnel rotation, combined with a doctors' draft, did nothing to improve military medical service in Korea. Like their non-medical counterparts, medical personnel were rotated out at about the time that they were beginning to know their jobs well. The doctors' draft brought in men whose skills were sometimes too specialized for military medicine, who were more often than not resentful of the military and its peculiar ways and who shared the general American ennui with this seemingly endless war. But there is no evidence that these sometimes bitter feelings affected their professional duties.

Inmin Gun and CPV medical personnel, on the other hand, would have been delighted to have had the problems that afflicted the UNC medical system. The Communist armies' medical services, such as they were, had collapsed by early 1951. Wounded troops could not be evacuated until nightfall and had to endure evacuation by truck over abominable roads or interminable train journeys that had to cease with the dawn. Many, of course, died on the way. Medicines and medical equipment were often interdicted by UNC air power and never reached the lines. The CPV and the North Koreans had nothing like the US Army's MASH or its first-rate equipment and, of course, no helicopter evacuation. Primitive or non-existent sanitation in the midst of a society that fertilized its fields with human waste, which almost universally lacked modern sewage and potable water, along with poor nutrition rendered the huge Communist armies in Korea easy prey to disease. In fact, as noted, many authorities now presume that it was the massive inroads of typhus and other diseases that impelled the Communists globally to trumpet charges of a vile US conspiracy to use bacteriological warfare on the battlefields and over North Korea. Although there is good evidence that the Communist leadership actually believed most of these charges, the fact remains that the CPV and the *Inmin Gun* commands had lost control of the health of their armies in the field. When they regained such control, more or less, the charges dissipated.

By the signing of the armistice the UNC could look back upon solid military medical advances and could pride itself on the care it had given its soldiers in a relatively unhealthy environment. The Communists could make no such claims, and military medicine must be adjudged one of the greatest failures of their armies. The exhortation of the commissar could hardly substitute for timely, efficient medical evacuation and treatment. Few conflicts have seen such a disparity between the medical services of the belligerents.

Considering the aerial blitz over North Korea that rivalled the bombardments of Germany or Japan in the Second World War, as well as the guerrilla wars in both North and South Korea, the POW camp uprisings, and the propaganda wars waged by both sides, it is obvious that peace hardly reigned behind the lines of either Koreas during the Korean War.

Chapter Twelve

Home fronts

The Koreas and China

The Korean War bore most harshly on the home fronts of North and South Korea. Nonetheless, the DPRK's wartime experience remains closed to any objective analysis by the lack of open archives.

In South Korea the problem is not so much a lack of documentation, although official accounts minimize the authoritarian nature of the Rhee regime and the sufferings of the South Koreans. South Korea was overpopulated even before the conflict erupted, as nearly two million refugees from the North had made their way to the ROK between 1945 and 1950. Although much of the ROK population seemed willing to make their peace with the Communist invaders in the summer of 1950, by January 1951 *another* two million North Koreans (who presumably by then knew what a Communist regime was like) were fleeing Southward along with the retreating UNC armies. At Suwon alone, just south of Seoul, some 100,000 refugees, desperately hoping for transport further south, jammed the railway yards. In addition to the refugees from the North, several millions more were displaced from their homes by the violence of the fighting.

The only bright spot in all of this, if it can be so termed, was that the pre-war high unemployment evaporated, as most able-bodied South Korean men found themselves either in the ROK Army or in some type of war work. Many men and women obtained relatively lucrative employment with the other UNC forces as labourers, translators, secretaries, laundresses, seamstresses, and so on. But even this good fortune was tarnished by inflation throughout the war years, fuelled by high levels of UNC troop spending and reconstruction funding. The UNC and the US government were well aware of the problem but could never convince the Rhee regime to undertake the austerity programme necessary to check it. In fact, except for official payments and transportation fares, black market goods such as US cigarettes, army blankets or rations became the true medium of exchange. At its simplest, a civil servant might exchange some US relief fertilizer for a few bags of rice from a farmer. At its more complex, an entrepreneur might supply a trucking firm with petroleum and lubricants pilfered from US Army fuel dumps while Korean guards looked the other way in exchange for US cigarettes. The trucking owner might then repay the entrepreneur with no-questions-asked transport for his ill-gotten goods. Although such officials might justify their illicit activities by arguing that their families came first and could not be supported on salaries that did not begin to catch up with inflation, the black market and its attendant corruption bred cynicism and despair. It also did nothing for the development of a healthy, above-board ROK economy. (Pilfering had become so endemic that an entire infantry regiment of the 1st Cavalry was brought to Korea from Japan to mount guard on the vast UNC supply dumps at Pusan and Taegu.)

With the stalemate of the battlelines, the political life of the ROK revived, temporarily. Rhee's term of office was due to expire in 1952. His opponents, who now dominated the National Assembly, gathered strength for his defeat. Certainly Rhee's regime provided more than enough ammunition for its own downfall. In one of the regime's worst scandals, the National Defense Corps (NDC), organized along military lines with the coming of the war, practically dissolved as members found themselves clothed in rags, starved, diseased and abandoned. Many would have starved or frozen to death had it not been for the ministrations of US Army civil affairs teams. It transpired that funds for the proper outfitting of these unfortunates had been shamelessly embezzled by the unit's own commander, a son-in-law of Rhee's defence minister. An equally horrific scandal occurred when an ROK Army unit, furious that a band of guerrillas had escaped its net, turned on a local village and shot all of its men. Attempts by Rhee's opponents to investigate this undoubted massacre were thwarted by "Tiger" Kim, a Rhee favourite, fresh from beheading some 50 NKPA captives and whom Rhee "rewarded" by appointing him to head the national police.

The Americans were hesitant to criticize a beleaguered ally, in effect legitimizing his regime and its brutalities. Rhee's opponents were flayed as being in league with the Communists. Many went into hiding or were hunted down and imprisoned. It is an accurate measure of Rhee's nearly unlimited power, based his total control of the army and the police, that the National Assembly, once a stronghold of his opponents, unanimously voted in June 1952 to extend his term of office. Kim Il Sung could not have done much better.

His home front secure, Rhee could now turn without threat of distraction to his goal of unification of the peninsula under his regime. The same types of "spontaneous demonstrations" that had demanded his perpetuation in office were now organized to demand PUK CHIN – "Drive North!", "Unification or Death!" and down with the Panmunjom negotiations. The UNC tried to mollify Rhee with offers of large-scale funding for ROK reconstruction and a buildup of the army, but he disdainfully rejected the offers. As the armistice agreements were eventually finalized, Rhee made his last gesture of defiance by releasing 27,000 non-repatriate North Korean POWs from their UNC compounds. But the release had little lasting effect; both sides denounced Rhee. Marathon negotiating sessions between US State Department representatives and the ROK president resulted in substantial financial aid for the Rhee regime in exchange for Rhee's commitment not to impede armistice negotiations further.

To make matters worse for Rhee, at about this time the Communists launched a series of strong offensives specifically directed against ROK Army units. The offensives were blunted only by heavy non-ROK UNC air and ground bombardment and counterattacks. Even then some ground was permanently lost.

There can be little doubt that the war stunted Korean political life, as Rhee and the masses of refugees from the North almost automatically equated any demands for personal and political freedom with "Communism". The real power in South Korea thus remained in the army and with the police until the 1990s.

The people of the DPRK suffered about as much as their Southern compatriots although far more from UNC aerial bombardment than from ground combat, the mirror image of the situation in the ROK. The major cities of the North, particularly Pyongyang and Sinuiju, were nearly reduced to ashes in strategic and tactical bombings that resembled what the Allies had inflicted on the cities of Germany and Japan during the Second World War. Rail and road centres were blasted from the air many times and were just about as many times patiently rebuilt.

With few hard-fought land battles in the North, the peasant economy was less disrupted, but the North must have felt the absence of some two million of its people who had fled South. Further, the peasants who were not drafted into the *Inmin Gun* were subjected to heavy taxes for the Communist state and for the war effort. The Soviet Union did supply some capital and consumer goods, but these were hardly in plenteous supply in the USSR itself, still very much in the process of recovering from the disaster of the Second World War. But details of the Korean War experience in the DPRK still remain obscure.

The wartime PRC, fully aware that the nation was exhausted after nearly two decades of intermittent warfare, made every effort to maintain morale as well as to build support for its Korean incursion. PVA soldiers' families had preference in obtaining food, consumer goods and jobs. The government even opened special shops for their needs. A "Hero's' Family" or a "Glorious Family" was expected to write to its PVA menfolk, exhorting them to achieve ever more glorious feats on the battlefront, or to inquire as to why the laggards had not done so. Nation-wide campaigns were mounted to provide much-needed gifts of clothing and personal effects to the troops. ("I saved this cake of soap for you so that you can clean off the enemy's blood on your clothes and prepare for another battle.") Soviet equipment had to be paid for, and on one well-publicized occasion, citizens raised 250,000 *renminbi* to buy one Russian tank. Workers were exhorted to produce more and to donate the difference to arms purchases. The government claimed that such sacrifices enabled it to buy no fewer than 3,710 MiG jet fighters. The "Learn from Yang Gensi" propaganda campaign extolled the virtue of a PVA peasant lad who charged down from his destroyed position with an explosive device in his hands, sending panicky US Marine survivors (most improbably) tearing for the rear.

Still, morale flagged after the early victories in late 1950. The PRC government, in late 1951, embarked upon its internal propaganda "anti" programmes. The first, "The Three Antis" was to wipe out bribery and tax evasion, waste, and bureaucratism. (The latter "anti" was a foreshadowing of the disastrous "Great Proletarian Revolution" which proclaimed the line "Better Red Than Expert", a policy that could prove catastrophic if applied in, say, a Chinese hydro-electric plant.) The "Five Antis" fought again against bribery and tax evasion, as well as theft of state property and the more esoteric sins of cheating on government contracts and stealing economic information. (Privately, Mao seemed to confirm the problem, remarking that "perhaps only after [we] execute a few tens of thousands of those guilty of corruption throughout the entire nation can [we] resolve these problems".[1])

Whatever the failings of Chinese citizens, America was the main object of hate throughout the war. The official title for the Korean War to this day in the PRC is "The War to Resist America and Aid Korea". A "Hate America" campaign blamed most of the world's ills on the United States. Its soldiers were damned as blood-thirsty murderers and wanton destroyers in Korea, devoid of any culture or morals.

If the average Chinese worker or peasant was somewhat confused at the time about the official interpretation of the war, or the "party line", such confusion is hardly surprising. The Chinese people were supposedly "as one" in Marxist selflessness behind the CPV troops, yet there was presumably among them so much bribery, tax evasion, waste and bureaucratism, not to mention stealing of state property and economic information, that two major campaigns had to be mounted to stamp out these ills. American soldiers were basically destroying Korea, presumably out of sheer bloody-mindedness, yet the American people themselves were depicted as decent workers and peasants ground under the heel or thumb of their capitalist/monopolist "ruling circles". Further, although those "soft" Americans and other UNC troops were being ignominiously defeated on all fronts by the "ever-victorious" People's Volunteers and their undaunted Korean allies, yet the war showed no sign of ending and even greater sacrifices were constantly demanded by the government and the Party.

The United States

The United States was the only major belligerent for whom the Korean War came as a surprise. Previous American conflicts had been preceded by a period of tension and by a series of "incidents", and crises. No American was stupefied when William McKinley or Woodrow Wilson asked Congress for declarations of war. Even the surprise attack on Pearl Harbor had been preceded by several years of tense Japanese American relations. These months and years of pre-war crises and tensions had, at least before Pearl Harbor, given the nation some months to begin preparations for war. The outbreak of war in Korea, however, came in the midst of a drastic military draw-down common enough among democracies in the wake of a victorious war.

The North Korean invasion was apparently as much a surprise to the State and Defense Departments as to the average American. As noted, Secretary of State Acheson had placed South Korea outside the US defence perimeter, and the US Army had basically written off the Republic of Korea. High and low, the overwhelming majority of Americans saw Korea as indeed "a far-off country about which we know nothing". Nonetheless, President Truman's decision to send in the armed forces of the United States to the defence of the Republic was immensely popular for the first weeks of the conflict, while leftists and the handful of American Communists generally went to ground.

As the war degenerated into weary stalemate, however, the American public, according to practically all indicators, continued to accept the war with a sullen resignation, and the conflict faded, if not from the front pages at least out of the headlines. Americans picked up the thread of what would distinguish the decade of the 1950s: the motorized flight to suburbia amidst a prospering economy, punctuated only occasionally by a brief notice in a hometown newspaper of a local boy's death in Korea.

A visitor to the United States in, say, late 1951 would have found it difficult to credit that this nation was in the midst of its fourth most bloody war. He would see no rationing and no curtailment of the production and sale of consumer goods, no screaming billboards exhorting Americans to produce more, consume less, or to "Remember Task Force Smith". Even the armed services' recruiting posters would emphasize the benefits of "joining up", rather than playing on the horrors of Communism. Visitors would hear no Korean War songs, no equivalents to the First and Second World Wars' "Over There", "Praise the Lord and Pass the Ammunition", or "Bell-Bottom Trousers". However, if they entered a film theatre they might find that Hollywood, which only a few years earlier had been investigated for "Communist influence" in its products had, in reaction to the war, turned out some obvious anti-Communist themes along with its more usual escapist fare. *I Married a Communist* and *My Son John* were representative of this undistinguished vein. Films about the Korean War itself, oddly enough, were sometimes more sophisticated. *The Steel Helmet* and *A Yank in Korea*, both 1951 releases, were two of the best. But Hollywood produced no mythic Korean screen images, no *Red Badge of Courage* (Civil War), no *Sergeant York* (First World War), no *Sands of Iwo Jima*, or *Thirty Seconds Over Tokyo* (Second World War). The so-called "forgotten war" was featured for the most part in forgettable films, perhaps because Hollywood, for whatever reason, did not produce a single John Wayne Korean War film.

If they watched any television, visitors would note also the surprising scarcity of war news except in the Korean War's first weeks. This conflict touched the overwhelming majority of Americans mainly through the conscription, which took their young men who were not in college or in deferred occupations.

The war sustained an economic boom throughout its three years. Americans went about their business, buying and selling, job-hopping and moving to the suburbs with little more than a passing concern with the war news they encountered. Once it became obvious that this war would not end with UNC victory parades in Pyongyang, Tokyo and Washington, Americans seemed to lose interest in the conflict, retaining only a vague dissatisfaction, a feeling that it should be concluded "one way or the other". A sizeable proportion of Americans spoke as if they believed that "one way or the other" might well include war with China and even the use of nuclear weapons. On the other hand, very few seemed prepared to pay the price in blood, resources and government controls that such a wider war would demand.

This sullen resignation to the war on the American home front seemed to provoke those who made it their job to deal with questions of high national policy, and they embarked upon apocalyptic imaginings of Communist threat and nuclear annihilation that seem almost ludicrous in the light of subsequent history (i.e. hindsight). These visions actually commenced some months before the war's outbreak, beginning with the Soviets' explosion of a nuclear "device" in August 1949, an achievement well ahead of the predictions of most "experts". A little more than one month before the outbreak of war, the commanding general of the USAF Continental Air Command, Lieutenant General Ennis C. Whitehead, concluded that by 1952 the Soviet Union's atomic bomb and its supposed huge fleet of jet fighters and heavy bombers could destroy the United States, a looming crisis as great as anything since the American Revolution. General Whitehead's opinion was only slightly more extreme than that of many other Air Force officers.

At about the same time, such fears were given more official expression in National Security document NSC-68, one of the major state papers of the Cold War. NSC-68 postulated, accurately enough, that the globe was divided by the two competing ideologies, and that while the United States still had the edge over the Soviet Union, the immediate future would see a deterioration of that superiority. From 20 atomic bombs in 1950, the Soviet nuclear arsenal would expand to 200 by 1954. Western Europe could be overrun at any time by the enormous Soviet conventional land and air numerical superiority. Ruling out the extremes of preventive war and isolation for the United States, NSC-68 proposed, and in the end obtained, a massive US programme of rearmament for the nation and for its allies. The document claimed that the nation could afford the expense of defending itself and "the forces of freedom" more easily than many had imagined, although the cost would be high. NSC-68's conclusions were true in everything but their main argument. The Soviet stockpile of nuclear weapons would indeed grow, but so then would that of the United States, and the US did shoulder much heavier military expenses than imagined possible in 1950. But all this was carried out in the absence of any Soviet attack, either on the United States or on Western Europe. In the end, four decades later, it was the Soviet Union that would collapse, financially, industrially, militarily, and literally as a nation, an historical denouement that even NSC-68's most anti-Soviet creators could hardly have dreamed possible.

The coming of the war itself seemed to confirm the worst fears of the more belligerent Americans. As early as late August 1950, with the UN forces at least holding the line at the Pusan Perimeter, the Secretary of the Navy, Francis P. Matthews, unnervingly declared in a public speech that the US should pay any price for peace, including "instituting a war to compel cooperation for peace". Such sentiments were immediately disavowed by the State Department. President Truman privately rapped his Navy Secretary's knuckles and the matter died. But with singularly inept timing the

Commandant of the Air War College a few days later stated in an interview with the local newspaper "Give me the order to do it, and I can break up Russia's five A-bomb nests in a week". Commandant Major General Orvil Anderson then added:

> When I went up to Christ I think I could explain to him why I wanted to do it – now before it's too late. I think I could explain to him that I had saved civilization.

(The general failed to indicate if his going "up to Christ" might come as the result of natural causes or an all-out nuclear exchange.) After his bizarre musings were widely publicized, he was relieved of duty by the USAF Chief of Staff. (In all the publicity, no one seems to have pointed out that the bumbling general did preface his remarks with the significant phrase, "Give me the order".[2]) Apparently the Secretary of Defense, Louis Johnson, also favoured a preventive war at the time with the Soviet Union, but only after public opinion had been prepared for such an horrific eventuality.

Such matters only got worse with the entry of China and the long UN retreat southward in late 1950. Former Secretary of the Air Force Stuart Symington, a most influential member of the National Security Council and normally one of the most sober of leaders, forwarded a memo to President Truman in which he proposed not only the UN evacuation of Korea and attacks on the Chinese mainland, but the making of explicit nuclear threats against the Soviet Union itself. President Truman publicly ignored the bellicose document, but his marginalia revealed his common-sense evaluation: "bunk!", "[as] big a lot of Top Secret malarkey as I've ever read".[3] The President showed less wisdom and more militancy, however, when he ignorantly told British Prime Minister Attlee early in 1951 that Communist China was a:

> satellite of Russia and will be a satellite as long as the present Peiping regime is in power. . . . they were a complete satellite. The only way to meet communism is to eliminate it.[4]

Congressman H. F. Edward Hébert of Louisiana also wrote to Truman, in early December, that the nation was in "what I believe to be the Gethsemane of our existence". The Speaker of the House of Representatives, Sam Rayburn, unoriginally warned early in 1951 that the nation faced perhaps "the beginning of World War III". Even the normally sober military correspondent Hanson W. Baldwin hysterically claimed that the nation faced "the greatest danger in our history. . . . Western civilization and our American way of life" faced deadly peril. Truman himself, perhaps by now more influenced by Symington and Hébert than he realized, confided to his diary that "it looks like World War III is near". Such sentiments were not confined to Washington politicians. The commander of the 1st Cavalry Division in Korea startled arriving Australian officers with the news that "The Chinese are in, the Third World War has started!"

Life magazine, in a deliberately unsettling editorial ("Let's Get Down to Cases", 8 January 1951) proclaimed that "Life sees no choice but to acknowledge the existence of war with Red China and to set about its defeat *in full awareness that this course will probably involve war with the Soviet Union as well*" (emphasis added). *Colliers* magazine helped along the sentiment with its series of the same year, "The War We Hope Never to Have to Fight", which depicted nuclear conflict between the Soviet Union and the United States with Washington laid in ruins – along with Moscow.

Still the Apocalypse tarried despite the perfervid alarums generated by those with a vested interest in such matters. However, disturbing events much closer to home did catch their attention. A few months before the outbreak of war Alger Hiss had been convicted for lying under oath about his part in a pre-war espionage ring. Hiss, a New Dealer and a State Department official in the Roosevelt and Truman administrations, had been one of the stellar members of the US public policy "establishment". As a high State Department officer, he had been a major behind-the-scenes arranger of the Yalta Conference and the first session of the United Nations. The charges originated with a somewhat seedy former Communist and *Time* magazine writer, Whittaker Chambers. When Hiss sued for libel after Chambers repeated his charges away from the immunity conferred by the House Un-American Activities Committee, Chambers produced incriminating documents he had secreted when he had broken with the Communist Party before the war. The fact that prominent Democrats, starting with President Truman, had spoken up for Hiss badly wounded that political party, making all the more credible the Republican charges that the Democrats were "soft on Communism". Never mind the fact that President Truman himself had instituted a loyalty investigation programme to ferret out Communists as early as 1947.

It was in this atmosphere that the odious and irresponsible Senator Joseph McCarthy (R–Wisconsin) flourished, tarring with his reckless brush the most improbable of Americans with unsubstantiated charges of Communist sympathies or even Party membership. Careers were ruined, but in the end, not one known Communist was exposed by the junior Senator from Wisconsin. Something of a pall of fear fell over the land, in which the cantankerous and the cross-grained, the village atheist, the labour union activist, the socialist, the dissenter went about in fear of their jobs and their good name although not of their lives and only rarely of their liberty. In 1950 Congress passed the McCarran Internal Security Act over President Truman's veto. This enactment made it a federal offence "to perform any act which would substantially contribute [to] the establishment of a totalitarian dictatorship". Truman exclaimed that the act had more in common with Moscow than with Washington, but few commentators noted that most democratic nations had even more broad-based security legislation, such as Great Britain's Defence of the Realm Act, going back to the First World War.

The overwhelming majority of Americans cheered, in many cases literally, the 1953 simultaneous electrocutions of the two "atom spies", Julius Rosenberg, who had delivered nuclear secrets to the Soviet Union during the Second World War, and his wife Ethel, the tougher of the two, but apparently little more than a very witting accomplice. Their treachery was compounded by seeming British incompetence in uncovering their own atomic spies until they had done their dirty work or had actually decamped to the Soviet Union under the noses of British "security". All of this did make it easier for Americans to comprehend how the Soviets had developed a nuclear bomb of their own, years before such a thing could have been possible: treason.

If President Truman's decision to commit US military forces to the defence of South Korea was initially cheered by Americans, there were few accolades for his handling of domestic issues. In the wake of the sharpest one-year rise in prices since the First World War and following the Chinese entry into the war, the Truman administration imposed wage and price controls. Initially, the move was generally popular, what with the Third World War seemingly around the corner. But as the Korean War settled into stalemate, more and more criticism was heard of "stifling bureaucratic controls", "government interference" and so on. Such sentiments seemed verified when President Truman moved to take the steel industry under federal control as a major strike in 1952 threatened to unleash another round of inflation and hamper the war effort. The Supreme Court's voiding of the President's action gave the Republicans that much more political ammunition. Thus even the concrete steps that Truman had taken to strengthen the home front were used against him.

Matters were not helped by the President's insouciance about those of his officials accused of corruption; his own military aide, General Harry Vaughan, stood accused of influence peddling. Americans, rather proud of their high tax compliance rate, were more outraged by the corruption unearthed in the Internal Revenue Service. It seemed as if the federal government itself were for sale.

Even with a Third World War, the US Constitution mandated national elections in 1952. The Republicans had found an effective slogan to use against the Democrats: "Communism, Korea, and Corruption", the two "C's" of which could be subsumed by Truman's enemies as "the mess in Washington". When the war hero, General Eisenhower, revealed himself a candidate for the Republican nomination for President, it seemed fairly obvious that his party would win in November. Nonetheless, bitter 1948 GOP memories of going to bed winners in all of the polls and awakening in reality losers in the cold dawn, gave them all the more cause to fight a vigorous campaign.

Eisenhower's nomination was not foreordained, however. His supporters had to wrest the prize from the party "regulars", who preferred Senator Robert A. Taft (Ohio), the representative of the more isolationist or "Asia First" wing of the GOP. General MacArthur had deflated his own presidential boomlet with a hall-emptying speech. He never returned to the public arena, an "old soldier" who did indeed "fade away". The Democrats nominated the popular Governor of Illinois, Adlai Stevenson. He remained handicapped by the Truman record, which he could hardly repudiate as a committed Democrat, and by "Mr Truman's War" in Korea.

The Republican campaign plan was that Eisenhower would take the "high road" of lofty internationalism. "Ike's" running mate, the committed anti-Communist California Senator, Richard Nixon, would follow the "low road" of excoriating the Democrats for their sins: "twenty years of treason" and "Communist, Korea, and Corruption".

Whatever course the GOP took in the campaign, Eisenhower's election was assured when the Republican standard-bearer made his momentous public declaration that "If elected, I will go to Korea". Just why neither President Truman nor Adlai Stevenson had never made such a promise remains a mystery. Candidate Eisenhower made no promises to end the war nor did he even hint at any plan to bring the boys home. By late 1952 Americans were so sick and tired of Korea that Ike's promise simply to go there was sufficient to arouse enthusiastic approval. Stevenson went down to foreordained defeat. Eisenhower did go to Korea as President-elect, toured the battle zone and behind the lines, looked knowledgeable, and returned home amid the usual publicity.

The inauguration of Eisenhower and the death of Joseph Stalin a few months later lowered the temperature of political dissention considerably, both at home and abroad. Americans overwhelmingly "liked Ike" – although not enough for the Republicans to retain control of Congress two years later. With Ike at the helm it was difficult for Americans any longer to believe that the government was honeycombed with Communists or that traitors controlled the State Department under Eisenhower's Secretary of State, the lugubrious old Cold Warrior, John Foster Dulles.

Although the new President spoke on at least one occasion rather casually of perhaps using a few nuclear weapons in Korea, he, of course, did nothing of the kind. Defence spending declined as the Eisenhower administration put its money into the unimaginatively termed defence "New Look", which emphasized nuclear deterrence and drastically downplayed ground combat. This "New Look" also had the benefit of lower costs over the maintenance of large ground forces. In fact, as a proportion of gross national product, defence spending in time of relative peace had reached an all-time-high level in Truman's last budget, for 1953. Americans were pleased at the tax reductions that Eisenhower's defence policies permitted and with the lower draft calls. The Cold War "thaw" was beginning and even though the Korean armistice was signed in the seventh month of Eisenhower's first term, that administration's history basically belongs to the post-Korean War era.

Great Britain

The domestic scene in the United Kingdom during the Korean War years was dominated by the political struggle between the resurgent Conservative Party and Labour, which had won a landslide victory in 1945 but which was now clearly losing ground. Rather surprisingly, the Labour government of Clement Attlee fully supported the initial American efforts to assemble a coalition to repel the North Korean invasion. For the most part, UK political leaders, Labour and Conservative alike, were fearful that the United States might revert to its old pre-war anti-Europe attitude (termed "isolationism" by those who didn't know better). At first, the British Cabinet was about as clueless as to the very whereabouts of Korea as were their US brethren. For the more radical Labourites, their party's decision to join with the Americans in Korea was rendered the more palatable by the fact that the anti-Communist forces would fight under the UN banner. Most British political leaders had little sympathy for the rightist, authoritarian Rhee regime, nor did they wish to be seen as supinely following in the train of unthinking American anti-Communism. In fact, anti-Americanism was one feeling that cut across party and class lines; Tories resented America taking up Great Britain's leading power mantle, while Labourites saw in the Great Republic a centre of reaction that extended aid to every rightist warlord who would say the magic word, "anti-Communist". After their initial support, Labour leftists tabled a motion calling for the immediate mediation of the conflict in Korea, withdrawal of Nationalist forces from Taiwan (then "Formosa") and the admission of Communist China to the UN. The Prime Minister himself privately expressed his reservations about America's Asian policies and particularly about General MacArthur's sabre-rattling. In fact, in his early December 1950 talks with President Truman, Attlee let the President know that he had no objection to the Chinese Communists assuming Taiwan's seat in the United Nations. More than one American high official, including US Secretary of State Acheson, privately spoke of "another Munich" and maliciously wondered if this Prime Minister had brought along his umbrella. Truman had a stouter British Prime Minister in mind when he proclaimed to Attlee that UNC troops would have to be driven bodily off the beaches of Korea in another Dunkirk and that he would never condemn to death (or Communism – it made little difference to him) the millions of Koreans who had placed their trust in the United States. Donald MacLean, the eminent British diplomat-spy, routinely received his uncensored copy of the talks and Attlee's report to the Cabinet upon his return from Washington. He presumably forwarded the lot to Moscow.

Basically, the highest British political leadership had little concern for Korea once the initial reaction of outrage at overt aggression had passed. Rhee was a corrupt dictator, and even if the Communists were thrown out, his regime would probably fall soon enough to Communist subversion. Both Labourites and Tories seemed to believe that the Koreans had little ability for self-government and had probably been better off under the Japanese, anyway. The British government of the time was considerably more concerned with Hong Kong and consistently sought to placate China to protect the *status quo* in their Crown Colony.

Governments of both parties looked to Great Britain's "special relationship" with America as well as their own greater "maturity" and "realism" to help restrain the "brash" Americans from going over the brink into some nuclear nightmare. Few Britons or Americans realized at the time that in Dean Acheson, American Secretary of State until early 1953, they were dealing with someone fully as mature and sophisticated as any European. Acheson's immediate successor, the evangelical anti-Communist John Foster Dulles, was for them emphatically and frighteningly another matter.

In January 1951, at the height of the crisis sparked by China's intervention in the war, Mr Attlee flew to Washington to press for negotiations and for the avoiding of anything that might lead to the Third World War. Irresponsible American talk about loosing "the bomb" in Korea was unnerving to those whose nations were considerably closer to the Soviet Union than was the United States – and which were still recovering from the Second World War. These were facts of geography and current history that many Europeans felt had escaped the more isolated Americans. However, by this time, the British public, like the American, was tired of the war, now hardening into stalemate. Britons were strongly favourable to the concept of a basically *status quo* armistice. Truman's firing of General MacArthur was met in the UK with a collective sigh of relief.

Communism and Communists in the UK were treated with considerably less hysteria than in the USA. Viewed objectively, the threat at home certainly seemed minuscule. The only two avowed Communist Members of Parliament had been defeated in the February 1950 elections. On the other hand, it could be argued that the Communists did not need open Party members; the extreme left-wing members faithfully followed the Communist "Party Line" closely enough for them. The Koje riots of May 1952 were greeted with delight by such members and their fellow-travellers who wasted no time in terming the Koje camp "another Belsen" and in blasting the "reactionary" Rhee regime. A prominent British academic, Professor Joseph Needham, lent his name and prestige to the most improbable Communist "germ warfare" charges. Undoubtedly the most visible Communist fellow-traveller in the UK was the Very Reverend Hewlett Johnson, Dean of Westminster and Stalin Peace Prize laureate, in some ways a typical English upper-class eccentric. This cleric discerned in the Soviet Union the closest thing to the Kingdom of God on Earth. Anglo–American relations were helped even less by Americans ignorantly confusing the "Red Dean" with the Archbishop of Canterbury, the latter an ecclesiastic eminence of impeccable non-Communist views. The government did prosecute some strike leaders under the Companies Act (1875) but certainly did not pursue any vulgar anti-Communist McCarthyite "witch hunt" as in the United States. In fact, there was a tacit cross-party agreement to keep the domestic Communism issue out of electoral politics. Even the most reasonable step of the prior checking of the backgrounds of candidates for sensitive government posts was not instituted – until the disappearance of Burgess and MacLean.

British "calm" in these troubled years was admirable in many respects, but it did nothing to unmask those willing to betray the land for reasons of ideology and perhaps of sheer bloody-mindedness. Although British security finally uncovered such agents of the Soviet Union as Klaus Fuchs and Alan Nunn May after they had done their dirty work, it failed to prevent the defection of the nuclear scientist Bruno Pontecorvo or the diplomats Burgess and MacLean (and much later, "Kim" Philby) who, MacLean in particular, had enjoyed access to high Allied government secrets despite their daffy private lives. The fact that Pontecorvo, Burgess and MacLean subsequently surfaced in the Soviet Union (Fuchs flew off to East Germany after his prison sentence had been served) did nothing to help Anglo–American relations. All had been repeatedly cleared by British intelligence despite the Americans' doubts about the lot. The diplomats seemed to have lived a charmed, drunken life, beloved by a certain Whitehall–Mayfair set who found them "amusing", "clever" and, of course, "brilliant".

The Korean War caused the most serious crisis of the Attlee government. The need for increased defence expenditures led to the imposition of fees for dentures and spectacles previously distributed gratis by the National Health

Service. These imposts, in turn, prompted, in April 1951, the resignation of the Minister of Health, Aneurin Bevan, and other leftist Labourites from the government. The ark of the covenant for this generation of socialists was a nationalized health service, "free" for all, regardless of ability to pay. But what made these imposts pure wormwood to the "Bevanites" was the fact that they were to finance British rearmament at America's direction. In fact, Bevan himself probably resigned less because of the fees and more in disgust at his government's "truckling to the Yanks". For the more leftist Labourites, the UN was the best hope for world peace, not weapons, which the Soviets could match anyway. Oddly, the Bevanites had not publicly complained, much less resigned, when the Attlee Labour Government had embarked upon its own very expensive development of an atomic bomb, which had also diverted funds from social programmes to a weapons system obviously designed with the Soviet Union in mind.

However, the British electorate's allegiance was determined more by domestic concerns than by events in Asia, particularly after the relief of General MacArthur eased fears of a nuclear holocaust. Britain had finally shed her expensive burdens of India, Palestine and Greece, although still holding on in her African colonies and to her Egyptian Suez bases, where a nasty guerrilla war sought to prise the British military out of the Suez Canal Zone. An expensive insurgency in Malaya saw the assassination of the High Commissioner, Sir Henry Gurney, in 1951. Without the public realizing it, the British Empire was winding down by the early 1950s.

The public was tired after six years of socialist austerity that seemed more severe in some ways than the deprivations of the Second World War. Bread, for example, was never rationed during the war, but went "on points" after it. Citizens were still mindlessly required long after the end of the war to carry identification cards as an "administrative convenience" to the huge government bureaucracy. Businessmen complained of punitive taxation and a strangle-hold of regulations at the same time that they were being exhorted to produce ever more for export. The private motorist was treated as a selfish public nuisance. Almost no one wished to dismantle the National Health Service, expensive as it was, or even to reverse such measures as the nationalization of the coal mining industry or the railroads, money-losers as these industries were from the start. But overall, the 1945 socialist dream of "fair shares for all" now seemed to have declined into simply a threadbare austerity, punctuated by the official preachings to work harder, spend less and save more. Looking at the unrationed, now-booming economy of Germany, more than one irate Briton was moved to wonder "Who won the bloody war, anyway?"

For all of this discontent, the victory of the Tories in the October 1951 national elections was not by a majority of the popular vote; Labour gained its highest poll to date. The victors simply had a thin majority of Parliamentary seats. But it was the beginning of the long Tory ascendancy and an end to austerity. The old warrior, Winston Churchill, returned as Prime Minister.

Just four months after the Conservative victory, on 6 February 1952, the beloved monarch, King George VI, died in his sleep. His reign had come to be associated with years of trial and sacrifice. His successor, the youthful and beautiful Queen Elizabeth II, seemed to symbolize a renewed Great Britain. Certainly the immediate years after her coronation did see vastly increased prosperity at home and, a little more than one month after the Queen's coronation, an end to the Korean War and its British participation.

Domestically, Australia, Canada and New Zealand were hardly touched by the Korean War. None of these nations conscripted young men to serve in that conflict or imposed much in the way of controls on the economy. The war did spark economic recovery from the first, mild, post-war recession and brought high prices for their raw materials. The greatest impact of this conflict was in the bringing of these three self-governing Commonwealth dominions closer into the US anti-Communist defence orbit. Paradoxically, this closer defence relationship sparked a moderate increase in anti-American sentiment. Politically aware groups self-consciously shuddered at the more bellicose pronouncements of right-wing American politicians and congratulated themselves that they lived in civilized societies that were above the vulgarities of anything like McCarthyism or the threatening of nuclear cataclysm to bring peace.

It is a paradox that we understand far more about the relatively modest effect of the Korean War on the home fronts of the USA and the UK than we know about its obviously much greater impact upon North Korea and Communist China. The DPRK endured enemy invasion and occupation of much of its territory, as well as continuous aerial bombardment for three years. Along with the Chinese, they mourned the deaths in battle of hundreds of thousands of their young men. Very little is known about conditions in the Democratic Republic of Korea once the UN forces had been expelled. In the absence of objective documentation, it is only possible at this time to write of what the UNC was doing to North Korea, and that means mainly the air war over the North. It is certainly true that its major cities were heavily battered from the air and may have suffered more proportionally than had Germany or Japan during the Second World War. By 1953, the USAF was restricting raids over North Korea simply because of the lack of targets. The Democratic People's Republic of Korea and the People's Republic of China do their peoples no favour by continuing to withhold the documentation that would verify their own wartime endurance and accomplishments.

Chapter Thirteen

Fighting and negotiating

By the early summer of 1951 even Mao conceded that the time for large-scale offensives, at least for the moment, was past and that his armies must go over to "piecemeal" warfare. He cabled Peng that

> The [immediate] past campaigns have shown that our enveloping, outflanking and penetrating operations at both campaign and battle levels have encountered such great difficulties that we were prevented from achieving the goals of completely annihilating several US divisions or even a whole US division or regiment.

In an unconscious tribute to Ridgway's reforms, Mao conceded that this failure came "because the American armed forces still maintain a very strong confidence. . . . [Therefore] we must not be too ambitious in every battle".[1] He later compared his "piecemeal" strategy to "eating *niupitang*", a sticky candy from Mao's home province, Hunan, that was best cut up and consumed bit by bit.

Now the Chinese military commanders found themselves commending their troops for their defensive capabilities in the face of the UN counter-offensive north of the 38th Parallel in October. Even so, the Chinese had lost 91,000 of those troops to the UN. From then on, the emphasis would be on tunnelling, bunkers and deep trenches, measures at which the Chinese and North Koreans would prove masters compared to the UN forces.

The PLA/CPV leadership had indeed entered Korea in 1950 expecting to fight a defensive battle, but from the first found themselves drawn into offensive operations to clear North Korea of the UNC. Their military unpreparedness for this type of operation caused their troops to suffer heavily and needlessly for the most part. The CPV/PVA leadership generally believed that their numerical and moral superiority would yield complete victory, never expecting that the UN forces would recover so quickly from their long retreat. Further, they vastly underestimated their enemy's superior weaponry. And finally, their political and military leaders had expected practically unlimited support from their ally, the Soviet Union. What they got was too little and generally too late. By early 1951 "active defence"/"piecemeal", or *niupitang* had become the only feasible strategy for the CPV and the *Inmin Gun*, but it took one million casualties for their leadership to learn this lesson.

Early during the interminable armistice negotiations at Kaesong, the UN Command learned its own lessons from their counterparts as to the value of symbolism and propaganda. One would have thought the white flag incident might have made the UNC more aware, but once again they were tripped up. In China during any peace talks the loser traditionally sits facing north, the victor south. At the first negotiating sessions Communist propaganda was careful to show the Americans facing north towards the chief negotiator, Nam Il, who was seated on a higher chair: the victor dictating to the vanquished. The UNC delegates, in their innocence, assumed the northward-facing position simply because they were on the south side of the battle line. That the UNC, beaten on the battlefield, implored their enemies for an armistice was certainly the Communists' official "line": "Having suffered the repeated ignominious defeats of the powerful attack of our People's Army units, the US imperialists were thrown into confusion and have proposed armistice negotiations to our side."[2]

The Communists were also punctilious regarding matters of prestige and "face". When the UNC delegation brought in a small UN flag and stand to the meetings, the Communists responded with their own larger flag and stand. The erection of a modest UNC sanitary facility led to a construction "war" with the Communists, who promptly built their own facility, brightly painted and landscaped as well. The senior UNC delegate was transported to the meetings by a sedan; General Nam Il quickly saw to it that a luxury America sedan was transported from the Soviet Union so that he, too, could arrive in comparable style.

The businesslike UNC commissioned purely military men as their negotiators. But the Communists deputed personnel such as General Nam Il, not only Chief of Staff of the *Inmin Gun*, but Vice Premier of the Pyongyang regime. He was assisted by Major General Lee Sang Cho, Chief of the Reconnaissance Bureau of the KPA and a former minister of commerce. Major General Hsieh Fang's more modest formal credentials as chief of propaganda of the Northeast Military District of China belied his true position as the director of Communist truce negotiations and arrangements at Kaesong. These were the "open" leaders of the Communist delegation. The Chinese also established a "negotiation direction group", headed by the long-term head of PVA military intelligence and vice Foreign Minister, and the chief of the PRC's International Information Bureau, who had experience in negotiating with the Americans in the abortive attempts to negotiate an end to the Chinese civil war in 1945–6. It is significant that North Korea was not represented in this group. Perhaps as a way of getting even for this "slight", Kim Il Sung's official biography makes no mention of the Chinese as negotiators or in any other capacity. ("The cease-fire talks opened at Kaesong from July 10, 1951. The talk was between the Democratic People's Republic of Korea and US imperialism, the ring-leaders of world reaction."[3])

It is significant that none of the UNC negotiating team had any experience in dealing with a Communist regime. Furthermore, Nam Il and KPA Major General Lee Sang Cho were in the negotiations from the beginning to the end, and General Fang missed the final signing by only three months. Not one UN delegate could make that claim, and several remained for only a few months. As a reflection of the mindless personnel churning that afflicted the US Army then and now, the UN negotiators changed frequently. The ROK Army delegates experienced similarly brief tours of duty.

Still, the UNC delegates, changing as they were, eventually proved as tough a group of negotiators as the Communists themselves. In the initial negotiations they firmly resisted Communist demands for the withdrawal of all foreign troops and that the demarcation line be the 38th Parallel. When the chief UNC negotiator, Vice-Admiral C. Turner Joy, acidly responded that this supposedly sacrosanct international boundary had been crossed four times by Communist armies in the preceding 13 months, the issue went into abeyance. We now know that the Chinese and the North Koreans were willing to make peace in 1951 if the 38th Parallel were accepted as the demarcation line. Their negotiators never really dropped the subject. But if this condition were not met, the Sino–Korean side was prepared to prolong the negotiations.

At the same time, the Communists were well aware of their continuing heavy losses at the hands of UN bombardment. Kim Il Sung later complained to Stalin that "the enemy, almost without suffering any kind of losses, constantly inflicts on us huge losses in manpower and material values".[4]

Yet the Communists, even in private, blamed the UNC for prolonging the talks. Both sides had to settle in for difficult negotiations on the four major topics: the establishment of a military demarcation line and a demilitarized zone, arrangements for the establishment of a supervisory organization to oversee the carrying out of the armistice terms, the disposition of POWs and recommendations to the governments involved on actions to take in the post-armistice period. To save time, a subcommittee was assigned to each of these major topics so that negotiations could proceed concurrently, rather than serially. In fact, both sides and their general publics assumed that an armistice

agreement would come in a matter of months. At the opening of the negotiations, "pessimistic" newsmen accredited to the UNC, thought that an
armistice agreement might be as long as six weeks in the making, and the
Chinese delegates brought only summer clothing. Both sides were to be sorely
and equally disappointed.

The UNC delegates soon discovered that the Communists knew exactly
what they wanted and would stand firm on matters of substance but that they
could be flexible on procedures and formats. When the Communists had
uncovered the basic positions of the UNC team, they would push no further
and could prove businesslike. The UNC delegates also learned that, as long
as their adversaries would argue a point, they had not ruled out compromise;
when the Communists refused to discuss the matter further, they had reached
their bedrock position. All of this negotiating was generally to the accom-
paniment of rudeness, bluster and even profanity, although much of the latter
was lost in translation. The English language capabilities of the Communist
delegates were never determined. It is indicative of the charged atmosphere
of the talks that when the negotiations had reached an impasse on 10 August
on the question of the 38th Parallel, the two delegations faced each other in
frozen silence for two hours and ten minutes, the palpable tension broken
only by General Nam Il nervously tapping his cigarette lighter on the table.
On another such "frozen" occasion, the chief UNC negotiator watched in
fascination as a fly carefully explored Nam Il's face. The Communist negotiator never blinked.

Syngman Rhee and his government were resolutely opposed to the truce
talks. They could see no reason to return to the pre-war *status quo* that had
proved so unsatisfactory and had led to the near-loss of the Republic. As far
as Dr Rhee was concerned, now was the time to press for the reunification
of the nation, under ROK hegemony of course, as the only UN-recognized
government of the peninsula. Rhee publicly set out his terms on 20 September:
withdrawal of all Chinese forces and the disarmament of the North Koreans.
The latter would, however, generously be extended full representation in
the (South) Korean National Assembly and thus should have no grounds for
complaint. In the light of this attitude, the ROK representative to the armistice
negotiations merely served as an observer.

The course of the negotiations was not furthered in the early weeks by a
series of violations or supposed violations of the neutral zone. On 4 August
a company of fully-armed Communist troops marched through the conference site. The UNC filed a strong denunciation, the world press gave the
incident unfavourable publicity, and it was not repeated. On the other hand,
several Communist truck convoys, marked with white crosses, were strafed
by UN warplanes just outside the neutral zone. Flatly rejecting Communist

protests, the UNC pointed out that their command had not been notified of such movements, as stipulated in preliminary agreements. (General Ridgway also suspected that these marked convoys were being used for more than innocently bringing non-military supplies to Kaesong.) But the Communists could more justly protest when a Chinese military police platoon was ambushed and the platoon leader killed. The UNC denied all responsibility, and considering that some witnesses described several of the attackers as wearing civilian clothes, this mysterious incident might have been the result of anti-Communist guerrillas acting on their own, or possibly, as Mao believed, it might have been at the instigation of the Rhee regime to break up the talks. At any rate, the UNC would have had no reason to sabotage the talks. (The Communist delegation invited two chief UNC delegates to attend the slain platoon leader's funeral, but they, now wise to their adversary's propaganda machinations, politely refused.)

Perhaps as another propaganda manoeuvre, the Communists then bitterly protested a supposed UN bombing of the conference site and pointed out several small holes and a few so-called bomb fragments. UNC investigators, after a technical investigation, termed the whole business "nonsense".

The Communists then indefinitely suspended the negotiations on 22 August, although liaison officers continued to meet to discuss changing the current volatile site and to formulate agreements that would prevent a repetition of the distracting violations that had marred the earlier talks. Mao, in his reports to Stalin, seemed to believe that the Americans were indeed guilty of provocations and wished "to use the period of the break in negotiations for conducting a cold war in order to expose the impudent provocational acts of the enemy".[5]

To make matters worse, on 10 September a USAF warplane from the 3rd Bomb Group did indeed strafe Kaesong through a navigational error. No damage was inflicted. Ridgway promptly apologized and received an almost friendly response from the Communist side and an offer to resume negotiations at Kaesong immediately. But the UN Commander, tired of the imagined and real violations of security by both sides at Kaesong, demanded a more secure site. Eventually the delegates agreed on the tiny, mud-hut village of Panmunjom, about five miles to the west of Kaesong, and the "provocations" ceased. In the years to come, the "Panmunjom" heading on a news story could prove as important as that of "Washington" or "Moscow".

General Van Fleet, meanwhile, concerned that his troops were losing their "fighting edge", mounted a series of offensive actions to improve his lines. The fighting around the Punchbowl and Bloody and Heartbreak Ridges was fierce, for the Communists' forces in accordance with Mao and Peng's directives had burrowed in well with concealed, interlocking bunkers and dug-in

artillery positions, most of which had not been spotted by UN aerial reconnaissance. The cost was heavy. The 2nd Division alone suffered some 6,000
casualties at the aptly named Bloody and Heartbreak Ridges. The KPA 6th,
12th, and 13th divisions and the Chinese 204th Division incurred losses
estimated at nearly 25,000 men. These local battles showed that the UNC
had underestimated Communist strength and tenacity, and that the Chinese
and the North Koreans had more or less recovered from their pounding in
the spring of 1951 and were fighting with courage and tenacity. The UNC
troops were in little danger of losing their "fighting edge".

Perhaps as a way of sending its own "message" to Premier Stalin, the
USAF finally received permission to bomb the North Korean port of Rashin
(Najin), which lay within 19 air miles of the Soviet border. General MacArthur
had been forbidden to mount any air raids against the city because of the
possibility of attacking the Soviet Union itself through navigational error.
Air reconnaissance had reported extensive military stockpiling, and Rashin
itself was an important railway and highway centre with oil storage and rail
equipment repair shops that served the Communist war effort. Earlier, the
Far East Air Force Commander had termed Rashin/Najin the keystone of
North Korea's logistics system. The question of the city's bombing went
right up through the Joint Chiefs and the Secretary of Defense to President
Truman, all of whom approved. On 25 August, 35 B-29s, escorted by US
Navy fighters for the first time in the Korean War, struck the railway
marshalling yards with "excellent" results and with no USAF losses. There
was also no overt Soviet response, although observers on Russian soil less
than a score of miles away must have seen the smoke plumes and heard the
thunderous explosions. A later raid in December 1952 also provoked no
Soviet response.

Presumably the UNC's "elbowing forward", along with the intensive air
and naval bombardment, had its effect on the Communist side, for on 25
October the talks were resumed at Panmunjom. Although the negotiators
did not repeat their earlier wordless episode, they did have this enlightening
exchange during the first meeting:

Major General Lee Sang Cho: Do you have any idea about the military
demarcation line?

Major General Henry Hodes: We ended the last conference before
the suspension by asking for your proposal. Do you have one?

General Lee: We would like your opinion first.

General Hodes: We gave our opinion many times, and asked for your
proposal based on our proposal. As it was your proposal to have the sub-
delegation meeting, we expected you to have a proposal. Let's have it.

General Lee: You said you had made a new proposal, but we have heard nothing new which will break the deadlock.

General Hodes: That's right, you haven't.

General Lee: We have established a subcommittee to break the deadlock. The deadlock can be broken only if we have a mutually satisfactory proposal.

In the same session General Nam Il took it upon himself to deride the point made by Admiral Joy that the United States had defeated Japan in the Second World War without one US soldier setting foot on Japan proper. Nam Il seriously maintained that "anyone knew" that the mere four days of Soviet combat against Japan had really won the war in the Pacific, a testimony to either that high-ranking officer's ignorance of recent history or his devotion to propaganda when opposed to inconvenient facts.

But the Communists' rejection of the UNC proposals to trade territory and the UNC's refusal to discuss the 38th Parallel as a demarcation line finally induced the Communists to accept the current battleline as the line of demarcation, a major concession on their part. Almost immediately, military operations slowed drastically. The Communists were certainly taking the long-range view here. In a ciphered telegram to "Flippov", the Chinese leader explained that:

> Expecting that the negotiations will be drawn out for another half year or year and, we have moved toward economizing on our human and material forces in the Korean theater of military operations and we are pursuing the tactics of a long, active defense, with the goal of holding the positions we presently occupy and inflicting great manpower losses on the enemy, *in order to gain victory in the war.*[6]

By December the negotiations had turned to the establishment of a neutral nations supervisory organization to oversee and report on both sides' observance of the armistice. With a straight face the Communist side proposed the Soviet Union as a member. The Communists just as resolutely rejected the UNC demand that all airfield construction or rehabilitation in Korea cease. This deadlock was broken by some hard bargaining in which the UNC dropped the airfield demand, the Communists abandoned their insistence on the Soviet Union as a "neutral nation", and the UNC accepted Czechoslovakia and Poland instead. These two nations were hardly neutral in their wholehearted support for the Communist side throughout the Korean War, but they at least did not arm and finance that side to any great extent. The Communists accepted Sweden and Switzerland, more truly neutral countries, as the UNC nominees for the supervisory nations. In addition, the negotiators established a military armistice commission which would operate out of Panmunjom to handle all truce violations and to supervise and administer the demilitarized zone.

This progress reflected the desire of the belligerent parties to arrive at some sort of a cease-fire and armistice. Mao and Kim had by now abandoned their earlier view of the armistice negotiations as a stall manoeuvre until they could mount an offensive in the autumn of 1951. They finally realized that they could not deliver a severe defeat to the UN forces, let alone drive them from the peninsula.

Stalin, however, remained adamant on spinning out the talks indefinitely. In November he cabled Mao that

> Americans are more in need of the early completion of negotiations. . . . We consider it proper . . . to continue to stick to a firm line without haste and without a strong interest in the early completion of negotiations.

This despite the sufferings of the DPRK people. For example, on 16 January 1952, the North Korean Foreign Minister made a heartfelt complaint to Peng DeHuai that

> The Korean people throughout the country demand peace [demand?] and don't want to continue the war, [but dutifully concluded that] If the Soviet Union and China consider it fruitful to carry on the war, then the Central Committee of the Labour Party [Communist Party of North Korea] will be able to overcome any difficulties and stick to the present position.[7]

But neither the Chinese nor the North Korean leadership could prevail. Two months later the Soviet Politburo passed a resolution coldly stating that "We should not hurry the process of negotiations. It is not in our interests". A 20 August 1952 meeting between Stalin and Chou En-lai, PRC foreign minister and a Mao comrade and confidante, indicates that Mao had come back at least partially to Stalin's views on the talks. Chou quoted Mao as saying that "continuation of the war was favorable to us because it prevented the United States from preparation of a new world war; for the USA continuation of the war was not favorable". Chou also noted that "the North Korean leadership did not want to continue the war because their daily losses were bigger than the number of POWs that we wanted to get back from the Americans".[8] Considering that the UNC POW camps held more than 75,800 North Koreans, somebody must have been wildly exaggerating for effect here. Stalin coldly retorted that the "North Koreans have not lost anything, except losses in killed". (He obviously had not visited blitzed Pyongyang recently.) But, his humanity getting the better of him, Stalin added that

Of course, we should understand Koreans – they have big losses in killed. But they must be told that this is an important cause. It is necessary to persevere, to have patience. The war in Korea has shown the weakness of Americans.[9]

Stalin then entered into a rambling monologue about Americans and American soldiers that bore some eerie resemblance to the ignorant "thoughts" of his erstwhile comrade and enemy, Adolph Hitler:

Americans are merchants. Every American soldier is a speculator, occupied with buying and selling. Germans conquered France in 20 days [not quite]. It's been already two years, and the USA has still not subdued little Korea. What kind of strength is that? America's primary weapons, . . . are stockings, cigarettes and other merchandise. They want to subjugate the world, yet they cannot subdue little Korea. No, Americans don't know how to fight.[10]

Basically, Stalin favoured continuation of the war because it tied America's hands ("this war is getting on America's nerves"), provoked tension with America's allies and cemented the Sino–Soviet alliance, forestalling any possibility of Mao becoming "another Tito", lured from the socialist camp by the much greater economic aid that the Americans could offer a defector. Stalin was undoubtedly aware of the Chinese Communist leadership meeting with American representatives in the 1930s and with a special US Office of Strategic Services team during the Second World War. (On the other hand, there was a similar team with the Red Army during the same conflict.) He was also looking in the long term to a war with the United States, a war that the Soviet Union was not yet prepared to fight victoriously. And because Stalin was paying the bills for North Korea and China in this war, both "fraternal socialist" nations had to defer to his will.

It could be argued that the armistice negotiations did not need Stalin to become deadlocked: the POW issue would serve that end quite adequately. The background to this most vexatious question was that the United States had signed the Geneva Convention of 1949, although Congress had not yet ratified it. North Korea's foreign minister had stated early in the war that his nation would abide by the same convention. That international treaty had provided that "Prisoners of war shall be released and repatriated without delay after the cessation of hostilities".

But things historically had not always proven that simple. After the American War for Independence, for example, thousands of Hessian and British prisoners and deserters had remained in the New World, in contravention of the Treaty of Paris, lured from their military service for the most part by the

247

promise of free land. After the Second World War, the Soviet Union had held on to its prisoners for as much as a full decade or even later; many never returned. Less well known was the British and the French retention of their German POWs for something like slave labour until 1948 and 1949, respectively. There was the then-unpublicized and distinctly unpleasant story of tens of thousands of Soviet former POWs of the Germans who bitterly refused repatriation, many to the point of suicide, but were nonetheless frog-marched by the Western Allies into Soviet transports.

The UK in this war again saw no problem with forcible repatriation. A Foreign Office Minute perceptively noted that the anti-Communist POWs would wind up in Chiang Kai-shek's military and concluded that Great Britain had "no interest at all in UK and Communist POWs having to stay captive in order to build up Guomingdang forces". (No mention of other UN POWs here.) At roughly the same time, a Foreign Office official, one J. M. Adds, coldly noted that "the humanitarian argument, that we could not have it on our conscience to force POWs to return to death or slavery, has been given too much importance".[11] The *Inmin Gun* had press-ganged tens of thousands of ROK civilians and captured military personnel into its service during its occupation of South Korea. Most of these were still in the UNC POW camps. It would have been monstrous forcibly to return these *South* Koreans to North Korean jurisdiction. Then, the People's Liberation Army had also impressed many Chinese Nationalist troops into its armies during the Chinese civil war, and their commitment to the Communist cause was generally weaker than that of troops who had served only in the Chinese People's Liberation Army.

Fittingly, Brigadier General Robert McClure, the Army Chief of Psychological Warfare, was the first ranking US officer to seize upon the propaganda value of the Chinese Nationalist POWs. For the Chinese, General McClure proposed a clever legalistic ploy: in that the United States recognized the regime of Chiang Kai-shek as the only legitimate government of China, the release of these thousands of prisoners to Taiwan would not be a violation of the Geneva Convention. General McClure was certainly well aware of the psychological warfare gains that could be reaped by the UNC over the repatriation issue, and conversely, the damage that could be inflicted by forcible repatriation. The UNC psywar effort in leaflet, loudspeaker and radio broadcast emphasized "Come over to our side and you will be well treated". What would be the reaction of possible defectors to the news that they would eventually be returned to the Communist overlords that they had emphatically rejected?

US Army Chief of Staff, General J. Lawton Collins, went General McClure one better. He proposed that no Chinese or North Korean prisoner of war should be returned to the Communists against his will. They could worry about the Geneva Convention later. General Ridgway, while favourable to his superior's idea in general, wondered if it might work to America's disadvantage in future wars (that is, the holder of US POWs could claim that many had "seen the light" and now refused to return to the horrors of capitalism). But the initiative here lay with the Communist side. If they insisted on a "one for one" exchange, all would be well, for there were far more POWs held by the UNC than vice versa; the UNC could hand over all who desired repatriation and still have many "left over" who might wish to remain. But if the Communists insisted on "all for all", things would get much more complicated and bitter. In fact, General Collins and Ridgway both soon backed away from their ideas. In the end, it was President Truman who prevailed with his adamant opposition to the forced repatriation of any POW, whatever the consequences.

The Communists agreed to furnish a list of their POWs on 18 December 1951. But the eagerly awaited list provoked bitterness and grief in South Korea and the United States. For although the Communists had boasted that their all-conquering armies had rounded up some 65,000 UNC prisoners in the first months of the war, their list showed a mere 11,559; the ROK Army alone carried some 88,000 as missing and the US Army more than 11,500. By way of contrast, the UNC listed their holding of 132,000 POWs and had classified another 37,000 as civilian internees, leaving 19,000 unaccounted for. This was a remarkable correlation of figures considering the savagery and widespread nature of this war, not that the Communists ever expressed any satisfaction in the matter. The chief Communist negotiator, General Lee, explained that his side held such a small number of POWs because most of these POWs had been "re-educated" and had volunteered for the front. Standing logic on its head, he denounced the principle of voluntary repatriation as some sort of "slave trade"! The Chief UNC negotiator, Admiral Ruthven Libby, tried some "bourgeois logic" on General Lee: he solicitously informed Lee that he could not understand why the Communists were concerned about any of these POWs refusing repatriation. If, as the Communist side insisted, all Chinese troops in Korea were "composed of men eager to fight for the Korean People's Army", then there was nothing to worry about; all such POWs would obviously desire to return to the socialist motherland. General Lee, no fool he, refused to rise to the bait. But later he did become so choked in trying to suppress his own laughter while attempting to explain the Communist "righteous and benevolent" system of prisoner education that he could hardly finish his remarks.

The talks were clearly going nowhere. In some desperation, several high US Army officials proposed in early 1952 the unilateral release of those UN

POWs who refused repatriation. This proposal had the value of allowing the Communists to save face and yet of presenting them with a *fait accompli*. The idea was shelved, but the UNC had not seen the last of it.

Matters became more complicated when, in February 1952, an estimate based more on guesswork than actual nose-counting, determined that of 132,000 UN POWs about 28,000 would not wish to return home, but that only about 16,000 of those would actually resist repatriation. The Communists were so notified. But during the April screening period the final total astounded both sides: only about 70,000 of the POWs indicated that they would not resist repatriation. And this figure was arrived at after UNC staff had spent considerable time trying to persuade as many of those POWs as possible that they *should* return. (There is no indication that the Communists ever tried to dissuade any of their captives from remaining.) The Communists, understandably, felt that they had been deceived by some vile "imperialist" machination. They were particularly concerned about the low number of Chinese POWs who wished to return and feared these troops would likely be used to strengthen the army of the unspeakable Chiang Kai-shek. At about this time the chief UNC negotiator had to admonish his Communist counterpart to curb his screaming; the American enjoyed good hearing but he did not understand Chinese and the dramatic effect unfortunately lost much of its edge in translation.

In May 1952 violence erupted at the Koje-do UNC POW camp when the camp commandant was seized by militant Communist prisoners. Under such duress, the acting commandant "admitted" that POWs had been abused. The negotiating atmosphere at Panmunjom was thus even further poisoned, although the Communist side obviously enjoyed its propaganda windfall.

A new and more careful UNC screening after the worst of the POW camp riots had been put down, showed that about 83,000 Communist prisoners would return to their homes, but even this higher figure was rejected by the Communist delegates, who made it clear that the Chinese POWs were the real bone of contention. The Communist side refused further UNC proposals on the issue and shut down the negotiations on 8 October, amid little hope that they would reopen in the foreseeable future.

Military racial integration in wartime

It was during the Korean battlefield lull in the autumn of 1951 that the US Army took up some unfinished racial business. That Army had fought through the Second World War primarily on a racially segregated basis. But the generally mediocre performance of the larger all-black units in that conflict led to a somewhat grudging examination of US military racial policies in the immediate post-war years. Most higher-ranking Army officers would have been just as happy to have *no* blacks in the Army or to employ them simply as service troops. But the post-war generation of black Americans proved much less ready to accept the racial *status quo*.

The American armed forces entered the Korean War basically segregated by race, but ended that conflict more or less racially integrated. Despite President Harry S. Truman's 1948 executive order mandating equality of treatment in the US military and the integrationist recommendations of the President's Fahy Committee, little had been accomplished by the beginning of the Korean War. In fact, the Army preferred to follow the regressive conclusions of its Chamberlain Board, which claimed that although black Americans comprised about 10 per cent of the US population, they fell "well below 10% of the leadership and skills of the nation as a whole". The "white man" had to fill the gap.

The all-black 24th Infantry Regiment of the 25th Infantry Division was early in battle in Korea and early acquired a bad reputation for its "bug out fever". On different occasions, almost an entire company of the 24th had left their positions, and a complete battalion later drifted off. But it should be remembered that in that disastrous summer of 1950, precipitous retreat was an "equal opportunity" UNC phenomenon, sparing no racial group. Nonetheless, it could hardly be argued that the 24th was a crack outfit. Those who later tried to depict that unit as an effective fighting force should have remembered the comment of Walter White, Executive Director of the NAACP, while defending himself for admitting that the all-black 92nd Infantry Division of the Second World War occasionally "melted away" in the face of enemy attacks: "How can one denounce segregation and then defend the product of segregation?"

The problems with the 24th and other such segregated combat units were the same. On the one hand there was no larger pool to draw upon to replace those who had failed or fallen in leadership. On the other, what was the incentive to excel when the regiment (and not command of that regiment, either) was as high as any black could go? Battalion or division command slots were closed, and the higher service schools, a requirement for higher command, such as the Command and General Staff College, the Army War College, the Air War College, or the Naval War College remained still *de facto* segregated. For both white and black officers command of black troops was a career dead end. Further, due to lack of battle experience in the Second World War, combat-wise black NCOs were comparatively rare. This situation was something that the black trooper in the ranks quickly picked up

251

on. Finally, black units held more than their share of low-scorers on Army tests because of the poor educational opportunities open to blacks at the time. Black low-scorers could not be distributed throughout the Army, as could whites, but had to be concentrated in a few units.

Blacks also had more severe punishments meted out to them by Army courts-martial. Thurgood Marshall, representing the NAACP, and with the co-operation of General MacArthur, found ample confirmation of unequal military justice for blacks, including the conspicuous absence of blacks on those courts-martial and the swiftness of their proceedings. Marshall gave as one example, a black trooper tried, convicted and sentenced to life imprisonment in 42 minutes. He remarked that "even in Mississippi a Negro will get a trial longer than 42 minutes, if he is fortunate enough to be brought to trial" (that is, if he were not killed on the way).

Despite individual instances of heroism and self-sacrifice, the 24th was considered by the 25th's commanding general, Major General William Kean, with some justification, as by far the worst of his regiments, a threat not only to the parent division but to the entire United Nations' defence of South Korea. His solution was not to bar blacks from combat, but rather to spread them through combat units. There was a war on and combat soldiers were desperately needed. Yet there was an abundance of able-bodied black troops, as always, in the service branches: graves registration, stevedoring, food service, security, and so on. Obviously here was a gross imbalance in the Army's personnel policies and equally obviously, this imbalance stemmed from racial segregation.

General Kean received little support from General MacArthur, whose own command had few if any blacks in positions of authority. However, by the autumn of 1950 many black troopers were being assigned to understrength white units in Korea. MacArthur's successor, General Matthew B. Ridgway, proved to be an entirely different commander in more than one way. He early went on record as believing that racial segregation was "both un-American and un-Christian". But Ridgway had practical concerns in mind as well. The Eighth Army in Korea desperately needed combat replacements, while able-bodied black troops were serving in food lines, burying the dead, or mopping floors in Japan. For Ridgway this was no way to run an army. In the spring of 1951, when he had been in command for only a few months, he formally requested the Army for permission to integrate his command. This request was granted quickly enough; Secretary of Defense George C. Marshall had already ordered all of the armed services to share low-scoring draftees proportionately. This wiped out at one stroke the Navy's discriminatory selection standards and the Army's argument that its high proportion of low-scoring inductees made segregated units a necessity.

In October 1951, the 24th was inactivated. Its troops were distributed throughout other US Army units. By May 1952 with little, if any, of the troubles or problems predicted, the Far East Command had achieved 100 per cent racial integration. (The entire US Army was racially integrated within the next few years.)

In something of an "apology" to the men of the 24th and in an impressive effort to set the historical record straight, the US Army Center of Military History, many years after the Korean War, published a devastating critique of the ineptitude and racism that had permeated so many white officers of the 24th while not excusing the depressingly numerous instances of straggling and panic among black troops. Although the study was denounced by some 24th veterans who claimed that their regiment was no worse than most other US Army units in 1950, it could also be pointed out once again, that few, if any, other armies in the world would have disseminated, under official imprimatur, a study so critical of its own leadership.[12]

The US Air Force was well on the way to racial integration by the time of the outbreak of the Korean War, and that conflict simply accelerated the process. Although the Marine Corps lagged behind the Air Force in integration, by the time of the Pusan Perimeter battles the corps was, for the first time, assigned large numbers of black Marines as individual replacements. The Corps Commandant assessed them as "good people" and specifically ascribed their sterling combat performance to racial integration. The Navy proved to be not as enlightened in such matters. Most black seamen were clustered in the stewards' branch. Blacks entered the Navy in increasing numbers primarily because they wanted to avoid conscription into the dead end of the combat infantry, not because of any basic change in Navy brass attitudes. On the personal level, the first black naval aviator, Ensign Jesse L. Brown, was shot down near the Chosin Reservoir in December. Heroic attempts by his white wing man to rescue Ensign Brown from his burning aircraft failed, but the wing man was awarded the Medal of Honor.

A major impulse to end racial segregation in the US military was the recognition that such an anachronism presented the Communists with a ready-made propaganda advantage, particularly in Asia and Africa. Any American expounding on the horrors of Communism was setting himself up for "Well, what about your Negroes?" Complete and immediate military racial integration could certainly weaken this argument and would demonstrate that the United States was taking a major, albeit long overdue, step to end a long-standing pattern of injustice. Despite Navy foot dragging, by a little more than a year after the end of the Korean War the American military establishment had completely abolished official racial segregation and had done so at least a full decade ahead of American civil society.

Stalemate

On the battlefront, in the absence of any armistice agreement, the fighting went on. After a year of sweeping movement from north to south, south to north, then back south again, the conflict had stabilized into a "new war", a war of position, of outposts, trenches and bunkers, of night patrols and raids, in many ways a reprise of the First World War on the European Western Front. As in that earlier conflict, territorial gains were measured in hundreds of yards. Of course, there were significant differences between Korea and northern France: for one, the availability of DDT meant that the previous war's ubiquitous louse was happily absent – at least on the UNC side. Medical treatment and evacuation had improved enormously, as the UNC death rate from all causes showed. And the "Big R" (troop rotation) saw to it that whatever the battlefield conditions, they were endured by non-ROK UNC troops for no more than nine months. All of these positive differences were enjoyed almost exclusively by UNC troops; the Communist soldier would have noted no particular improvement over any earlier war. If anything, he might have considered that conditions were worse in the light of the UNC's overwhelming superiority in air power, artillery and logistics, which made him more likely in this war, despite his peasant toughness, to die on the battlefield or to expire from untreated wounds or disease.

Surveying the battlefield, the commanders and political leaders of both sides knew that any significant battlefield gains would cost too much in blood and treasure. The UNC democracies also realized that their civil populations would not stand for the sacrifices that victory or even a major advance would now cost. The UNC did dust off its old proposal for an advance to the Wonsan–Pyongyang line but quickly put it back on the shelf when the Joint Chiefs of Staff estimated it would cost some 200,000 casualties. Instead, the fighting took place around minor moves to straighten a bulge here or protect a line of supply there; the opposing force would react, both sides would throw in more troops and finally one side would concede that retaking the lost position was not worth the cost. In the battle for White Horse Mountain in November 1951, for example, the ROK 9th Division lost the hill on 5 November, retook it the following day, lost it again on 16 November and retook it on the following day. General Van Fleet, still concerned about Eighth Army's "fighting edge", instructed his corps commanders "to keep the Army sharp through smell of gunpowder" by intensifying patrols and laying ambushes to catch prisoners.

Almost as though searching about for something to do, the UNC hit upon Operation Clam-Up, in which silence was imposed along the line of battle from 10 to 15 February 1952. Not a patrol was dispatched, not an artillery round fired, not an air strike within 20,000 yards of the front. The idea was to confuse the Communists into thinking that the UN forces had withdrawn from their positions, to lure him towards the UN lines and then to ambush him and seize prisoners. The idea was probably too clever by half; for whatever reason, the Communists did not rise to the bait and Clam-Up was called off.

By this time US Army troops were the beneficiaries of another morale-boosting innovation that ranked up there with DDT or even rotation: the armoured vest. This was a relatively lightweight nylon outer garment that could resist shell, grenade, or mortar fragments. (The Army and the Marine vest, typically, were somewhat different in design.) Soon after the vest was introduced, some unsung genius did even more for soldier morale by adding a resistant flap to the bottom of the vest that protected the trooper's nether regions.

Both sides remained well matched in numbers of troops across the peninsula, again despite continued references to "human tidal-waves". By mid-1952, eight Chinese armies, numbering an estimated 207,800 men, stretched from the west coast to the Taebek range and were anchored on the eastern end of the line by three *Inmin Gun* corps of 83,000 troops. Facing them were four US Army divisions, the 1st US Marine Division, the Commonwealth Division and nine ROK Army divisions, for a total of 247,554 troops; not that much of a front-line disparity between the UNC and Communist side.

But behind the Communist lines were no fewer than 422,000 Chinese, 185,300 North Koreans, and some 10,000 Soviet or satellite troops, giving the Communists an incredible 617,000 rear-echelon troops for a total of 908,100 troops. UNC troops totalled a little fewer than 700,000, with some 453,000 behind the lines. In other words, both UNC and Communist front-line forces were supported by about the same ratio of "tooth-to-tail" troops. Those who even today rhapsodize the Communist Chinese soldier, able to cover great distances on a sock of rice every couple of days, could well ponder on what those 617,000 rear-echelon troops were doing. And judging from a new Chinese law that permitted a wife unilaterally to divorce her soldier husband if she had not heard from him in two years, not too many Communist rear-echelon troops were burdened with delivering soldiers' mail, the bedrock of any troops' morale.

Triangle Hill, Old Baldy, Jane Russell Hill, Jackson Heights, Pike's Peak, Hill 598 and Sniper Ridge were all totally undistinguished prominences, but soldiers fought and died for them to "straighten the line", seize prisoners, nip off a threatening Communist salient, or simply to "keep the fighting edge". Between these sharp little battles, the fighting could die down to almost an armed truce level. One UNC report in the summer of 1952 solemnly relayed the news that "an enemy soldier approached our lines. We threw grenades, he went away".

The air and naval war, however, was in no such hiatus. In the spring of 1952 the question of the great hydro-electric generating plant complex at Supong/Suiho on the Yalu came up once again. Suiho was no ordinary target; it was the largest hydro-electric generating plant in East Asia and the fourth largest in the world. Something between one-half and three-quarters of its output was utilized by industry in Manchuria and thus any attack on the plant would be seen as a direct blow against China. General Ridgway had been against attacking the plant because of a possible adverse effect on the armistice negotiations.

But Ridgway's successor as UNC Commander, General Mark Clark, decided to intensify the air pressure on the Communists. General Clark had considerable experience with the Communists during his tenure as commander of US forces in Austria, then divided into four Allied zones of occupation. He was convinced that they respected and understood force only. He also knew first-hand of the human consequences of forcible repatriation in Austria and Italy after the Second World War.

Washington, badly embarrassed by the Koje incident, also saw this bombing campaign as a means of putting pressure on the Communists at Panmunjom. The decision was approved by President Truman himself. The Joint Chiefs warned the USAF that the ban on air operations within 12 miles of the Soviet border still applied and that all precautions should also be taken to prevent any inadvertent bombing of Manchurian territory as well. In a well co-ordinated joint USAF–USN strike on 23 June, 25 giant AD-Skyraider dive bombers struck the dam, while USAF F-86 Sabrejets provided overhead cover and Navy Panther carrier jet fighters suppressed anti-aircraft fire. After this first round, 79 F-84 Thunderjet fighters and 45 F-80 Shooting Stars flew over and dropped their loads. More than 200 Communist jet fighters across the Yalu on Manchurian airfields did not stir themselves to interfere. The Communists later lamely explained that the weather was bad, but the weather did not seem to have particularly hampered the UNC pilots. (A sympathetic author claimed that the Soviets were not expected to defend the Suiho complex, but does not explain who was supposed to do so.[13] Most likely, the poor showing of the Communists was because of their markedly inferior electronics that did not give them all-weather capabilities. The USAF and the USN flew more than 1,400 sorties between them over the next three days, whatever the weather, badly damaging the generating plants.

In addition USN and USAF warplanes attacked the less politically sensitive hydro-electric plants at Fusen, Chosin and Kyosen. Eleven of the 13 plants in the four attacked complexes ceased operation. For two weeks North Korea was blacked out. In the coming months North Korea could only restore some 10 per cent of its electric power and no longer could export electricity to Manchuria or Siberia. Consequently, many factories in those provinces failed to meet their annual production norms.

The raids failed to bring about the desired change in attitude on the Communist side, however. In fact, the strongest reaction came from the UK, where even members of the Conservative government protested the lack of consultation with an ally whose troops were also fighting and dying in Korea. (Secretary of State Acheson more or less apologized for the raids before a gathering of irate MPs in Westminster Hall.) The Americans never revealed why they had kept their British ally in the dark, but it was speculated that the sensational disappearance of the two left-wing Foreign Office diplomats well after US security services had voiced their suspicions may have caused Washington to play its Korea cards close to its own chest. But it is also possible that the Americans knew of and wished to disrupt secret UK–China talks on ending the war.

The following month UNC naval Task Force 77 was equipped, in secrecy, with nuclear weapons. At roughly the same time, B 36 intercontinental bombers, nuclear-equipped, were deployed to Okinawa. The Communist leaders probably knew about TF 77's new weapons (the information may have been deliberately "leaked") and their intelligence sources could hardly have missed the gigantic bombers on Okinawa. These moves were designed to hasten the Communists to close the armistice negotiations or face an uncertain future at the hands of an exasperated enemy, who had now brought to the Pacific rim of Asia nuclear weapons and the means for their delivery.

On the Panmunjom negotiations front, both sides had finally agreed that the cease-fire line would follow the battlelines. By February 1952, the UNC, in turn, had assented to the Communist proposal for the convening of a political conference to determine Korea's future after a cease-fire. The issue of forcible POW repatriation remained the only significant obstacle to achieving that cease-fire. The Communists were still in the awkward position, from a propaganda viewpoint, of having far more of their many prisoners in the UN camps unwilling to return, compared to the much smaller number of the far fewer UN POWs in the Communist camps who would refuse repatriation.

Syngman Rhee was himself busily attempting to sabotage any possible cease-fire. He addressed several mammoth "spontaneous" demonstrations in Seoul, calling not only for an end to any negotiations with the Communists, but, most unrealistically, for PUK CHIN, "Go North!"

The unexpected death of Joseph Stalin, on 5 March 1953, did throw the Kremlin leadership into some disarray and made them more amenable to dealing with the West. On 19 March the Council of Ministers of the USSR approved a letter to Kim Il Sung and Mao concluding that "We must achieve the exit of Korea and China from this war according to the basic interests of other peace-loving peoples", and instructed these Communist leaders exactly what they had to do to achieve an end to the war. Even the fire-eating Kim Il Sung "was happy to hear the good news", pointing out that his forces were losing some 300 to 400 troops per day, so that it was hardly advisable to continue discussion with the Americans about repatriation of the controversial number of POWs.[14] The first public straw in the wind indicating a shift in Soviet strategy came in a Radio Moscow broadcast conceding for the first time since 1945 that the efforts of the United States and Great Britain in the Second World War might actually have had something to do with the defeat of the Axis Powers.

On 11 April liaison officers from both sides at Panmunjom signed an agreement for the exchange of ill and wounded POWs. Within ten days Operation LITTLE SWITCH (the UN term) had commenced at Panmunjom. But even this humanitarian gesture had its political overtones. Many of the Communist POWs refused DDT-dusting, and demonstrated, chanted and threw away their rations of tooth powder, soap and cigarettes, often including in these articles hand-written messages accusing their captors of "starvation, oppression, and barbarous acts against the Korean People". Some Chinese POWs went on a hunger strike, claiming their food had been poisoned. On their final train ride many of the prisoners tore their UN-issued clothing to suggest poor treatment. In fact, these well-publicized images probably served rather to reinforce images of Communist fanaticism. More truly indicative was the often-emaciated condition of so many of the UNC returnees. These were quietly repatriated by the UNC, which feared that any publicity about poor treatment in the Communist POW camps might jeopardize the main prisoner repatriation process, still under negotiation. In all, LITTLE SWITCH saw the UNC turn over 6,670 of its POWs and the Communists release 684.

In the meantime, the recessed armistice talks had been resumed on 26 April, and the negotiations proceeded smoothly for a change. Both sides reached an agreement on voluntary POW repatriation on 8 June. A week later the military staffs of the two sides had worked out the demarcation line between the two armies. Later the same day, Peng, in the name of the commander of the joint CPV–KPA headquarters, ordered all Chinese and North Korean forces to cease offensive operations the next day. The end of the war seemed very close.

Two days later, however, hope for a quick end to the conflict was dashed. In an effort to derail the pending armistice signing, President Rhee released more than 25,000 anti-Communist North Korean POWs who had been in the custody of ROK forces. The Communist side professed itself convinced that the UNC had plotted with Rhee for just this operation although, with their many agents in Seoul, they must have known that in actuality the UNC had long dreaded just such an eventuality. Moscow's interpretation of Rhee's action was in standard Soviet-Marxist boiler-plate: "It is absolutely clear that latest actions of Rhee Syngman's clique, the fuss around them is the implementation of certain ruling circles of the USA, who are doing this to appease the most aggressive part of American monopolists." Beijing, on the other hand, had a much more accurate view: the Americans indeed wanted to end the war and were preoccupied with suppressing Rhee's machinations.[15] The rage of the UNC, in fact, easily surpassed that of the Communists. President Eisenhower intemperately confided to his diary that "Both the Communists and the South Korean government have raised so many difficulties in the prosecution of the negotiations intended to end the fighting that it raises in my mind a serious question as to whether or not the United Nations will ever again go into an arena to protect the inhabitants against Communist attack."[16] The UNC and the US government must have wished on more than one occasion that Syngman Rhee would truly live up to the Communists' "puppet" charges and do what he was told. Indeed, there was some talk then of actuating Operation EVERREADY, the overthrow of Rhee, which the US government had drawn up about one year earlier and which remained under consideration. Overall, however, the Communist reaction to Rhee's action was surprisingly muted. Mao shrewdly predicted that the US would not support Rhee's efforts to prolong the conflict because this would put the Eisenhower administration under "tremendous pressure" at home and abroad, and the US would pressure Rhee to accept the armistice, which was what actually ensued.

The Communists certainly took advantage of the perceived UNC disarray by mounting a series of ferocious, albeit short-lived offensives against the ROK lines. This final offensive was probably mounted as much to forestall a feared "Inchon II" as to teach Rhee the lesson that he could still lose the war and that he had better not hinder the armistice negotiations. Peng's final series of offensives did inflict frightful casualties upon ROK forces while suffering some 28,000 of their own. While ROK commanders often would hold positions against heavy odds and at great cost to retain "face", other UNC forces tended to "roll with the punch". Even the indomitable Turks, after sweeping the Chinese off outpost Vegas in a hand-to-hand counter-attack with cold steel, were pulled back along with accompanying US troops. American troops later also abandoned famous Pork Chop Hill after withstanding numerous Chinese assaults. Unwilling to accept further losses so late in a war that was about over, the US forces left the hill to the CPV. Then, as the Chinese milled about the blasted bunkers, the 7th Division's artillery practically obliterated the crest and all on it. In the end it had taken nine ROK and US divisions, blocking and counter-attacking, to halt the Communist offensive and to regain some of the lost, relatively useless, terrain. At the end of the offensive and of the war itself, the Communists remained in fairly good condition, eating three meals per day, compared to two in the early stages of the war, and shooting off their highest total of artillery fire of the war.

The ROK forces had usually retreated in fairly good order or had stubbornly held out too long. But the Communists' late war offensive had indeed proved that PUK CHIN was not likely to come through the efforts of the ROK and Dr Rhee unaided anytime in the foreseeable future. The hopes for an early signing of the armistice after Operation LITTLE SWITCH had been cruelly dashed at great cost in human life.

But the Communists had made their point and so had the Americans. The incoming Eisenhower administration had publicly not ruled out the use of nuclear weapons in Korea. The Joint Chiefs of Staff favoured an air and naval operations against China, and the use of nuclear weapons, although the President was not entirely convinced of the efficacy of such weapons on the Korean battlefield. Further, the conclusions of NSC-147, a National Security Council paper (2 April 1953) which seriously considered the nuclear option, was diplomatically "leaked" and undoubtedly reached China and North Korea, although to what effect is unknown.[17] Whatever the reasons, both sides finally agreed to an armistice in July 1953.

Typically, controversy attended even what should have been a straightforward armistice-signing ceremony. The Communist side, still concerned with symbolism, provided only one entrance in the original plans of the building housing the signing ceremony, a door which faced north, requiring the UNC delegates to cross into Communist territory to enter. The UNC successfully argued for a southern entrance, as well as for the removal of two "peace doves", a Communist symbol created by the fellow-travelling artist Pablo Picasso and used throughout the world in Communist-led peace demonstrations. These UNC complaints appear to have been a straightforward resistance to Communist attempts to dominate the ceremony marking a war in which no side had emerged as the winner. But the Communist insistence on an absolutely equal exchange of the armistice agreements seemed simply petulant. In that there were 18 copies of the agreement, nine for each side, a UNC staff officer suggested that six each be forwarded to Kim Il Sung and Peng for their signatures and returned to the UNC, and 12 documents be given at once to General Clark for his signature and then returned to the two Communist leaders. But the Communist side insisted on an equal exchange of nine documents for countersignature, even though this would require two exchanges of the documents. The UNC delegation wearily acceded to the Communist position. Some symbolism remained to the end: the nine UN copies, blue-bound, reposed under a small UN flag, and the nine Communist maroon copies were under a DPRK flag.

That piece of trivia out of the way, the stage was set for the actual signing, on 27 July 1953. The delegations themselves presented a strong contrast. Both entered on the minute at the agreed 10.00 hours. The UNC members were dressed in casual uniforms, tieless. They also stood on little ceremony, except for passing through an honour guard representing the different UNC military services in Korea (with the significant exception of those of South Korea). The Communist delegates, by contrast, were in full-dress uniform buttoned to the neck. They filed stiffly into the signing hall and sat down straight and rigid, arranged by size. The two chief delegates, (still) Nam Il for the Communists and Lieutenant General William K. Harrison for the UNC, completed the signing ceremony. Both chief delegates exchanged no words, locked glances momentarily and then simultaneously departed. General Clark signed the documents at the Musan-ni UNC base camp three hours later. Photographs of this signing show such a collection of lugubrious expressions that one would have thought that the UNC had been ignominiously defeated. (According to Kim Il Sung's official biographer, that is exactly what had happened: "On July 27, 1953 the US imperialists were taken to Panmunjom, where they bent their knees to the national flag of the Democratic People's Republic of Korea and signed the armistice agreement."[18] Again, no mention of China.) The Chinese were only a little more restrained. Mao a few years later claimed that "We have fought them [the US] for thirty-three months and got to know them for what they are worth. U.S. imperialism is not terrifying, nothing to make a fuss about".[19]

As provided in the Armistice agreement, at 22.00 hours, 27 July 1953, the overt combat of the Korean War ended. Korea would remain basically divided in two as it had been on 25 June 1950. But no POW from either side would be unwillingly repatriated. Tens of thousands on both sides had died over just that point.

Operation BIG SWITCH, the exchange of the able-bodied POWs of both sides, took place between 5 August and 23 December 1953. The term "able-bodied" proved something of a misnomer for those prisoners handed over by the Communist side. Many were emaciated and most suffered some type of disability. Communist prisoners, by contrast, and for all the pandemonium of the UNC camps, presented a picture of health, even while some demonstrated against their "barbaric" treatment at the hands of the "imperialists".

The UNC returned 75,823 POWs: 70,183 Koreans and 5,640 Chinese. The Communist side repatriated 12,773 of its prisoners: 7,862 Koreans,

3,597 US, 946 UK, 229 Turks, 40 Filipinos, 30 Canadians, 22 Colombians, 21 Australians, 12 Frenchmen, 8 South Africans, 2 Greeks and Netherlanders, and 1 each Belgian, New Zealander and Japanese. One of the UK repatriates, the British civilian George Blake, later proved to be a true "Manchurian Candidate". Blake, most improbably, had been converted to Communism in the camps and returned to a position in British intelligence specifically to betray his country. His treason uncovered, Blake was sentenced to a long term of imprisonment. But he was rescued from his durance vile and spirited to the Soviet Union where he consorted with another British traitor, "Kim" Philby. After the fall of the USSR, Blake proclaimed that he still believed in the dream, although he admitted that its fulfillment might take a while longer than he had thought at first.

Non-repatriates, those for whom the war had gone on for more than a year after all other major obstacles to an armistice had been overcome, totalled 14,704 Chinese and 7,900 Koreans. A total of 359 prisoners of the Communist side also refused repatriation: 23 US, 1 UK and 335 Koreans.

Although it is generally conceded that both sides were heartily tired of this stalemated conflict and signed the armistice in something like good faith, Mao Tse-tung did speculate to the Soviet Foreign Ministry official, Fedorenko Kuznetsov, two days after the signing, "that from a purely military point of view it would not be bad to continue to strike the Americans for approximately another year in order to occupy more favorable borders along the Changan river". Fortunately for all concerned these musings were not translated into action and the armistice has held, despite armed probes from the DPRK, for something approaching 45 years.

Chapter Fourteen

Conclusions

The Korean War itself was primarily a conventional conflict. Nuclear weapons, which featured so dominantly in those late 1940s' "War of Tomorrow" scenarios, both official and popular, were, of course, not employed. Few, if any, "push-button" weapons were deployed. (Senator Brian McMahon remarked at the time that "We don't even have the push-buttons for push-button war!") In fact, the overwhelming bulk of the weapons employed in Korea were not only conventional on both sides, but most were left-overs from the Second World War. The American GI was issued the same fine M-1 Garand semi-automatic rifle that his older brother or father had drawn in the Second World War. There were no "Flying Wings" or even the more conventional B-36 intercontinental heavy nuclear bombers over Korea. Rather, B-29s, the same bombers that had burned the heart out of Japan's cities five or six years earlier, torched Pyongyang and Sinuiju in incendiary raids that would have been thoroughly familiar to any bombardier from the Tokyo fire raids. Even the uniforms on both sides (except for the North Koreans) were identical to those of Second World War belligerents, if not actual surplus stock. In fact, the only major new military equipment items were the latest jet fighters employed by the contending forces over "MiG Alley", the 3.5in anti-armour "bazooka", the 75mm recoilless rifle, some post-war model tanks – and the US armoured combat vest.

This war did not just look back to the Second World War. By the summer of 1951 the fighting had hardened into a stalemate with trench lines, night raids, heavy bombardments and limited offensives that won limited terrain. It all was in many ways reminiscent of the Western Front of the First World War.

Both the US Army and the CPV had their lessons to learn in this war, particularly those involving the power of mass attack by underarmed armies in the face of enemy firepower and the courage and quality of their opponents. It is a tribute to both armies that they came out of the Korean War as considerably better forces than when they went in.

The war rested much more easily on the United States than on China or the two Koreas, for as in both World Wars, the American homeland was spared physical ravages. This situation likely explains why Americans seemed more willing to consider the strategic bombing of civilian targets, or even to use nuclear weapons. Europeans, who had themselves been the victims of heavy city bombing in the Second World War, pointed out that most of them were under the Soviet flight path to the West.

Few wars in modern history have concluded with such an even distribution of gains and losses as the Korean War. The Republic of Korea and the UN side could take satisfaction in having driven the invader from most of the territory of the ROK while the Communists could rejoice that the UNC forces had been almost completely expelled from the DPRK. The armistice line itself pushed north into the former DPRK in the east, but down into previously ROK territory in the west. Both sides had initially fought for total victory and the actual destruction of their enemy's government; both sides by 1951 had reluctantly come to accept the military fact that total victory would of necessity involve a considerably greater war than either the Chinese or the UN coalition were willing to fight. Significantly, both the governments of the ROK and the DPRK held out the longest for complete victory – and unification of Korea. And both were overruled by their more powerful allies.

The symmetry of both sides in the Korean War holds when it comes to the human cost of the conflict. South Korea's losses of something like one million dead were probably matched by the civilian and military deaths suffered by the North, both on the battlefield and from unrelenting UNC aerial bombardment. The North's figures have remained just an estimate to everyone dealing with the subject outside the archives of Pyongyang itself; the twentieth-century Hermit Kingdom was not about to give out accurate statistics on any matter. The Chinese suffered the most battle and disease deaths, although the ground and airs war had halted at China's borders. The war affected the homeland of both China and the USA primarily through higher taxes and the casualty lists.

A major consequence of the Korean War was an increased militarization of both Communist and anti-Communist global camps. By the end of that war much of the world was more divided between the two super-powers than ever before and was considerably more of an armed camp than in June 1950. Large numbers of US troops were dispatched to Europe at the same time that the US forces in Korea were also being built up. In 1950 81,000 troops and one infantry division were stationed in Western Europe and were mostly concerned with occupation duties in Germany. But by the middle 1950s the US military presence there had increased to six divisions and 260,000 men oriented to the "defence of the West", somewhat more than the 238,600 soldiers in Korea.

In the immediate post-war years an enormous outcry was raised in the USA over the few "turncoat" Americans who had, incredibly, turned their backs on their own country for an alien ideology and an enemy nation. Certainly nothing like this had ever happened in America's previous wars, which had mostly ended in victory anyway. (Actually, it had; enough Americans had deserted from the US Army during the Mexican War to form the San Patricio Brigade/Battalion of the Mexican Army.) Was there something wrong with "the present generation"? Was America's youth "going soft"?

Something even worse was to follow. Soon after repatriation came reports and allegations of wholesale co-operation by US POWs in the camps, talk of "giveupitis", of "everyman for himself" attitudes that made the death rate for the prisoners so high. These charges were brought together by the journalists Eugene Kinkhead and W. L. White (*In every war but one* [1959]/*Why they collaborated* [1960]). But these sensational allegations were effectively refuted a few years later in the much more sober and better-researched conclusions of Alfred D. Biderman (*March to calumny: the story of American POWs in the Korean War* [1963]). Biderman and, later, others, pointed out that many US POWs had been captured early in the war and had endured much longer periods of captivity by the brutal North Koreans than had their non-ROK allies. Most US Army troops were conscripts and not particularly motivated in a war against a nation whose threat to the United States seemed as remote as its location across the globe. The US Marines, the Turks and the Commonwealth forces were in the main troops motivated enough to volunteer for military service in the first place and many had been given some training in resistance to the Communists if captured. Further, there were incidents of collaboration among the Commonwealth troops, but these were officially played down. The Turks simply executed their informers.

Much pseudo-science was exhibited sensationally in the controversy over the alleged "brainwashing" of US POWs. Prisoner indoctrination and "retraining" were indeed a part of the Chinese means of waging war. (The North Koreans did not waste their time with such niceties; their camp regime consisted simply of varying degrees of brutality.) But there is little if any evidence of any Communist use of drugs, hypnotic methods or sex in their programmes. The Communists' methods did enjoy some success in modifying

POW behaviour, but only temporarily. They accomplished very little in making any lasting change in prisoner beliefs, and in fact, in most cases, the results were a lasting disgust with Communism.

Perhaps more tragically, strong evidence from returning POWs began to reach the UNC that the Communists had not repatriated all US POWs who wished to return. There was very little official US protest at this appalling discovery and almost no public outcry; nothing must be permitted to interfere with the workings of the armistice process. When the question was finally raised in the 1990s, the Communists insisted that there had never been any involuntary unrepatriated American POWs in the PRC or the USSR. The DPRK simply refused to discuss the subject or issued boiler-plate rejections of the question. After the fall of the Soviet Union, the successor Russian government did admit that a small number of American POWs had indeed been taken to the USSR during the war for interrogation, but they insisted, probably in truth, that all had eventually died there. However, despite belated Pentagon efforts to resolve the issue, the question remains open about Americans remaining involuntarily in North Korea itself. These attempts later included talks with DPRK and the return (for cash) of the remains of US servicemen buried in North Korea. The DPRK for its part professed itself completely unconcerned about the repatriation of the remains of any of its troops buried in South Korea; they are in Korean soil and that is all that matters.

For the first two decades after the armistice it could have been argued that the symmetry of the war extended to both post-war Koreas. Both were dictatorships. The ROK was admittedly more disorderly, with some glimmerings' of hope for political freedom. But it was still ruled by a succession of ROK Army generals who employed varying degrees of brutality in putting down pro-democracy demonstrations.

In the meantime, the supposedly monolithic Sino–Soviet axis fissured, and the two great powers eventually came briefly to blows along their border. By contrast, relations between the PRC and the USA, after President Richard Nixon's opening to China, became almost cordial at times. After the decade of the 1960s, the Soviet Union began its long, slow decline towards national collapse, although few of the specialists on the USSR predicted the denouement that today has about it such an air of inevitability.

Through these years the peace held, and the great fear of the 1950s, nuclear Armageddon, never came. Nuclear weapons were never used after the Second World War. In fact nuclear war came closest during the Cuban Missile Crisis of 1962, well after the Korean War.

For the next two decades the Korean War also confirmed the belief in a monolithic Communist bloc ruled from Moscow. Assistant Secretary of State,

Dean Rusk, who had confidently informed a Congressional Committee a few days before the outbreak of war in 1950 that he could see no evidence of a large-scale invasion from the North, continued his miscalls by insultingly referring to the PRC as the "Manchukuo" of the Soviet Union, a cruel reference to the Japanese puppet-state torn from China by Japanese aggression in 1931. (Rusk was apparently rewarded for these egregious miscalls by becoming Secretary of State in the Kennedy and Johnson administrations, where he proved a tireless defender of the US role in Vietnam.) Stalin had ordered Kim to attack South Korea, or so the reasoning in high places at the time went, in order to draw attention from Western Europe. Mao also was simply doing Stalin's bidding. But in all the Soviet documents released or uncovered in the 1990s, nothing has come to light in which Stalin used the argument of diverting the US from Western Europe by a war in Korea. Even at the time, a close reading of Sino–Soviet relations could have revealed significant strains between these allies that would lead to a bitter break a little more than a decade later.

The seeds of the Second Vietnam War were sown when the United States, as a result of the Korean War military buildup, dispatched a Military Assistance Advisory Group in September 1950 to advise the French on dealing with their Communist insurgency. That MAAG, of several score troops, would eventually become the 500,000-man US Military Assistance Command, Vietnam.

In line with its global, near-apocalyptic strategic vision of the Cold War, the United States opted for a strategy that came to be known as "massive retaliation", that is, aerial nuclear bombardment of the Soviet Union in case of war. The mere threat of such a response by the United States was deemed sufficient to keep the Communists at bay. The frustrations of the Korean War were considered a "lesson" for future confrontations with the Communists. At the end of the war, Secretary of the US Air Force, Thomas K. Finletter, asserted that "Korea was a unique, never-to-be-repeated diversion from the true course of strategic air power". Strategic air power would keep the peace, and if need be, win the next war. Consideration of anything less than a major confrontation with the Soviet Union was given short shrift. Later, the Kennedy administration's reaction to this nuclear emphasis was to fight "global Communism" and its "wars of national liberation" by means of counter-insurgency. Such a course would supposedly avoid a Korean-type major Asian land war. To the contrary, fashionable counter-insurgency doctrines were a major reason for the US involvement in a second major war on the Asian mainland, this time in Vietnam. Only with the Gulf War of 1991 would the United States, again under UN auspices, fight another conventional, non-nuclear war to victory.

The sustained economic expansion of the Western industrialized nations was joined by Japan and the so-called "Asian Tigers" of Singapore, Taiwan, Hong Kong – and The Republic of Korea. By the mid-1960s the ROK was making impressive economic strides and within another decade its booming automobile manufacturing industry would be competing with the Japanese within the United States, a development that would have seemed flatly imposs- ible to any observer of the 1950s. Further, South Korea became a major trading partner with the People's Republic of China and the Soviet Union/Russia. Admittedly, this development in the ROK was aided immensely by large amounts of US economic aid, but the DPRK had also received substantial assistance from the Soviet Union and China.

Political progress took a much longer time in coming, as the ROK govern- ment massacre of demonstrators in Kwangju of 1980 showed. But eventually military rule was overthrown, and the ROK emerged into a reasonably free and democratic regime. In fact, the opposition leader, a veteran of South Korea's jails, Kim Dae Jong, was freely elected to the premiership in 1997, with the belated blessings of the former military rulers who had put him there in the first place.

North Korea did not replicate the prosperity and eventual democracy of the ROK. In the immediate post-war years Kim Il Sung purged any poten- tial rivals. Yi Sung Yop, former Minister of Justice, who had engaged in secret talks with ROK leftists, was condemned in 1953 as a "state enemy who colluded with the American imperialists", and was shot. Pak Tu Bong, never having recovered his prestige and power after his disastrous assurances that the exploited masses of South Korea would rise and welcome their liberators from the North, was executed in December 1955. Kim Tu Bong had remained a member of the North Korean Politburo until 1956. But with Kim Il Sung's purge of the Yenan faction in 1957, Kim Tu Bong lost all of his official positions, was expelled from the Korean Workers' Party and was reported to have expired several years later while toiling as a labourer on an agricultural co-operative near Pyongyang. Once again, the revolution had "devoured its own".

For a time after the Korean War the DPRK was one Communist state which "progressive" analysts could point to as having perhaps greater econ- omic development, if not a higher individual standard of living, than its non-Communist counterpart. This progress was undoubtedly brought about more by that nation's hydro-electric complex and its disciplined workers than by the wonders of *juche* ("self-reliance"), Kim Il Sung's mantra for every citizen. Kim ("The Great Leader") himself was deified to an extent that would have made even Josef Stalin envious. According to his publicists/ panegyrists, the very trees would bow low as Kim's aircraft passed over the hills. North Korea was officially proclaimed a "paradise" in which all selfishness, all religious feeling had vanished, as all citizens laboured selflessly to achieve *juche* under the perfect guidance of the perfect Kim. "Progressive" visitors to Pyongyang marvelled at the cleanliness, the lack of beggars, the civic dedication, the true devotion to the leader, much as their spiritual brethren had beamed over the joys of Moscow, Beijing, or Jonestown. However, a more perspicacious observer accurately described the Democratic People's Republic of Korea as "more of a cult than a country". The flavour of the DPRK cult can be seen in a 1975 nonsensical panegyric to Pyongyang and to Kim himself:

> Pyongyang, the capital of our socialist homeland, boundlessly loved by the entire Korean people and admired by the revolutionary people of the world, will prosper forever as a city of eternal youth in the infinite loyalty of the people who devote their all to the country's reunification, the nationwide victory of the revolution, the building and completion of socialism and communism in our country under the inspiring, brilliant guidance of the great leader Comrade Kim Il Sung, attending him till the end of the sun.[1]

But by the 1970s the DPRK was suffering the same sclerotic leadership and lack of economic development that was concurrently afflicting the Soviet Union. The DPRK leadership lashed out in sheer frustration with bombings, assassinations, and violent border incursions. ROK and US troops were killed in these incidents, and numerous tunnels running from North to South were uncovered, burrowed beneath the "Demilitarized Zone", that scar tissue of the long-past war.

Kim Il Sung died in 1994, a passing which must have surprised the more credulous DPRK citizens who had every reason to believe that "The Great Leader" should have lasted at least "to the end of the sun". But they could take some comfort in the presence of his mummy in its elaborate Lenin-like monument and in its ominous inscription, "The great leader comrade Kim Il Sung will always be with us".

Kim Il Sung was succeeded, at least officially, by his son, Kim Jong Il. Under "The Dear Leader" the economy of the DPRK neared collapse. The nation reached such dire straits that it was actually reduced to appealing for food aid from the traditional enemy, the Japanese, the "puppet" South Koreans, and even from the unspeakable Americans. Pyongyang blamed disastrous floods for food shortages that were causing near-starvation in the countryside. This excuse presented something of a problem for the more thoughtful, in that "The Dear Leader" supposedly could rebuke storms and cause them to cease, and weather in the southern half of the peninsula seemed generally unexceptionable. At any rate, the North Korean Army, something like the world's third largest, appeared well-nourished and possessed enough energy in early 1997 to dispatch a troop of commandos by submarine to the ROK, where they proceeded to bludgeon to death three inoffensive South Korean civilians before they were tracked down and killed by security forces.

The DPRK in the late 1990s was the most militarized nation on earth, with a soldier-to-citizen ratio of one soldier for every civilian man, woman, or child. Numerically, North Korea had some 1,128,000 persons in its active forces and could call upon another 115,000 from its security forces and border guards. Its ground forces were divided into 26 infantry divisions, 14 armoured brigades and 23 separate motorized and mechanized infantry brigades. "Special Purpose" corps contained commando, reconnaissance, river crossing, amphibious and airborne units, and 22 separate light infantry battalions, some 100,000 troops that are to fight behind ROK lines. Perhaps even more ominously, since the 1960s the North had concentrated on 13 different strains of bacteria and toxins. On the other hand, most of the equipment of these forces had become obsolete and spare parts would soon run out in any future sustained combat.

For all the DPRK militarism, any invasion of the ROK would face much greater obstacles than those in 1950, when Seoul was taken in three days. Highways could be more easily blocked and ROK forces hold substantially more territory north of the 38th Parallel than they did in June 1950. Most importantly, the North could no longer count on Soviet or Chinese sustenance, either in equipment or oil, for any invasion scheme. And US forces are on the peninsula in strength. As one US Marine commander noted of the North, "They remember Inchon".

In the long-range view, the Korean War, for all of its destruction, waste and human cost, was not fought in vain. Whatever the failings of the Rhee regime and its immediate successors, South Korea was spared the worst of the Stalinist regimes and eventually emerged with something far better. Other Asian nations after June 1950 felt that they could count on some tangible US reaction at least to overt aggression. Aside from the collapse of the pro-West regimes of the Vietnam peninsula, the Asian "dominoes" did *not* fall.

Rather, it was the Soviet Union and its Potemkin Village empire that fell in 1991. The beginnings of this denouement, unimaginable in 1950, can be traced to President Harry Truman's decision in July that year, with the support of the United Nations, to dispatch troops to the defence of the Republic of Korea. Yet in that war itself there would be no victors and no vanquished.

Notes

Chapter One

1. R. V. Appleman, *South to the Naktong, north to the Yalu* (Washington: US Army Office of the Chief of Military History, 1961). Colonel Appleman has continued his good historical work in a commercially published series of volumes dealing with the entire war.
2. Lloyd C. Gardner (ed.), *The Korean War* (New York, 1972), p. 5.
3. Quoted in Peter Hennessy, *Never again: Britain 1945–1951* (New York, 1993), p. 231.
4. M. B. Ridgway, *The Korean War* (Garden City, NY, 1967), p. vi.
5. J. L. Collins, *War in peacetime: The history and lessons of Korea* (1969), p. 4.
6. Quoted in Appleman, *South to the Naktong, north to the Yalu*, p. 720. The quotation had been repeated frequently, with some glee by those interested in denigrating the American soldier. But following this advice could get a Chinese soldier killed later in the war.
7. W. G. Hermes, *Truce tent and fighting front. The United States Army in the Korean War* (Washington: Office of the Chief of Military History, 1966), p. 511.
8. For what it may be worth, it might be noted that the ineffable rightist British MP, Sir Waldron Smithers, called for a House Committee on "Un-English Activities", a proposal quickly shot down.

Chapter Two

1. XIV Corps G-2, report for 11 December 1948, US National Archives and Record Service R 332, records of US Forces in Korea, box 47, G-2 periodic reports.
2. US Army Forces in Korea, "History of USAFIK, Pt. 2" (Seoul, December 1946), Chapter 4, p. 166, emphasis added.

271

3. K. Weathersby, "Korea, 1949–50: to attack or not to attack? Stalin, Kim Il Sung, and the prelude to war", *Working paper of the Cold War International History Project* (Woodrow Wilson International Center for Scholars, Spring 1995), p. 9.

4. Weathersby, "Korea, 1949–50" (Spring 1995), p. 37.

5. S. Goncharov, W. Lewis and X. Litai, *Uncertain partners: Stalin, Mao, and the Korean War* (Stanford, 1993), pp. 144–5.

6. Weathersby, "Korea, 1949–50" (Spring 1993), p. 16.

7. GHQ, FEC, Military Intelligence Section, "Intelligence plan of the North Korean Army for an attack operation", "20 June 1950" [obviously an arbitrary date and thus given in quotation marks; no such plan could have been put into effect in its preparatory stage in the five days remaining to 25 June and the start of the invasion.] Record Group 242, National Archives, Collection of Foreign Records Seized, Korean War Documents, Item 200686, declassified. Material kindly supplied by Mr Richard Boylan, National Archives 2.

8. C. E. Hoag, "American Military Government in Korea: war policy and the first year of independence, 1941–1946" (Washington: US Army Office of the Chief of Military History, 1970), p. 434.

9. H. Summers, "The Korean War: a fresh perspective", *Military History*, April 1996, p. 2.

10. XXIV Corps Staff Conference, 10 September 1948, US National Archives and Record Service, Record Group 332, United States Army Forces in Korea, box 28, "Historical Journal of Korea" folder.

11. Quoted in RG 332, USAFIK, box 28, "Historical Journal of Korea" folder.

12. *New York Times*, 10 October 1949.

13. Quoted in John R. Merrill, *Internal warfare in Korea, 1948–1950*, PhD thesis, University of Delaware, 1982.

14. CIA, Intelligence Memorandum No. 197, pp. 19–20, quoted in T. Lineer, *Evolution of Cold War rules of engagement: the Soviet combat role in the Korean War, 1950–1953*, Master of Military Art and Science thesis, US Army Command and General Staff College (1993).

15. Goncharov, Lewis and Xue Litai, *Uncertain partners: Stalin, Mao, and the Korean War*, p. 87.

16. Far East Command, *Operations of the Military Intelligence Section*, GHQ, SWPAR/FEC/SCAP, Supplement: Korea 1950–1951, vol. III, Intelligence Series (III).

17. Gye-Dong Kim, "Who initiated the Korean War?", in James Cotton and Ian Neary (eds.), *The Korean War in history* (Atlantic Highlands, New Jersey, 1989), pp. 42–3.

Chapter Three

1. Baik Bong, *Kim Il Sung* (Pyongyang/Tokyo, 1970), vol. 2, p. 289.

2. There is some indication that Mr Stone was not too "independent" to turn away an offer of a Soviet subvention made about the time of his speculations

on the origins of the Korean War. In 1992, that is after the fall of the Soviet Union, several former Soviet intelligence officers claimed that their agency had made such an offer to Mr Stone, although they were unclear as to whether he had indeed accepted it. Stone was dead by then and could not defend himself, but others did. Nonetheless, it is difficult to see what the former security agents would have to gain by such a false claim about a journalist practically unknown to the general public. Further, it is strange that Mr Stone never made any public mention of such an offer, which if exposed, would have enhanced his reputation. (*New York Times*, 13 and 31 August, 26 September 1992.)

3. Top Secret, Shtykov To Comrade Zakarov, 26 June 1950, in K. Weathersby, "New Russian documents on the Korean War", CWIHP *Bulletin*, Winter 1995, p. 39.
4. General Yoo Sung Chul, quoted in Goncharov, Lewis and Xue Litai, *Uncertain partners: Stalin, Mao, and the Korean War*, p. 150.
5. Kim, "Who initiated the Korean War?", p. 35.
6. Kim, "Who initiated the Korean War?", p. 44.
7. T. F. Shtykov to Zakharov, 26 June 1950, in Weathersby, "New Russian documents", pp. 39–40.
8. R. Humphrey, Fight the Cold War; Korean Supplement, [Tokyo?], n.d., p. 12.
9. "Report of the First OCAFF [Office of Chief of Army Field Forces] Observer Team to the Far East Command", 16 August 1950, National Archives, Record Group 387, entry 55, box 171.
10. Ciphered telegram, Shtykov to Comrade Fyn-Si, 7 July 1950, in Weathersby, "New Russian documents", p. 42.

Chapter Four

1. Baik Bong, *Kim Il Sung*, vol. 2, p. 305.
2. Ciphered telegram, Fyn-Si to Kim Il Sung [via Shtykov], in Weathersby, "New Russian documents", p. 45.

Chapter Five

1. The quotation has been widely repeated, with the latest in C. Utz, *Assault from the sea: the amphibious landing at Inchon* (US Naval Historical Center, 1994), p. 5. Emphasis added.
2. Baik Bong, *Kim Il Sung*, vol. 2, pp. 307–8.
3. A. Hamby, "Public opinion: Korea and Vietnam", *Wilson Quarterly*, Summer 1978).

Chapter Six

1. Fynsi [another Stalin alias] to [Red Army General] Zakaharov and [Soviet Ambassador to North Korea] Shtykov, 27 September 1950. Papers distributed at New Evidence on Korean War conference, Woodrow Wilson Center, Washington, DC, July 1996.

2. A. Y. Mansourov, "Stalin, Mao, Kim, and China's decision to enter the Korean War, September 16–October 15, 1950", paper presented at Woodrow Wilson Center conference on New Evidence on Korean War.

3. Mansourov, "Stalin, Mao, Kim, and China's decision to enter the Korean War, September 16–October 15, 1950: new evidence from the Russian Archives", *CWIHPB* (Winter 1998).

4. Baik Bong, *Kim Il Sung*, vol. 2, p. 311.

5. Draft, Far East Command, "Civil Information and Education Policy for North Korea", n.d., 8201st report, 15 October 1950–31 August 1951, 2, RG 470, entry 368, box 4995.

6. *Ibid.*

7. Mansourov. Note that Stalin seems to be saying that the issue of war or peace would be in his hands, not in those of the Americans.

8. *Ibid.*

9. S. Zhang, *Mao's Military Romanticism: China and the Korean War, 1950–1953* (Lawrence, Kansas: 1995), p. 91.

10. V. Newton, *The Cambridge spies: the untold story of MacLean, Philby, and Burgess in America* (London 1991), p. 332.

11. Quoted in B. Mossman, *Ebb and Flow, November 1950–July 1951, United States Army in the Korean War*, US Army Center of Military History (1990), p. 58, note 24.

12. "Threat of full Chinese communist intervention in Korea", 12 October 1950, in Michael Warner (ed.), *CIA Cold War Records: The CIA Under Harry Truman* (Washington: 1994), p. 1.

13. B. Mossman, *Ebb and flow*. US Army Center of Military History, Washington, DC (1990), p. 47, note 30.

14. Zhang, *Mao's Military Romanticism*, p. 215.

15. *Ibid.*, p. 198.

Chapter Seven

1. Appleman, *South to the Naktong, north to the Yalu*, p. 720.

2. Mossman, *Ebb and flow*, pp. 53–5.

Chapter Eight

1. Baik Bong, *Kim Il Sung*, vol. 2, p. 325.

2. Quoted in Mossman, *Ebb and flow*, p. 229.

3. "Special estimate: probable developments in the world situation through mid-1953", in Warner, *CIA Cold War Records*, p. 4.
4. K. Weathersby, "The Soviet role in prolonging the Korean War, 1951–53", paper presented at the Conference "The Korean War: An Assessment of the Historical Record, Washington, 24–25 July 1995, pp. 14–15.
5. *Ibid.*, p. 17.
6. *Ibid.*, p. 19.

Chapter Nine

1. Quoted in J. Grey, *The Commonwealth armies and the Korean War: an alliance study* (Manchester 1988), p. 189.
2. Telegram, Peng to Mao, 4 December 1950, quoted in Shu Guang Zhang, "China's military strategy during the Korean War", in "The Korean War: an assessment of the historical record", Korea Society – Korea-America Society and Georgetown University symposium, 24 and 25 July 1995, n.p.
3. Telegram, Mao to Peng, 26 May 1951, *ibid.*

Chapter Ten

1. Captain Boris Abakumov, quoted in P. Lashmoar, "POW's, Soviet intelligence, and the MIA question", in "The Korean War: an assessment for the historical record", n.p.
2. M. McCarthy, "Uncertain enemies: Soviet pilots in the Korean War", *Airpower History*, Spring 1997, p. 38.
3. Oral interview with Captain (Retired) Jack Gifford, PhD, 14 April 1992, in T. A. Lineer, "Evolution of Cold War rules of engagement: the Soviet combat role in the Korean War, 1950–53", Master of Military Art and Science, US Army Command and General Staff School, Fort Leavenworth, Kansas, 1993. This author knows and can vouch for the veracity of Dr Gifford.
4. H. S. Craig, "Memorandum for the Record, Subject: returned POWs at Valley Forge General Hospital, 12 May 1953"; Operations Coordinating Board, "Meeting of POW Working Group[,] Tuesday, 10 November 1953" [quotation]; Jesse MacKnight, "Government Memorandum, Subject: Department of the Army fact sheet 'Communist mistreatment of United States prisoners of war' – October 23 1953'"; Charles Norberg, "Comments on atrocity item draft speech", 20 November 1953, all in Papers of Dwight D. Eisenhower, White House National Security Papers, quoted in Lineer, "Evolution of Cold War rules of engagement", pp. 105–6.

5. Laurence Jolidon, *Last seen alive: the search for missing POWs from the Korean War* (1995).
6. Baik Bong, *Kim Il Sung*, vol. 2, p. 289.
7. Gorshkov, in *Morskaya Moshch' Gosudarstva* [Sea Power of the State] (Moscow, 1976), p. 390, cited in K. Hagan, *In peace and war, interpretations of American naval history, 1775–1978* (Westport, CT and London, 1978), p. 305.

Chapter Eleven

1. G. S. Pettee, *Psywar operations in the Korean War* (Operational Research Office, Fort McNair, Washington, 23 January 1951), p. 4.
2. Loudspeaker leaflet scripts from US Army Special Operations Command History Archives, Fort Bragg, North Carolina.
3. Communist leaflet examples in US Army Special Operations Command History Archives.
4. Leaflet examples in US Army Special Operations Command Historical Archives.
5. Gan Siqi and Li Zhimin (eds), *Zhongguo Renmin Zhiyianjun Kangmei Yuanchao Zhanaheng Ahengzhi Gongquo Zongie [A summary of the CPV political work in the war to resist US aggression and aid Korea]*, Beijing: People's Liberation Army Press, quoted in Shu Guang Zhang, *Mao's military romanticism* (Lawrence, Kansas, 1995), pp. 159–60.
6. Quoted in R. Futrell, *The United States Air Force in Korea 1950–1953* (New York, 1961), p. 686.

Chapter Twelve

1. Zang, *Mao's Military Romanticism*, p. 251.
2. *New York Times*, 2, 4, 6 and 10 September 1950.
3. Quoted in Walton S. Moody, *Building a strategic Air Force* (Air Force History and Museums Program, 1996), p. 146.
4. Peter Lowe, "Britain, the US and the Korean War", in J. Cotton and I. Neary (eds), *The Korean War in history* (Atlantic Highlands, NY, 1989), p. 87.

Chapter Thirteen

1. Shu Guang Zhang, "China's military strategy during the Korean War".
2. "On strengthening our defence", 13 July 1951, *Kim Il Sung's works* (Pyongyang, 1981), vol. 6.

3. Baik Bong, *Kim Il Sung*, vol. 2, p. 352.
4. Kim Il Sung to Stalin, 16 July 1952, in Weathersby, "New Russian documents", p. 77.
5. *Ibid.*, p. 78.
6. Mao to Stalin, 14 November 1951, *ibid.*, p. 71, emphasis added.
7. N. Bajanova, "Assessing the conclusion and outcome of the Korean War", paper presented at "The Korean War: an assessment of the historical record" symposium, p. 6.
8. *Ibid.*
9. *Ibid.*, p. 7.
10. K. Weathersby, "Stalin and a negotiated settlement in Korea, 1950–53", paper presented at conference "The Cold War in Asia", sponsored by the Cold War International History Project, University of Hong Kong (9–12 January), p. 35.
11. C. McDonald, *Britain and the Korean War* (London, 1990), pp. 144–5, 73.
12. William T. Bowers, William M. Hammond and George MacGarrigle, *Black soldier white army: the 24th Infantry Regiment in Korea* (Washington, DC: US Army Center of Military History, 1997).
13. J. Halliday, "Air operations in Korea: the Soviet side of the story", in William J. Williams (ed.), *A revolutionary war: Korea and the transformation of the postwar world* (1993), p. 170.
14. This letter is reproduced in Weathersby, "New Russian documents", pp. 80–1. Kim's reaction in ciphered telegram from Federenko and Kuznetsov in Pyongyang to Moscow, in *ibid.*, p. 83.
15. Bajanova, "Assessing the conclusion and outcome of the Korean War", p. 8.
16. Entry for 24 July 1953, *The Eisenhower diaries*, Robert Ferrell (ed.) (1981).
17. Edward C. Keefer, "NSC-147: an analysis of possible courses of action in Korea", in James I. Matray (ed.), *An historical dictionary of the Korean War* (1991); Edward C. Keefer, "Eisenhower and the end of the Korean War", *Diplomatic History* (Summer 1986) pp. 41–53; *Foreign Relations of the United States, 1952–1954*, vol. 15.
18. Baik Bong, *Kim Il Sung*, p. 404.
19. *Mao's Military Romanticism*, p. 251.

Chapter Fourteen

1. Foreign Languages Publishing House, *Pyongyang* (1975), p. 7.

Select bibliography

The following are works that pertain primarily to the Korean War. The ephemeral has been omitted, along with unit histories.

Bibliographies

Blanshard, C. *Korean War bibliography and maps of Korea* (Albany, NY, 1964).

Brune, L. & R. Higham (eds). *The Korean War: handbook of the literature and research* (Westport, CN, 1994).

Edwards, P. M. *The Korean War: an annotated bibliography* (Westwood, Connecticut, 1998).

Higham, R. & D. Mrozek, *Guide to the sources of U.S. military history, supplement III* (North Haven, CT, 1993).

Hyatt, J. (comp.). *Korean War, 1950–1953: selected references* (The Air University Library, USAF, Maxwell AFB, AL, 1990).

Koh, H. & J. Steffens (eds). *Korea: an analytical guide to bibliographies* (New Haven, CT, 1971).

Korean War Studies Association. *Bibliographies related with the Korean War* (Seoul, 1985).

Kwak, T.-H., Tae-Han, John Chay, Cho Soon-Sung & Shannon McCune (eds). *U.S.–Korean-relations* (Seoul: Institute for Far Eastern Studies, 1982).

Lee, C.-k. Bibliographic essay on Korean War. *Tong Il Mun Je Yon Ku* (*A study of unification affairs*) 2 (Seoul, 1990).

McFarland, K. *The Korean War: an annotated bibliography* (New York, 1986).

Millett, A. A reader's guide to the Korean War. *Journal of Military History* (Lexington, VA, 1997).

Park, H.-K. *The Korean War: an annotated bibliography* (New York, 1971).

Rhee, S., P. Chong-Chun & Ohn Chang-Il (eds). Selected bibliography of the Korean War. *Korea and World Affairs* (Seoul, 1984).

Swartout, R., Jr. American historians and the outbreak of the Korean War: an international essay. *Asia Quarterly* **1** (Brussells, 1979).

Korean War in general and background

Ahn, C. *The study on the day of the outbreak of war: a critique on the inducement theory of the war* (Seoul, 1993).

Alexander, B. *Korea: the first war we lost* (New York, 1986).

Allen, R. *Korea's Syngman Rhee: an unauthorized biography* (Rutland, UT, 1960).

Baldwin, F. (ed.). *Without parallel: the American–Korean relationship since 1945* (New York, 1973).

Beach, K. *Tokyo and points east* (Garden City, NY, 1954).

Berger, C. *The Korea knot: a military and political history* (Westport, CN, 1957).

Blair, C. *The forgotten war: Americans in Korea, 1950–1953* (New York, 1987).

Blum, R. *Drawing the line: the origins of the American containment policy in east Asia* (New York, 1982).

Chae-Jin, L. (ed.). *The Korean War: a 40-year perspective* (Claremont, CA, 1991).

Chengwen, C. & Z. Yongtian. *A factual record of the Korean War* (Seoul, 1990).

Cho, S. *Korea in world politics, 1940–1950: an evaluation of American responsibility* (Seoul, 1967).

Choi, T-h. & Park Hye-kang. *A study on the Korean War: understanding Korean modern history* (Seoul, 1990).

Choo, Y-b. *The Korean War I had experienced* (Seoul, 1990).

ChullBaum, K. (ed.). *Truth and testimonies: the true picture of the Korean War unmasked 40 years later* (Seoul, 1990).

ChullBaum, K. (ed.). *Korean War and the United States* (Seoul, 1990).

ChullBaum, K. (ed.). *Perspectives of the Korean War* (Seoul, 1990).

ChullBaum, K. (ed.). U.S. withdrawal decision from Korea, 1945–1949. PhD diss., State University of New York at Buffalo (1984).

ChullBaum, K. (ed.). *The Korean War: Great Power Politics and North–South discord* (Seoul, 1989).

Chung, I.-K. *A secret record: war and truce* (Seoul, 1986).

Collins, J. *War in peacetime: The history and lessons of Korea* (Boston, 1969).

Cotton, J. & I. Neary (eds). *The Korean War in history* (Atlantic Highlands, NY, 1989).

Cumings, B. *Child of Conflict: The Korean–American Relationship, 1943–1953* (Seattle, 1983).

Cumings, B. *Korea's place in the sun* (New York, 1997).

Cumings, B. *The origins of the Korean War*, vol. 1, *Liberation and the emergence of separate regimes, 1945–1947* (Princeton, 1981), vol. 2, *The roaring of the cataract, 1947–1950* (1990).

Cumings, B. *War and television* (New York, 1992).

Daisaburo, Y. *Chosen senso to katamen kowa* (The Korean War and the one-sided peace). In Rekishigaku Kenkyukai (ed.) *Koza nihon rekishi II gendai I* (*Lectures on Japanese history*) (Tokyo, 1985).

Dobbs, C. *The unwanted symbol: American foreign policy, the Cold War, and Korea, 1945–1950* (Kent, Ohio, 1981).

Fehrenbach, T. *This kind of war: A study in unpreparedness* (1963, reprint by US Army, New York, 1993).

Foot, R. *A substitute for victory: the politics of peacemaking at the Korean armistice talks* (Ithaca, NY, 1990).

Foot, R. *The wrong war: American policy and the dimensions of the Korean conflict* (Ithaca, NY, 1985).

Goodman, A. (ed.). *Negotiating while fighting: the diary of Admiral C. Turner Joy at the Korean armistice conference* (Standford, CA, 1978).

Goulden, J. *Korea: the untold story of the war* (NY, 1982).

Guttman, A. (comp.). *Korea and the theory of limited war* (Boston, 1988).

Gye-Dong, K. *Foreign intervention in Korea* (Aldershot, UK, 1993).

Ha, Y. *New approaches to the study of Korean War: beyond traditionalism and revisionism* (Seoul, 1990).

Hankuk, J. *History of the Korean War* [5 vols] (Seoul, 1990–1992).

Hastings, M. *The Korean War* (NY, 1987).

Haynes, R. *The awesome power: Harry S. Truman as Commander in Chief* (Baton Rouse, LA, 1973).

Heller F. (ed.). *The Korean War: a 25-year perspective* (Lawrence, KS, 1977).

Hermes, W. *Truce tent and fighting front. United States Army in the Korean War* (Office of the Chief of Military History, US Army, Washington, DC, 1966).

Institute of Far Eastern Studies. *Korean War and the construction of the socialist system in North Korea* (Kyung Nam University, Seoul, 1992).

Institute for Social Sciences (Seoul). *War and revolution: Korean War and April student revolution* (June 1990).

Iriye, A. *The Cold War in Asia: a historical introduction* (Englewood Cliffs, NY, 1974).

Joint Chiefs of Staff (Republic of Korea). *The Korean War History* [8 vols] (Seoul, 1984).

Joy, C. *How Communists negotiate* (New York, 1955).

Kaufman, B. *The Korean War: challenges in crisis, credibility, and command* (Philadelphia, 1986).

Kim, C. *Korean War and the United States* (Seoul, 1990, 1995).

Kim, C. *Truth and testimonies: the true picture of the Korean War unmasked 40 years after* (Seoul, 1990).

Kim, C. (ed.). *The Korean War: great power politics and South–North discord* (Seoul, 1989).

Kim, C. (ed.). *Perspectives of the Korean War* (Seoul, 1990).

Kim, C. & James Matray (eds). *Korea and the Cold War: division, destruction and disarmament* (Seoul, 1991; Claremont, CA, 1993).

Kim, H. & H. K. Park (eds). *Studies on Korea: a scholar's guide* (Seoul, 1980).

Kim, J. K. *The Korean War and workers party strategy* (Seoul, 1973).

Kim, S. *History of the Korean War: reevaluation of modern history* (Tokyo, 1967).

Kim, Y. H. *Secret records: division and war* (Seoul, 1994).

Kim, Y. M. *History of the Korean War* (Seoul, 1976).

Kim, Y. M. *The Korean War* (Seoul, 1973).

Knox, D. *The Korean War – an oral history: Pusan to Chosin* (New York, 1985).

Knox, D. & A. Coppel. *The Korean War: an oral history, uncertain victory* (San Diego, CA, 1988).

Korean Association of International Studies. *Historical reevaluation of the Korean War* (Seoul, 1990).

Korean Political Science Research Association. *A collection of treaties: the 40th anniversary of the Korean War* (Seoul, 1990).

Korean Society of Diplomatic History. *The Korean War seen from the context of diplomatic history* (Seoul, 1989).

Korean Sociological Association. *The Korean War and the changes in Korean society* (Seoul, 1992).

Korean Sociological Association. *The Korean War and the construction of a socialist system in North Korea* (Seoul, 1992).

Korean War Research Committee. *The historical re-illumination of the Korean War* (Seoul: War Memorial Service, Seoul, 1990).

Leckie, R. *Conflict: the history of the Korean War, 1950–1953* (NY, 1962).

Lee, S.-k. *The Korean War must be rewritten* (Seoul, 1990).

Lowe, P. *The origins of the Korean War* (London, 1986, 1997).

Lyons, G. *Military policy and economic aid: the Korean case, 1950–1953* (Columbus, OH, 1961).

McCune, G. *Korea today* (Cambridge, MA, 1950).

MacDonald, C. *Korea: the war before Vietnam* (New York, 1987).

McGovern, J. *To the Yalu: from the Chinese invasion of Korea to MacArthur's dismissal* (New York, 1972).

McGovern, J. *Historical dictionary of the Korean War* (New York, 1991).

Masao, O. *The Korean War: the process of U.S. intervention* (Seoul, 1986).

Matray, J. *Historical dictionary of the Korean War* (Westport, CN, 1991).

Matray, J. *The reluctant crusade: American foreign policy in Korea, 1941–1950* (Honolulu, 1985).

Mayers, D. *Cracking the monolith, US policy against the Sino–Soviet alliance, 1949–1955* (Baton Rouge, LA, 1986).

Merrill, J. *Internal Warfare in Korea, 1948–1950: the local settings of the Korean War* (Seoul, 1988).

Merrill, J. *Korea: the peninsular origins of the war* (Newark, Delaware, 1989).

Mossman, B. *Ebb and flow: November 1950–July 1951. U.S. Army in the Korean War* (US Army Center of Military History, Washington, DC, 1990).

Myung-ki, K. *The Korean War and international law* (Clairmont, CA, 1991).

Nimmo, W. (ed.). *The occupation of Japan: the impact of the Korean War.* Proceedings of a symposium sponsored by the General Douglas MacArthur Memorial, 16–17 October 1986 (Norfolk, VA, 1990).

Noh, M.-y. *Reevaluation of the Korean War: unfinished war* (Seoul, 1991).

O'Ballance, E. *Korea, 1950–1953* (Hamden, CN, 1960).

Oliver, R. *Korean report, 1948–1952; a review of governmental procedures during the two years of peace and two of war* (Washington, 1952).

Oliver, R. *Syngman Rhee: the man behind the myth* (New York, 1955).

Oliver, R. *Syngman Rhee and American involvement in Korea, 1942–1960: a personal narrative* (Seoul, 1978).

Oliver, R. *Why war came in Korea* (1950).

Paige, G. *The Korean decision (June 24–30, 1950)* (New York, 1968).

Park, G.-d. *The Korean War and Kim Il Sung* (Seoul, 1990).

Ra, J.-y. *The Korean War seen through testimonies* (Seoul, 1991).

Ra, J.-y. *The unfinished war: Korea and great power politics, 1950–1990* (Seoul, 1994).

Rees, D. *Korea: the limited war* (New York, 1964).

Republic of Korea, Ministry of Defense. *The account of defensive operations along the Nak Dong River* (Seoul, 1970).

Republic of Korea, Ministry of Defense. *All out counter attack operations* (Seoul, 1971).

Republic of Korea, Ministry of Defense. *The brief history of ROK armed forces* (Seoul, 1986).

Republic of Korea, Ministry of Defense. *The invasion by Chinese forces* (Seoul, 1972).

Republic of Korea, Ministry of Defense. *The invasion of the North Korean puppet forces* (Seoul, 1967).

Republic of Korea, Ministry of Defense. *Liberation and the building of armed forces* (Seoul, 1967).

Republic of Korea, Ministry of Defense. *The participation of UN forces* (Seoul, 1980).

Republic of Korea, Ministry of Defense. Information and Education Bureau, *The Korean War* (Seoul, 1951–1955).

Republic of Korea, Ministry of Information. *The origins and truth of the Korean War: an analysis of false perspective by revisionists* (Seoul, 1990).

Sandler, S. *The Korean War: an encyclopedia* (New York, 1995).

Scalapino, R. & Lee Chong-Sik. *Communism in Korea* [2 vols] (Berkeley, CA, 1973).

Schnable, J. *U.S. Army in the Korean War, policy and direction: the first year* (US Army Center of Military History, Washington, DC, 1972).

Schnable, J. & R. J. Watson. *The Korean War*, vol. 3 of *The history of the Joint Chiefs of Staff: The Joint Chiefs of Staff and national policy* [5 vols] (Washington, DC, 1978–86).

Seoul National University, Institute for International Affairs. *Reevaluation of the Korean War: a critique of Communist theory* (Seoul, 1990).

Shinn, B. *The forgotten war remembered, Korea: 1950–1953* (Elizabeth, NY, 1996).

Shuguang, Z. *Deterrence and strategic culture: Chinese–American confrontation, 1949–1958* (Ithaca, NY, 1992).

Silberson, B. *Korean conflict: A collection of historical manuscripts on the Korean campaign held by the U.S. Army Center of Military History* (Library of Congress Photo-duplication Service, Washington, DC, 1975).

Spanier, J. *The Truman–MacArthur controversy and the Korean War* (Cambridge, MA, 1959).

Stokesbury, J. *A short history of the Korean War* (New York, 1988).

Stueck, W. *The Korean War: an international history* (Princeton, 1995).

Stueck, W. *The road to confrontation: American policy toward China and Korea, 1947–1950* (Chapel Hill, NC, 1981).

Summers, H. *Korean War almanac* (New York, 1990).

Sung Sin Women's University Press. *The impact of the Korean War on the people and society of Korea* (Seoul, 1986).

Toland, J. *In mortal combat: Korea, 1950–1953* (New York, 1991).

Truman, H. *Memoirs: years of hope and trial* (New York, 1956).

United Nations Command. *Report of the United Nations Command on the operations of the Neutral Nations Repatriation Commission* (New York, 1954).

US Army. *The handling of prisoners of war during the Korean War.* (US National Archives, 1 micro reel, Washington, DC, 1960).

US Army. *Terrain study no. 6, northern Korea* (Tokyo, 1950?).

US Army. *Terrain study no. 26, southern Korea* (Tokyo, 1950?).

US Army. Comptroller of the Army. *Pocket data book supplement* (Tokyo, 1959).

US Army Walter Reed Army Medical Center. *Some observations on the Chinese indoctrination program for prisoners of war* (Washington, DC, 1955).

US State Department. *American policy 1950–1953: basic documents*, 2 vols (Washington, DC, 1957).

US State Department. *Foreign relations of the United States, 1950*, vol. 7, *Korea* (Washington, DC, 1976).

US State Department. *Foreign relations of the United States, 1950*, vol. 7, *Korea and China* (Washington, DC, 1983).

US State Department. *The record on Korean unification 1943–1960: narrative summary with principal documents* (Washington, DC, 1960).

US State Department. Far Eastern Series. *A historical summary of United States–Korean relations, 1934–1962* (Washington, DC, 1962).

Vatcher, W. *Panmunjom: the story of the Korean military armistice negotiations* (New York, Westport, CN, 1958).

Whelan, R. *Drawing the line: the Korean War, 1950–1953* (Boston, 1990).

Williams, W. J. (ed.). *A revolutionary war: Korea and the transformation of the postwar world* (Military History Symposium, US Air Force Academy, Colorado Springs, CO, 1993).

Yang-Myong, K. *The history of the Korean War* (Seoul, 1976).

Yim, L. *My forty year fight for Korea* (London, 1952).

Korean War in general, articles

Allegations on POWs denied. *Beijing Review* (January 1993).

Bajanova, N. Assessing the conclusion and outcome of the Korean War. In The Korean War: an assessment of the historical record, Symposium, Georgetown University, 24–25 July 1995.

Bernstein, B. New light on the Korean War. *International History Review* (April 1981).

Bernstein, B. The struggle over the Korean armistice: prisoners of repatriation. In B. Cumings (ed.), *Child of Conflict* (1983).

Bernstein, B. Truman's secret thoughts on ending the Korean War. *Foreign Service Journal* (November 1980).

Bernstein, B. The week that we went to war: American intervention in the Korean War. *Foreign Service Journal* (January, February 1977).

Blechman, B. & R. Powell. What in the name of God is strategic superiority? *Orbis* (Summer 1973).

Buhite, R. Major interests: American policy toward China, Taiwan, and Korea, 1945–1950. *Pacific Historical Review* (August 1978).

Caine, P. The United States in Korea and Vietnam: a study in public opinion. *Air University Review* (January, February 1968).

Calingaert, D. Nuclear weapons and the Korean War. *The Journal of Strategic Studies* (June 1988).

Chaffee, W. Two hypotheses of Sino–Soviet relations as concerns the instigation of the Korean War. *Journal of Korean Affairs* (October 1976–January 1977).

Cohen, W. Conversations with Chinese friends: Zhou Enlai's associates reflect on Chinese–American relations in the 1940s and the Korean War. *Diplomatic History* (Summer 1987).

Crofts, A. The state of the Korean War reconsidered. *Rocky Mountain Social Science Journal* (April 1974).

Cumings, B. & K. Weathersby. An exchange on Korean War origins. *Cold War International History Project Bulletin (CWIHPB)* (Winter 1995).

Cumings, B. American policy and Korean liberation. In F. Baldwin (ed.), *Without parallel* (New York, 1973).

DeWeerd, H. Strategic surprise in the Korean War. *Orbis* (Fall 1962).

Dingman, R. Atomic diplomacy during the Korean War. *International Security* (Winter 1988–9).

Dingman, R. The dagger and the gift: the impact of the Korean War on Japan. In W. J. Williams (ed.), *A revolutionary war* (1993).

Dingman, R. Korea at forty plus: the origins of the Korean War reconsidered. *The Journal of American–East Asian Relations* (Spring 1992).

Dingman, R. Truman, Attlee and the Korean War crisis. In *The East Asian crisis, 1945–1951* (London School of Economics, 1982).

Dobbs, C. Limiting room to maneuver: the Korea Assistance Act of 1949. *Historian* (August 1986).

Drifte, R. Japan's involvement in the Korean War. In J. Cotton & I. Neary (eds), *The Korean War in history* (1989).

Elowitz, L. & J. Spanier. Korea and Vietnam: limited war and the American political system. *Orbis* **18**(2) (1974).

Endicott, D. Germ warfare and "plausible denial": the Korean War 1952–53. *Modern China* (January 1979).

Farrar-Hockley, A. Notes on the successive strategies employed during the Korean War. In The Korean War: an assessment of the historical record, Symposium, Georgetown University, 24–25 July 1995.

Foot, R. Anglo-American relations in the Korean crisis: the British effort to avert an expanded war, December 1950–January 1951. *Diplomatic History* (Winter 1986).

Foot, R. Making known the unknown war: policy analysis of the Korean conflict in the last decade. *Diplomatic History* (Summer 1991).

Foot, R. Nuclear coercion and the ending of the Korean Conflict. *International Security* (Winter 1988–9).

Gittlesohn, J. War and remembrance: forty years on the origins of the Korean inspire debate and reassessment. *Far Eastern Economic Review* (19 July 1990).

Gupta, K. How did the Korean War begin? *China Quarterly* (October–December 1972).

Hwang, B.-M. Misperception and the causes of the Korean War. *Review Internationale d'Histoire Militaire* (1988).

Jervis, R. The impact of the Korean War on the Cold War. *Journal of Conflict Resolution* (December 1980).

Keefer, E. Eisenhower and the end of the Korean War. *Diplomatic History* (Summer 1986).

Kim, C. An inquiry into the origins of the Korean War: a critique of the revisionist view. *East Asia Review* (Summer 1994).

Kim, C. U.S. policy on the eve of the Korean War: abandonment or safeguard? In P. Williamson (ed.), *Security in Korea: war, stalemate, and negotiations* (1994).

Kim, G.-D. Who initiated the Korean War? In J. Cotton & I. Neary (eds), *The Korean War in history* (1989).

Kim, K. Russian foreign ministry documents on the origins of the Korean War. In The Korean War: an assessment of the historical record, Symposium, Georgetown University, 24–25 July 1995.

Lafeber, W. NATO and the Korean War: a context. *Diplomatic History* (Fall 1989).

Lashmar, P. POWs, Soviet intelligence and the MIA question. In The Korean War: an assessment of the historical record, Symposium, Georgetown University, 24–25 July 1995.

Lee, W. Domestic trends regarding the Korean War study. *Korea and International Politics*, Chung Nam University Institute of Eastern Studies (Autumn 1990).

Leffler, M. The American conception of national security and the beginnings of the Cold War, 1945–48. *The American Historical Review* (April 1984).

Leopold, R. The historian's task. In F. Heller (ed.), *The Korean War: a 25-year perspective* (1977).

McGlothan, R. Acheson, economics, and the American commitment in Korea, 1947–50. *Pacific Historical Review* (February 1989).

Matray, J. America's reluctant crusade: Truman's commitment of combat troops in the Korean War. *Historian* (May 1980).

Matray, J. Captive of the Cold War: the decision to divide Korea at the 38th Parallel. *Pacific Historical Review* (May 1981).

Matray, J. Civil is a dumb name for a war. In The Korean War: an assessment of the historical record, Symposium, Georgetown University, 24–25 July 1995.

Munro-Leighton, J. A postrevisionist scrutiny of America's role in the Cold War in Asia, 1945–1950. *Journal of American–East Asian Relations* 1 (Spring 1992).

Ohn, C. Military objectives and strategies of the two Koreas and the Korean War. In The Korean War: an assessment of the historical record, Symposium, Georgetown University, 24–25 July 1995.

Park, K. From Pearl Harbor to Cairo: American Korean diplomacy. *Diplomatic History* (Summer 1989).

Park, M.-r. The point of argument regarding Korean War history. In *The view of Korean history before and after liberation* (1989).

Park, M.-s. Stalin's foreign policy and the Korean War: history revised. *Korean Observer* (Autumn 1994).

Pike, D. & B. Ward. Losing and winning: Korea and Vietnam as success stories. *Washington Quarterly* (Summer 1987).

Pollack, J. The Korean War and Sino–American relations. In H. Harding & Y. Ming (eds), *Sino–American Relations, 1945–1955: a joint reassessment of a critical decade* (1989).

Simmons, R. The Korean civil war. In F. Heller (ed.), *The Korean War* (1977).

Simmons, R. Some myths about June 1950. *China Quarterly* (April–June 1973).

Soh, J. The role of the Soviet Union in preparation for the Korean War. *Journal of Korean Affairs* (January 1974).

Spanier, J. The Korean War as a civil war. *Orbis* (Winter 1976).

Stairs, D. The United Nations and the politics of the Korean War. *International Journal* (Spring 1970).

Stueck, W., Jr. Cold War revisionism and the origins of the Korean conflict: the Kolko thesis. *Pacific Historical Review* (November 1973).

Stueck, W., Jr. The Korean War and international history. *Diplomatic History* (Fall 1986).

Stueck, W., Jr. The Korean War in historical perspective. In Chae-jin Lee (ed.), *The Korean War: forty-year perspective* (Keck Center for International and Strategic Studies, 1991).

Stueck, W., Jr. The Korean War, NATO, and rearmament. In W. J. Williams (ed.), *A revolutionary war* (1993).

Stueck, W., Jr. The Soviet Union and the origins of the Korean War. *World Politics* (July 1976).

Summers, H. The Korean War paradigm. In The Korean War: an assessment of the historical record, Symposium, Georgetown University, 24–25 July 1995.

Warner, G. The Korean War. *International Affairs* (January 1980).

Wedemeyer, A. 1947 Wedemeyer report on Korea. *Current History* **20**(118) (1951).

Wilz, J. Encountering Korea: American perceptions and policies to June 25 1950. In W. J. Williams (ed.), *Revolutionary war* (1993).

Wilz, J. Truman and MacArthur: the Wake Island meeting. *Military Affairs* (December 1978).

A UN war

Bailey, S. *The Korean armistice* (London, 1993).

Goodrich, L. *Korea: a study of US policy in the United Nations* (New York, 1979).

Gordenker, L. *The United Nations and the peaceful unification of Korea: the politics of field operations, 1947–1950* (Den Hague, 1959).

O'Neill, R. *Australia in the Korean War, 1950–53* [2 vols] *Strategy and diplomacy* (Australian Government Publishing Service, 1981), *Combat operations* (Canberra, 1985).

Ovendale, R. *The English-speaking alliance: Britain, the United States, the Dominions, and the Cold War, 1945–1951* (London, 1985).

Republic of Korea, Ministry of National Defense, *The history of the United Nations forces in the Korean War* [6 vols] (Seoul, 1975).

United Nations, *General Assembly, Reports of the neutral nations repatriation commission covering the period ending 9 September 1954* (New York, 1954).

A UN war, articles

Goodrich, L. Collective action in Korea: evaluating the results of the UN Collective action. *Current History* **38**(226) (1960).

Gordenker, L. The United Nations, the United States occupation, and the 1948 election in Korea. *Political Science Review* **73** (1958).

Halliday, J. The United Nations and Korea. In F. Baldwin (ed.), *Without parallel* (1973).

Hoyt, E. The United States' reaction to the Korean attack: a study of the principle of the UN Charter as a factor in American policy-making. *American Political Science Review* (January 1961).

Kaplan, L. The Korean War and US foreign relations: the case of NATO. In F. Heller (ed.), *The Korean War* (1977).

Ra, J. The politics of conference: the political conference at Geneva, April 26–June 15, 1954. In The Korean War: an assessment of the historical record, Symposium, Georgetown University, 24–25 July 1995.

US military

Acheson, D. *The Korean War* (New York, 1971).

Alexander, B. *Korea: the first war we lost* (New York, 1986).

Appleman, R. *Disaster in Korea: the Chinese confront MacArthur* (University Station, TX, 1989).

Appleman, R. *East of Chosin: entrapment and breakout in Korea, 1950* (University Station, TX, 1987).

Appleman, R. *Escaping the trap: the U.S. Army X Corps in northeast Korea, 1950* (University Station, TX, 1990).

Appleman, R. *Ridgway Duels for Korea* (University Station, TX, 1990).

Appleman, R. *South to the Naktong, north to the Yalu. The US Army in Korea* (Office of the Chief of Military History, Washington, DC, 1961).

Berebitsky, W. *A very long weekend: the Army National Guard in Korea* (Shippensburg, PA, 1996).

Berger, F. *et al. Chosin Reservoir: defensive retrograde winter, 1st Marine Division, 27 November–11 December 1950* (US Army Command and General Staff College, Combat Studies Institute, Leavenworth, KS, 1983).

Biderman, A. *March to Calumny; the story of American POWs in the Korean War* (New York, 1963).

Blakeley, H. *Marine Corps operations in Korea, 1950–1953* [5 vols] (US Marine Corps Historical Branch, Washington, DC, 1954–1972).

Bok, L. *The impact of U.S. forces in Korea* (US National Defense University, Washington, DC, 1987).

Bruer, W. *Shadow warriors: the covert war in Korea* (New York, 1996).

Brown, D. *The United States Air Force in Korea, 1950–1953* (Office of Air Force History, Washington, DC, 1983).

Bowers, W., W. Hammond & G. MacGarrigle. *Black soldier white army: The 24th Infantry Regiment in Korea* (US Army Center of Military History, Washington, DC, 1996).

Bureau of Social Research. *Further analysis of POW follow-up study data report* (New York, 1965).

Bussey, C. *Firefight at Yechon: courage and racism in the Korean War* (Washington, DC, 1991).

Cagle, M. & F. Mason. *The sea war in Korea* (Annapolis, MD, 1957).

Condit, D. *History of the Office of the Secretary of Defense*, vol. 2, *The test of war, 1950–1952* (Washington, DC, 1988).

Cowart, G. *Miracle in Korea: the evacuation of X Corps from the Hungnam beachead* (Washington, DC, 1992).

Cowdrey, A. *The medics' war. United States Army in the Korean War* (US Army Center of Military History, Washington, DC, 1987).

Dean, W. *General Dean's Story* (New York, 1954).

Dixon, J. (ed.). *The American military and the Far East: Proceedings of the ninth Military History Symposium, United States Air Force Academy* (Office of Air Force History, Washington, DC, 1980).

Day, J. *[UN] Partisan operations in the Korean War.* (MA thesis, University of Georgia, 1989).

Evanhoe, E. *Dark moon: Eighth Army special operations in the Korean War* (Annapolis, MD, 1995).

289

Field, J. *History of United States Naval operations: Korea* (Office of Naval History, Washington, DC, 1962).

Flint, R. *The tragic flaw: MacArthur, the Joint Chiefs, and the Korean War* (PhD thesis, Duke University, 1975).

Fondataro, S. *A strategic analysis of U.S. special operations during the Korean conflict, 1950–1953* (Thesis, US Army Command and General Staff College, Leavenworth, KS, 1988).

Fox, W. *Interallied operations during combat operations: history of the Korean War*. Headquarters, Far East Command, Military History Section, vol. 3, part 2, Section B. (Tokyo, n.d.).

Futrell, R. *The United States Air Force in Korea 1950–1953* (Office of Air Force History, Washington, DC, 1961).

Gardner, L. ed. *The Korean War* (New York, 1972).

Giangreco, D. *War in Korea* (New York, 1990).

Gugelar, R. *Combat actions in Korea* (Office of the Chief of Military History, Washington, DC, 1970).

Gunther, J. *The riddle of MacArthur: Japan, Korea and the Far East* (Westport, CN, 1950, 1974).

Hansen, K. *Heroes behind barbed wire* (New York, 1957).

Hansen, K. Psywar in Korea. Unpublished typescript (Office of the Joint Chiefs of Staff, Washington, DC, 1960).

Harris, W. W. *Puerto Rico fighting 65th U.S. Infantry: From San Juan to Chorwon* (San Juan, PR, 1980).

Heinl, R. *Victory at high tide: the Inchon–Seoul campaign* (Philadelphia, 1968).

Higgins, M. *War in Korea: the report of a woman combat correspondent* (New York, 1951).

Hinshaw, A. *Heartbreak Ridge* (New York, 1989).

Hopkins W. & S. Marshall. *One bugle, no drums: the Marines at Chosin Reservoir* (Chapel Hill, NC, 1986).

Hoyt, E. *The Pusan Perimeter* (New York, 1984).

Hoyt, E. *On to the Yalu* (New York, 1984).

Hoyt, E. *The bloody road to Panmunjom* (New York, 1985).

Hoyt, E. *The day the Chinese attacked: Korea, 1950* (New York, 1990).

Huston, J. *Guns and butter, powder and rice: U.S. Army logistics in the Korean War* (Selinsgrove, PA, 1989).

James, D. *Refighting the last war: command and crisis in Korea, 1950–1953* (New York, 1992).

James, D. *Triumph and disaster, 1945–1964*, vol. 3 of *The years of MacArthur* (Boston, 1970).

Kemp, R. *Combined operations in the Korea war* (US Army War College, Carlisle, PA, 1989).

Kinkhead, E. *In every war but one* (New York, 1959).

Kinkhead, E. *Why they collaborated* (London, 1960).

Langley, M. *Inchon landing: MacArthur's last triumph* (New York, 1979).

Little, R. *Building an atomic Air Force, 1949–1953*, vol. 3 in L. Bowen and R. Little, *The history of Air Force participation in the atomic energy program, 1943–1953* (Office of Air Force History, Washington, DC, n.d.).

Long, G. *MacArthur as military commander* (London, 1959).

Lowitt, R. (comp.). *The Truman–MacArthur controversy* (Chicago, 1967).

MacArthur, D. *Reminiscences* (New York, 1964).

MacArthur, D. *A soldier speaks: public papers and speeches of General of the Army Douglas MacArthur* (New York, 1965).

Malcom, B. *White tigers: my secret war in North Korea* (Washington, DC, 1996).

Manchester, W. *American Caesar: Douglas MacArthur (1880–1964)* (Boston, 1978).

Marshall, S. *Infantry operations and weapons in Korea* (1988), US Army Office of Chief of Army History.

Marshall, S. *Military history of the Korean War* (1963).

Marshall, S. *Pork Chop Hill: the American fighting man in action, Korea, Spring 1953* (New York, 1956).

Marshall, S. *The river and the gauntlet: defeat of the Eighth Army by the Chinese Communist forces, November 1950, in the battle of the Chongchon river, Korea* (New York, 1953).

Meade, E. *American military government in Korea* (US Army Office of Chief of Military History, Washington, DC, 1951).

Montross, L. & N. Canzona. *The Inchon–Seoul operation* (Historical Branch, US Marine Corps, Washington, DC, 1954).

Montross, L. *Cavalry of the sky: the story of U.S. Marine combat helicopters* (New York, 1954).

Mossman, B. *Ebb and flow: November 1950–July 1951, United States Army in the Korean War* (US Army Center of Military History, Washington, DC, 1990)

Mossman, B. *EUSAK propaganda operations, 13 July 1950–1 September 1952* (Far East United States Army forces, 3rd Historical Detachment, Tokyo, n.d.).

Nicholls, J. & W. Thompson. *Korea: the air war 1950–1953* (London, 1991).

Noble, H. *Embassy at war: an account of the early weeks of the Korean War*, F. Baldwin (ed.) (Seattle, 1975).

Pasley, V. *22 stayed* (London, 1955).

Pease, S. *Psywar: psychological warfare in Korea, 1950–1953* (Harrisburg, PA, 1992).

Pettee, G. *Psywar operations in the Korean War* (Operational Research Office, Fort McNair, Washington, 23 January 1951).

Politello, D. *Operation Grasshopper* (Wichita, KS, 1958).

Poole, W. *The history of the Joint Chiefs of Staff: the Joint Chiefs of Staff and national policy, 1950–1952*, vol. 4 (Joint Chiefs of Staff Directorate of History, Washington, DC, 1979).

Potter, A. *The Truman–MacArthur controversy: a study in political–military relations* (Thesis, US Army Command and General Staff College, 1972).

Reister, F. *Battle casualties and medical statistics: U.S. Army experience in the Korean War* (The Surgeon General, Department of the Army, Washington, DC, 1973).

Ridgway, M. *The Korean War: history and tactics* (New York, 1967).

Ridgway, M. *Soldier: the memoirs of Matthew B. Ridgway, as told to Harold H. Martin* (New York, 1956).

Roberston, W. *Counterattack on the Naktong, 1950* (US Army Command and General Staff College, Combat Studies Institute, Washington, DC, 1985).

Rush, E. *Military strategic lessons learned from the Korean War as they related to limited warfare* (US Army War College, Carlisle, PA, 1975).

Sarafan, B. Military government: Korea. *Far Eastern Survey* (20 November 1947).

Sawyer, R. *Military advisors in Korea: KMAG in peace and war* (Office of the Chief of Military History, Washington, DC, n.d.).

Schaller, R. *Douglas MacArthur: the Far Eastern general* (New York, 1989).

Schnabel, J. *Policy and direction: the first year* (US Army in the Korean War, Office of the Chief of Military History, Washington, DC, 1972).

Schnabel, J. & R. Watson. *The history of the Joint Chiefs of Staff: The Joint Chiefs of Staff and national policy*, vol. 3, *The Korean War* (Washington, DC, 1979).

Smith, R. *MacArthur in Korea: the naked emperor* (New York, 1982).

Soderbergh, P. *Women Marines in the Korean War era* (Westport, CN, 1994).

Spanier, J. *The Truman–MacArthur controversy and the Korean War* (Cambridge, MA, 1959).

Stanton, S. *America's tenth legion: X Corps in Korea, 1950* (Novato, CA, 1989).

Steuck, W., Jr. *The road to confrontation: American policy toward China and Korea, 1947–1950* (Chapel Hill, NC, 1981).

Stewart, R. *Staff operations: the X Corps in Korea, December 1950* (US Army Combat Studies Institute, Leavenworth, KS, 1991).

Thornton, J. *Believed to be alive* (Middlebury, VT, 1981).

Tomedi, R. *No bugles, no drums: an oral history of the Korean War* (New York, 1993).

United Nations Command. *United Nations civil affairs activities in Korea* (Tokyo, n.d.).

US Air Force, Aerospace Studies Institute, Air University. *Guerrilla warfare and airpower in Korea, 1950–1953* (Montgomery, Al, 1964).

US Army Center of Military History. *Korean conflict: a collection of historical manuscripts on the Korean campaign held by the U.S. Army Center of Military History* [9 reels] (Washington, DC, 1979).

US Congress, Senate, Committee on Armed Services and Committee on Foreign Relations. *Hearings . . . to conduct an inquiry into the military situation in the Far East and the facts surrounding the relief of General of the Army Douglas MacArthur from his assignments in that area* (Washington, DC, 1951).

US Congress, Senate, Committee on Armed Services and Committee on Foreign Relations. *The military situation in the Far East and the relief of General MacArthur* [8 reels with guide] (Washington, DC; Newark, DE, 1977).

US Department of the Army, Civil Affairs Division. *Liberated Korea: a summary* (Washington, DC, 1948?).

US Far East Command. *United Nations civil affairs activities in Korea* (Tokyo, 1952–4).

US Government. *Military situation in the Far East.* Hearings before the Committee on Armed Services and the Committee on Foreign Relations, US Senate, 82nd Congress, First Session (Washington, DC, 1951).

US Joint Chiefs of Staff. *Records of the Joint Chiefs of Staff*, Part 2 (1946–53). Microform: *The Far East* [13 reels with guide] (Washington, DC; Newark, DE, 1979–83).

(US Navy) CINCPACFLT. *Korean interim evaluation reports, 1950–1953* [6 reels] (Washington, DC, 1987).

US State Department. Communist war in POW camps (Washington, DC, 1953).

Weintraub, S. *War in the wards*, 2nd edn (Korea's unknown Battle in a Prisoner-of-War Hospital Camp, San Rafael, 1976).

Westover, J. *Combat support in Korea* (US Army Center of Military History, Washington, DC, 1987).

White, W. *Captives of Korea* (NY, Westport, 1955, 1978).

Wilkinson, A. *Up front, Korea* (New York, 1967).

Zellers, L. *In enemy hands: a prisoner in North Korea* (Lexington, KY, 1991).

Zimmerman, L. *Korean War logistics, Eighth United States Army* (US Army War College, Carlisle, PA, 1986).

US military, articles

Amody, F. Skyknights, nightmares, and MIGs. *American Aviation Historical Society Journal* (Winter 1989).

Avedon, H. War for men's minds. *Military Review* (March 1954).

Baldwin, R. Our blunder in Korea. *The Nation* (2 August 1947).

Blakeleu, M. Disaster along the Chongchon: intelligence breakdown in Korea. *Military Intelligence* (July–September 1992).

Boatner, H. The lessons of Koje-do. *Army* (March 1972).

Brinton, J. Small Korea is a big test. *New Republic* (14 March 1949).

Collins, J. A dismantled army goes to war. *Army* (December 1969).

Connor, A., Jr. The Army debacle in Korea, 1950, implications for today. *Parameters* (Summer 1992).

Connor, A., Jr. Breakout and pursuit: the drive from the Pusan Perimeter by the 1st Cavalry Division and Task Force Lynch. *Armor* (July–August 1993).

Cowdrey, A. Germ warfare and public health in the Korean conflict. *Journal of the History of Medicine and Allied Sciences* (April 1984).

Darragh, S. Hwanghae-do: the war of the donkeys. *Armor* (November 1984).

Flint, R. Task Force Smith and the 24th division: delay and withdrawal 5–19 July 1950. In C. E. Heller & W. A. Stofft (eds), *America's first battles 1776–1965* (1986).

Gardner, L. Review: Korea: the unknown war. *Journal of American History* (December 1991).

Gayle, J. Korea: honor without war. *Military Review* 31(10) (1951).

George, A. American policy-making and the North Korean aggression. *World Politics* (January 1955).

Gooodman, W. Review of television program: "Korea: the unknown war". *New York Times* (12 November 1990).

Huppert, H. Korean occupational problems. *Military Review* (December 1949).

Huston, J. Korea and logistics. *Military Review* (February 1957).

James, C. Command crisis: MacArthur and the Korean War. In *The Harmon memorial lectures in military history*, No. 240 (US Air Force Academy, 1982).

Jensen, A. To the Yalu. US Naval Institute *Proceedings* (February 1990).

Karsten, P. American POWs in Korea and the citizen soldier: triumph or disaster? *Military Affairs* (June 1966).

Kepley, D. The Senate and the great debate of 1951. *Prologue: Journal of the National Archives* (Winter 1982).

Kmiecik, R. Task Force Smith: a revised perspective. *Armor* (March–April 1990).

Kropf, R. US Air Force in Korea: problems that hindered the effectiveness of air power. *Air Power Journal* (Spring 1990).

Kwak, T.-H. *United States–Korean relations: a core interest analysis prior to United States intervention in the Korean War* (PhD thesis, Claremont Graduate School, 1969).

Larew, K. Inchon invasion not a stroke of genius or even necessary. *Army* (December 1988).

Lauterbach, R. Hodge's Korea. *Virginia Quarterly* (Summer 1947).

Liem, C. United States rule in Korea. *Far Eastern Survey* (6 April 1949).

Lofgren, C. Mr. Truman's war: a debate and its aftermath. *Review of Politics* (April 1969).

Lowe, P. An ally and a recalcitrant general: Douglas MacArthur and the Korean War. *English Historical Review* (July 1990).

Ludgvigsen, E. An arrogant display of strength: the failed bluff of Task Force Smith. *Army* (May 1992).

McClellan, D. Dean Acheson and the Korean War. *Political Science Quarterly* (March 1968).

McCune, G. Post-war government and politics in Korea. *The Journal of Politics* **9** (1947).

Malkin, L. Murderers of Koje-do! *MHQ: The Quarterly Journal of Military History* (Summer 1993).

Marion, F. The grand experiment: Detachment F's helicopter combat operations in Korea, 1950–1953. *Air Power History* (Summer 1993).

Marshall, T. Summary justice: the Negro in Korea. *Crisis* **58** (1951).

Matray, J. Truman's plan for victory: national self-determination and the thirty-eighth parallel decision in Korea. *Journal of American History* (September 1979).

Mayer, W. Brainwashing. In Symposium of the Neuropsychiatric Conference, Far East Command, US Army Hospital, 8167th Army Unit, Tokyo, Japan (3–4 May 1954).

Mentzer, R. Research from the battlefield: military history detachments in wartime Korea. *Army History* (Summer 1991).

Merloo, J. The crime of menticide. *American Journal of Psychiatry* **107** (1952).

Paschall, R. Special operations in Korea. *Conflict* **7** (1987).

Pirnie, B. The Inchon landing: how great was the risk? *Joint Perspectives* (Summer 1982).

Ridgway, M. Troop leadership at the operational level: the Eighth Army in Korea. *Military Review* (April 1990).

Schein, E., W. Hill, H. Williams & A. Lublin. Distinguishing characteristics of collaborators and resistors among American prisoners of war. *Journal of Abnormal and Social Psychology* **55** (1957).

Simmons, E. The Marines: survival and accommodation. In *Evolution of the American Military Establishment since World War II* (P. Schratz (ed.), New York, 1978).

Sinclair, D. The occupation of Korea – operations and accomplishments. *Military Review* (August 1947).

Skaggs, D. (originally R. Weinert). The KATUSA experiment: the integration of Korean nationals into the U.S. Army, 1950–1965. *Military Affairs* (April 1974).

Sutker, P. *et al*. Cognitive deficits and psychopathology among former prisoners of war and combat veterans of the Korean War. *American Journal of Psychiatry* (January 1991).

Tosch, D. Sustainment of the 24th Infantry Division in the Korean War: first 90 days vs. last 90 days. Student paper, US Army Command and General Staff College, 21 May 1986.

Truman, H. MacArthur was ready to risk general war. I was not. *U.S. News and World Report* (17 February 1956).

US Armed Forces Far East. The armistice negotiations, Korean conflict, 1951, 1952, and 1953. Typescript (n.d.).

Walker, S. Logistics of the Inchon landing. *Army Logistician* (July–August 1981).

West, P. Interpreting the Korean War. *American Historical Review* **94** (1989).

Wilz, J. The MacArthur hearings of 1951: the secret testimony. *Military Affairs* (December 1975).

Wilz, J. The MacArthur inquiry, 1951. In A. Schlesinger & R. Bruns (eds), *Congress investigates* (1975).

Winocur, G. The germ warfare statements: a synthesis of a method of and the extortion of false confessions. *Journal of Nervous and Mental Diseases* (July 1955).

Wubben, H. American prisoners of war in Korea: a second look at the "something new in history" theme. *American Quarterly* (Spring 1970).

Other UN forces

Anderson, E. *Banner over Pusan* (London, 1960).

Ayres, C. *The US Army and the development of the ROK Army: 1945–1950*. Report by the [US] Army–Air Force Center for Low-Intensity Conflict, Langley Air Force Base (Hampton, VA, n.d.).

Barclay, C. *The First Commonwealth Division* (Aldershot, UK, 1954).

Barker, A. *Fortune favors the brave* (London, 1974).

Bartlett, N. (ed.). *With the Australians in Korea*. (Australian War Memorial, Canberra, Australia, 1954).

Breen, B. *The battle of Maryang San* (Australian Army Training Command, Sydney, Australia, 1991).

Caine, M. *What it's all about* (London, 1992).

Canada, Army General Staff, Historical Section. *Canada's Army in Korea: a short official history* (Queen's Printers, Ottawa, 1956).

Canada, Army General Staff, Historical Section. *Canada's Army in Korea, the United Nations operations, 1950–1953, and their aftermath* (Ottawa, 1956).

Carew, T. *The Commonwealth at war* (London, 1967).

Clemov, C. *New Zealand, the Commonwealth, and the Korean War: a study in government policy and unofficial opinion* (Thesis, University of Auckland, 1967).

Davies, S. *In spite of dungeons* (London, 1955).

Dyal, S. *India's role in the Korean question* (New Delhi, 1959).

Farrar-Hockley, A. *The British part in the Korean War*, vol. 1, *A distant obligation* (HMSO, London, 1990), vol. 2, *An honorable discharge* (HMSO, London, 1994).

Farrar-Hockley, A. *The edge of the sword* (1954).

Fox, W. *History of the Korean War: inter-allied co-operation during combat operations* (Far East Command, Tokyo, n.d.).

Great Britain. *The experience of British prisoners of war in Korea* (HMSO, London, 1953).

Great Britain. *Report concerning the disappearance of two former Foreign Office officials* (HMSO, London, 1955).

Great Britain. *The Royal Ulster Rifles in Korea* (London, 1953).

Great Britain, Ministry of Defence. *Treatment of British prisoners of war in Korea* (London, 1955).

Grey, J. *The Commonwealth armies: an alliance study* (Manchester, 1989).

Grimsson, T. & E. Russell. *Canadian naval operations in the Korean War, 1950–1953* (Queen's Printer, Ottawa, 1965).

Heimsath, C. *India's role in the Korean War* (PhD thesis, Yale University, 1957).

Hennessy, P. *Never again: Britain, 1945–1951* (London, 1993).

Jones, F. *No rice for rebels* (London, 1956).

Kahn, E. *The peculiar war* (London, 1952).

Kaushik, R. *The crucial years of non-alignment: USA, the Korean War, and India* (New Delhi, 1972).

Lansdown, J. *With the carriers in Korea, 1950–1953* (London, 1992).

Lankford, D. *I defy* (London, 1954).

Linklater, E. *Our men in Korea* (HMSO, London, 1954).

McCormack, G. *Cold War, hot war: an Australian perspective on the Korean War* (Sydney, 1983).

MacDonald, C. *Britain and the Korean War* (Oxford, 1983).

McGibbon, I. *New Zealand and the Korean War*, vol. 1, *Politics and diplomacy* (Oxford, 1992).

Melady, J. *Canada's forgotten war* (Toronto, 1983).

Meyers, E. C. *Thunder in the morning calm: the Royal Canadian Navy in Korea, 1950–1953* (Toronto, 1997).

Motyn, J. & D. Kooiman. *A lamb to slaughter* (London, 1985).

Odgers, G. *Across the Parallel: the Australian 77th Squadron in the United States Air Force in the Korean War* (London, 1954).

Paik, S. *From Pusan to Panmunjom* (Washington, 1992).

Paik, S. *Reflections on the Korean War: the Army and I* (Seoul, 1989).

Shipster, J. *The die-hards in Korea* (London, 1994).

Skordiles, K. *Kagnew: the story of the Ethiopian fighters in Korea* (Tokyo, 1954).

Stairs, D. *The diplomacy of constraint: Canada, the Korean War, and the United States* (Toronto, 1974).

Stairs, D. *The role of Canada in the Korean War* (PhD thesis, University of Toronto, 1969).

Tae-Hoo, Y. *The Korean War and the United Nations* (Seoul, 1965).

Thorgrimsson, T. & E. Russell. *Canadian naval operations in Korean waters, 1950–1953* (Department of National Defence, Canadian Forces Headquarters, Naval Historical Section, Ottawa, 1965).

Tucker, E. & P. McGregor. *Per noctem per diem: the story of 24 Squadron, South African Air Force* (Pretoria, 1961).

United Kingdom, Ministry of Defence. *British Commonwealth naval operations, Korea, 1950–1953* (London, 1967).

United Nations Allies in the Korean War. *Army Information Digest* **8**(9) (Washington, DC, 1953).

Villansanta, J. *Dateline Korea: stories of the Philippine battalion* (Bacolod City, PI, 1954).

Walker, A. *A barren place: national servicemen in Korea, 1950–1954* (1994).

Wilson, D. *Lion over Korea: 77 Fighter Squadron RAAF, 1950–1953* (Canberra, 1994).

Wood, H. *Strange battleground: the operations in Korea and their effect on the defence policy of Canada* (Queen's Printer, Ottawa, 1966).

Other UN forces, articles

Boyle, P. Britain, America, and the transition from economic to military assistance, 1948–1951. *Journal of Contemporary History* (July 1987).

Boyle, P. Oliver Franks and the Washington Embassy, 1948–1952. In John Zametica, *British officials and British foreign policy, 1945–51* (1990).

Bullen, R. Great Britain, the United States and the Indian armistice resolution on the Korean War, November 1952. In *Aspects of Anglo–Korean relations, international studies* (London School of Economics, 1983).

Canada's Army in Korea. *Canada's Army Journal* **9** (1955).

Cooling, B. Allied interoperability in the Korean War. *Military Review* (June 1983).

Devaney, C. Know your allies. *Military Review* **32**(12) (1953).

Dockrill, M. The Foreign Office, Anglo–American relations and the Korean War, June 1950–June 1951. *International Affairs* (1986).

Dockrill, M. The Foreign Office, Anglo–American relations and the Korean War, July 1951–July 1953. In J. Cotton & I. Neary (eds), *The Korean War in history* (1989).

Farrar, P. Britain's proposal for a buffer zone south of the Yalu in November 1950. *Journal of Contemporary History* **18** (1983).

Farrar, P. A pause for peace negotiations: the British buffer zone plan of November 1950. In J. Cotton & I. Neary (eds), *The Korean War in history* (1989).

Foot, R. Anglo–American relations in the Korean crisis: the British effort to avert an expanded war, December 1950–January 1951. *Diplomatic History* (Winter 1986).

Gallaway, J. *The last call of the bugle: the long road to Kapyong* (1994).

Grey, J. Commonwealth prisoners of war and British policy during the Korean War. *Royal United Services Institute Journal* (Spring 1988).

Hall, T. KMAG and the 7th ROK Division. *Infantry* (November–December 1989).

Harbron, J. Royal Canadian Navy at peace, 1945–1955: the uncertain heritage. *Queen's Quarterly* **73** (1966).

Hausman, J. Formation of the Korean Army, 1945–1950, *Armed Forces and Society* (Summer 1997).

Hoare, J. British public opinion and the Korean War. *British Association on Korean Studies*, Papers 2 (1992).

Lee, D. Australia and Allied strategy in the Far East, 1952–1957. *Journal of Strategic Studies* (December 1993).

Lee, D. The national security planning and defence preparations of the Menzies government, 1950–1953. *War and Society* (October 1992).

Lee, Y. Birth of the Korean Army, 1945–1950: evaluation of the role of United States occupation forces. *Korean and World Affairs* **4** (1980).

Lowe, P. The frustrations of alliance, the United States and the Korean War, 1950–51. In J. Cotton & I. Neary (eds), *The Korean War in history* (Manchester, 1989).

Lowe, P. The significance of the Korean War in Anglo–American relations. In M. Dockrill & J. W. Young (eds), *The Korean War in history* (Manchester, 1989).

McGregor, P. History of No. 2 Squadron, SAAF in the Korean War. *Military History Journal* (June 1978).

Merrill, J. The Chedu-do rebellion. *Journal of Korean Studies* **2** (1982).

Ozselcuk, N. The Turkish Brigade in the Korean War, 25th June 1950–27 July 1953. *Review Internationale d'Histoire Militaire* **46** (1980).

Prince, R. The limits of constraint: Canadian–American relations and the Korean War, 1950–1951. *Journal of Canadian Studies/Revue d'etudes Canadiennes* (Winter 1992–3).

Prince, S. The Royal Navy's contribution to the Korean War. *Journal of Strategic Studies* (June 1994).

Ra, J.-I. Special relationship at war: the Anglo-American relationship during the Korean War. *Journal of Strategic Studies* (September 1984).

Ra, J.-I. Political settlement in Korea: British views and policies, Autumn 1950. In J. Cotton & I. Neary (eds), *The Korean War in history* (Manchester, 1989).

Ramsey, R. The Columbian battalion in Korea and Suez. *Journal of Inter-American Studies* (October 1967).

Smith, H. The BBC television newsreel and the Korean War. *Historical Journal of Film, Radio and Television* **8** (1988).

Stairs, D. Canada and the Korean War: the boundaries of diplomacy. *International Perspective* **6** (1972).

Steinberg, B. The Korean War: a case study in Indian neutralism. *Orbis* (Winter 1965).

The Communist side

Atkins, E., H. Griggs & R. Sessums. *North Korean logistics and methods of accomplishment* (Baltimore, Johns Hopkins University, Operations Research Office, for US Army, 1951).

Bacteriological warfare. Special edition of *Chinese Medical Journal* (English language) (Peking, 1952).

Bermudez, J. *North Korean Special Forces* (New York, 1988, 1998).

Biderman, A. *Communist techniques of coercive interrogation*, Lackland Air Force Base (Lackland, TX, 1956).

Biderman, A. & H. Zimmer (eds). *The manipulation of human behavior* (Washington, DC, 1961).

Blake, G. *No other choice* (London, 1990).

Bong, B. *Kim Il Sung* [2 vols] (Pyongyang/Tokyo, Beruit, Lebanon, 1973).

Bradbury, W. *Mass behavior in battle and captivity: the Communist soldier in the Korean War*. S. Meyers & A. Biderman (eds), *The Manipulation of Human Behaviour* (Chicago, 1968).

Brooks, R. Russian air power in the Korean War, the impact of tactical intervention and strategic threat on United States objectives. ([US] Air War College thesis, 1964).

Burchett, W. *This monstrous war* (London, 1953).

Burchett, W. & A. Winnington. *Koje unscreened* (London, 1953).

Chen, J. *China's road to the Korean War: the making of the Sino–American confrontation* (Chicago, 1994).

Chinese People's Committee for World Peace. *Statements by two captured US Air Force officers on their participation in germ warfare in Korea* (Peking, 1952).

Christiansen, T. Threats, assurances, and the last chance for peace: the lessons of Mao's Korean War telegrams. *International Security* (Summer 1992).

Commission on International Association of Democratic Lawyers report on war crimes in Korea (10 April 1952).

Cookridge, E. *George Blake: double agent* (London, 1970).

Cutforth, R. *Korean reporter* (London, 1955).

Dae-Sook, S. *Kim Il Sung: The North Korean Leader* (New York, 1988).

Democratic People's Republic of Korea. *Documents and materials exposing the instigators of the civil war in Korea: documents from the archives of the Rhee Syngman government* (Pyongyang, 1950).

Democratic People's Republic of Korea. *Facts tell* (Pyongyang, 1960).

Democratic People's Republic of Korea. *History of the just fatherland liberation war of the Korean people* (1961).

Democratic People's Republic of Korea. *History of the just fatherland war of the Korean people* (Social Science Institute Korea, 1961).

Democratic People's Republic of Korea. *Panmunjom* (Pyongyang, 1960).

Democratic People's Republic of Korea. *The U.S. imperialists started the Korean War* (Pyongyang, 1977).

Democratic People's Republic of Korea, Department of Cultural Relations with Foreign Countries, Ministry of Culture and Propaganda. *Depositions of nineteen captured US airmen on their participation in germ warfare in Korea* (Pyongyang, 1954).

Felton, M. *Korea: how to bring the boys home* (London, 1952).

Felton, M. *That's why I went* (London, 1953).

Felton, M. *What I saw in Korea* (Watford, 1952).

George, A. *The Chinese Communist army in action: the Korean War and its aftermath* (New York, 1967).

Goncharov, S., W. Lewis & X. Litai. *Uncertain partners: Stalin, Mao, and the Korean War* (Stanford, CA, 1993).

Griffith, S. *The Chinese People's Liberation Army* (New York, 1967).

Halliday, J. & B. Cumings. *Korea: the unknown war* (New York, 1988).

Hong Xuezhi. *Kangmei yuanchao zhanzheng huiyi* (Recollections of the War to Resist America and Assist Korea) (People's Liberation Army Literature Press, Beijing, 1990).

Jencks, H. *From muskets to missiles: politics and professionalism in the Chinese army, 1945–1981* (Boulder, CO; Westview, CT, 1982).

Jian, C. *China's Road to the Korean War: the making of the Sino–American confrontation* (New York, 1994).

Kahn, L. *et al. A study of North Korean and Chinese soldiers' attitudes toward the Korean War* (Baltimore, Operations Research Office, 1952).

Khrushchev, N. The Korean War. *Ogonek* (January 1991).

Kiernan, B. (ed.). *Burchett: reporting the other side of the world* (London, 1986).

Kim, C.-K. *The Korean War* (Seoul, 1973).

Lim, U. [pseud.]. *The founding of a dynasty in North Korea: an authentic bibliography of Kim Il Sung* (Seoul, 1982).

McMichael, S. *An historical perspective on light infantry* (US Army Command and General Staff College, Combat Studies Institute, Leavenworth, KS, 1987).

Meyers, S. & A. Biderman (eds). *Mass behavior in battle and captivity: the Communist soldier in the Korean War* (Baltimore, Operations Research Office, 1968).

Meyers, S. & W. Bradbury. *The political behavior of Korean and Chinese prisoners of war in the Korean conflict: an historical analysis* (Baltimore, Operations Research Office, 1958).

Moakley, G. *US Army Code of Conduct training: let the POWs tell their stories* (Thesis, US Army Command and General Staff College, Leavenworth, KS, 1976).

Newton, V. *The butcher's embrace: the Philby conspirators in Washington* (London, 1991).

Pak, H. *Documents and materials exposing the instigators of the civil war in Korea* (DPRK Ministry of Foreign Affairs, Pyongyang, 1950).

Pratt, Sir J. *Korea: the lie that led to war* (London, 1951).

Pritt, D. *Light on Korea* (London, 1950).

Pritt, D. *New light on Korea* (London, 1951).

Peng Dehuai. *Memoirs of a Chinese marshal: the autobiographical notes of Peng Dehuai (1898–1974)* (Beijing, 1984).

Petrov, V. Soviet role in the Korean War confirmed: secret documents declassified. *Journal of Northeast Asian Studies* (Fall 1994).

Preston, H. *Study of ineffective soldier performance under fire in Korea 1951* (Washington, DC, Operations Research Office, 1954).

van Ree, E. *Socialism in one zone: Stalin's policy in Korea, 1945–1947* (Oxford, 1989).

Ryan, M. *Chinese attitudes toward nuclear weapons: China and the United States during the Korean War* (Armonk, NY, 1989).

Scalapino, R. & C.-Sik Lee. *Communism in Korea* [2 vols] (Berkeley, CA, 1972).

Shrader, C. *Communist logistics in the Korean War* (Westport, CT, 1995).

Shu-gang, Z. *Mao's military romanticism: China and the Korean War, 1950–1953* (Lawrence, KS, 1995).

Simmons, R. *The strained alliance: Peking, Pyongyang, Moscow, and the politics of the Korean civil war* (New York, 1975).

Siqi, G. & Li Zhimin (eds). *Zhongguo Renmin Zhiyianjun Kangmei Yuanchao Zhanaheng Ahengzhi Gongquo Zongie* (A summary of the CPV Political Work in the War to Resist U.S. aggression and aid Korea) (Beijing, People's Liberation Army Press, 1985).

Souris, P. The transfer of US Korean War POWs to the Soviet Union. Working papers (Joint Support Commission Support Branch, Research and Analysis Division, US POW/MIA Office, Washington, DC, 1993).

Spurr, R. *Enter the dragon: China's undeclared war against the U.S. in Korea, 1950–1951* (New York, 1988).

Stone, I. *The hidden history of the Korean War* (New York, 1952).

Suh, D.-S. *The Korean Communist movement, 1918–1948* (Princeton, 1967).

Sung, K. I. *Kim Il Sung's works*, vol. 6 (Pyongyang, 1981).

Taylor, R. *MiG operations in Korea* ([US] Air University, Colorado Springs, CO, 1986).

Tunstall, J. *I fought in Korea* (London, 1953).

United Nations Command. *The Communist war in POW camps* (New York, 1953).

US Air Force, Far East Air Force. *Intelligence Roundup* (Issues, Tokyo, 1951–4).

US Army. *Handbook on the Chinese Communist army* (Washington, DC, 1952).

US Army. *History of the north Korean army* (Washington, DC, 1952).

US Army, Far East Command. *Order of battle handbook: Chinese Communist forces, Korea and the North Korean army* (Far East Command and Eighth US Army, G2, Tokyo, 1955).

Yin-Hsieh, C. *The Truman administration's military budgets during the Korean War* (PhD thesis, University of California, Berkeley, 1978).

Zang, S. *Mao's Military Romanticism: China and the Korean War, 1950–1953* (Lawrence, Kansas, 1995).

Zelman, W. *Chinese intervention in the Korean War: a bilateral failure of deterrence* (1967).

Zong-hong, S. & M. Zhaohui *et al. Zhongguo renmin Zhiguanjun Kangmei yuanchao zhanshi* (A history of the war to resist America and assist Korea by the Chinese People's Volunteers) (Beijing, 1988).

Zhongguo renmin Zhiyuanjum knagMei yuanChao (A battle history of resistance to America and aid to Korea by the Chinese People's Volunteer Army) (Beijing, 1998).

The Communist side, articles

Biderman, A. Communist attempts to elicit false confessions from Air Force prisoners of war. *Bulletin*, New York Academy of Medicine, no. 33 (1957).

Biderman, A. Effects of Communist indoctrination attempts: some comments based on Air Force prisoner of war study. *Social Problems* **6**(4) (1959).

Bo, Y. The making of the "lean to one side" decision. Trans. Zhai Qiamg. *Chinese Historians* (Spring 1992).

Chai, C. & Zhao Yongtian. *Banmendian tanpan* (The Panmunjom negotiations) (People's Liberation Army Press, 1989).

Christiansen, T. Threats, assurances, and the last chance for peace: the lessons of Mao's Korean War telegrams. *International Security* (Summer 1992).

Chen, J. Why and how China entered the Korean War: in light of new evidence. In The Korean War: an assessment of the historical record, Symposium, Georgetown University, 24–25 July 1995.

Cohen, W. Conversations with Chinese friends: Zhou Enlai's associates reflect on Chinese American relations in the 1940s and the Korean War. *Diplomatic History* **11**(2) (1987).

Ding, X. *et al.* Recalling the Northeast Bureau's Special Office in North Korea during the War of Liberation in the Northeast. *Zhonggong dangshi ziliao* (Materials of CCP History, March 1986).

Dokuchayev, A. The time has come to tell the story: it was Korea. *Krasnaya zvezda* (25 June 1989). Trans. *JPRS Report Soviet Union Military Affairs*, JPRS-UMA-89-019 (31 July 1989).

Dokuchayev, A. Missile ambushes. *Ibid.* (13 February 1991).

Du Ping. Zai zhiyuanjun zongbu: Du Ping huiyilu (My days at the headquarters of the Chinese People's Volunteers: Du Ping's memoirs) (People's Liberation Army Press, 1988).

Entry into the Korean War remembered. *Beijing Review* (9 November 1990).

Farrar-Hockley, A. A reminiscence of the Chinese People's Volunteers in the Korean War. *China Quarterly* (June 1984).

Halliday, J. Air operations in Korea: the Soviet side of the story. In *A revolutionary war: Korea and the transformation of the postwar world* (1993). Papers originally presented at the 15th Military History Symposium, USAF Academy, 14–16 April 1962.

Hao Yufan & Zhai Ahihai. China's decision to enter the Korean War: history revisited. *China Quarterly* (March 1990).

Harris, W. Chinese nuclear doctrine: the decade prior to weapons development (1945–1955). *China Quarterly* (January–March 1965).

Hitchcock, W. North Korea jumps the gun. *Current History* (March 1951).

Hunt, M. Beijing and the Korean crisis, June 1950–June 1951. *Political Science Quarterly* (Fall 1992).

Iriye, A. Introduction: the Korean War in the domestic context. *Journal of American–East Asian Relations* (Spring 1993).

Jeon, H. & G. Kahng. The Shtykov diaries: new evidence on Soviet policy in Korea. *CWIHPB* (Winter 1995).

Jian, C. China's changing aims during the Korean War, 1950–1951. *Journal of American–East Asian Relations* (Spring 1992).

Jian, C. China's road to the Korean War. *CWIHPB* (Winter 1995).

Johnson, H. *I appeal* (London, 1952).

Jolidan, I. Soviet interrogation of U.S. POWs in the Korean War. *CWIHPB* (Winter 1995).

Kim, H.-J. China's non-involvement in the origins of the Korean War: a critical reassessment of the traditionalist and revisionist literature. In J. Cotton & I. Neary (eds), *The Korean War in history* (Atlantic Highlands, NY, 1989).

Kim, H.-J. An inquiry into the origins of the Korean War – a critique of the revisionist view. *East Asian Review* (Summer 1994).

Li, X. & G. Tracy, trans. Mao's telegrams during the Korean War, October 1950–December 1950. *Chinese Historians* (Fall 1992).

Lineer, T. Evolution of Cold War rules of engagement: the Soviet combat role in the Korean War. (US Army Command and General Staff College thesis, Leavenworth, KS, 1993).

McCarthy, M. Uncertain enemies: Soviet pilots in the Korean War. *Airpower Historian* (Spring 1997).

McCormack, G. Korea: Wilfred Burchett's thirty years' war. In B. Kiernan (ed.), Burchett: reporting the other side of the world (1986).

Mansourov, A. Did conventional deterrence work? Why the Korean War did not erupt in the summer of 1949. CWIHP conference paper, Hong Kong, January 1996.

Mansourov, A. Stalin, Mao, Kim, and China's decision to enter the Korean War, September 16–October 15, 1950: new evidence from the Russian archives. *CWIHPB* (Winter 1995).

Monat, P. Russians in Korea: the hidden bases. *Life* (27 June 1960).

Park, M. Stalin's foreign policy and the Korean War. *Korea Observer* (Autumn 1994).

Petrov, V. Soviet role in the Korean War confirmed: secret documents declassified. *Journal of Northeast Asian Studies* (Fall 1994).

Ruban, S. Soviet fliers in the Korean sky. Unpublished paper in Russian and translated (US Department of Defense, MIA/POW Office, Washington, DC, n.d.).

Simmons, R. The Communist side: an exploratory sketch. In F. Heller (ed.), *The Korean War* (Lawrence, KS, 1977).

Slusser, R. Soviet Far Eastern policy, 1945–1950: Stalin's goals in Korea. In Y. Nagai and A. Iriye (eds), *The Origins of the Cold War in Asia* (Englewood Cliffs, NJ, 1977).

Smorchkov, A. Heroic pilot recalls his days in Korea. Radio Moscow international broadcast Service, 11 June 1990, trans. in FBIS SOV-90-121 (22 June 1990).

Soh, J. The role of the Soviet Union in preparation for the Korean War. *Journal of Korean Affairs* (January 1974).

Thach, J., Jr. Modernization and conflict: Soviet military assistance to the PRC, 1950–1960. *Military Review* (January 1978).

United Nations Command. The Communist war in POW camps (Tokyo, 1953).

Weathersby, K. Korea, 1949–50: to attack or not to attack? Stalin, Kim Il Sung and the prelude to war. *CWIHP* (Spring 1995).

Weathersby, K. Soviet aims in Korea and the outbreak of the Korean War, 1945–1950: new evidence from the Russian archives. Working Paper of the Cold War International History Project, Woodrow Wilson International Center for Scholars (1993).

Weathersby, K. The Soviet role in prolonging the Korean War. In The Korean War: an assessment of the historical record, Symposium, Georgetown University, 24–25 July 1995.

Weathersby, K. The Soviet role in the early phase of the Korean War: new documentary evidence. *Journal of American–East Asian Relations* (Winter, 1993).

Xiaobing, Li, Wang Xi & Chen Jian, trans. Mao's dispatch of Chinese troops to Korea: forty-six telegrams July–October 1950. *Chinese Historians* (Spring 1992).

Xu, Li. The Chinese forces and their casualties in the Korean War: facts and statistics. Trans. Li Xiaobing. *Chinese Historians* (Fall 1993).

Yi, K.-T. It took Mao Zedong three agonizing, sleepless nights to decide to dispatch troops to the Korean War. (US) Foreign Broadcast Information Service, *FBIS Daily Report – East Asia* (29 March 1991).

Yufan, H. & Zhai Ahihai. China's decision to enter the Korean War: history revisited. *China Quarterly* (March 1990).

Zaloga, S. The Russians in MiG Alley. *Air Force Magazine* (February 1994).

Zhang, S. China's military strategy during the Korean War. In The Korean War: an assessment of the historical record, Symposium, Georgetown University, 24–25 July 1995.

Air and naval

Alling, F. *History of modification of USAF aircraft for atomic weapon delivery 1948–1954* (Historical Division, Office of Information Services, Air Matériel Command, February 1955).

Breuer, W. *Shadow warriors: the covert war in Korea* (1996).

Cardwell, T. III. *Command structure for theater warfare: the quest for unity of command* (Air University Press, Montgomery, AL, 1984).

Carter, G. *Some historical notes on air interdiction in Korea* (Rand Corporation, Santa Monica, CA, 1966).

Crews, T. Thunderbird through Ripper: joint operations in Korea, 25 January–31 March 1951 (US Army War College, Carlisle, PA, 1991).

Degovanni, G. Air Force support of Army ground operations: lessons learned during World War II, Korea, and Vietnam (US Army War College, Carlisle, PA, 1989).

Dews, E. & F. Kozaczka. *Air interdiction: lessons from past campaigns* (Rand Corporation, Santa Monica, CA, 1981).

Dixon, J. (ed.). *The American military and the Far East: proceedings of the Ninth Military History Symposium, United States Air Force Academy, 1–3 October 1980* (Office of Air Force History, Colorado Springs, CO., 1980).

Evans, D. *Sabre jets over Korea: a first-hand account* (1984).

Farmer, J. & M. Strumwasser. *The evolution of the Airborne Forward Air Controller: an analysis of Mosquito operations in Korea* (Rand, 1967).

Futrell, R. *Ideas, concepts, doctrine: basic thinking in the United States Air Force, 1907–1960* (Air University Press, Washington, 1989).

Futrell, R. *The United States Air Force in Korea*, rev. ed. (Office of Air Force History, 1983).

Hallion, R. *The naval air war in Korea* (Baltimore, 1986).

Hightower, C. *The history of the United States Airborne Forward Air Controller in World War II, the Korean War, and the Vietnam conflict* (US Army Command and General Staff College, Leavenworth, KS, 1984).

Jackson, R. *Air war over Korea* (New York, 1973).

Kirtland, M. *Air University Review index*, 1 May 1947 through January–March 1987 (Air University Press, Montgomery, AL, 1990).

Kirtland, M. *Airpower Journal index, 1987–1991* (Air University Press, Montgomery, AL, 1993).

Kohn, R. & J. Harahan (eds). *Air interdiction World War II, Korea, and Vietnam: an interview with General Earle E. Partridge, General Jacob E. Smart, General John W. Vogt, Jr.* (Office of Air Force History, Washington, DC, 1986).

Kohn, R. & J. Harahan (eds). *Air superiority in World War II and Korea: an interview with General James Ferguson, General Robert M. Lee, General William W. Momyer, and General Elwood R. Quesada* (Office of Air Force History, 1983).

Maurer, M. *USAF credits for destruction of enemy aircraft, Korean War.* USAF Historical Study No. 81 (Washington, DC, 1963).

Meilinger, P. *Hoyt S. Vandenberg: the life of a general* (Bloomington, IN, 1989).

Merrill, F. *A study of the aerial interdiction of railways during the Korean War* (US Army Command and General Staff College, Leavenworth, KS, 1965).

Millar, W. *Valley of the shadow* (New York, 1955).

Momyer, W. *Air power in three wars: WWII, Korea, Vietnam* (Department of the Air Force, 1978).

Nichols, J. & W. Thompson. *Korea: the air war, 1950–1953* (New York, 1991).

Parrish, N. Hoyt S. Vandenberg: building the new Air Force. In J. Frisbee (ed.), *Makers of the United States Air Force* (Office of Air Force History, Washington, DC, 1987).

Scutts, J. *Air war over Korea* (London, 1982).

Sherwood, J. *Officers in flight suits: the story of American Air Force fighter pilots in the Korean War* (New York, 1996).

Stewart, J. *Airpower: the decisive force in Korea* (Princeton, 1957).

Taylor, R. *MiG operations in Korea* ([USAF] Air War College, Air University, Montgomery, AL, 1986).

Utz, C. *Assault from the sea: the amphibious landing at Inchon* (US Naval Historical Center, Washington, DC, 1994).

Air and naval, articles

Almody, F. We got ours at night: the story of the Lockheed F-94 Starfire in combat. *American Aviation Historical Society Journal* **27** (1982).

Almody, F. Skynights, nightmares and MiGs. *Ibid.* (Winter 1989).

Benson, L. The USAF's Korean War recruiting rush . . . and the great tent city at Lackland Air Force Base. *Aerospace Historian* **25** (1978).

Bowers, R. Korea: proving ground for combat air transportation. *Defence Management Journal* (July 1976).

Brooks, J. That day over the Yalu. *Aerospace Historian* (June 1975).

Cable, D. Air support in the Korean War. *Aerospace History* (Summer 1969).

Calingaert, D. Nuclear weapons and the Korean War. *Journal of Strategic Studies* (June 1988).

Cline, T. Forward air control in the Korean War. *American Aviation Historical Society Journal* (Fall 1976).

Cole, J., Jr. Lamplighters and gypsies. *Aerospace Historian* (March 1973).

Dokuchayev, A. The time has come to tell the story: it was in Korea. *Krasnaya zvezda* (25 June 1989).

Fithian, B. The F-94 first kill in Korea. *Navigator* (Winter 1981).

Fogleman, R. Modernization for Korean War stopped post–WWII reduction, made US ready. *Officer* (December 1991).

Futrell, R. A case study: USAF intelligence in the Korean War. In W. Hitchcock (ed.), *The intelligence revolution: a historical perspective.* Proceedings of the Thirteenth Military History Symposium, US Air Force Academy, October 1988 (Office of Air Force History, 1991).

Futrell, R. The Korean War. In A. Goldberg, *A history of the United States Air Force, 1907–1957* (1957).

Futrell, R. Tactical employment of strategic airpower in Korea. *Airpower Journal* (Winter 1988).

Halliday, J. A secret war: US and Soviet air forces clashed directly in the Korean War. *Far Eastern Economic Review* (22 April 1993).

Hinkle, C. Air sanctuaries in limited war: a Korean War case study ([US] Air War College thesis, 1985).

Holm, S. Yalu River raider. *Air Progress* (September 1984).

Jamieson, T. Nightmare of the Korean hills: Douglas B-26 Invader operations in the Korean War, 1950–1953. *American Aviation Historical Society Journal* (Summer 1989).

Junji, T. The Soviet Air Force participated in the war. In K. Chullbaum (ed.), *The Truth about the Korean War. Truth and testimonies* (Seoul, 1991).

Kirtland, M. Planning air operations: lessons from Operation Strangle in the Korean War. *Airpower Journal* (Summer 1992).

Kropf, R. The U.S. Air Force in Korea: problems that hindered the effectiveness of air power. *Air Power Journal* (Spring 1990).

Kuehl, D. Refighting the last war: electronic warfare and the U.S. Air Force operations in the Korean War. *Journal of Military History* (January 1992).

Launius, R. MATS and the Korean airlift. *Airlift* (Summer 1990).

Lobov, G. Blank spots in history: in the skies of North Korea. *Aviatsiya i kosmonavtika* (October 1990).

Lobov, G. U.S. air actions in Korea recalled. Moscow radio broadcast in Korean (2 September 1991) FBIX SOV-91-97 (10 October 1991).

Lobov, G. V nebe Severnoy Koreiji (In the sky of North Korea). *Aviatsiya i kosmonavtika* (Aviation and Cosmonautics) (October 1990).

McLaren, D. Air support in Korea: Mustang style. *Aerospace Historian* (June 1986).

McLaren, D. Mustangs in aerial combat: the Korean War. *American Aviation Historical Society Journal* (Summer 1985).

Marion, F. The grand experiment: Detachment F's helicopter combat operations in Korea, 1950–1953. *Air Power History* (Summer 1993).

Millett, A. Korea, 1950–1953. In B. Cooling (ed.), *Case studies in close air support* (Office of Air Force History, 1990).

Milton, T. The equalizer in Korea. *Air Force Magazine* (October 1991).

Mo, K. The implications of the sea war in Korea (from the standpoint of the Korean Navy). *Naval War College Review* (Summer 1967).

Newman, P. The Royal Canadian Navy. *United States Naval Institute Proceedings* **80** (1954).

Poe, B. Korean War combat support: a lieutenant's journal. *Air Force Journal of Logistics* (Fall 1989).

Reid, W. Tactical air in limited war. *Air University Quarterly Review* (Spring 1956).

Risedorph, G. Mosquito. *American Aviation Historical Society Journal* (Spring 1979).

Rivera, M. Airlift of cargo and passengers in the Korean War. *Air Force Journal of Logistics* (Fall 1989).

Rosenberg, D. U.S. nuclear stockpile, 1945–1950. *Bulletin of the Atomic Scientists* (May 1982).

Yaffe, M. A higher priority than the Korean War! The crash programs to modify the bombers for the bomb. *Diplomacy and Statecraft* (July 1994).

Zaloga, S. The Russians in MiG Alley. *Air Force History Magazine* (February 1991).

Zhang, X. China and the air war in Korea, 1950–1953. *The Journal of Military History* (April 1998).

Home fronts

Axelsson, A. *Restrained response: American novels of the Cold War and Korea, 1945–1960* (NY, 1990).

Caridi, R. *The Korean War and American politics: the Republican Party as a case study* (Philadelphia, 1969).

Condit, D. *The test of war 1950–1953*, vol. 2, *History of the Office of the Secretary of Defense* (Washington, DC, 1988).

DiCola, L. *The Korean War as seen by the Chicago Tribune, the New York Times, and The Times of London* (PhD thesis, Kent State University, 1981).

Donovan, R. *Tumultuous years: the presidency of Harry S. Truman, 1949–1953* (New York, 1982).

Edwards, P. M. *A guide to films on the Korean War* (1997).

Gietschier, S. *Limited war and the home front: Ohio during the Korean War* (PhD thesis, Ohio State University, 1977).

Mantell, E. *Opposition to the Korean War: a study in American dissent* (PhD thesis, New York University, 1973).

Notopoulos, J. *The influence of the principles of the containment policy upon the military strategy of the Korean War* (PhD thesis, The American University, 1964).

Osmer, H. *Religious journalism and the Korean War* (Washington, DC, 1980).

Riggs, J. *Congress and the conduct of the Korean War* (PhD thesis, Purdue University, 1972).

Titus, J. (ed.). *The home front and war in the twentieth century: the American experience in comparative perspective*. Proceedings of the Tenth Military History Symposium, 20–22 October 1982, US Air Force Academy (Colorado Springs, CO., 1984).

Home fronts, articles

Banks, S. The Korean conflict. *Negro History Bulletin* **6** (1973).

Caine, P. The United States in Korea and Vietnam: a study in public opinion. *Air University Quarterly Review* (November–December 1968).

Caridi, R. The GOP and the Korean War. *Pacific Historical Review* **37** (1968).

Elowitz, L. & J. Spanier. Korea and Vietnam: limited war and the American political system. *Orbis* (Summer 1974).

Flynn, G. The draft and college deferments during the Korean War. *Historian* (May 1988).

Hamby, A. Public opinion: Korea and Vietnam. *Wilson Quarterly* (Summer 1978).

Herzon, F. *et al.* Personality and public opinion: the case of authoritarianism, prejudice and support for the Korean Wars. *Polity* **11**(1) (1978).

Lofgren, C. "Mr. Truman's war": a debate and its aftermath. *Review of Politics* (April 1969).

McClellan, D. Dean Acheson and the Korean War. *Political Science Quarterly* (March 1968).

Mee, C. Are you telling us that it is an utterly useless war? *Horizon* (Winter 1976).

Mueller, J. Trends in popular support for the wars in Korea and Vietnam. *American Political Science Review* **65**(2) (1971).

Perkins, D. Dissent in time of war. *Virginia Quarterly* (Spring 1974).

Ruddick, P. Stopping the war: the Eisenhower administration and the search for an armistice in Korea. *Paradigms* (Spring 1992).

Spanier, J. The Korean War as a civil war. *Orbis* (Winter 1976).

Suchman, E., A. Rose, K. Goldsen & R. Williams. Attitudes toward the Korean War. *Public Opinion Quarterly* (Summer 1953).

Thomas, J. The collapse of the defensive war argument. *Military Review* (May 1973).

Toner, J. American society and the American way of war: Korea and beyond. *Parameters* (May 1981).

Wilz, J. The Korean War and American society. In F. Heller (ed.), *The Korean War: a 25-year perspective* (Lawrence, KS, 1977).

Additional Works (unpublished)

Soviet direction of Korean War and prisoner of war control. 14 April 1955. Dwight Eisenhower Papers, White House National Security Papers, 1948–1961, OCB Central File Series, ACT 387.4 Korea (4-14-55), Eisenhower Presidential Library (cited in T. Lineer, Evolution of Cold War rules of engagement (US Army Command and General Staff College thesis, 1993).

Baum, K. US withdrawal decision from South Korea, 1945–1949. (PhD thesis, State University of New York at Buffalo, 1984).

CIA 2-50. Review of the World Situation. Published 15 February 1950. Papers of Harry S. Truman, President Secretary's File, Intelligence File, Box 257, Harry S. Truman Presidential Library (cited in Lineer).

CIA 6-50. Review of the World Situation, published 14 June 1950. *Ibid.*

CIA 8-50. Review of the World Situation, August 1950. Box 1. *Ibid.*

PRE 18-50. Current capabilities of the Northern Korean regime. *Ibid.*

Critical situations in the Far East. 12 October 1950. Box 267. *Ibid.*

Threat of Soviet intervention in Korea. 14 October 1950. *Ibid.*

International implications of maintaining a beachead in South Korea. Special Estimate 1. 1 January 1951. Truman Papers, Records of the National Security Council, CIA File, Box 258.

Current Soviet activities with particular reference to the Far East. Special intelligence estimate (sanitized copy). 6 April 1951. Box 257. *Ibid.*

The conflict in Korea: events prior to the attack of June 25, 1950. Selected records relating to the Korean War, US policy in Korea. June 1951. Box 2. *Ibid.*

Ibid. July 1951. *Ibid.*

United States policy regarding Korea, Pt. III: December 1945–June 1950. Box 1. *Ibid.*

Minutes of the 34th, 40th, 41st, 50th, 104th, 144th meetings of the National Security Council. *Ibid.*, National Security Staff Papers 1948–1961. Box 1. *Ibid.*

National Security Council 48/5. The position of the United States with respect to Asia. 23 December 1949. *Ibid.*

National Security Council 81/1. United States courses of action with respect to Korea. HST Papers. 9 September 1950. Box 267.

National Security Council 100. Recommended policies and actions in light of the grave world situation. 11 January 1951. *Ibid.*

National Security Council. Current Policies of the Government of the United States of America relating to national security, vol. 1, pt. 3. Far East and Communist China. 1 November 1952. *Ibid.*

American Institutes for Research. U.S. military response to overseas insurgencies. By Carl Rosenthal (Kensington, Maryland, n.d.).

Eaddy, R. New Zealand in the Korean War: a study in official government policy (Master's thesis, University of Otago, 1983).

Hoag, C. American military government in Korea, 1941–1946 (Office of the Chief of Military History, 1970).

Huh, M. La constance de l'unite nationale coreene: essai d'une novelle interpretation de la guerre de Coree (PhD thesis, Ecole des Hautes Etudes en Science Sociales, 1988).

Kang, H. The United States military government in Korea, 1945–1948 (PhD thesis, University of Cincinnati, 1970).

Kim, C. U.S. withdrawal decision from South Korea, 1945–1949 (PhD thesis, State University of New York at Buffalo, 1984).

Kim, C. The role of the USSR and China in the outbreak of the Korean War. Paper presented at seminar at the University of California, Berkeley, November 1994.

Kim, G.-y. Foreign intervention in Korea 1950–1954 (PhD thesis, Oxford University, 1988).

Kim, J. The study of Communist struggle pattern in Korea 1945–1950: with emphasis on armed struggle (PhD thesis, Kyong Hee University, 1972).

Kim, J. K. The evolution of the Korean War and the dynamics of Chinese entry (PhD thesis, University of Hawaii, 1996).

Kim, J.-m. (Shomei Ichikawa). A study of the Korean War and the United Nations (PhD thesis, Meiji University, 1965).

Kim, M.-w. Prisoners of war as a major problem of the Korean armistice, 1953 (PhD thesis, New York University, 1960).

Kim, R. (Kim Ung-taek). Sino–Soviet Dispute and North Korea (PhD thesis, University of Pennsylvania, 1967).

Kim, T.-h. Die Vereinten Nationen and ihre kollektiven sicherheitsmassnahme: studie under die UN-aktion gegen die intervention der VR China inm Koreakrieg (The United Nations and collective security: a study of UN action against the intervention of the People's Republic of China in the Korean War) (PhD thesis, Munich University, 1968).

Kim, Y. Power and prestige: explaining American intervention in the Korean War (PhD thesis, University of Virginia, 1996).

Lee, C.-s. Communist satellite politics: the case study of the Korean War (1966).

Lee, K. A study of the United Nations' Commission for the Unification and Rehabilitation of Korea: the Cold War and the United Nations subsidiary organ (PhD thesis, University of Pittsburgh, 1974).

Lee, S. A study on the origins of the Korean War in connection with Sino–Soviet confrontation (Korea University, 1980).

Lineer, T. Evolution of Cold War rules of engagement. the Soviet combat role in the Korean War, 1950–1953 (Master of Military Art and Science, US Army Command and General Staff College, 1993).

Lowe, D. Australia, Southeast Asia and the Cold War, 1948–1954 (PhD thesis, University of Cambridge, 1991).

Mantell, M. Opposition to the Korean War: a study in American dissent (PhD thesis, New York University, 1973).

Marshall, S. Commentary on infantry weapons usage in Korea Winter of 1950–51. ORO-R-13 (27 October 1951).

Merrill, J. Internal warfare in Korea, 1948–1950: the local setting of the Korean War (PhD thesis, University of Delaware, 1982).

O'Neill, M. The other side of the Yalu: Soviet pilots in the Korean War (PhD thesis, Florida State University, 1996).

O'Shaughnessy, J., Jr. The Chinese intervention in Korea: an analysis of warning (Thesis, Defence Intelligence College, 1985).

Park, D. A study of Chinese participation in the Korean War (PhD thesis, Mun Hwa University, 1975).

Perrin, K. The problem of Korean unification and the United Nations, 1945–1955 (PhD thesis, University of Utah, 1971).

Ra, J.-y. British–American relations during the Korean War (PhD thesis, Cambridge University, 1971).

Soh, J. Some causes of the Korean War of 1950: a case of Soviet foreign policy in Korea (1945–1950) with emphasis on Sino–Soviet collaboration (PhD thesis, University of Oklahoma, 1963).

Special Operations Research Office. A study of rear area security measures: Korea (American University, Washington, DC, n.d.).

Suh, J.-m. The influence of the Korean War on Turkish foreign policy (PhD thesis, Ankara University, 1973).

US Air Force, Air University, Human Research Institute. A preliminary study of the impact of Communism upon Korea. Psychological Warfare Research, Report No. 1.

[US Army] XXIV Corps G-2 report. History of left-wing Korean political parties to 01 June 1947. Typescript, US National Archives, RG 332, USAFIK, Box 97, Criticism of U.S. MG folder.

US Army Forces, Commander-in-Chief Far East. Summation of United States Army Military Government activities in Korea. Monthly 1946–8.

US Army, 8086 Army Unit (Armed Forces Far East), Military History Detachment. UN partisan forces in the Korean conflict, 1951–1952 – a study of their characteristics and operations (1954).

US Army Military Government in Korea. Monthly reports for September 1945 to August 1948.

US Army, Psychological Warfare Center. Propaganda and germ warfare (n.d.).

Wood, H. American reaction to limited war in Asia: Korea and Vietnam, 1950–1968 (PhD thesis, University of Colorado, 1974).

Yang, D.-h. Korean truce talks: multi-dimensional situational analysis (PhD thesis, Munich University, 1982).

Yoo, T.-h. The Korean War and the United Nations: a legal and diplomatic historical study (PhD thesis, University of Louvain, 1965).

Yoon, Y. United Nations participation in Korean affairs, 1945–1954 (PhD thesis, American University, 1959).

Chronology

c. 2000 BC	Minuscule kingdom of Chosun ("land of the morning calm") established.
July 1844	Treaty establishing commercial relations between Kingdom of Korea and the United States signed.
August 1866	Crew of US schooner *General Sherman* massacred by Korean soldiers.
June 1870	US punitive attacks on Korean fortresses along the Yom-ha River. More than 250 Koreans killed.
1876	Treaty of Kanghwa between Korean and Japan.
May 1882	Treaty of Chemulpo between Korea and USA.
1904–1905	Russo-Japanese War. US President Theodore Roosevelt brokers the Treaty of Portsmouth (September 1905) ending that war. Russia agrees to Japan's exercising a free hand in Korea.
November 1905	The Japanese coerce the Korean king to allow his nation to become a protectorate of Japan.
1908	Root–Takahira agreement recognizes Japan's primacy in Korea and southern Manchuria.
1910	Japan annexes Korea.
December 1918	Koreans resident in the United States petition President Wilson "to aid the Koreans in their aspirations for self-determination" as a moral obligation resulting from the unabrogated Treaty of Chemulpo.
April 1919	Provisional government-in-exile established in Shanghai.
March–April 1919	"Mansei Revolution". Korean patriotic demonstrations put down by Japanese occupation forces.
1 December 1943	Cairo Conference Declaration affirms that "in due course Korea shall become free and independent.

313

Korean nationalists object to "in due course" qualifying phrase.

1945
15 August   Premier Stalin approves President Harry Truman's General Order Number One, providing for the temporary division of Korea at the Thirty-eighth Parallel of latitude into two temporary zones of military occupation, Soviet and United States.

2 September   Instrument of Japanese unconditional surrender signed in Tokyo Bay.

First week in
September   US occupation troops land at Inchon.

December   US and Soviet Union draw up agreement providing for five-year trusteeship for Korea. Large-scale demonstrations by resentful Korean patriots.

1946   Activation of "Peace Preservation Officers' Training Schools", nucleus of North Korean Army.

September   US State Department agrees that South Korea should be left to its fate.

1947
17 September   US refers issue of reunification and independence of Korea to the UN.

29 September   US Joint Chiefs of Staff agree that South Korea has too little strategic value to justify the stationing of 45,000 US occupation troops.

14 November   General Assembly of the UN, over Soviet objections, approves American-sponsored resolution calling for one government for all of Korea, and providing for a UN Temporary Commission (UNTCOK) to supervise national elections to lead to independence and unification.

1948
24 January   Refusal of Soviet occupation commander in North Korea to permit entry of UNTCOK into his jurisdiction prevents Korea-wide elections.

February   Joint Chiefs of Staff recommend pulling out of all American troops, even though this move will probably result in the "eventual domination of Korea by the USSR".

February   [North] Korean People's Army formally activated.

April	Opening of Chedu-Do rebellion, lasting until at least autumn of 1949.
2 April	US National Security Council paper NSC-8 agrees that the US should help build up the Korean economy and armed forces, but beyond that, the South Koreans would have to maintain their own security against the Communist north. Paper approved by President Truman as basis for US Korea policy.
10 May	With the Soviets refusing to admit United Nations commissioners to North Korea, UN-sponsored elections in Southern Korea return representatives to a National Assembly, which elected Syngman Rhee the first President of a new republic.
15 August	Republic of Korea (ROK) formally inaugurated.
9 September	Establishment of the Democratic People's Republic of Korea (DPRK).
October	Yosu-Sunchon Communist-led uprising brutally suppressed by ROK forces.
December	Arrival of small but high-level Soviet military mission in Pyongyang.
31 December	Soviets announce that their forces have been withdrawn from North Korea.
1949	
January	General MacArthur informs the Joint Chiefs of Staff that ROK armed forces could not turn back an invasion from the North, that the US should not commit troops in case of such an invasion, and that the US should remove all of its combat forces as soon as possible.
2 May	US–Korean Military Advisory Group (KMAG) activated.
27 June	US State Department concludes that US should respond to an invasion from the North by submitting the matter to the UN.
29 June	Last US occupation troops leave ROK.
10 October	Activation of South Korean Air Force.
1950	
12 January	US Secretary of State Dean Acheson, in a speech before the National Press Club in Washington, omits South Korea from America's defence perimeter in Asia. Those omitted states would have to rely upon their own resources until the UN could mobilize against an aggressor.

19 January	US House of Representatives defeats Korean aid bill for 1949–1950.
January–March	MacArthur's Intelligence Section evaluates reports of impending invasion of the ROK from the North (including one that pinpoints the month of June 1950), but does not believe that an invasion is imminent.
14 February	Sino–Soviet Treaty of Friendship and Alliance signed.
15 March	The Commanding Officer of Korean Military Advisory Group concedes that the DPRK would give the ROK "a bloody nose", that the southern civil population would accede to the new regime and that the ROK "would be gobbled up to be added to the rest of Red Asia".
2 May	The Chairman of the Senate Foreign Relations Committee (Senator Tom Connally of Texas), in an interview with *U.S. News and World Report*, concedes that the Republic of Korea would be abandoned in case of enemy aggression and that the security of that nation was not essential to America's defensive Asian strategy.
30 May	ROK-wide elections produce a majority of National Assembly representatives opposed to the Rhee government.
1 June	The Intelligence Section of the USAF Far East Air Force (FEAF) concludes that "South Korea will fall before a North Korean invasion".
19 June	The Central Intelligence Agency (CIA) determines that North Korea could seize and hold at least the upper reaches of South Korea, including Seoul, without Chinese or Soviet military units.
25 June	Military forces of the Democratic Republic of (North) Korea invade the Republic of (South) Korea, opening the Korean War.
27 June	USAF provides evacuation and air cover for US nationals from Seoul and Inchon; first use of US military forces in Korean War.
28 June	Seoul falls to invading North Korean military forces.
29 June	President Truman agrees with reporter's characterization of the conflict as a "police action". Eighteen B-26 light bombers raid airfield near Pyongyang
30 June	President Truman commits ground forces to the Korean conflict.

3 July	First UN naval operations against North Koreans. Aircraft carriers USS *Valley Forge* and HMS *Triumph* launch air strikes against enemy airfields and the North Korean capital of Pyongyang.
2 July	UN naval forces destroy North Korean torpedo and motor gunboats in the only naval engagement of the Korean War.
5 July	Task Force Smith, the US Army's first attempt to blunt North Korean advance, scattered, three miles north of Osan.
6–12 July	US Army fights delaying, but also losing, actions at Pyongtaek, Chonan and Chochiwon.
8 July	General Douglas MacArthur appointed United Nations Commander in Chief to repel North Korean aggression against South Korea.
14–20 July	US ground forces defeated at Taejon-Kum River. The commander of the US 24th Infantry Division captured, but some time is won to form perimeter along Naktong River further south.
25 July	US Naval aircraft make first emergency close support air strikes against North Korean forces.
4 August	UN troops take up defensive positions around the Pusan Perimeter.
15 August	Eighth Army directed to employ native recruits in US Army divisions, beginning the Korean Augmentation to the US Army (KATUSA).
18 August	First tank-to-tank battle of the war.
12 September	George C. Marshall becomes third US Secretary of Defense, succeeding Louis Johnson.
15 September	MacArthur's Inchon landings far behind the enemy's lines open a temporary turn of the war in favour of UN forces.
16–22 September	UN forces break out from the Pusan Perimeter in the wake of the Inchon landings to their enemy's rear.
27 September	Seoul falls to UN forces, three months to the day after it was occupied by North Korean military.
October	Arrival of first Greek Army forces in Korea.
19 October	Pyongyang falls to UN forces.
24 October	Arrival of first Netherlands forces in Korea.
25 October	Chinese [Communist] People's Volunteer Forces launch their First Phase offensive.
5 November	British Commonwealth ground forces (Australian) first enter ground combat.
8 November	History's first jet-to-jet air combat.

20 November	Arrival of Indian 60th Field Ambulance and Surgical Unit, India's sole, but much valued, contribution to the UN Korean War effort.
23 November	Full battalion of the Netherlands forces reaches Korea.
25 November	First battle between US and Chinese Communist forces. US 8th Cavalry Regiment badly mauled.
27 November–9 December	Battle of Changjin (Chosin) Reservoir. Encircled 1st US Marine Division and attached US and ROK Army elements fight their way to the sea.
29 November	Arrival of first French forces in Korea. 2nd US Infantry Division almost destroyed at Kunu-ri.
9 December	Arrival of Greek Battalion at Pusan.
16 December	President Truman declares State of National Emergency.
21 December	UNC imposes full military censorship.
23 December	Lt. Gen. Walton Walker, 8th US Army Commander, killed in motor accident. Walker is immediately replaced by General Matthew B. Ridgway.
24 December	Hungnam evacuated without loss of men or equipment.
31 December	New Chinese offensive begins. UN forces retreat eventually to as far as 70 miles south of the 38th Parallel. Arrival of first New Zealand forces.

1951	
1–15 January	Third Phase CPV offensive. UN forces pushed south of 38th Parallel.
4 January	Seoul falls again to Communist forces.
25 January	First UN counter-offensives since entry of Chinese Communist forces, ending talk of evacuating UN forces from Korea. Series of such offensives, lasting through the spring of 1951, eventually drives Communist forces to positions mostly north of the 38th Parallel by the end of March.
11–13 February	Battle of Hoengsong. War's heaviest concentration of US Army battle deaths.
13 February	General MacArthur issues statement critical of UN/US military policy. Makes similar statement on 7 March.
16 February	Beginning of 861-day blockade of Wonsan, the longest effective maritime siege of modern history.
21 February–4 April	Operations Killer and Ripper. Successive UNC offensives that drive Communists out of most of South Korea and retake Seoul.

318

14 March	Seoul retaken by UN forces.
24 March	General MacArthur issues demand for Communist surrender.
5 April	House Republican Minority Leader Joseph W. Martin releases letter from General MacArthur calling for victory in the Korean War.
10 April	General MacArthur relieved by President Harry Truman. General Ridgway succeeds MacArthur as UN commander.
14 April	Lt. Gen. James A. Van Fleet arrives in Korea to succeed General Ridgway as 8th Army commander.
19 April	General MacArthur delivers "No Substitute for Victory"/"Old Soldiers Never Die" speech before joint session of US Congress.
22 April	Chinese Communist forces open first stage of their fifth offensive, drive almost to outskirts of Seoul before being stopped by the end of May. Chinese suffer extremely heavy casualties. US military rotation plan introduced.
3 May	US Senate opens committee hearings on the dismissal of General MacArthur and US strategy in Korea.
2 June	UN Command initiates Operation Strangle, an attempt to interdict Communist supply lines through air action, with only problematic success.
1 June	US Secretary of State, Dean Acheson, indicates that the US is prepared to accept truce line in vicinity of the 38th Parallel.
23 June	Soviet UN Ambassador, J. Malik, calls for negotiations for a cease-fire.
2 July	Communist authorities agree to cease-fire negotiations at Kaesong.
10 July	First meeting of complete delegations from opposing sides in the Korean War.
28 July	Commonwealth Division activated from smaller British Commonwealth units in Korea.
8 September	Japanese Peace Treaty signed at San Francisco.
13 September	Opening of battle of Heartbreak Ridge.
25 October	Truce talks transferred to Panmunjom.
12 November	General Ridgway orders end of UN ground offensive military action and implements "active defence" strategy.
27 November	Agreement reached at Panmunjom on line of military demarcation and Demilitarized Zone. Agreement subsequently invalidated on 27th December.

1952

2 January UN Command proposes voluntary repatriation of all POWs at Panmunjom negotiations.

18 February Major clash between UN guards and POWs at Koje-do prison camp. Also, opening of Communist campaign claiming that US was waging biological warfare in the Korean War.

8 April President Truman seizes control of strike-bound American steel mills.

7 May Kidnapping of commander of Koje-do prisoner camp and subsequent negotiations with kidnappers leads to humiliation of UN command, but in a military operation the command takes back control of the camp compounds and vastly improves security and living conditions.

7 May Truce negotiations stall over question of repatriation of Chinese and North Korean prisoners.

12 May General Mark Clark succeeds General Ridgway as UN Commander.

2 June US Supreme Court declares unconstitutional President Truman's seizure of steel mills.

23–24 June UN air attacks on North Korean Suiho power generation complex to hasten armistice negotiations.

July–August Heavy UN air strikes on Pyongyang practically destroy North Korean capital.

November Dogfight between US Naval aircraft and Soviet MiG-15s near carrier *Oriskany*; only known direct attempt by Soviet airpower to attack UN sea forces.

4 November Dwight Eisenhower elected President of the US.

2–5 December President-Elect Eisenhower tours Korea to fulfill his election pledge, "I Will Go to Korea".

1953

23 March–7 July Battle of Pork Chop Hill.

20 April–3 May Operation Little Switch exchanges sick and wounded POWs.

June Series of Chinese offensives against ROK forces demonstrate that South Korea could not survive on its own militarily, despite President Rhee's bluster of "on to the North".

July USN Task Force 77 equipped with nuclear weapons.

27 July Signing of the Korean armistice agreements.

28 July

First meeting of the Military Armistice Commission. The armistice holds through the decades, and these meetings continue to the present time.

August–23 December

Operation Big Switch exchanges all POWs willing to be repatriated.

1954
26 April

Opening of fifth Geneva Conference on the reunification of Korea and other Asian matters.

Index